# World Societies

## The Evolution of Human Social Life

**Stephen K. Sanderson**
*Indiana University of Pennsylvania*

**Arthur S. Alderson**
*Indiana University, Bloomington*

D1710872

PEARSON

Boston   New York   San Francisco
Mexico City   Montreal   Toronto   London   Madrid   Munich   Paris
Hong Kong   Singapore   Tokyo   Cape Town   Sydney

**Senior Editor:** *Jeff Lasser*
**Editorial Assistant:** *Heather McNally*
**Senior Marketing Manager:** *Kelly May*
**Editorial-Production Administrator:** *Annette Joseph*
**Editorial-Production Coordinator:** *Holly Crawford*
**Editorial-Production Service:** *Lynda Griffiths*
**Photo Researcher:** *Katharine S. Cook and Leah M. Eisenstadt*
**Composition Buyer:** *Linda Cox*
**Electronic Composition and Art:** *Cabot Computer Services*
**Manufacturing Buyer:** *JoAnne Sweeney*
**Cover Administrator and Designer:** *Kristina Mose-Libon*

For related titles and support materials, visit our online catalog at www.ablongman.com.

Between the time website information is gathered and then published, it is not unusual for some sites to have closed. Also, the transcription of URLs can result in typographical errors. The publisher would appreciate notification where these errors occur so that they may be corrected in subsequent editions.

*Library of Congress Cataloging-in-Publication Data*

Sanderson, Stephen K.
 World societies : the evolution of human social life / Stephen K. Sanderson, Arthur S.
Alderson
 p. cm.
Includes bibliographical references and index.
ISBN 0-205-35948-5
 1. Macrosociology. 2. Social evolution. I. Alderson, Arthur S. II. Title.

HM490.S26 2005
303.4—dc22                                        2004057323


Printed in the United States of America
10 9 8 7 6 5 4 3 2 1    RRD-VA    09 08 07 06 05 04

**Photo credits:**  page 7: Courtesy of Stephen Sanderson; pages 9, 12, 67, 107: Library of Congress; page 44: EMG Education Management Group; page 55: American Museum of Natural History; pages 58, 132, 172: Corbis/ Bettmann; page 70: Rossi, Guido Alberto/Getty Images Inc.—Image Bank; page 83: The Image Works; page 91: Philip de Bay/Corbis/Bettmann; page 102: Erich Lessing/Art Resource, N.Y.; page 111: Ken Usami/Getty Images, Inc.—Photodisc; page 115: Digital Vision Ltd.; page 135: Brad Markel/Getty Images, Inc.—Liaison; page 148: Courtesy of Randall Collins; page 167: Cary Wolinsky/Aurora & Quanta Productions Inc.; page 180: National Academy of Sciences; page 190: Edgar Cleijne/Peter Arnold, Inc.; page 201: Courtesy of Immanuel Wallerstein; page 206: China Tourism Press.Xie, Guang Hui/Getty Images, Inc. - Image Bank; pages 224, 255: AP/Wide World Photos; page 226: AFP Photo/Rabih Moghrabi/Getty Images, Inc. - Agence France Presse; page 234: Ontario Ministry of Tourism; page 260: French Government Tourist Office; page 263: Wally McNamee/ Corbis/Bettmann.

*For Derek, Sarah, Meera, and Neal*

# CONTENTS

# PREFACE

This book started out with the title *Macrosociology: An Introduction to Human Societies*, published in 1988 by Harper and Row. Second and third editions were published in 1991 and 1995, respectively, by HarperCollins, and a fourth edition appeared in 1999 under the imprint of Addison Wesley Longman. The current version is a major revision of *Macrosociology*, and because the revision is so substantial the book now carries a new title, *World Societies: The Evolution of Human Social Life*, and Arthur Alderson has been added as a coauthor. It was decided to give the book greater flexibility by retaining the core parts of the original book, mainly those that focused on the political economy of human societies and its evolution over the long term. Material on race and ethnicity, family, gender, kinship, and education has been been almost completely eliminated, although some of the materials on education were reincorporated into the chapter on modern industrial capitalist societies.

This book has also been thoroughly reorganized. The old organization was topical, whereas the new organization is historical or evolutionary. We start with hunter-gatherer societies, move from there to discuss horticultural, agrarian, and pastoral societies, and then turn to the emergence of capitalism and industrialism, the rise and demise of state socialism, development and underdevelopment, globalization, and the future. The book has been thoroughly updated where necessary, and the materials on globalization have been expanded into an entire chapter. The original chapter on the future has been dramatically revised, with 13 bold predictions for the next 25 to 50 years. Because of the book's reorganization, an entirely new chapter on theories of social evolution and development has been added, and appears as Chapter 2. This chapter might be too difficult for some students. If so, it can be eliminated without much loss, or the main points can be briefly summarized by the instructor. However, we believe it is important to include the chapter because some instructors will find it useful.

*World Societies* has also been substantially shortened and now appears in paperback at a much lower price. For those who used *Macrosociology* and felt committed to it, *World Societies* can still be used as a stand-alone text. But its much shorter length now makes it appropriate as a supplement to full-scale textbooks. Introductory sociology textbooks focus mostly on modern U.S. society. Some have comparative and historical content, but this is quite limited in the vast majority of cases. *World Societies* would serve as a very useful supplement for those who want to use a conventional text but who would like much more in the way of comparative and historical materials. This book could also be used very nicely as a supplement to the one other textbook that takes a fully comparative and historical approach, Nolan and Lenski's *Human Societies*. Both of these books are evolutionary in approach, but take rather different perspectives and cover quite a different range of materials. They would complement each other very well for those who are teaching the introductory course in a comparative and evolutionary fashion, or other courses that have a comparative and evolutionary format. *World Societies* would also be very appropriate for courses in social change and for courses in economic or political sociology.

For those instructors who have not used a comparative, historical, or evolutionary approach in teaching the introductory course, but who might have an interest in doing so, the merits of such an approach are discussed in Sanderson (1985).

A test bank of multiple-choice, true-false, and essay questions is available from the publisher.

Stephen K. Sanderson
Arthur S. Alderson

# ACKNOWLEDGMENTS

Thank you to the sociology editor at Allyn and Bacon, Jeff Lasser, for seeing this book to completion and for being understanding when we submitted the manuscript over a year late. Very special thanks are due to Christopher Chase-Dunn for his useful critical comments on this book, for using every edition of its predecessor, and for his unflagging support over the years.

I also thank the following people for their intellectual collegiality and friendship, which have contributed in important ways to this book and various editions of its predecessor: Chris Chase-Dunn, Tom Hall, Randy Collins, Pierre van den Berghe, Jon Turner, Sandy Maryanski, Andre Gunder Frank, Al Bergesen, Sing Chew, Ed Bell, Sam Clark, Mike Hammond, Josh Dubrow, Wes Roberts, Gerry Lenski, Victor Garcia, Jeff Kentor, Tom Reifer, Herb Hunter, Bruce Lerro, Manuela Boatca, Harvey Holtz, Tom Conelly, Bob Carneiro, and Paul Kamolnick. I am especially grateful to my son, Derek Sanderson, for numerous stimulating conversations about issues of sociological relevance over many years. Although not a sociologist or a student of sociology, he has a keen sociological mind and eye nonetheless.

It is a special pleasure to be able to add Arthur Alderson as my coauthor. He took the introductory sociology course with me in 1984. *Macrosociology* was still in the process of completion (four years away from publication), and he and the other students used a manuscript version of the book as the course's main text. He seemed fascinated by the comparative and historical focus of the manuscript, not realizing that all of these other types of societies existed and could be studied systematically. After the course, he became a sociology major and took several more courses with me. Few authors are as fortunate as I am to be able to add as a coauthor a former student who learned his first sociology from one of the earliest possible versions of the book in question. In the future, I hope he will have the opportunity to shape the direction of the book more and more.

Stephen K. Sanderson

*No description can even begin to lead to a valid explanation*
*if it does not effectively encompass the whole world.*

—Fernand Braudel

# CHAPTER

# 1

# 10,000 Years of Social Evolution

$T$oday people live in a globalizing world in which the world's societies are rapidly becoming interconnected economically, politically, militarily, and culturally. There are fewer than 190 autonomous nation-states in the contemporary world, although many of these states contain communities that maintain old-fashioned ways of life based on hunting and gathering, preindustrial agriculture, animal herding, or some combination thereof. Prior to 10,000 years ago, hunting and gathering was the subsistence mode by which all humans on earth lived, and there were tens of thousands of hunter-gatherer communities. In the intervening 10 millennia, agriculture developed, civilizations and states emerged, and an industrial revolution occurred throughout much of the world. How and why did these things happen? How did the world go from tens of thousands of tiny hunter-gatherer societies to just a handful of huge nation-states? Why is the world becoming increasingly interconnected, and why is the pace of this interconnection constantly accelerating? These questions and others are the central focus of this book, which is an introduction to human societies past and present and their evolution over the past 10,000 years.

## The Ancestral Environment

*Hominids*—members of the human family—began to separate from the common ancestor of modern apes and humans some 5 to 7 million years ago, but it was not until after 200,000 years ago that anatomically modern humans—*Homo sapiens*, the genus and species to which all living humans belong—appeared on the scene. The predominant line of thinking, generally known as the "Out of Africa" hypothesis, is that all anatomically modern humans originated in Africa and that sometime around 100,000 years ago some groups began to migrate north into Asia and then later into Europe (Stringer and Gamble, 1993; Shreeve, 1995; Klein, 1999). Despite their differences, all of these groups led a common way of life centered on the hunting of wild animals and the gathering of wild plants. We know much more about the social patterns of modern hunter-gatherer societies than we do about their ancient counterparts. Most modern hunter-gatherer societies live in small bands or camps that seldom exceed 50 individuals and that may average only about 25. Economic life revolves around the band, with men doing most of the hunting and women doing most of the gathering. Bands move frequently in search of game

1

and plant food and thus lead a nomadic existence, and most groups are highly egalitarian in their social relations and worldviews. Undoubtedly, many hunter-gatherers in the ancient past lived similarly, but it is likely that many others lived in larger groups that moved less frequently because they enjoyed richer and more productive environments than those inhabited by the majority of modern hunter-gatherers. Many ancient hunter-gatherers may also have been less egalitarian because of the greater productivity of their environments.

## The Neolithic Revolution

Although ancient hunters and gatherers probably knew for tens of thousands of years how plants and animals could be domesticated (Cohen, 1977), it was not until about 10,000 years ago that some of them began to devote themselves to the practice of agriculture. Although some ancient hunter-gatherers lived in settled villages, once the transition to agriculture was made settled village life became the norm. This transition of humankind to an agricultural (technically, **horticultural**) mode of existence based on settled villages is known as the **Neolithic Revolution.** Actually, this term is somewhat misleading, since there was not a single revolutionary transition. The transition to agriculture occurred on an independent basis in several different regions of the world and at somewhat different times.

It is widely understood that the adoption of agriculture occurred first in southwest Asia (the Middle East) around 10,000 years ago, or perhaps slightly earlier. Somewhat later, around 9,000 years ago, agricultural communities began to develop in southeast Asia (M. Cohen, 1977; Fagan, 1989), and by 8000–7000 BP ("before the present") agriculture emerged in China (Chang, 1986). Agriculture also arose in two other areas of the Old World. In Europe, agriculture developed earliest in Greece and its adjacent regions, possibly as early as 8000 BP (Milisauskas, 1978; Fagan, 1989). After about 7000 BP, farmers migrating into temperate Europe carried agriculture with them, and by approximately 5500 BP, agriculture had reached northern Europe (Scandinavia and the British Isles) (Fagan, 1989). In Africa, agriculture developed earliest in Egypt (around 7000 BP) and slightly later in west and central Africa (around 6500 BP), the Sudan and Ethiopia (around 6000 BP), and northern Kenya (around 4500 BP). In most of Africa below the equator, agriculture developed much later, not beginning until after about 2000 BP (Phillipson, 1985).

Agriculture was also independently invented or adopted in several regions of the New World: Mesoamerica (what is now Mexico and parts of Central America), South America, and North America. In Mesoamerica, agriculture can be dated from about 7000 BP (MacNeish, 1978), although it is possible that it might have begun in some regions as early as 9000 BP (Fiedel, 1987). Settled village life, however, did not emerge until several thousand years later. This is a striking contrast with the Old World, where agriculture and sedentary village life usually emerged together (M. Harris, 1977). Another contrast between Old World agriculture and that in Mesoamerica was the absence of any large animal domesticates in the latter, apparently because of a lack of species suitable for domestication (M. Harris, 1977). In South America, especially Peru, agriculture arose around 8000 BP. In Ecuador, it is possible that maize was being grown as early as 5000 BP, and in the Amazon Basin, it is thought that manioc was being cultivated perhaps as early as 4000 BP (Fiedel, 1987). In North America, the cultivation of such crops as squash and sunflowers arose sometime after 4500 BP in the eastern part of the continent, and the cultivation of maize, along with beans and squash, began in the western part of the continent perhaps as early as 3500 BP (Bogucki, 1999).

As recently as the 1960s, it was believed that agriculture was invented only once, in the Middle East, and then spread from that agricultural center to other world regions. The argument was basically that it was agricultural knowledge, or the *idea* of agriculture, that spread. Researchers now know that this older view is incorrect. It has come to be generally accepted that agriculture was invented independently in at least four different world regions: the Middle East, North China, Mesoamerica, and eastern North America (Bogucki, 1999). It has been argued that agriculture was independently invented in almost every place where it first appeared (cf. Sanderson, 1999b:23–34), but this is probably overstating the case. It is now well established that agriculture arose in Europe because of the influence of Middle Eastern agricultural communities. In some European regions, agriculture was introduced as the direct result of the migration of agricultural groups from the Middle East, who brought with them their own crops, livestock, and sedentary lifestyles. In other parts of Europe, people adopted agriculture as a result of contact with groups already practicing it (Bogucki, 1999). Bogucki (1999) points out that the wild ancestors of wheat and barley were not indigenous to Europe, nor were there any wild sheep or goats in Europe. Since these were among the major cultigens and livestock of European agriculture, they had to have been introduced from elsewhere. Similarly, the western part of North America was not home to the wild ancestors of their principal cultigens, maize and beans, thus the conclusion is that these domesticates were adopted from Mesoamerican agricultural communities (Bogucki, 1999).

## The Rise of Civilization and the State

Agriculture developed slowly and gradually in virtually all regions of the world. Hunter-gatherers did not become agriculturalists overnight, but gradually added cultivated plants to their diet while continuing to hunt and to gather. In some regions, it took several thousand years before agriculture became the only, or even the primary, mode of subsistence. However, once agriculture was adopted as the primary or only subsistence mode, its practice was intensified over time in many regions of the world, largely as a result of expanding populations. People began to adopt new tools and methods of production, and the scale of social life increased.

Early horticultural societies were usually not politically organized beyond the village level. The many villages that may have constituted a tribe interacted, but there was no centralized coordination among them. In later horticultural societies, however, centralized coordination often developed, and societies known as **chiefdoms** began to arise. Early chiefdoms may have numbered only a few thousand people, but later and more complex ones sometimes reached 100,000 members. Chiefdoms themselves were precursors to still more complex forms of social organization known as **civilizations,** which were politically ruled by **states** (Carneiro, 1981). Civilizations were complex and large-scale societies characterized by such features as towns and cities, monumental architecture, craft specialization and occupational differentiation, writing and record keeping, and extreme social and economic inequalities. States were political bodies that, like chiefdoms, centrally coordinated large populations, but they were different in several crucial respects. They typically organized much larger populations, contained more numerous and more specialized political officials, and possessed much more power to contend with rebellion and revolt from dissatisfied groups.

Civilizations arose in at least six regions of the Old World and at least two regions of the New World. For the most part, these were the same regions where agriculture first emerged. The earliest of the Old World civilizations evolved in Mesopotamia (what is now mainly Iraq) and Egypt in approximately 5000 BP (Fagan, 1989; Wenke, 1990). Civilizations arose in other parts of Africa somewhat later—for example, in 3600 BP in Kerma on the middle Nile, in 2500 BP in Ethiopia, and in west Africa in approximately CE 200 (Connah, 1987). In China, an indigenous civilization began to emerge with the creation of the Shang Dynasty around 3800 BP (Chang, 1986). In north India (in what is now Pakistan), the famous civilization known as the Harappan was evolving around 4600 BP (Possehl, 1990). There were also early civilizations in Europe. In Mediterranean Europe (mainly Greece), the first civilizations arose no later than 2700 BP (Champion, Gamble, Shennan, and White, 1984) and possibly as early as 4000 BP (Milisauskas, 1978; Fagan, 1989). In temperate Europe, the first states, those of the Celts, were emerging around 2200 BP (Champion et al., 1984). Many of these Old World civilizations emerged in geographical regions dominated by major rivers, or, in the case of Mediterranean Europe, in the vicinity of a large sea. Thus, the earliest Mesopotamian civilizations arose in the fertile area between the Tigris and Euphrates Rivers, civilization in China evolved along the Yellow River in northern China, and the Harappan civilization emerged along the Indus River in northern India.

In the New World, civilizations evolved somewhat later. The two regions of civilizational origins in the New World were Mesoamerica and Peru. In the Mesoamerican lowlands, the first civilizations to emerge were those created by the Olmec and Maya. Olmec civilization flourished between 3200 and 2800 BP, whereas Mayan civilization achieved its peak between approximately CE 300 and 900 (Fiedel, 1987). In the Mesoamerican highlands, just north of what is now Mexico City, the first civilization formed around the city of Teotihuacán in approximately CE 1 (Fiedel, 1987). The most powerful of the Mesoamerican highland civilizations, though, was established by the Aztecs, whose capital city was known as Tenochtitlán. The Aztecs reached the apex of their development in the early sixteenth century. Sometime around CE 1 in Peru, a series of wars and conquests led to the formation of more complex and extensive political units. These eventually reached imperial scope and culminated in the establishment of the Inca empire, which reached its zenith in the fifteenth and sixteenth centuries (Fiedel, 1987).

A classic study by Robert Adams (1966) provides a clear picture of the nature of early civilizations and their parallel development in the Old and New Worlds. Adams's study is devoted to a comparative analysis of the formation of civilizations in one Old World case, Mesopotamia, and one New World case, central Mexico. It is quite likely that the evolutionary processes at work in Mesopotamia and Mexico were broadly similar to those involved in the emergence of early civilizations elsewhere. Basic to the emergence of civilization in these two cases was the development of social stratification, or class distinctions. At the pinnacle of Mesopotamian society stood princely families who, during late Early Dynastic and Akkadian times, were increasingly extending their control of land. These ruling families apparently headed manorial estates. A significant proportion of the labor force employed on these estates consisted of slaves. At the top of the Aztec social hierarchy were royal households that in due time evolved into an endogamous (in-marrying) nobility sharply distinguished from the rest of the population by wealth, education, diet, and dress. Great estates were at the king's disposal; large amounts of surplus production were generated by these estates, the surplus flowing as tribute from commoners to the ruling class. At an intermediate level in the social hierarchy were groups of warriors and merchants. Below them were localized kin groups that were internally stratified and held corporate (collective) title to land. Below these, in turn, were persons who cultivated the private lands of the nobility and who have been likened to medieval serfs. At the very bottom of the social order were slaves.

In both Mesopotamia and Mexico we find a general pattern of political evolution characterized by the emergence of theocratic polities—ones in which religion and politics were fused—and their eventual transformation into militaristic and, ultimately, conquest states. The early formation of civilization in both cases was marked by a decidedly religious focus, with much emphasis on temple building and governance by priesthoods. The dominance of religious groups, however, soon gave way to the rise to power of militaristic groups. Political power came to be increasingly concentrated in dynastic institutions at the expense of earlier communal and religious bodies. Archaeological evidence demonstrates the existence of palaces containing private apartments for the ruling family and the families of top-ranking administrative officials and personal servants. In Mesopotamia there is good evidence for the existence of an array of political functionaries such as gatekeepers, cooks, servants, messengers, and slaves. Clearly, the palace structure associated with both civilizations indicates the development of highly stratified societies in which the power and complexity of governing bodies had been erected on a major scale. Both societies had parallel conceptions of kingship, and both evolved into major conquest states that extended territorial control over wide regions. This increasing conquest of neighboring lands and peoples brought greater demands for tribute, increasing stratification, and yet further intensification of the autocratic features of the state.

## The Rise of Modern Capitalism and Industrialism

The era dominated by these kinds of civilizations lasted several thousand years. Many things changed—for example, technology advanced, states got bigger and more powerful, and trade between civilizations expanded—but the overall character of social life remained much the same. Life was rural and most people lived by cultivating the soil. Towns and cities existed, within which merchants and artisans were the center of economic life, but the members of these occupational groups played a secondary role in the vast majority of societies. But by the sixteenth century CE, a dramatic evolutionary transformation was underway: the rise of modern capitalism. The production of goods and their sale in markets began to gain the upper hand in economic life, whereas for thousands of years this kind of mercantile activity had been held in check almost everywhere. By the eighteenth century, the new capitalist development led to a dramatic technological revolution, the Industrial Revolution, which began in England around 1760 and eventually occurred throughout much of Europe and North America in the nineteenth and twentieth centuries. The Industrial Revolution was characterized by the replacement of manual labor with machinery and the large-scale development of the factory system. A new type of society, industrial capitalist society, came into being.

Industrialization had enormous consequences for the organization of social life, with virtually every aspect of social life being touched by it. One was an increase in economic productivity on a scale totally unprecedented in human history. To take a simple case, in England in 1750 the import of raw cotton for spinning amounted to £3 million, but by 1784 the figure had climbed to £11 million, by 1799 to £43 million, and by 1802 to £60 million (Heilbroner, 1972). Likewise, the production of pig iron increased dramatically from 68,000 tons in 1788 to 1,347,000 tons in 1839 (Heilbroner, 1972). Moreover, the productivity of labor increased continually from these early days of industrial capitalism to the present and is vastly greater today than it was in the early nineteenth century.

Another consequence of industrialization was the creation of an industrial proletariat, or working class. This proletariat consisted of the mass of workers—men, women, and children—who worked in the factories. In the early days of industrial capitalism, these workers labored under conditions of severe hardship (Engels, 1973; orig. 1845). They were brutally overworked in the factories and paid extremely low wages, in many cases barely enough to keep them alive. They lived in overcrowded slums and suffered frequently from malnutrition and disease. Many of them were children, who could be paid even lower wages than adult men and women. The situation in industrial England in the first half of the nineteenth century was thus one characterized by the exploitation and degradation of a large mass of the population. It was precisely this situation that led to Karl Marx's scathing critique of capitalism.

A third result of industrialization occurred within the realm of work: the increasing specialization of labor. This phenomenon, whereby the worker has increasingly become a small cog in a large machine, developed especially rapidly and extensively since the late nineteenth century. In Marx's view, this growing specialization of labor made work more and more meaningless and stifling for the worker. This was another feature of industrial capitalism that led him to be extremely critical of it. The *alienation* of the worker that Marx observed in the nineteenth century became far more prominent in the twentieth (Braverman, 1974).

A fourth consequence of the emergence of industrial capitalism was the extensive urbanization of society. Social life shifted from the rural countryside to cities, many of them of vast scale. As Heilbroner (1972) notes in regard to the urban development of the United States, in 1790 only 24 towns and cities exceeded 2,500 citizens,

*Five specialists in the study of very long-term social change. Left to right: Stephen K. Sanderson, Thomas D. Hall, Christopher Chase-Dunn, Albert Bergesen, and Andre Gunder Frank.*

and collectively these towns constituted only 6 percent of the total population. But by 1860, 20 percent of the population was located in the 392 largest cities, and by 1970, much of the eastern seaboard had evolved into practically one gigantic city containing more than 60 percent of the total population of the country.

In the view of Immanuel Wallerstein (1974a, 1974b), capitalism was born as a world-economy and was never a phenomenon confined to individual nation-states. It has always been global, he says. This is true so long as we do not use the term *global* in its literal sense, for the capitalist world-economy in the sixteenth and seventeenth centuries doubtless made up no more than 20 percent of the habitable earth. By the late twentieth century, though, it had become literally global, having gobbled up the whole world. And now this globalization process is continuing on a massive scale. And where will it end? With the extension of industrial capitalism to every society and nation-state? With a single world-government? With everyone speaking a single language? Or, on the other hand, with the collapse of capitalist civilization (Sanderson, 1999b) and the transition to a very different mode of economic life (Wallerstein, 1998)? No one knows the answers to these questions today, and it may be a long time before anyone does. But let us go back to the beginning and see how we got to the point where we are at the present time.

## FOR FURTHER READING

*The Evolution of Human Societies* (1987; 2nd ed. 2000), by anthropologists Allen W. Johnson and Timothy Earle, is a very good overview of the main lines of social evolution from the simplest foraging societies to complex agrarian states. Robert Wenke's *Patterns in Prehistory* (1990; 4th ed. 1996) treats the main lines of social evolution from an archaeological perspective. Peter Bogucki's *The Origins of Human Society* (1999) is a similar work. Stephen Sanderson's *Social Transformations* (1999b) develops a general theory of social evolution and applies it to the three major evolutionary transformations discussed in this chapter. *The Social Cage: Human Nature and the Evolution of Society* (1992), by sociologists Alexandra Maryanski and Jonathan Turner, provides an interesting perspective on long-term social evolution from the authors' unique perspective on human nature.

# CHAPTER

# 2

# Theories of Social Evolution and Development

Evolutionary theories are those that attempt to describe and explain sequences of long-term social change. Evolutionists generally argue that many societies have undergone broadly similar changes from earliest times to the present, and they are concerned with identifying the nature of these changes and explaining why they have occurred. Erik Olin Wright (1983) provides a more precise conception of an **evolutionary theory.** He suggests that all evolutionary theories share the following characteristics:

- They organize history into a typology of stages.
- They assume that this stage ordering represents a direction along which societies tend to evolve.
- They postulate that the probability of movement to a later (or "higher") stage exceeds the probability of movement back to an earlier (or "lower") stage.
- They identify a mechanism or set of mechanisms that is intended to explain the movement from one stage to another.

As Wright is at pains to point out, evolutionary theories need not assume that the sequence of stages through which societies move is a rigid one that is the same for all societies, or that **social evolution** is some sort of automatic process of the unfolding of latent tendencies or potentialities inherent in the nature of societies. They do not even need to assume that forward movement always occurs. Regression is acknowledged as a possible (and sometimes actual) occurrence, and it is fully recognized that for many societies and at many times in history long-term steady states (rather than social transformation) may be the normal order of things. It is important that these points be established and well understood, because there are still many misconceptions concerning the nature of evolutionary theories (Sanderson, 1990).

## Classical Evolutionism

Evolutionary approaches to social life were extremely popular among both sociologists and anthropologists in the second half of the nineteenth century. In fact, evolutionary theorizing dominated these two disciplines at that time. One of the most famous of the nineteenth-century evolutionists was the English philosopher and sociologist Herbert Spencer (1820–1903), who developed a theory of social evolution that was similar in some ways to Darwin's theory of biological evolution (Spencer, 1972). Spencer attempted to understand the operation of all things in the universe by reducing them to a single universal principle that he called the *Law of Evolution*. According to this law, all things in the universe have a tendency to "evolve from a state of indefinite, incoherent, homogeneity to a state of definite, coherent, heterogeneity." What Spencer meant was that all things tend to develop from simple and unspecialized forms into more complex and specialized ones. Spencer saw this universal tendency as the master key to unlocking all the great riddles of the universe. He considered the evolution of human societies as but a special instance of a great cosmological tendency inherent in the nature of the universe itself.

With respect to the evolution of societies, what Spencer was describing was a process of *increasing social differentiation*. Societies could be placed on an evolutionary ladder in which there were four main societal stages or types. *Simple* societies have no, or only very rudimentary, formal political leadership. *Compound* societies have formal leadership and centralized political control, systematic social ranking, and a more complex division of labor. *Doubly compound* societies extend the process of differentiation even further. They have more complex government and are much more technologically advanced. They also have laws, towns, and roads. *Trebly compound* societies are characterized by the great ancient civilizations, such as the Egyptian and Roman empires and by modern-day Britain and France, and are the most differentiated of all societies.

Spencer also had another evolutionary scheme, which involved the distinction between *militant* and *industrial* societies. *Militant societies* are ones in which warfare and military organization dominate social life, whereas in *industrial societies* militarism and warfare take second place to economic activities in the areas of agriculture,

*Herbert Spencer (1820–1903). This English philosopher and social theorist developed a grandiose evolutionary scheme that is not acceptable by modern scholarly standards, but some of his more specific ideas about social evolution provide important insights.*

commerce, or industry. Militant societies are also characterized by the subordination of individual freedom to the group, but in industrial societies the individual has a much greater capacity to stand apart from the group or rise above it. Spencer thought that there was a generalized tendency for militant societies to give way to industrial ones in the process of social evolution; however, he was never quite able to connect this evolutionary typology with his four levels of social differentiation.

Another well-known nineteenth-century evolutionist was the American anthropologist Lewis Henry Morgan (1818–1881). Morgan (1974; orig. 1877) was much concerned with the evolution of technology. He divided human history into three great stages, each of which was associated with a different level of technological development: Savagery, Barbarism, and Civilization. The stage of *Savagery* was characteristic of peoples who subsisted primarily by hunting wild animals and gathering wild plants. The transition to *Barbarism* was marked by the domestication of plants and animals and the development of additional improvements in overall technology. The emergence of *Civilization* marked the transition from "primitive society" (what Morgan called *societas*) to "civil society" (what Morgan called *civitas*). Morgan saw the development of the phonetic alphabet and writing as a major characteristic of this stage.

Morgan's distinction between *societas* and *civitas* was an important contribution. Societies at the stage of *societas* are organized on the basis of kinship ties and are characterized by highly egalitarian and democratic social relations. With the passage to *civitas*, kinship declined in importance as an organizing principle and was replaced by property and territory as the mechanisms that held society together. Social and economic inequalities became prominent and societies were based much more on the use of force, often being ruled by despots.

The third major nineteenth-century evolutionist was Edward Burnett Tylor (1832–1917), an English anthropologist. Tylor (1871, 1878, 1924) was committed to a general evolutionary perspective and employed the same evolutionary stages as those used by Morgan (Savagery, Barbarism, and Civilization). However, unlike Morgan, he was more interested in the ideational or mental aspects of social life than in the evolution of technology, economics, and politics. He had a special concern for the evolution of language, myth, and religion. With respect to religion, Tylor thought that there had been an overall evolution from a belief in souls to a belief in spirits, which was then followed by polytheistic and later by monotheistic religions (i.e., from religions with a pantheon of several high gods to religions with a single high god). Tylor argued that the evolution of religion was a rational and progressive process whereby humans achieved a better and better understanding of the world.

Although the ideas of these and other early evolutionists were provocative, they contained a number of serious flaws. One of these was the tendency to pass off mere descriptions of evolutionary transformations as explanations for those transformations. They thought that social evolution was inherent in the very nature of things, and often seemed to regard this observation as sufficient to explain why social evolution occurred. But merely to note that evolution tends to occur says nothing about why it does so. Another flaw in the thinking of the nineteenth-century evolutionists was their ethnocentrism. They viewed their own society (Western civilization) as superior to all others, holding that societies at earlier evolutionary stages represented various gradations of inferiority to their own. They therefore claimed that social evolution was indicative of progress, of a general improvement in human rationality, happiness, and morality. They tended to see Western civilization as the end point of social evolution, as the culmination of millennia of human progress. These are views that are rejected, or at least questioned, by many modern sociologists and anthropologists.

## Marxian Evolutionism

An important evolutionary approach to social life was also developed by the famous nineteenth-century German social theorists Karl Marx (1818–1883) and Friedrich Engels (1820–1895). Marx and Engels (1970; orig. 1846) developed a theoretical perspective that they referred to as the "materialist conception of history," and what has since come to be known as *historical materialism* (sometimes called *dialectical materialism*). This was a theoretical approach to social life developed in direct opposition to the current of **idealism** that prevailed at that time in German philosophy. The leading advocate of idealism was German philosopher G. W. F. Hegel (1770–1831). Hegel (1956, orig. 1830–31; 1953, orig. 1837) held the view that the foundation of every society consisted in its basic way of viewing the world, especially as this was embodied in its religion, philosophy, and art. Although Marx and Engels accepted a good deal of Hegelian philosophy, they turned its idealism upside down and replaced it with a **materialist** conception of social life.

Historical materialism was constructed primarily as a means of understanding modern capitalist societies, but Marx and Engels understood it to be applicable as well to the whole range of human societies in both the past and the present. They divided human societies into two major components. One of these they referred to as the *infrastructure* or *base*, sometimes also called the *mode of production*. The base was in turn divided into two categories: the forces of production and the relations of production. The *forces of production* consisted of the raw materials and social creations necessary for a society to engage in economic production: the available level of technology and the specific nature of natural resources, such as the quality of the land. The *relations of production*, on the other hand, referred to the ownership of the forces of production. Marx and Engels noted that in some societies the forces of production were owned communally (by the entire group), but in other societies private ownership of the productive forces had emerged. The group that acquired ownership of the productive forces was able to compel other groups to work for it. Marx and Engels noted that several different forms of private relations of production existed in different societies.

The other major component of human societies identified by Marx and Engels was the *superstructure*. This component consisted of all those aspects of a society not included in the base, especially politics, law, family life, religion, and ideas and ideals.

Marx and Engels held that a society's base and its superstructure were directly related. Although they noted that the superstructure could occasionally influence the base, they argued that the primary direction of causation ran from the economic

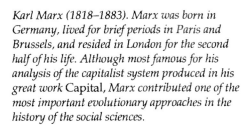

*Karl Marx (1818–1883). Marx was born in Germany, lived for brief periods in Paris and Brussels, and resided in London for the second half of his life. Although most famous for his analysis of the capitalist system produced in his great work* Capital, *Marx contributed one of the most important evolutionary approaches in the history of the social sciences.*

base to the superstructure. They believed, in other words, that the patterns of human thought and action found within a society's superstructure were largely shaped by the features of that society's economic base. In his famous eulogy at Marx's funeral, Engels (1963:188–189; orig. 1883) explained why this must be the case:

> Just as Darwin discovered the law of evolution in organic nature, so Marx discovered the law of evolution in human history; he discovered the simple fact . . . that mankind must first of all eat and drink, have shelter and clothing, before it can pursue politics, science, religion, art, etc., and that therefore the production of the immediate material means of subsistence and consequently the degree of economic development attained by a given people or during a given epoch, form the foundation upon which the state institutions, the legal conceptions, the art and even the religious ideas of the people concerned have been evolved, and in the light of which these things must therefore be explained.

If this is how societies are organized or put together, how then did they change? Here is where Marx and Engels borrowed directly from Hegel. Hegel's view of historical change was *dialectical,* by which he meant that it occurs through the inner contradictions or conflicts that something contains. For Hegel, dialectical contradictions occurred within the realm of the human mind, within ideas. Any idea that humans put forth (a thesis) contains its own logic opposite (or antithesis). For example, the idea of freedom implies its opposite, the idea of slavery. The idea "all people are free" implies its polar opposite "no people are free." The human mind wishes to resolve such contradictions, and so produces a third idea that is partly like the thesis and partly like the antithesis. This is the synthesis. In the preceding example it could be the idea "some people are free." But the new synthesis is also a second thesis, which produces a second antithesis, out of which emerges a second synthesis, which is itself yet a third thesis, and so on. This process produced increasingly better ideas and would continue, Hegel thought, until thought had been perfected. There would then be a society that had perfect religious, artistic, and philosophical institutions, and these institutions would form the basis for an ideal society.

Marx and Engels accepted Hegel's notion that historical change was dialectical, but they thought that the contradictions occurred within the economic base, not in the realm of ideas. Contradictions within the economic base led to changes within it that eventually led to its disintegration, and as the old economic base distintegrated it gave rise to a new economic base. Since economic bases condition or determine superstructures, the emergence of a new economic base led to the emergence of a new superstructure. Thus, changes within the superstructure were brought about mainly by changes that had already occurred within the base.

Marx and Engels marked off four major stages of social life, with one still to come. *Primitive communism* was the earliest stage of history and the simplest form of society. It was characterized by a rudimentary subsistence technology based on hunting and gathering, simple agriculture, or animal herding. The relations of production were communal and no social class divisions existed. The main contradiction of this stage was that between humans and nature—the limited nature of technology, making life a continual struggle for bare subsistence. With technological advance, humans were able to overcome their bare existence, but with this change also came private property and class divisions. *Slavery*, or the *ancient mode of production*, was the result. Here, class divisions existed in the form of masters and slaves. Ancient Greece and Rome were the leading representatives of this mode of production. In time, the contradictions of the slave mode led to its disintegration and the formation of the *feudal mode of production*. This occurred in the centuries after the fall of the Roman Empire. Feudalism was characteristic of Europe until the fifteenth or sixteenth centuries and was based on a class division between landlords and serfs. But this system, like previous modes of production, was unstable, and its contradictions eventually led to its downfall and the gradual emergence of *capitalism*. Capitalism was based on the production of goods and their sale in markets in order to make the maximum profit. Industrialization occurred on a massive scale and a new class, the capitalist class, came to dominate society and to subordinate a working class to its economic aims. But capitalism, too, contained fatal contradictions that would tear it apart in the end. Workers would revolt against capitalism and establish a workers' state that would end class divisions and exploitation. Thus, *socialism* was born, which would mark the end of history because socialism would not contain any fundamental contradictions.

This theory leaves much to be desired. Its stages of historical development pertain more to European history than to world social evolution, and it greatly oversimplifies the evolutionary process by seeing it as the result of a dialectic of class struggle. Important causal factors, especially population growth and environmental change, are ignored. Moreover, Marx's predictions about the transition from capitalism to socialism have failed miserably. The working class has shown little if any revolutionary potential in advanced capitalist societies, and socialist revolutions have occurred instead in much less developed agrarian societies where the peasantry was the largest and most revolutionary class. To make matters worse, socialism has not fulfilled Marx's expectations at all (with the possible exception of being more egalitarian than capitalism), and the major socialist societies broke down in the late 1980s and early 1990s and began evolving back toward capitalism. Nevertheless, the theory is moving in the right direction with its materialist understanding of social life and its view that material conditions are the driving forces of social change. Even though its predictions of the nature of capitalist breakdown have failed, it does pinpoint some of the problems that capitalism continues to confront, and it is indeed a distinct possibility that capitalism could break down in the longer run and give way to some other mode of production (Wallerstein, 1998). So the theory cannot be thrown on the intellectual junkpile just yet. It contains important insights even though a better overall theory of social evolution is needed.

## Twentieth-Century Evolutionism: First Generation

Toward the end of the nineteenth century, evolutionary thinking began to come under severe criticism, and as the criticisms mounted against it, evolutionism was ultimately abandoned by most social scientists. Throughout the early decades of the twentieth century, social scientists turned their attention to questions and problems other than those dealing with long-term social change. But evolutionism was not dead; it was only dormant. A number of scholars began to see that this "antievolutionary reaction" was a gross overreaction; it made many exaggerated claims based on a superficial reading of the works of the classical evolutionists, and some of its accusations were just flatly wrong (see Sanderson, 1990:36–49; 1997). Beginning in the 1930s and 1940s, it staged a significant revival, and the whole problem of long-term evolutionary change began once again to preoccupy the minds of many social scientists.

### V. Gordon Childe

The first major figure in the evolutionary revival was archaeologist V. Gordon Childe (1936, 1951, 1954), an Australian who spent his career at the University of Edinburgh in Scotland. Childe identified two great technological and social revolutions in human history and prehistory. The first, what he called the *Neolithic Revolution*, was so named because it was associated with the development of polished stone tools. However, its real importance was that it involved the domestication of plants and animals and thus the emergence of the first agricultural societies. The transition from food collection to food *production* allowed for the production of an economic surplus—a quantity of food above and beyond that necessary for survival—and the support of larger and denser populations.

As Neolithic communities continued to evolve over the millennia in several parts of the world, the way was paved for a second revolution, or the so-called *Urban Revolution*. The Urban Revolution was made possible by the invention of the plow.

The plow brought about dramatic increases in soil fertility; much greater quantities of food could be produced, which meant much bigger economic surpluses and still larger and denser populations. All of this led to the development of cities and urban life, craft specialization, sharp class divisions, and the creation of powerful governments needed to contain increasing social conflict and advance the interests of wealthy classes.

What was the driving force of social evolution? Childe considered himself a Marxist and advocated what he referred to as the "realist conception of history." However, he was a Marxist in only the most general sense of emphasizing technological and economic factors as the primary evolutionary forces. Technology seemed to loom larger than economics. He often spoke of the different forms of social organization that followed from the use of stone, bronze, or iron tools. His discussion of the Urban Revolution focused more on the causal significance of technological factors, especially the invention of the plow, than on anything else.

## Leslie White

After Childe came the American anthropologist Leslie White (1943, 1945, 1949, 1959). White refused to call himself a neoevolutionist because he insisted that his ideas were simply a reconstruction and restatement of the basic ideas of the classical evolutionists, Lewis Henry Morgan in particular. White distinguished between evolutionary and historical modes of explanation. *Historical accounts* are those that attempt to trace out and explain unique sequences of events, whereas *evolutionary accounts* ignore historical uniqueness and focus on the evolution of human culture as a whole. White adopted a threefold classification of the components of cultural systems: technology, social systems, and ideology. *Technology* consisted of the tools and techniques people had developed with respect to both subsistence and military aggression and defense. *Social systems* were the patterned social relationships that people carried on—kinship and family life, political organization, religious ritual, and the like. *Ideology* was mental rather than behavioral and consisted of the beliefs, values, philosophies, and symbolic systems that people shared.

White was a vigorous materialist and thus regarded the technological component as the foundation of culture and as determining both social systems and ideology. His technology-social systems-ideology compartmentalization of culture, in fact, recalls Marx's base-superstructure distinction, and many features of his analysis, especially as found in his major evolutionary work *The Evolution of Culture* (1959), are decidedly Marxist in tone. However, White gave technology a much greater causal role in social evolution than Marx ever did. This is obvious in White's formulation of his so-called *Law of Evolution:* Culture evolves as humans increase the amount of energy they harnessed per capita and per year, or as they increase the efficiency with which they put energy to work. Technological change, of course, is what makes the harnessing of increased energy and its more efficient use possible.

Like Childe, White identified two great technological revolutions in human history. The first, the *Agricultural Revolution*, was simply Childe's Neolithic Revolution. But whereas Childe's second revolution was the Urban Revolution, White's was what he called the *Fuel Revolution*, which has been more commonly called the Industrial Revolution. This second revolution began in England in the eighteenth century and was associated with the replacement of human manual power by machine power. Each of White's two technological revolutions had enormous consequences for the evolution of the other dimensions of culture.

White's evolutionary thinking was also permeated by Morgan's famous distinction between *societas* and *civitas*. The transition from *societas*, or primitive society, to *civitas*, or civil society, was brought about by the Agricultural Revolution. The development of an agricultural technology led to increasing population sizes and densities, and societies became more complex and occupationally specialized. There emerged carpenters, potters, weavers, metalworkers, and so on. Private ownership of the means of production replaced communal ownership, and class divisions and class struggles emerged and intensified. For White, the transition to civil society was associated with a number of economic, political, and social evils; here, he clearly reveals his more Marxist side.

## Julian Steward

Julian Steward (1949, 1955, 1977) was the third main figure in the evolutionary revival. Despite contributing to this revival, though, Steward clearly tried to distance himself from both Childe and White. Steward drew a distinction between three types of evolutionary analysis, which he called unilinear, universal, and multilinear evolutionism. By *unilinear* evolutionism Steward meant the theories of the nineteenth-century evolutionists. These he rejected as much too simplistic and as overstating parallel changes in human societies. *Universal* evolutionism involved the theories of Childe and Steward, which he thought operated at such an abstract and general level that they were of little real use—not wrong, necessarily, but at the same time not telling us very much. In place of these forms of evolutionary theorizing Steward proposed *multilinear* evolutionism. Multilinear evolutionism was much less sweeping in its generalizations, and instead concentrated on "those limited parallels of form, function, and sequence which have empirical validity" (Steward, 1955:19). Steward actually started out as a kind of unilinear evolutionist (Carneiro, 1973), but in time he became increasingly timid and nervous about it. His multilinear evolutionism was intended to be a sort of compromise between unilinear and universal evolutionism on the one hand and the analysis of unique historical sequences on the other. He wanted to generalize about long-term social change, but he also wanted to particularize, or take into account the unique features of societies and their historical sequences.

A good example of Steward's multilinear evolutionism is his analysis of parallel changes between two Indian tribes, the Algonkians of North America and the Mundurucu of South America. These societies were once very different but over time converged on similar patterns as they were influenced by outside pressures. The Algonkians lived by hunting and gathering and had no permanent settlements. The Mundurucu, by contrast, practiced a simple kind of tropical forest agriculture and lived in semipermanent villages. Both societies got sucked into commercial networks, the Mundurucu as rubber producers and the Algonkians as fur trappers, and as a result began to produce goods for sale in outside economic markets. This involvement in commercialism produced similar changes in both societies. Most significantly, their traditional kinship networks decayed in favor of the development of small nuclear families as the primary social group.

Steward was a materialist like Childe and White before him, but he put more causal emphasis on *ecological factors* than on technology and economics. In a famous early essay (1949), Steward adopted the famous hypothesis of Karl Wittfogel (1957) that highly despotic societies evolved in especially dry regions of the world to coordinate the irrigation works people had constructed in order to be able to farm the land at all. Steward gave such consistent emphasis to the causal role of ecology that he has long been recognized as the founder of the anthropological school of thought known as *cultural ecology* (Harris, 1968).

# Twentieth-Century Evolutionism: Second Generation

Childe, White, and Steward can be criticized for a number of false steps, outright errors, and confusions of various sorts. Nevertheless, their thinking reestablished the legitimacy of evolutionary thinking in the social sciences, and they set the stage for later theorists who could improve on their works. They also reestablished the legitimacy of a materialist mode of explanation, which had gone into hiding during the early decades of the twentieth century. All three thinkers had a profound influence on the next generation of evolutionary theorizing.

## Talcott Parsons's Idealist Evolutionism

The most famous sociological theorist of the middle of the twentieth century was a man by the name of Talcott Parsons. For most of his career Parsons showed little interest in social change, and his theories were often severely criticized because they seemed unable to explain why social change should occur at all. However, in the 1960s and 1970s, Parsons reformulated his thinking so that it could account for change. In fact, he went much further and developed a very elaborate theory of long-term social evolution (Parsons, 1966, 1971). Unlike the two thinkers whom we shall discuss next, Parsons showed no knowledge at all of the works of Childe, White, and Steward. Parsons's theory of social evolution owed much more to the ideas of the early sociologists Max Weber (1864–1920) and Emile Durkheim (1858–1917), and in unacknowledged ways to the philosophical idealism of Hegel.

The key concepts in Parsons's evolutionary theory are social differentiation, adaptive upgrading, and evolutionary universals. Social evolution for Parsons is primarily a process of *differentiation*, or one in which societies develop greater and greater levels of functional specialization and more elaborate forms of integration of their specialized parts. As societies become more differentiated, they undergo *adaptive upgrading*, which means that they experience improvements in the functional efficiency with which they operate. *Evolutionary universals* are social innovations that allow a society to function better and that provide the foundation for additional adaptive upgrading.

In Parsons's thinking, all of these concepts are closely intertwined. Three types of societies, and thus three stages of social evolution, are identified. *Primitive societies* are highly undifferentiated. Social life revolves around kinship and other dimensions of society, such as politics, economics, or religion; all occur within the framework of kinship relations. At some point in the development of primitive societies the evolutionary universal *social stratification* emerges. By rewarding some people more than others, primitive societies are able to develop more effective forms of leadership and thus function better. A second evolutionary universal at this early stage is *cultural legitimation*. This allows a society to develop a distinct identity separate from the cultural identities of other societies, and to develop core values and goals and establish means of realizing them.

The stage is then set for the emergence of *intermediate societies*. Parsons distinguishes two subtypes of these societies: archaic societies and historic empires. *Archaic societies* have literate priesthoods, which represents a religious differentiation between specialists and laypersons. Archaic societies are also characterized by a third evolutionary universal, *adminstrative bureaucracy*, and there is substantial separation between the political officials who staff this bureaucracy and religious officials. Egypt and Mesopotamia are the two leading examples of this type of society. *Historic empires*, of which the leading four examples are historic China, India, Islamic civilization, and ancient Rome, differ from archaic societies largely in terms of what Parsons calls their *philosophical breakthroughs*. China, India, and Islam developed much more advanced philosophical and religious systems than any society before them, and they were also characterized by the substantial development of a fourth evolutionary universal, *money and markets*. Ancient Roman society retained a polytheistic religious system, but it went much farther than the other three empires in terms of the development of money and markets. Its major philosophical breakthroughs were made with respect to concepts of law and citizenship. It developed an elaborate system of law that formed the basis for modern legal systems, and it developed an early form of citizenship and democracy.

*Modern societies* represent the third and final stage of social evolution. The first modern societies, England, France, and Holland, emerged in the sixteenth century. England was the most modern of these three because it was the most differentiated. Commercial farming arose, and the newly established Protestantism played a role in breaking down the traditional fusion of religion and government. Parliamentary government and legal changes emphasizing individual rights also developed. The most important developments in the emergence of modern societies were the industrial and democratic revolutions. The Industrial Revolution was extremely important because it led to massive differentiation within the economy and freed labor from the constraints to which it had been subject in earlier medieval society. The democratic revolution established a whole new value system, one emphasizing achievement and equality of opportunity.

The development of modern societies was also closely tied to the emergence of the final two evolutionary universals: generalized universalistic norms and the democratic association. *Generalized universalistic norms* are abstract legal rules that apply to a whole society. Rome pioneered in this area, but English common law took things much further. The *democratic association* involves the election of political leaders to office and it allowed power to be based on a broad societal consensus.

Although England led the way into modernity, modernity is epitomized today by the United States, which Parsons refers to as "the new lead society of contemporary modernity." This society is the most highly differentiated society that has ever existed, and it has carried universalistic norms farther than ever before. Its emphasis on achievement has been greater than that of any other society in human history.

So much for how the evolutionary process works according to Parsons. What is driving it? Here, Parsons departs radically from the materialists of the evolutionary revival—whose work he probably never bothered to read—and formulates a distinctively idealist theoretical argument in the tradition of Hegel. Parsons emphasizes as the primary causal factors in social evolution such things as symbolic codes, philosophical and religious systems, and legal norms. For example, the transition to the historic empires was made possible by important philosophical breakthroughs, and Judaism and Christianity were important to the development of modernity because they were universalistic monotheistic religions. Moreover, modernity was only made possible by the emergence of generalized universalistic norms and democratic values. All throughout social evolution, it appears, the human mind has been doing most of the work. It has been thinking itself to higher and higher levels and creating societies with greater and greater levels of adaptive capacity.

There are many problems with Parsons's theory of social evolution, only the most serious of which can be noted here (cf. Sanderson, 1990:118–130). His master concept is that of social differentiation. For Parsons, this is overwhelmingly the great trend of the evolutionary process. There is little doubt that increasing differentiation has been *one* trend in long-term social evolution, but is it the master trend? We think not. There are many aspects of social evolution that have little or nothing to do with differentiation. The evolution of increasingly sophisticated subsistence technologies, for example, represents the emergence of new *kinds* of technology whose differences involve much more than just increasing complexity. Moreover, as Charles Tilly (1984) points out, much of social evolution involves decreasing rather than increasing differentiation. Such evolutionary processes as the steadily decreasing number of political units in the world over the past several thousand years, the development of capitalist mass consumption, and increasing linguistic standardization are actually processes of *de*differentiation.

The problems with the differentiation concept become more serious when it is linked with the notion of adaptive upgrading. There are two difficulties here. First, Parsons thinks of entire societies as the units that do the adapting. We would argue that this is a logical error, a form of what is called *reification*. To reify something is to give it a type or level of reality that it cannot logically possess. Parsons does this with societies. But societies cannot do any adapting, only individuals can. Only individuals possess a brain and consciousness, and thus only they can adjust themselves to circumstances in ways designed to meet their needs and promote their goals.

The second difficulty involves Parsons's notion that the level of adaptiveness somehow increases throughout social evolution. Parsons clearly states that primitive societies have the lowest adaptive capacity, whereas modern capitalist and industrial societies have the most (thus implying that the latter are "better" than the former). It is certainly true that modern societies have improved the quality of human life in many ways compared to primitive societies (e.g., improving the standard of living, reducing infant mortality, lengthening the life span). But primitive societies lasted for tens of thousands of years, and modern societies—which have been around only a very short time by comparison—are rapidly damaging their environments and live with the continual threat of ecological collapse and nuclear holocaust; they are therefore at risk of having the shortest existence of all known societies. In what sense is this an increase in a society's adaptive abilities? Parsons has fallen into the trap that has snared many a social evolutionist—that bigger and later are necessarily better than smaller and earlier. It isn't always the case, by any means.

Finally, Parsons's explanatory account of social evolution leaves a great deal to be desired. Here, Parsons largely falls back on an old chestnut—the notion that the evolution of society is driven by the expanding powers of the human mind. But if this is the case, why does the mind itself evolve? Parsons provides no clear answer to this critical question. He seems to be implicitly saying that the mind just has some sort of natural tendency to advance, to think itself to higher and higher levels. This is extremely unconvincing and unsatisfying. In this regard, Parsonian evolutionism closely resembles Hegel's philosophy of history, although without the concept of dialectics. (At least Hegel provided a mechanism of mental change, no matter how wrong his philosophy of history may have been!) It will be our contention in this book that the evolution of ideas is not much of an independent driving force, and that mental evolution is itself largely a product of other, more basic, evolutionary changes.

## Gerhard Lenski's Technological Evolutionism

Although a sociologist, Gerhard Lenski's (1966, 1970) evolutionism was little influenced by sociologists, despite resembling Parsonian evolutionism in some respects. Rather, his ideas bear the unmistakable imprint of Childe and White and, indeed, are substantially derived from them.

In Lenski's view, social evolution is primarily a process whereby societies mobilize increasing levels of *energy* and especially *information* in adapting to their environments. Lenski borrowed White's compartmentalization of societies into technology, social systems, and ideology, and restated as well White's notion that social systems and ideologies are largely shaped by the nature of technologies. Technological advance produces a wide range of important consequences for social systems and ideologies. Because it allows societies to utilize their environments more efficiently, technological advance leads to population growth. More mouths can be fed and more lives supported. As people gain increasing control over their food supply, they begin to live in larger and more permanent settlements.

Technological advance also leads to increases in economic productivity, and as a result social and economic inequalities open up and progressively widen because people struggle for control over the wealth that is being created. As the stakes get larger, people have more incentives to compete to get more for themselves. Increasing technological sophistication also leads to social differentiation and increasing occupational specialization. Many people become freed from the necessity of producing their own living by hunting, farming, or herding and move into specialized roles involving managing the economy and coordinating governmental activity. And as all of these things happen, people experience an overall increase in the amount of leisure time available to them, time that can be used to develop the non-economic dimensions of society and culture. Some people become, for example, priests, artists, or educators. The symbolic and ideational aspects of culture become increasingly elaborate. Lenski has repudiated the label *technological determinist*, which he has often been given, because he says that technology is not the only important causal force. Nevertheless, technological change is clearly the primary force of social evolution for Lenski.

A very important contribution made by Lenski was the development of a better and more precise evolutionary typology of societies (he actually borrowed from the anthropologist Walter Goldschmidt, 1959, in this regard). He distinguishes six major types of societies on the main evolutionary line of development. *Hunting and gathering societies* are the simplest and earliest. Their members live in small, nomadic bands and hunt wild game and collect wild plants. With the Neolithic Revolution that began some 10,000 years ago came the earliest and crudest agriculture, and thus were born *horticultural societies*. They cultivated the land in the form of small gardens using hand tools. *Simple horticultural societies* used only digging sticks as cultivating implements, but *advanced horticultural societies* used metal hoes, which allowed them to work the land more efficiently.

As agricultural methods improved, *agrarian societies* emerged between about 4,000 and 5,000 years ago. The key technological advance here was the development of the plow and the harnessing of animal energy for plowing. Agrarian societies without iron plows or other tools Lenski refers to as *simple agrarian societies;* those with iron plows and other tools he calls *advanced agrarian societies. Industrial societies* began to arise two and a half centuries ago with the English industrial revolution. They are based on the substitution of machine power for manual power and the factory system. As industrialization intensified, people moved off the land into towns and cities, and thus industrial societies became highly urbanized societies.

Lenski also distinguishes three types of societies not on the main line of social evolution. *Fishing societies* are nonagricultural societies, but they depend on fishing rather than hunting for their supply of meat. *Herding societies* specialize in animal herding rather than agriculture in dry environments not suitable for cultivation. *Industrializing societies* are the less-developed societies of the contemporary world.

Lenski's evolutionism was a major contribution to sociology when it first emerged in the mid-1960s. It helped to recapture the comparative and historical outlook that sociology had once had but had lost in the early part of the twentieth century. Nevertheless, his evolutionary perspective is not without flaw. We note only in passing that Lenski's evolutionism is similar to Parsons's in that society is the unit that is doing the adapting, and societies increase their adaptive capacity as they evolve. We have already criticized this idea.

The most serious problem with Lenski's theory is that it gives far too much emphasis to technological change as the primary causal force. It is certainly true that technological advance is a major part of the evolutionary process and that it is closely intertwined with the other dimensions of social evolution. However, Lenski is never able to demonstrate that technological change is what is causing the other changes. More recent work, in fact, suggests that technological change is itself more often—perhaps much more often—an effect rather than a cause. Moreover, if technological change is a primary, first cause, as Lenski claims, what is driving it? Lenski's tacit assumption is that technological change is basically a matter of improving human knowledge. Lenski is a technological Socratic: The society that knows the good chooses the good. Technological change is almost always a good thing because it allows people to adapt more efficiently to nature, and once people have invented new technologies they will almost always put them to use.

As will be seen in the discussion that follows and elsewhere in this book, there are good reasons for questioning not only Lenski's claim about the causal role of technological change but also his claim that people always perceive technological change as good and will automatically use new technologies when they become available. In fact, people often resist them because, contrary to Lenski, new technologies usually increase the workload and thus actually decrease the amount of leisure time most people have available to them.

## Marvin Harris's Cultural Materialism

Virtually all of the evolutionists we have discussed thus far have been *progressivists;* that is, they have all regarded social evolution as leading to overall **progress,** defined either as improved societal functioning or an improvement in the quality of the human condition. Even Marx, who was a bitter critic of capitalist society, regarded it as an improvement over feudalism in many respects and as a necessary way-station in the transition to socialism. With Marvin Harris (1968, 1977, 1979) one encounters a very different kind of thinker. Harris's evolutionary theorizing is the antithesis of the extreme progressivism of Parsonian evolutionism, and it differs from Parsonian theory in almost every other way possible. It is primarily individuals rather than societies that adapt, and societies do not experience increased adaptiveness as they evolve. Harris is one of the few social evolutionists who is a non- or antiprogressivist.

Harris was greatly influenced by Childe, White, and Steward, but also by Marx. Although Childe thought of himself as a Marxist, and although White showed Marxian influences that he never acknowledged, Harris is more Marxian than both without ever thinking of himself as a Marxist. He gives much more attention to economic relationships, and much less attention to technology, than either of these other thinkers.

In the 1950s, Harris began to create a general theoretical perspective that continued to develop throughout the 1960s and 1970s. He called this perspective *cultural materialism.* Cultural materialism divides all societies into three components that are reminiscent of Marx's base-superstructure distinction and White's distinction between technology, social systems, and ideology. For Harris, all societies have the components that he calls infrastructure, structure, and superstructure. The *infrastructure* consists of technology, ecosystems, technoenvironmental relationships, and the demographic features of societies (the features of a society's population, such as its size, density, growth rate, age and sex ratios, and the technology of birth control and population regulation). The *structure* contains two subcomponents, *political economy* (ownership of the means of production, class and caste structures, political organization, and war) and *domestic economy* (marriage and family patterns, gender relations, and age roles). The *superstructure* is the mental or ideational component of societies; it includes a society's basic beliefs, values, and norms, as well as philosophies, religion, science, art, music, and ritual.

Harris conceptualizes the relationship between these three major components in terms of his *principle of infrastructural determinism*. This holds that the infrastructure conditions the structure which in turn conditions the superstructure. The principle is probabilistic—this is what happens most but not all of the time—and allows for the occurrence of other causal relationships. As a principle applied to social evolution, it holds that changes are most often initiated within the infrastructure and these changes set off reverberating changes in the structure and superstructure.

Why should things work this way? Harris's answer is that the infrastructure has a logical causal priority because it involves those dimensions of human social life that are most fundamental to human survival and reproduction. Without the infrastructure, humans cannot live, nor can they produce more humans; this gives it a critical importance not possessed by the structure and superstructure, even though these other two components are very important in their own right. Since the parts of societies need to have a basic compatibility with one another so everything does not break down, the logically prior existence of the infrastructure constrains the ways in which the structure and superstructure can develop. They must develop in ways reasonably consistent with how the members of a society get a living and how they create the next generation.

Although Harris always had an evolutionary view of social life, with the publication of his book *Cannibals and Kings: The Origins of Cultures* (1977) he formulated a more precise theory of social evolution. Here, he attempts to explain the broad outlines of the past 10,000 years of social evolution by making use of the concepts of **environmental depletion** and **intensification of production**. The application of technology to the environment, and the steady (even if very slow) growth of population, invariably produce a situation in which people's environments become depleted, which means that they yield less energy (mostly less food) for the same effort. Living standards decline. People may tolerate decline for a while, but any further decline may make the situation unacceptable. At this point, people intensify their productive efforts. Initially, this need not involve any changes in the nature of technology; people simply work harder and longer and make more vigorous use of existing resources. This helps to prevent living standards from dropping even lower, but only for a while. Eventually, a new type of intensification, one based on advancing the level of technology, must be introduced. Hunter-gatherers start cultivating and eventually become virtually full-time horticulturalists. Simple horticulturalists gradually become more advanced horticulturalists. And so on and so forth. But in the long run, this technological intensification is a losing proposition. Like Alice in

Wonderland, people have to run faster and faster just to keep from falling further and further behind.

The trump card in this whole process is the growth of population. People have discovered a variety of ways of limiting childbirth and controlling population, but these techniques are seldom effective enough to prevent population from growing at all. Throughout the tens of thousands of years that humans lived as hunter-gatherers, their populations grew very slowly, but grew they did. As a result, hunter-gatherers eventually depleted their environments to the point where they had to start adopting plant and animal domestication (something they had heretofore resisted because it took more time and energy). With the transition to horticultural societies people relaxed their birth control techniques because now they could produce more food to feed many more people. But this was soon counterproductive, because the rate of population growth accelerated, leading to even more rapid depletion. The process of social evolution itself accelerated.

Agrarian societies eventually replaced horticultural ones, and eventually a massive form of technoenvironmental intensification occurred in the form of the Industrial Revolution, which is rapidly depleting the earth's resources on an unprecedented scale. What would have happened had humans been able to keep their populations from growing? The answer is, we would all still be hunting game and collecting plants (and no one would be reading this book, which would not exist). But we couldn't, and therefore we aren't. We are caught up in an evolutionary process that, Harris surmises, will threaten our very existence unless we can discover heretofore unimagined technologies.

It is important to see how different Harris's theory is from the technological determinism of Childe, White, and Lenski. For Harris, technology advances not simply because knowledge increases, but because humans are compelled by declining living standards to work harder and longer to feed more mouths. Moreover, technological advance is not producing continual improvement in Lenski's sense; on the contrary, living standards continue to go down in spite of technological advances (but would go down even more, and foreshadow human extinction, without technological advance). The Industrial Revolution involved such a massive technological advance that the quality of life has certainly improved for most people—they live longer, healthier, more interesting lives, for example—but most of this improvement has occurred within two centuries or less. For nearly all of the past ten millennia humans have been on a downward spiral, however much that conclusion may conflict with one's preconceptions about human history.

Harris's overall cultural materialist approach, and his more specific intensification-depletion-renewed intensification evolutionary model, represent a major intellectual advance in understanding long-term social change. Rather than engage in a general critique here (see Sanderson, 1990:164–168; 1994c; 2001:114–119), we shall limit ourselves to one main point. As an anthropologist, Harris has naturally focused his attention on preindustrial societies and preindustrial social evolution. His ideas have relevance for modern industrial societies, and he has applied them as such (see in particular Harris, 1981). However, Harris's strong emphasis on ecological and demographic factors has made his model much less useful for the analysis of the modern world than for its precursors.

The modern world got its start in the sixteenth century with the rise of the capitalist mode of production (Wallerstein, 1974a, 1974b, 1979), and this created an "evolutionary rupture" within the evolutionary process. The "rules of the evolutionary game," so to speak, were partially rewritten. Economics became a lot more important than demography and ecology. Harris recognizes this to some extent, but his models are not fully equipped to deal with it. Note that in the Marxian base-superstructure model the relations of production are part of the infrastructure or base, whereas in Harris's cultural materialist model these relations have been shifted to the structure (more specifically, into political economy). Whereas economic relations have now assumed center stage, and thus should be considered a crucial part of the insfrastructure in modern capitalism, Harris has relegated them to the structure, which does much less of the causal work.

Let us end this theoretical discussion before we overtax you. Suffice it to say that Harris's ideas are extremely important, but they can be improved on, especially by infusing them with ideas from other theoretical traditions. This leads us to what might be called the third phase of twentieth-century evolutionary thinking.

# Twentieth-Century Evolutionism: Third Generation

Since the late 1970s, a variety of evolutionary theories have been developed. An especially popular type of evolutionary theory relies on an analogy with Darwin's theory of biological evolution by natural selection. Theories such as this have been developed by, for example, Donald Campbell (1965), John Langton (1979), L. L. Cavalli-Sforza and Marcus Feldman (1981), and, in a slightly different form, W. G. Runciman (1989). Since these theories focus largely on the *process* of evolution rather than its *fact and course*, and, since they seem to draw much too close a connection between Darwinian natural selection and social evolution, we have not found them especially useful (see Sanderson, 1990:170–174, for a critique).

Another recent popular type of theory is what has been called a *coevolutionary* theory. Theories of this nature have been set forth by Charles Lumsden and E. O. Wilson (1981), Robert Boyd and Peter Richerson (1985), and William Durham (1991). These theories attempt to show that social evolution is a product of both genetic transmission and social or cultural transmission, and, indeed, that the two are often closely intertwined. Coevolutionary theories have certain valuable uses, but they, like natural selectionist theories, have not been especially effective in either describing or explaining social evolution over the long term (see Sanderson, 1990:174–180, for a critique).

One of the most ambitious recent attempts to explain the fact and course of long-term social evolution has been that of Stephen Sanderson. His theory, which he calls **evolutionary materialism,** is set forth in a highly detailed propositional manner (see Sanderson, 1994c, 1995, 1999b:3–16). Evolutionary materialism builds directly on Harris's cultural materialism and may be thought of as a formalization and extension of it. It accepts Harris's division of societies into infrastructure, structure, and superstructure but slightly reformulates the notion of infrastructure. Harris had divided "economy" into two major components: *subsistence economy* on the one hand and *political economy* on the other. The first was placed in the infrastructure, the second in the structure. Sanderson has kept these two components of economy together and placed them both in the infrastructure. This makes it possible to produce a much more logical infrastructural analysis of the contemporary world. Sanderson formulates infrastructure, structure, and superstructure as follows:

1. **Infrastructure:** The raw materials and social forms relevant to human survival and adaptation.
   - *Technology:* The information, tools, and techniques that underlie economic action.
   - *Economy:* The organized system whereby goods and services are produced, distributed, and exchanged among individuals and groups.
   - *Ecology:* The totality of the physical or natural environment to which humans must adapt.
   - *Demography:* The nature and dynamics of human populations and the technology of birth control.

2. **Structure:** The organized patterns of social behavior carried out among the members of a society, excluding those social patterns that belong to the infrastructure.
   - *Stratification systems:* Class and caste divisions and the relationships between such groups.
   - *Racial and ethnic stratification:* Social divisions based on putative physical and/or cultural differences between and among groups.
   - *Political organization:* Structures of leadership and rule characteristic of a society.
   - *Gender roles and relations:* Social arrangements between the sexes with respect to power, authority, and rights and perquisites.
   - *Family and kinship:* Patterns of marriage and the organization of people into households and groups based on descent and genealogical affiliation.

3. **Superstructure:** The shared ways in which the members of a society think, conceptualize, evaluate, and feel.
   - *Beliefs, values, and norms:* Shared cognitive assumptions about truth and falsehood, socially defined conceptions of worth, and shared standards or rules regarding proper or improper social conduct.
   - *Religion:* Shared beliefs, values, and norms pertaining to postulated supernatural beings, powers, or forces.
   - *Science:* Techniques for the acquisition and accumulation of knowledge relying on systematic observation and experience.
   - *Art:* Symbolic images or representations having aesthetic, emotional, or intellectual value for the artistic producers and other members of society. Broadly defined to include *music* and *literature*.

Evolutionary materialism also contains a **Principle of Infrastructural Determinism** (as well as Marx's and Harris's claim about why the infrastructure has logical priority) but modifies Harris's version slightly. Sanderson's version of the principle postulates that ecology and demography are the most frequent infrastructural determinants in small-scale societies resting on hunting and gathering, simple agriculture, or animal herding; that these factors plus technology and economy are all important causal forces in large-scale agrarian civilizations; and that economy, especially "political economy," is the most likely infrastructural determinant in the modern capitalist world. Sanderson emphasizes that throughout the process of social evolution there have been "evolutionary ruptures," so that with the transition to a new type of society there may be a reconstitution of the "evolutionary rules of the game" such that different "evolutionary logics" appear in different historical or prehistorical eras. In other words, the logic whereby modern capitalist society evolves is different in some crucial respects from the logic whereby hunter-gatherer or horticultural societies evolve.

Evolutionary materialism also accepts Harris's distinction (developed by earlier scholars) among parallel, convergent, and divergent evolution. **Parallel evolution** occurs when two or more societies evolve in basically similar ways and at similar rates. Beginning about 10,000 years ago, for example, human communities in various regions of the world independently began to domesticate plants and animals and to live increasingly by agriculture. The adoption of agriculture in these communities led to strikingly similar changes in their structures and superstructures. Likewise, several thousand years later, societies in many of the same regions where agriculture first arose underwent parallel changes in social and political structure that led to the emergence of civilizations. **Convergent evolution** results when societies that have originally been dissimilar evolve in ways that make them increasingly alike. The United States and Japan, for example, have evolved along convergent lines in the past 100 years or so, and other east Asian societies, such as Taiwan and South Korea, are beginning to converge with Western societies. **Divergent evolution** occurs when originally similar societies evolve along lines of increasing dissimilarity. Japan and Indonesia, for example, were much more similar in the sixteenth and seventeenth centuries than they are today (Geertz, 1963). Japan is a modern industrial nation with a very high standard of living, whereas Indonesia remains a poor, underdeveloped country. Harris has suggested that parallel and convergent evolution have figured more significantly in human history than divergent evolution, and evolutionary materialism accepts that premise. This book therefore concentrates on the first two evolutionary modes and says less about the third mode.

Any good evolutionary theory must also recognize three other processes or outcomes of human adaptation: continuity, devolution, and extinction (recognized explicitly by Lenski and implicitly by Harris). Evolutionary materialism explicitly acknowledges these outcomes. **Social continuity** is the relative lack of change from one generation, or a whole series of generations, to the next. There is no such thing as a totally unchanging society, but there are societies that change little over long periods of time. Some hunter-gatherer societies, for example, have survived into the modern era, as have some horticultural and pastoral societies. In general, the smaller a society is in scale, and the simpler its mode of technology and economic life, the less likely it is to undergo fundamental changes.

**Social devolution** is a reversal of evolutionary change; it involves the movement of a society back to an earlier evolutionary stage, or at least the adoption of some characteristics of societies at earlier stages of development. This might mean a decrease in complexity, a loss of social cohesion, or a reversion to subsistence methods more characteristic of an earlier evolutionary stage. The Ik of Uganda provide a striking illustration of a society that lost virtually all of its social cohesion (Turnbull, 1972). The Ik were a hunter-gatherer society that experienced economic disaster when their traditional hunting grounds were turned into a game preserve by the Ugandan government. This event precipitated the virtual collapse of Ik society. With the loss of their traditional means of subsistence, and with the shift to agriculture made difficult or impossible, the Ik experienced a substantial decline in population and lost their basis of political cohesion.

Ester Boserup (1965) points out that communities will often regress to earlier and simpler techniques of cultivation when their population densities decline. This has occurred in South America in recent centuries, and in parts of Africa and south and southeast Asia in the twentieth century. People will often shift back to simpler cultivation methods because they involve less work and are sufficient to feed a sparser population.

Sometimes large-scale societies undergo major collapses. Joseph Tainter (1988) has called attention to the frequency with which agrarian empires have collapsed, usually because they have invested so many resources in building a highly complex society that it becomes too costly to sustain it for more than a limited time. The most famous example of the collapse of an ancient empire is, of course, the collapse of the Roman Empire in the fifth century CE. Rome had created a huge empire, which extended all the way from Egypt in the south to the British Isles in the north. The diverse regions of the empire were linked by a marvelous system of roads, and the empire was centralized economically, politically, and militarily. When the empire finally fell apart after a long and slow period of decline, Europe devolved into a vast region filled with largely economically self-sufficient villages and principalities.

**Social extinction** involves the complete obliteration of a society. This has been the fate of numerous hunter-gatherer societies in recent times, as well as various societies of greater evolutionary complexity. A society can become extinct either through the physical extermination of its members or through its absorption into another society by means of political conquest. Both of these processes have occurred frequently in human history, especially since the rise of modern capitalism in the sixteenth century. The North American continent, for example, was once filled with hundreds of Indian tribes. With the emergence and expansion of the new American civilization, most of the members of these tribes were killed in bloody wars. Those who remained were eventually herded onto reservations, their aboriginal way of life largely lost.

Cultural materialism emphasizes the adaptive character of social evolution, and evolutionary materialism does likewise. What is meant by calling social evolution an **adaptive** process is that *social patterns are created by humans as rational responses* *to the problems of existence that they confront, and when the nature of these problems changes, as invariably happens, the responses must and will change as well.* Several important clarifications and qualifications of the concept of **adaptation** need to be made.

First, to say that a social pattern is adaptive is not to imply that it is therefore "good" or "morally desirable." A claim about adaptation is a scientific assessment of how various types of social patterns originate, persist, and change. A claim about "goodness," by contrast, is completely different. It is a judgment about whether one likes or approves of the things that people do. Thus, it is perfectly possible to identify a social pattern as adaptive and feel a moral repugnance for it. For example, in many societies in the contemporary Middle East, clitoridectomy (surgical removal of the clitoris) and infibulation (sewing the vaginal opening shut) are common practices. Members of Western societies usually find these practices repugnant, but they can be regarded as adaptations (at least for males) intended to reduce female sexual response and to control female sexual behavior. To understand this fact is to make a scientific statement, not a judgment of moral desirability.

Similarly, in all types of societies infanticide—the selective killing of infants, most commonly females—has been practiced, often with great frequency. Infanticide occurs even occasionally in modern industrial societies. Infanticide is adaptive for couples when they lack sophisticated birth control techniques and when the circumstances for rearing a child are poor. They may lack the economic resources to support another child, or attempting to support that child may have a negative impact on the well-being of older children. Infanticide may also occur when people want a child of the opposite sex; female infants may be killed when parents desire a son, male infants when they desire a daughter. These are the most common reasons why infanticide occurs (Hrdy, 1999), and thus mothers, couples, or older children benefit from it. But to explain infanticide is one thing; condoning or accepting it in a moral sense is quite another.

We also need to be clear about the kind of unit to which the concept of adaptation applies—about just what it is that does the adapting. Sociologists such as Parsons have assumed that the adaptive unit is an entire society. But such a notion is misplaced. As argued earlier in this chapter, societies are not comparable to organisms or individual persons; they do not have brains or consciousness, or needs and desires, and thus they cannot adapt to anything. Since only individual persons have these properties, only they can be units of adaptation. Of course, we sometimes speak about whether or not a social pattern is adaptive for a group or even a whole society, but when we do this it is clear that we can only be referring to an aggregate of individuals, and that it is from the point of view of each individual that the adaptation is judged.

This leads to another crucial point: An adaptive social pattern may not be equally beneficial for all individuals or groups within a society. It is frequently the case that a pattern that benefits some individuals or groups is maladaptive for others. Indeed, the more evolutionarily complex a society is, the more this is likely to be the case. In the earlier example, clitoridectomy and infibulation have been introduced because they benefit men at the expense of women, and men have sufficient power over women to have developed the social patterns and to keep them alive.

Moreover, early industrial capitalism was adaptive for wealthy factory owners, but it was highly maladaptive for the many factory workers who died from exhaustion, malnutrition, and disease (Engels, 1973; orig. 1845). And modern world capitalism is much more adaptive for the members of some societies than the members of others. It benefits people in the rich industrial countries much more than it does the members of poor ones.

As pointed out earlier with respect to Parsonian evolutionism, it is extremely important to recognize that it is inappropriate to claim that adaptation necessarily increases throughout social evolution. This notion of "increased adaptive capacity" has been a common one, being endorsed by some evolutionary materialists (cf. Childe, 1936; L. White, 1959) in addition to Parsons and his followers. This book rejects such a view, which is difficult to support by scientifically objective criteria (Granovetter, 1979). New social forms emerge as adaptations, but these altered adaptations should be regarded simply as new and different adaptations rather than as better ones. This does not mean that progress has never occurred. Indeed, it has, especially with the formation of modern industrial societies. But throughout much of social evolution, as stressed by Harris, things have often run downhill in terms of the quality of human life for most people. However, even with progress, *there is no warrant for claiming that society somehow functions better or more efficiently.* Such a statement involves a reification of society and contradicts the notion that it is individuals and their needs and desires that are the units of adaptation.

Finally, we must acknowledge that not all social patterns are adaptations, and thus the concept of adaptation does not have universal applicability. But even though we cannot use the concept everywhere and at all times, we are still far better off with it than without it. Indeed, by having a notion of adaptation as a guiding premise we will be in a position to identify which social traits are not adaptations and why they are not.

## FOR FURTHER READING

Sanderson's *Social Evolutionism: A Critical History* (1990) provides a detailed explication and critical evaluation of theories of social evolution from the mid-nineteenth century to the present. Bruce Trigger's *Sociocultural Evolution* (1998) is a similar effort. An article by Robert Carneiro (1973) lays out four types of social evolution that have been identified by social scientists, and his book *Evolutionism in Cultural Anthropology* (2003) is a good succinct history of evolutionary theorizing, especially classical evolutionism. G. A. Cohen's *Karl Marx's Theory of History: A Defence* (1978) is a celebrated analysis of the subtleties and nuances of Marxian historical materialism, although its arguments are highly controversial and rejected by many (see Sanderson, 1990:50–74, for a critique and reformulation). Parsons's theory of social evolution is discussed in a pair of books, *Societies: Evolutionary and Comparative Perspectives* (1966) and *The System of Modern Societies* (1971).

Harris's *The Rise of Anthropological Theory* (1968) is a classic history of anthropological theory with considerable emphasis on evolutionary theories. His *Cultural Materialism: The Struggle for a Science of Culture* (1979) lays out his general theoretical perspective in great detail, and his *Cannibals and Kings: The Origins of Cultures* (1977) presents his intensification-depletion-renewed intensification model of social evolution. Lenski's main arguments are presented in his *Power and Privilege: A Theory of Social Stratification* (1966) and *Human Societies: A Macro-level Introduction to Sociology* (1970). Sanderson's evolutionary materialism and its application to the major evolutionary changes in world history and prehistory is presented in *Social Transformations: A General Theory of Historical Development* (1995; expanded ed. 1999b). An article-length version of the same is Sanderson (1994c).

Graeme Donald Snooks, an economic historian, has written a trilogy of books that deal in important conceptual and theoretical ways with the whole problem of historical development over the past several thousand years: *The Dynamic Society: Exploring the Sources of Global Change* (1996), *The Ephemeral Civilization: Exploding the Myth of Social Evolution* (1997), and *The Laws of History* (1998). These books raise deep theoretical questions and are extremely provocative interpretations of long-term historical change. Snooks presents a resolutely materialist interpretation of history that reveals many crucial insights. Although he argues against an evolutionary interpretation of history, he is in fact a type of social evolutionist.

David Christian's *Maps of Time: An Introduction to Big History* (2004) is an extraordinary attempt to do what he calls "Big History." He not only provides an excellent analysis of the evolutionary dynamics of the past 10,000 years of human history but he also discusses the origin of the universe, the origin of life on earth, and human origins and evolution. Christian also projects the human future over the near, medium, and long term.

CHAPTER

3

# Preindustrial Societies

## Hunter-Gatherers and Horticulturalists

In order for their members to survive, all societies obviously must develop technology and establish some form of economic life. Technology and economy are very closely related in every society but are by no means the same thing. A society's **technology** consists of the tools, techniques, and knowledge that its members have created in order to meet their needs and wants. A society's **economy,** on the other hand, consists of the socially organized way in which goods and services are produced and distributed. This chapter and Chapter 4 discuss the evolution of preindustrial forms of technology, conceived here as *subsistence technology*, or the technology directly related to getting and maintaining a living, as well as the types of political economy that correspond to these technological forms. We will look at five types of societies arranged in a general evolutionary order: hunter-gatherer, simple horticultural, and intensive horticultural societies, and, in Chapter 4, agrarian and pastoral societies. At the end of Chapter 4 we will discuss the reasons one type of society has replaced another in the evolutionary history of the human species. Industrialism as a mode of technological, social, and economic life will be discussed in Chapter 6.

## Hunter-Gatherer Societies

### Subsistence Technology

For about 99 percent of their history, humans subsisted entirely by hunting wild animals and gathering wild plant foods. The total monopoly of the hunting and gathering way of life was not broken until some 10,000 years ago, when some societies began to subsist by the practice of agriculture. During the past 10,000 years, **hunter-gatherer societies** have grown fewer and fewer in number, and only a handful remain today. Most of these are found in relatively isolated geographical locations, such as the arid and semiarid regions of Australia, the central rain forest and southwestern desert regions of Africa, and the Arctic. It is unlikely that even these will survive more than a few decades longer. The hunting and gathering way of life is soon destined to be only a historical relic known to ethnography and archaeology.

Most of what is currently known about hunter-gatherers is based on fieldwork conducted among surviving hunting and gathering groups. It cannot be known with any certainty how similar these groups may be to hunting and gathering societies of prehistoric times. No doubt there are a number of differences, but it is also likely that there are many striking similarities. In any event, the description of the hunting and gathering way of life that follows is based primarily on the results of contemporary ethnographic research.

Hunter-gatherers live in small groups known as *local bands*. These are groups of about 25 to 50 men, women, and children who cooperate with each other in the quest for subsistence. Each local band is a more or less politically autonomous and economically self-sufficient unit. However, many local bands are usually connected by ties of intermarriage into a much larger cultural unit, sometimes known as a **tribe.** A tribe is a network of bands all of whose members share the same cultural patterns and speak the same language. Furthermore, the composition of each local band is constantly shifting, with people frequently moving from one band to another. Such movement may arise from marriage or from a need to create a more even balance between population size and the food supply.

How do hunter-gatherers divide their time between hunting and gathering? Some years ago Richard Lee (1968) estimated that contemporary hunting and gathering societies derive approximately two-thirds of their diet from gathered foods of all sorts, holding that this figure closely corresponds to the subsistence activities of prehistoric hunter-gatherers. This idea has come to be widely accepted by social scientists, even to the extent that the suggestion has been made that such societies might be more appropriately named "gatherer-hunter" societies.

However, a closer look suggests a rather different picture. Carol Ember (1978), using a sample of 181 contemporary hunter-gatherer societies drawn from the *Ethnographic Atlas* (Murdock, 1967), a larger and more inclusive sample than the one used by Lee, shows that hunter-gatherers are rather evenly divided in their emphasis on the activities of gathering, hunting, and fishing. Gathering is the most important activity in 30 percent of the societies, hunting most important in 25 percent, and fishing most important in 38 percent. However, if fishing is treated as a type of hunting, which is logical since fishing involves the procurement of wild animal protein, then 63 percent of hunter-gatherer societies emphasize hunting over gathering.

Another way of looking at this problem is to calculate the percentage of societies in which a particular subsistence activity contributes half or more of the calories that people consume. Ember (1978) shows that in only 23 percent of societies does gathering contribute more than half of the calories. If Ember's data are reliable, then, they show that in hunting and gathering societies hunting is clearly the dominant subsistence activity. This is consistent with what experts have long known about hunter-gatherers: They usually spend more time hunting than gathering and meat is more highly valued than plant food.

Since hunter-gatherers are food collectors rather than food producers, they must wander over wide geographical areas in search of food. They are thus

**Frank and Ernest**

*Hunter-gatherer societies are highly noteworthy for their low level of economic specialization.*

©1985 Thaves. Reprinted with permission. Newspaper dist. by NEA, Inc.

generally nomadic, and the establishment of permanent settlements is highly unusual.

The technological inventory of hunting and gathering societies is quite limited. The tools and weapons used directly for subsistence typically include spears, bows and arrows, nets, and traps used in hunting, as well as digging sticks used for plant collecting. Tools are crude and simple, generally being made of stone, wood, bone, or other natural materials. There are usually few or no techniques for food storage or preservation, and food is thus generally consumed immediately or within a short span of time.

Hunter-gatherer societies are the simplest in structure of all human societies, the division of labor being based almost exclusively on age and sex distinctions. Primary responsibility for subsistence ordinarily falls to persons who are in middle adulthood, with both young and old members contributing less to the subsistence needs of the group. Hunting is conducted by males, gathering by females. Although women may occasionally hunt or trap small game animals, they are seldom involved in big game hunting. Likewise, men sometimes share in gathering activities, but they are the principal gatherers in no hunter-gatherer society. Hunter-gatherers are notoriously lacking in occupational specialization beyond subsistence tasks. There are no specialized "arrow makers" or "bow makers," for example. Each man makes all of the tools that he needs in the subsistence quest, and the women do the same.

The primary unit of subsistence among hunter-gatherers is the family, and hence economic life may be termed *familistic* (Service, 1966). Yet individual families within each local band are linked together into a total economic unit, the local band itself. While individual families produce their own subsistence, they also contribute in significant ways to the subsistence of other families within their band.

Hunter-gatherers, or at least most of them, are well known for their failure to produce an **economic surplus,** an excess of goods over and above what is needed for subsistence. Until recently, it was widely believed that this was due simply to an inability to do so—an inability resulting from a marginal and precarious existence. Contemporary research contradicts this view. Social scientists now generally agree that the failure to produce a surplus is due to a lack of any real need. Since the resources of nature are always there for the taking, nature itself becomes a kind of great storehouse. However, in recent years it has come to be increasingly recognized that some hunter-gatherers do produce an economic surplus, in some cases a considerable one. This has led to an important distinction between hunter-gatherer societies that store food and those that do not (Testart, 1982, 1988). Although nonstoring hunter-gatherers predominate, hunter-gatherers who store food are probably more common than experts have realized, and in any event differ in important respects from those societies that do not. Storing hunter-gatherers are more likely to be sedentary rather than nomadic, to have bigger populations and higher population densities, and to be organized in a more complex way.

Contemporary hunter-gatherers who store food can be found, but such groups seem to have been particularly prominent in the last few millennia before the development of agriculture (around 15,000 to 10,000 years ago) (M. Cohen, 1985), and probably represented hunting and gathering societies on the verge of developing an agricultural economy. It might be useful to call both prehistoric and contemporary hunter-gatherers who do not store food *simple* hunter-gatherers, while referring to those who do store food as *complex* hunter-gatherers (cf. Kelly, 1995).

The !Kung San serve as an excellent example of a contemporary hunter-gatherer society (the "!" stands for a "click" sound in the language). Some 45,000 San are found scattered throughout the territories of Botswana, Angola, and Namibia in southern Africa. These people are divided into several different linguistic groups, one of which is !Kung, spoken by about 13,000 people. Many of these people are now either under the direct control of local governments or heavily influenced in their way of life by means of contact with more technologically advanced peoples. The last of the hunting and gathering !Kung number some 1,600 clustered around water holes in northwestern Botswana. The ethnographic account that follows is based on a population of 466 !Kung located in the Dobe area of Botswana studied by Richard Lee (1972; cf. Lee, 1979, 1984).

!Kung life is organized around eight permanent water holes and 14 independent camps. These camps are moved about five or six times a year. The population density is approximately 0.4 person per square mile, a density typical for hunter-gatherers. The habitat is the Kalahari Desert, a region surprisingly abundant in resources. Nearly 500 species of plants and animals are known and named by the !Kung. The climate is characterized by hot summers with a four-month rainy season and by moderate winters with no rainfall.

The !Kung enjoy a secure existence. They depend primarily on vegetable foods (Lee estimates that about 37 percent of their diet consists of meat). Their most important food plant is the mongongo or mangetti nut, a highly nutritious and superabundant staple. Other major plant foods are also available, but the !Kung tend to eat only those that are more attractive in terms of taste or ease of collection. Game animals are less abundant and less predictable. A type of large antelope is regularly hunted, as are warthogs and smaller antelopes. Game birds are captured in ingenious snares, and a large tortoise is a great favorite.

The camp or local band is the basic residential unit and the primary focus of subsistence activities. Members of each local group move out each day individually or in small groups to exploit the surrounding area, returning each evening to pool collected resources. Women do the gathering in groups of three to five. The men do the hunting, which is primarily an individual activity. Bows and poisoned arrows serve as effective weapons. Food is extensively shared, although the sharing of meat is more formally organized than the sharing of vegetable foods. Large game is butchered and divided into three portions: about one-fifth remains with the family, one-fifth is cut into strips for drying, and the remaining three-fifths are distributed to closely related households. Meat division is carried out with considerable care. The hunter may call in other men to advise him, or he may even ask his father-in-law to conduct the division. Absolute sharing is the ideal in !Kung camps even though it is seldom attained in practice. It is noteworthy that the most common verbal disputes concern accusations of improper meat distribution and improper gift exchange.

## The Original Affluent Society?

Social scientists used to depict hunter-gatherers in largely negative terms. It was widely believed that they led a precarious and difficult life, one in which people had to work hard and long just to eke out a bare subsistence. As Marshall Sahlins noted over three decades ago (1972:1):

> Almost universally committed to the proposition that life was hard in the paleolithic, our textbooks compete to convey a sense of impending doom, leaving one to wonder not only how hunters managed to live, but whether, after all, this was living? The specter of starvation stalks the stalker through these pages. His technical incompetence is said to enjoin continuous work just to survive, affording him neither respite nor surplus, hence not even the "leisure" to "build culture."

Since the late 1960s, social scientists have radically altered this view of hunter-gatherers. In a famous argument, Sahlins (1972) dubbed them the "original affluent society." By this, he did not mean that they are rich and enjoy a great abundance of material possessions, which would be an absurd claim. That is affluence in the modern sense. What Sahlins meant was that hunter-gatherers have very limited needs and wants and are able to satisfy them with a minimum of effort. To assess Sahlins's claim, we need to look carefully at the hunter-gatherer standard of living and at how hard and long hunter-gatherers typically work.

Despite the fact that virtually all contemporary hunter-gatherers exist in marginal environments, these environments often turn out to be surprisingly abundant in resources. For example, Richard Lee (1968) notes that the !Kung San are able to rely on a wide variety of resources of considerable quality. As mentioned earlier, their most important food source is mongongo nuts, and thousands of pounds of these rot on the ground each year for want of picking. Furthermore, the !Kung habitat contains 84 other species of edible plants, and !Kung gathering never exhausts all the available plant foods of an area. Similarly, James Woodburn (1968) shows that the Hadza of Tanzania enjoy an exceptional abundance of game, and he thinks it is almost inconceivable that they would die of starvation. It would thus appear that both the !Kung and the Hadza obtain a standard of living that is perfectly adequate in meeting basic human subsistence requirements.

This impression is reinforced by Mark Cohen's (1989) survey of studies of diet and nutrition among many contemporary hunting and gathering groups. Cohen's review of numerous studies suggests to him that most hunter-gatherers generally enjoy diets that are fully adequate in nutrition. Some groups, such as the !Kung, may barely obtain a sufficient number of calories, but their diets are otherwise abundant in animal proteins and various nutrients. Many hunter-gatherers do experience seasonal bouts of hunger and food anxiety, and starvation may sometimes occur (Yesner, 1994). However, there is nothing unusual about hunter-gatherers in this respect. Settled agricultural populations also experience such difficulties, and often to an even greater extent.

Moreover, prehistoric hunter-gatherers seem to have been better nourished than prehistoric agricultural populations. Cohen and Armelagos (1984) summarize the findings from paleopathological studies—studies examining evidence of biological stress and disease in ancient skeletal and dental remains—carried out by over a dozen biological anthropologists. These studies were carried out on remains from virtually all major regions of the world, covering the time period after 30,000 BP. Most of the studies found that infection was a more frequent and severe problem for farming populations than for hunter-gatherers. Chronic malnutrition was also more common in agricultural populations. Indicators of biological stresses leading to the disruption of childhoold growth told basically the same story.

If hunter-gatherers generally enjoy adequate diets, how long and hard do they have to work to obtain them? A good deal of evidence suggests that many such groups work neither hard nor long. Reviewing data collected on the subsistence activities of the hunter-gatherers of Arnhem Land in northern Australia, Sahlins (1972) notes that these people do not work hard or continuously, that the subsistence quest is highly intermittent, and that plenty of spare time is available. Along the same lines, Lee (1979) has calculated that the typical !Kung adult spends an average of only 17 hours per week in direct food-getting activities. Woodburn (1968) shows that the Hadza obtain sufficient food with relative ease, and that life for them is anything but a difficult struggle for existence. His impression is that they spend less time and energy obtaining subsistence than do their agricultural neighbors.

Some other studies of hunter-gatherer workloads are not as encouraging, at least on the surface. Since Lee's data on !Kung work patterns were collected during the dry season, John Yellen (1977) studied a group of !Kung during the wet season. He found that during this time of year they worked considerably longer. In addition, Kim Hill, Hilliard Kaplan, Kristen Hawkes, and Ana Magdelena Hurtado (1985) find that men among the Aché, a hunter-gatherer society in Paraguay, spent perhaps 40 to 50 hours a week hunting. But this figure is probably highly atypical.

Robert Kelly (1995) presents data on the workload in 11 hunter-gatherer societies in five different world regions. These data show that the average amount of time both men and women spend foraging is only about 3.8 hours a day, which comes to slightly less than 27 hours a week (assuming that foraging is undertaken every day). If one calculates the total subsistence effort in these same 11 societies by adding in the amount of time people spend at such tasks as manufacturing and repairing tools and processing food, then people are spending only 6.5 hours a day (45.5 hours a week). This is well below the figure for the members of modern industrial societies, who work a 40-hour week and spend many more hours in such subsistence-related activities as getting to and from work, shopping for food, cooking, and maintaining their households. Most interestingly, Bruce Winterhalder (1993) shows that most hunter-gatherers must limit their subsistence efforts because failure to do so will be counterproductive. In most hunter-gatherer environments, if people work too hard they will deplete their resources and lower their productivity in the long run. As he notes, low to intermediate levels of effort are associated with the largest sustainable populations and the highest rates of food acquisition.

It would seem, when all is said and done, that Sahlins's original affluent society thesis holds up reasonably well. This appears to be especially true when we realize that most of what researchers know about the standard of living and the work patterns of hunter-gatherers is based on contemporary groups. Since nearly all of these groups live in marginal environments, prehistoric hunter-gatherers, most of whom would have existed in much more favorable environments, would have been even better off. It is crucial that we avoid romanticizing the hunting and gathering lifestyle as being some sort of primitive paradise. Clearly, that would be a gross oversimplification. Nonetheless, hunter-gatherers have fared much better than social scientists used to imagine. As Elizabeth Cashdan (1989:26) concludes, it is now possible to "demolish with confidence the old stereotype that hunter-gatherers had to work all the time simply to get enough food to eat." And it is also possible to demolish with confidence the old stereotype that hunter-gatherers did not eat well.

## Economic Life

When considering how goods are produced in all societies, a vital question concerns who owns the forces of production—that is, who owns those resources that are of greatest significance in carrying out productive activities. In the middle of the nineteenth century, Karl Marx speculated that the earliest mode of economic life in human history was what he termed **primitive communism.** By this, Marx meant a type of society in which people subsisted by hunting and gathering or by simple forms of agriculture or animal herding, and in which all of the vital resources of nature were held in common. Private ownership of resources by individuals or small groups was not found, he believed, in this type of society.

Although many social scientists over the years have challenged Marx's view on this matter, contemporary social science provides considerable evidence that Marx was basically correct. The vast majority of hunter-gatherers studied by modern anthropologists display a mode of resource ownership that can be adequately characterized by Marx's notion of primitive communism. Although much economic activity among hunter-gatherers is centered on the family, all individuals in such societies have equal access to those resources of nature that are necessary for their subsistence. No person in a hunter-gatherer band may be deprived by any other person or group of an equal opportunity to hunt game, collect plants, use a water hole, or camp on the land. Thus, everyone owns these resources collectively (it is sometimes said that since everyone has an equal right to their use, *no one* owns them). In fact, some hunter-gatherers do not even restrict the ownership of resources to their own local band; instead, they provide equal access to resources to all other individuals and groups who may have need for them (Woodburn, 1968). Even in those instances where resources may be "owned" privately by individual families, there are typically no restrictions on other families *using* these resources. Among the !Kung San, for instance, water holes are frequently said to be "owned" by individual families, but these families do not prevent other families from using them (Lee, 1968, 1972).

It is true that among hunter-gatherers items such as jewelry and art objects are owned privately, but this fact does not invalidate the claim that primitive communism is the principal ownership mode of hunting and gathering peoples. Jewelry and art objects are not part of the *forces of production*, as Marx called the vital resources necessary to economic production. Rather, they are items of what is more appropriately referred to as *personal property*. Since they are not used in the productive process, the nature of their ownership is irrelevant to the Marxian thesis of primitive communism. Even then, one finds that these items of personal property are seldom kept for long as private objects. Instead, they continually circulate among members of the group, and thus their use is community wide.

Hunter-gatherers generally distribute economic goods through a process known as **reciprocity**, which is the obligation to repay others for what they have given to or done for us, or the actual act of repaying others. Two distinct types of reciprocity, known as balanced and generalized reciprocity, exist. **Balanced reciprocity** occurs when individuals are obligated to provide equivalent and often immediate repayment to others. Balanced reciprocity can be identified by the fact that individuals deliberately and openly calculate what they are giving each other and openly declare the nature of the repayment to be made. Each party to the transaction expects to benefit in some way, but there is a clear expectation of mutual benefit and a lack of "exploitation."

**Generalized reciprocity** occurs when individuals are obligated to give to others without expecting any immediate or equivalent repayment. As opposed to balanced reciprocity, generalized reciprocity does not involve any direct or open agreement between the parties involved. There is a general expectation that equivalent repayment of a debt shall be made, but there is no particular time limit set for the repayment, nor is there any specification as to just how the repayment shall be made. The terms of repayment in generalized reciprocity are notoriously vague. Marvin Harris (1974) notes that one can tell whether generalized reciprocity is the prevailing mode of distribution by noticing whether people say "thank you." As Harris (1974:124) puts it, when generalized reciprocity is the distributive mode

> it is rude to be openly grateful for the receipt of material goods or services. Among the Semai of central Malaya, for example, no one ever expresses gratitude for the meat that a hunter gives away in exactly equal portions to his companions. Robert Dentan, who has lived with the Semai, found that to say thank you was very rude because it suggested either that you were calculating the size of the piece of meat you had been given, or that you were surprised by the success and generosity of the hunter.

One might also say that it is rude to express gratitude when generalized reciprocity is the distributive norm because under such circumstances giving things away to others is a social obligation, not an act of kindness.

Whereas generalized reciprocity occurs to some extent in all societies (it occurs among friends and family members in U.S. society, for instance), it constitutes the very essence of economic life among hunter-gatherers, where it is most frequently found. Hunting and gathering peoples are famed for their extensive food sharing. Individuals constantly give food to others and receive food in return. When a man returns to camp with an animal that he has killed, he will divide it into portions and then give these away, typically first to members of his family and then to other members of the band. Similarly, women constantly give away portions of food they have gathered. When a hunter gives meat to others, he expects only that he will probably be repaid in some way at some time. The hunter may give to others time after time without any repayment taking place and without any mention being made of this fact. He understands that the chances are excellent that his acts will eventually be reciprocated. A failure to reciprocate only becomes a cause for concern and conflict when it appears that one person is "freeloading" off another.

Where generalized reciprocity is a pervasive feature of economic life, sharing and individual humility become compulsory social habits. As Richard Lee comments in regard to the !Kung (1978:888):

> The most serious accusations that one !Kung can level against another are the charge of stinginess and the charge of arrogance. To be stingy or "far-hearted" is to hoard one's goods jealously and secretively, guarding them "like a hyena." The corrective for this in the !Kung view is to make the hoarder give "till it hurts," that is, to make him give generously and without stint until everyone can see that he is truly cleaned out. In order to ensure compliance with this cardinal rule, the !Kung browbeat each other constantly to be more generous and not to set themselves apart by hoarding a little nest-egg. . . .
>
> But as seriously as they regard the fault of stinginess, the !Kung's most scathing criticisms are reserved for an even more serious shortcoming: the crime of arrogance. . . . A boasting hunter who comes into camp announcing "I have killed a big animal in the bush" is being arrogant. A woman who gives a gift and announces her great generosity to all is being arrogant. Even an anthropologist who claims to have chosen the biggest ox of the year to slaughter for Christmas is being arrogant. The !Kung perceive this behavior as a danger sign, and they have evolved elaborate devices for puncturing the bubble of conceit and enforcing humility. These leveling devices are in constant daily use, minimizing the size of others' kills, downplaying the value of others' gifts, and treating one's own efforts in a self-deprecating way. "Please" and "thank you" are hardly ever found in their vocabulary; in their stead we find a vocabulary of rough humor, back-handed compliments, putdowns, and damning with faint praise.

What explains the pervasiveness of sharing among hunter-gatherers? The most commonly offered explanation is that it is a rationally chosen strategy of *variance reduction* (Cashdan, 1985; Winterhalder, 1986a, 1986b; Kelly, 1995). Hunter-gatherers intimately depend on one another for survival. Although resources are typically not highly scarce in a general sense, they are notoriously subject to marked fluctuations in availability. Thus, a man may encounter a long run of bad luck in hunting. If others do not give meat to him during this time, he must go without. They give meat to him because they know that they too will eventually have their turn with bad hunting luck, during which time they will expect to receive meat from him. Therefore, to give regularly to others is to help ensure one's own well-being in the long run (Weissner, 1982; Cashdan, 1985).

Generalized reciprocity, then, is a special instance of what is known as *enlightened self-interest*—cooperating with or assisting others when it is to one's own personal advantage to do so, not because one has natural altruistic feelings toward others. There can be nothing surprising in the fact that hunter-gatherers show great disdain for the occasional individual who is competitive, selfish, and boastful. Such a person is a serious threat to the economic well-being of others and must be subjected to strong pressure to change his or her ways.

## Social Inequalities and Political Life

Because of their emphasis on sharing and the absence of true private property among most hunter-gatherer societies, they usually lack **social stratification,** or structured inequalities of power and privilege. Yet the absence of class divisions does not mean that perfect equality prevails among the members of these societies. Inequalities do exist. These are mainly inequalities of prestige or social influence and are typically based on such factors as age, sex, and certain personal characteristics. As is the norm throughout the world, men tend to have higher status than women among hunter-gatherers, and, likewise, the older members of society are often given more honor and respect than the younger ones. In addition, the possession of certain personal traits is generally a basis for the acquisition of prestige. Men who are particularly skilled hunters, who show special courage, or who are thought of as having great wisdom are often accorded high prestige. Such individuals typically assume leadership functions because they are deemed to be worthy of the trust and confidence of others.

However, men of prestige and influence among hunter-gatherers are no more than "firsts among equals," and they typically have no special privileges not available to others. It must also be noted that the acquisition of prestige and influence comes from an individual's own abilities and efforts, not from any mechanism of social heredity. Prestige is both personally gained and personally lost. Individuals must continually justify such honor, and should their abilities or efforts fail them, their status will fall and others will replace them.

It must be stressed that the degree of prestige that can be gained among hunter-gatherers is very mild when compared to the nature of prestige in other societies. Hunter-gatherers loathe boasting and self-glorification, and they use strong sanctions against those persons who come to think too highly of themselves. Their emphasis is clearly on communal well-being and general social equality. In this sense, they are quite aptly described as **egalitarian societies** (Woodburn, 1982).

Yet not all hunter-gatherers have been egalitarian, and some have been characterized by considerable inequalities in privilege. The distinction made by Alain Testart (1982) between storing and nonstoring hunter-gatherers is relevant here. Using a representative sample of 40 hunter-gatherer societies, Testart has shown that

8 of the 10 that stored food were stratified, whereas only 2 of the 30 nonstoring societies had stratification. There is obviously a pronounced relationship between food storing and the presence of stratification.

By far the best examples of stratified hunter-gatherer societies are those Indian tribes that have inhabited the Northwest Coast of the United States. Although there has been some disagreement as to the actual nature and extent of the inequalities present, a number of anthropologists believe that the Northwest Coast was characterized by an exploitative class system. Anthropologist Eugene Ruyle (1973), for instance, makes a strong claim for the existence of a ruling class, rent or taxation, and slavery. These societies have been famous among social scientists for their elaborate competitive feasts known as *potlatches*. During these potlatches, Northwest Coast chiefs would attempt to shame rival chiefs by giving away large quantities of wealth and by ranting and raving about their own greatness. Among the Kwakiutl, for example, chiefs seemed obsessed with maintaining and enhancing their high status.

There is also strong evidence that a number of hunter-gatherer societies in late pre-Neolithic times (about 12,000–10,000 years ago) had crossed the threshold into stratification, or at least had developed extensive inequalities of social status or rank (Mellars, 1985). Like the Northwest Coast tribes, these societies very likely consisted of dense populations in regions of abundant resources that had adopted the practice of food storing. And, also like the Northwest Coast tribes, these prehistoric societies were uncharacteristic of hunter-gatherer societies the world over. Their uniqueness should not be allowed to detract from what is most commonly found at the hunting and gathering stage of social life—pervasive social and economic equality.

It might be suspected that the striking egalitarianism of hunter-gatherers is a "natural" phenomenon, or one that results from the absence of motivations toward status seeking and wealth acquisition at this stage of social life. Such motivations, it might be presumed, develop only at later evolutionary stages. But this would be an incorrect inference. As Elizabeth Cashdan (1980) and James Woodburn (1982) point out, social and economic equality is always threatened by individuals who seek to attain more than others, and it takes constant vigilance to maintain it. The equality that results from pervasive reciprocity and sharing seems to be an essential condition for human survival and well-being among most hunter-gatherers because it is a necessary means of overcoming temporal and spatial variations in the food supply. But since there is nothing natural about strict equality, powerful techniques of socialization must be used to bring it about and maintain it (Cashdan, 1980; Lee, 1978). The emergence of significant inequalities, then, results from the lifting of restrictions once placed on human motivations (Cashdan, 1980). It is among food-storing hunter-gatherers and, more significantly, horticultural and agrarian societies that these restrictions come to be lifted.

Political leadership in most hunter-gatherer societies rests on informal influence and typically lacks any sort of real power (Fried, 1967). In addition, leadership tends to be displayed in transient fashion, frequently shifting from one person to another. Political leaders, or *headmen* as they are usually called, seldom possess any real power or authority to command the actions of others. !Kung San leaders, for example, direct migration and subsistence activities and perform certain ceremonies, but the position they hold contains no power, honors, or rewards. Fried appears to catch the essence of political organization at the band level when he says (1967:83):

> It is difficult, in ethnographies of simple egalitarian societies, to find cases in which one individual tells one or more others, "Do this!" or some command equivalent. The literature is replete with examples of individuals saying the equivalent of "If this is done, it will be good," possibly or possibly not followed by somebody else doing it. More usually the person who initiates the idea also performs the activity. . . . The leader is unable to compel any of the others to carry out his wish.

# Simple Horticultural Societies

## Subsistence Technology

A number of **simple horticultural societies** can be found in the modern world. Most of these are found in Melanesia, a chain of islands in the southern Pacific (generally said to include New Guinea), and in various regions of South America. Extensive ethnographic research has been conducted among these societies, and the results of this research provide the basis for the discussion that follows.

Simple horticulturalists live in small villages ordinarily containing from 100 to 200 persons. Although villages substantially larger than this are known to exist, they are not common. Each village is in essence economically and politically self-sufficient. Nevertheless, important intervillage ties do exist. Marriage often takes place between individuals from different villages, and persons residing in separate villages often come together on ceremonial occasions. Members of culturally and linguistically related villages collectively constitute a tribe, a sociocultural unit that may contain tens of thousands or even hundreds of thousands of persons.

Most simple horticulturalists in recent times have lived in heavily forested environments and practice a form of cultivation known as **slash-and-burn** (also known as *shifting cultivation*). This cultivation technique involves cutting down a section of forest growth and then setting fire to the accumulated debris. The remaining ashes serve as a fertilizer, and usually no other fertilizer is added. The crops are then planted in these cleared plots (usually no more than an acre in size) with the aid of a digging stick, a long pole with a sharpened and fire-hardened end. A given plot may be devoted to a single crop, but a more common practice is to plant several minor crops along with one main staple (Sahlins, 1968). The task of clearing and preparing the plots generally falls to the men, while that of planting and harvesting is most often carried out by women.

Since wood ashes generally serve as the only fertilizer, slash-and-burn cultivation is associated with short-term soil fertility. Freshly produced ashes are washed away by rain after a year or two, and for this reason a plot of land can be cultivated only for that length of time. It must then be allowed to remain fallow long enough for the forest to regenerate so that new ashes can be produced. The fallow period ordinarily lasts approximately 20 to 30 years. When the forest growth has returned, the process of cutting, burning, and cultivating can begin again.

*Slash-and-burn cultivation. This area of tropical forest in the Amazon Basin has just been cleared for garden preparation.*

Because the slash-and-burn system requires lengthy fallow periods, any society practicing it must have much more land at its disposal than it will have under actual cultivation at any given time (Sahlins, 1968). The Tsembaga Maring of New Guinea, for example, had only 42 acres of land under actual cultivation in 1962–1963, but about 864 acres of their territory had been gardened at one time or another (M. Harris, 1975). Such land use requirements put limits on population density, and tropical forest cultivators often maintain population densities of less than 10 persons per square mile (Sahlins, 1968).

Cultivated plants constitute the bulk of the dietary intake among simple horticulturalists, but a number of simple horticultural societies also possess domesticated animals. Domesticated pigs, for instance, are found throughout Melanesia. But most simple horticulturalists lack domesticated animals, and such groups must rely on hunting or fishing for their supply of animal protein.

Simple horticulturalists produce more food per unit of land than do hunter-gatherers, and some even produce small economic surpluses. Yet it cannot be concluded that they enjoy a superior standard of living. Indeed, as noted earlier, it has been suggested that the standard of living for simple horticulturalists is *inferior* to that of hunter-gatherers (M. Cohen, 1977, 1989). They do not consume more calories, and their intake of protein appears to be lower. Furthermore, considerable evidence has accumulated in recent years to show that simple horticulturalists commonly work harder than hunters and gatherers (M. Cohen, 1977). It generally takes more time and energy to clear land and plant, tend, and harvest crops than to collect what nature automatically provides. Thus, simple horticulture is a more intensive system of technology than hunting and gathering, but it does not lead to greater material benefits.

The Yanomama (Chagnon, 1983, 1992) exemplify a surviving simple horticultural society. They are a South American Indian tribe living in southern Venezuela and adjacent portions of northern Brazil. There are perhaps some 125 widely scattered villages having populations ranging from 40 to 250 inhabitants, with an average village size of about 75 to 80 persons. Several hundred years ago, the Yanomama may have relied primarily on hunting and gathering, and so they may only have recently made the transition to a horticultural existence (Colchester, 1984). Be that as it may, their current subsistence practices nicely illustrate the simple horticultural mode of production. These practices have been described in some detail by Napoleon Chagnon (1983, 1992), one of their principal ethnographers.

The natural environment of the Yanomama is a relatively dense tropical forest. The land is entirely covered with jungle, even the tops of mountain ridges. The Yanomama survive in this environment with only a simple technology. All tools and techniques are uncomplicated, and none requires the use of specialized labor. Among the elements of technology the Yanomama have developed are crude clay pots, bows and arrows, agouti-tooth knives (made from the lower incisor of the agouti, a rodent), and canoes (which are so crude that they are generally used only once and then discarded). The Yanomama are slash-and-burn cultivators. In earlier times, they had only stone axes for clearing the land, but they now have steel axes that have been supplied by local missionaries. Each man clears his own land. Each village has a local headman, and he usually has the largest garden. The headman must produce larger quantities of food, as he is expected to give food away at feasts. By far the largest crop is plantains (similar to bananas), and each garden usually contains three or four varieties of both plantains and bananas. A root crop, sweet manioc, is also grown, and this is refined into a rough flour and then converted into a thick, baked bread. Other crops include taro, sweet potatoes, and a palm tree that produces a large crop of fruit. Maize is cultivated as an emergency crop, but it does not figure prominently in the daily diet. Tobacco is another cultivated crop, and the men, women, and children all chew it. Cotton is also grown and is used for making hammocks.

While perhaps 85 percent or more of the Yanomama diet consists of cultivated plants, the Yanomama spend almost as much time hunting as they do gardening. Since they have no domesticated animals, they rely exclusively on hunting (as well as some fishing and the collection of small animals and insects) for their source of animal protein. Game animals are not abundant, which is typical of tropical forest environments. The most frequently hunted game animals are several species of monkeys, two species of wild pig, armadillos, anteaters, deer, small alligators, small rodents, and several species of smaller birds. All game animals are shot with arrows. Several varieties of insects, some species of caterpillar, and large spiders are collected and eaten. Wild honey, considered a real delicacy, is collected in large quantities.

The suggestion that the Yanomama were hunter-gatherers in the recent past seems confirmed by the fact that some villages have made the transition to horticulture only very incompletely. People in these villages regularly leave them to spend long periods of time trekking through the forest, surviving largely on whatever game they can kill and plant foods they collect (Good, 1993). These treks may last anywhere from three to six weeks, and as many as six treks might be made in a year's time. It is easily seen that these groups of Yanomama spend nearly as much time away from their villages as in them.

## Economic Life

Among many small-scale horticultural peoples, primitive communism in the strict sense ordinarily does not prevail. Instead, most simple horticulturalists have a mode of property ownership that can best be designated **lineage ownership.** Lineage ownership occurs when large-scale kinship groups, known as *lineages* (or sometimes as clans), hold property in common. Of course, in such societies the most important form of property is land. When lineages own land in common, individual members of the group participate in the use of lineage land only because they are lineage members. Their right to the use of this land is granted only by the lineage itself as a corporate body; the leaders of the lineage, acting as representatives of the lineage as a whole, bestow these rights.

Lineage ownership is similar to primitive communism in that it is not a private form of property holding. Property is still held and used communally. But there is an important difference between lineage ownership and primitive communism. Lineage ownership is more exclusive or more restrictive inasmuch as it makes ownership and use of valuable resources dependent on kinship group membership. In societies resting on lineage ownership, not all members of the society have equal access to the forces of production, even though all members of the same lineage do. Lineage ownership is thus a small step away from primitive communism and toward private ownership. Still, it is closer to primitive communism than to private ownership, since in true lineage ownership the lineages themselves have relatively equal access to resources.

As you saw in the case of hunter-gatherers, as goes ownership so goes distribution. Reciprocity is a common practice in simple horticultural societies, but they are also characterized by another process that anthropologists have called **redistribution.** When redistribution occurs, products are funneled from individual households to a central source and then returned to those households in some sort of systematic manner. Redistribution differs from reciprocity in that redistribution is a more formalized process involving the movement of goods into the hands of some person or group that serves as the focal point for their reallocation.

Two types of redistribution may be identified: *pure* and *partial* (Moseley and Wallerstein, 1978), sometimes called *egalitarian* and *stratified* (M. Harris, 1975). In **pure redistribution,** the redistributive process is complete in the sense that the redistributive agent reallocates all goods and keeps no extra portion for himself. By contrast, where **partial redistribution** occurs the redistributive process is incomplete inasmuch as the redistributive agent retains a portion of goods for his own use.

Pure redistributive economies, which are most commonly associated with small-scale horticulturalists, work somewhat differently from one society to another. One version of a redistributive economy is widespread among simple horticultural groups in Melanesia. These societies contain extremely ambitious men known as **big men,** who seek prestige and renown through their roles as organizers of economic production. The typical aspiring big man begins his career by cultivating larger gardens and raising bigger pig herds. He does this by drawing on the help of close relatives and neighbors, who themselves have a stake in his success. If he is successful at his attempts to increase the productivity of his own gardens and herds, he will eventually have accumulated enough foodstuffs to hold a large feast, at which time these foodstuffs will be redistributed to other village members. Prestige and some renown fall upon him through the holding of a successful feast. But there are usually other individuals in his village with the same aspirations who are holding feasts of their own. If he is consistently able to hold larger feasts than those organized by his competitors, he is generally recognized as the village big man and given considerable prestige. But should he falter at this task, his status is quickly lost, and he will be replaced by one of the competitors who has outdone him. Also, he is expected to be generous in his distribution of products and must place considerable emphasis on the welfare of the entire village. Big men who are not sufficiently generous and keep too much for themselves are frequently killed (M. Harris, 1974, 1977).

The quest for high status on the part of aspiring Melanesian big men has definite economic consequences. Such a quest strongly enhances economic productivity, leading to a general increase in the quantity of garden products, domesticated animals, fish, and other economic products (Oliver, 1955). The circulation of goods is also substantially increased, as feast preparation involves numerous exchanges of goods and services. In addition, there is typically a notable increase in the consumption of many goods by the members of the entire village (Oliver, 1955). The process of competitive feasting is therefore a vital part of the economic systems of Melanesian horticulturalists.

The Kaoka-speakers, a simple horticultural group in Melanesia, are characterized by a classic big-man redistributive system (Hogbin, 1964). The native expression for a leader of prestige and renown is *mwanekama*, which literally means "man-big." The natives generally agree that there is at any given time only one real big man in a village. He is usually a man over 40 years old who carries himself with assurance and dignity, lives in the most solidly built house, extends extraordinary hospitality, and is shown deference by the villagers.

To win the support of relatives and neighbors in order to launch a career toward bigmanship, a man must be forceful, even tempered, tactful, industrious, and a good organizer. A man's ambition to pursue such a career usually becomes apparent in his early thirties. When a man intends to strive toward bigmanship, he begins by cultivating larger gardens, a task for which he enlists the aid of close relatives. He also attempts to increase the size of his pig herd. When in time his gardens are flourishing and he has perhaps 10 fat pigs and several smaller ones, the man makes it known that he wishes to build a new dwelling, one that is larger and better built than usual. This move is usually taken as a public declaration that he is a candidate for the highest honors of the village. The celebration to mark the end of the job, what the Kaoka-speakers call "the feast-to-remove-the-splinters," is highly elaborate (M. Harris, 1974, 1977).

One such feast was that of Atana, a man who was already notable but not as yet a rival to the acknowledged village big man. Toward this feast, Atana and his immediate kinsmen contributed 250 pounds of dried fish, 3,000 yam cakes, 11 bowls of yam pudding, and 8 pigs. Other villagers attending the feast also brought along additional foodstuffs. When these were added to what was provided by Atana and his kinsmen, the final count was 300 pounds of fish, almost 5,000 yam cakes, 19 bowls of pudding, and 13 pigs. It was then Atana's task to redistribute this food to all those who were in some way connected with the feast. By the time he was finished, he had made 257 separate presentations, and only the remnants were left for him.

The Kaoka-speakers considered this to be the proper result. As they said, "The giver of the feast takes the bones and the stale cakes; the meat and the fat go to others" (M. Harris, 1974, 1977).

Further progress toward village bigmanship requires that there be more and bigger feasts. If a man can continue to do this, he is eventually likely to become the village big man. If he does succeed, however, he can never rest on his laurels. As soon as the size of his gardens and pig herds begins to shrink, he subsides into insignificance. He is always faced with competitors who are waiting to take his place should he be unable to maintain a sufficiently intense level of economic productivity.

Marvin Harris (1974, 1977) points out that the big man is an economic intensifier. His actions lead to an increase in the level of production beyond what it would otherwise be. As such, it is easy to see why big men are not found among hunter-gatherers. Big men in hunter-gatherer societies would be economically maladaptive, for they would exploit the resources of nature beyond their natural recovery points and thus destroy the ecological and economic foundation of hunter-gatherer society. Thus, the very personalities that may be highly beneficial for many horticultural societies would produce disastrous consequences for hunter-gatherers.

## Social Inequalities and Politics

Like most hunter-gatherers, most simple horticulturalists lack hereditary class divisions and thus true social stratification. However, as should be clear from the preceding discussion, status-seeking behavior is carried considerably further in simple horticultural societies. They are examples of what Morton Fried (1967) has termed **rank societies.** As Fried defines it, "A rank society is one in which positions of valued status are somehow limited so that not all those of sufficient talent to occupy such statuses actually achieve them" (1967:109). Those who achieve high rank, or big men, come to be held in considerable respect, envy, and sometimes even awe. The Siuai of Bougainville in the Solomon Islands heap considerable praise on these men of high rank. They also show much respect for a high-ranking individual's name and person. He is generally not addressed by name, but usually called instead by a kinship term or simply *mumi* ("big man"). Even in reference his personal name may not be used, and on these occasions he may be referred to by the name of his clubhouse or by the name of one of his assistants. The respect given his name typically continues even after his death. Big men are also usually given considerable deference. As the Siuai's principal ethnographer, Douglas Oliver, comments (1955:401):

> Leaders are usually spared menial jobs; others fetch water for them, and climb palms to get coconuts and areca nuts for their refreshment. Boisterous talk usually becomes quieter when a leader approaches, and boys leave off rough-housing. In fact, one of the sternest lessons impressed upon a child is to stay away from a leader, or else remain quiet in his presence. ("Never play when a *mumi* is nearby; you might disturb him or hit him with your toys.") Females, especially, appear awed near the great men, often looking shyly to the ground. Men usually wait for a leader to open conversations, and take their cues from him concerning when to laugh, to commend, or to decry.

No supernaturally sanctioned taboos surround a leader's person in order to insulate him from plain physical contact with other natives, but few people would assume enough familiarity with him to place a friendly hand on his shoulder—a common gesture among equals.

Despite their prestige and the deference usually shown them, big men are like hunter-gatherer headmen in the sense that their leadership role confers no ability to command the actions of others. Big men advise, suggest, and cajole, and more often than not, their wishes will be followed. But since they lack the capacity to force others to do their bidding, they possess no real power or authority. The political structure of big-man leadership, therefore, rests on informal influence and requires the voluntary consent of those they attempt to lead. Lacking the capacity to command others, big men are successful leaders only to the extent that they serve the public good. In a real sense they are servants of the people, servants who depend on the good graces of their followers to retain high status. The status of a big man is symbiotic with society at large; in exchange for prestige and renown, big men must serve long-range societal interests, or else they will not continue to be big men. Failure to serve the public good ends in demotion from big-man status.

# Intensive Horticultural Societies

## Subsistence Technology

Many of the simple horticultural societies that were ushered into existence by the Neolithic Revolution in due time evolved into **intensive horticultural societies.** No doubt, hundreds of intensive horticultural societies have existed during the past several thousand years of human history. Until the influx of the Europeans in the late eighteenth century, such societies were widespread throughout Polynesia, a vast island chain in the southern Pacific that includes the islands of Hawaii, Tahiti, and Tonga, among many others. Prior to the end of the nineteenth century, they flourished throughout large parts of sub-Saharan Africa. South America and southeast Asia are also regions where numerous intensive horticulturalists were once located. Today, however, few remain. Most of these are found in parts of sub-Saharan Africa, and perhaps in some portions of South America and southeast Asia.

Like simple horticulturalists, intensive horticulturalists are dependent on cultivated garden products for the bulk of their food supply, and they cultivate by the slash-and-burn method. Some of them keep domesticated animals, whereas others hunt or fish to obtain their supply of meat. However, intensive horticulturalists differ in several significant ways from simple horticulturalists. One principal difference involves the length of time that land is allowed to remain fallow. Simple horticulturalists generally permit the land to lie fallow for 20 or 30 years before using it again. Intensive horticulturalists, by contrast, shorten the fallow period to perhaps as little as 5 to 10 years, thus cropping a given plot of land more frequently. Some intensive horticulturalists have reduced the length of the fallow period even further, occasionally to the point of cultivating land almost continuously. Ancient Hawaii, for example, fell into this category. To compensate for the decrease in soil fertility that accompanies more frequent cropping, intensive horticulturalists further fertilize the soil by adding such things as humus or animal manure.

The shortening of the fallow period has the effect of eventually converting thick forest growth to bush. Land that has been cleared of bush must be prepared for cultivation in a way that is unnecessary for land cleared of forest. Thus, many intensive horticulturalists have invented or adopted hoes for the purpose of properly preparing land for cultivation. As Boserup explains, "After the burning of real forest the soil is loose and free of weeds and hoeing of the land is unnecessary. By contrast, when the period of fallow is shortened and, therefore, the natural vegetation before clearing is thin or grassy the land must be prepared with a hoe or similar instrument before the seeds or roots can be placed" (1965:24).

Some intensive horticulturalists employ elements of technology in addition to, or instead of, the ones just mentioned. Polynesian intensive horticulturalists, for example, although they never made use of hoes, did engage in the terracing and irrigation of land. It is clear, then, that intensive horticulturalists have achieved a level of technological development beyond what is typical for simple horticulturalists. It is also clear that people work harder and longer under intensive horticulture. Preparing the land by hoeing and terracing and irrigating land are demanding and time-consuming activities. Since people work harder and longer, and since any given area of land is cultivated more frequently, it is obvious why this mode of subsistence technology is referred to as *intensive* horticulture.

Compared to simple horticulture, intensive horticulture is considerably more productive per unit of land. Intensive horticulturalists, in fact, produce sizable economic surpluses, and these surpluses are used to support a class of persons who are freed from direct involvement in agricultural production. In many intensive horticultural societies, the members of this class are regarded, theoretically at least, as the owners of all the land, and in all such societies they direct many economic activities. Their standard of living is higher than that of everyone else. The standard of living of most of the members of intensive horticultural societies is difficult to determine, but it seems likely that it differs little from that typically found among simple horticulturalists. Yet it should not be forgotten that intensive horticulturalists work significantly harder just to achieve the same material results.

As noted earlier, aboriginal Polynesia contained many simple horticultural societies. Most of the population of this region lived on the so-called high islands, which are rugged, eroded remnants of great volcanic cones. The arable land is very rich and covered with dense tropical growth. One of these high islands is Tahiti, a member of the Society Islands group. Tahiti is about 35 miles long and about half as wide. In the eighteenth century the island supported a population of approximately 100,000 (Service, 1963).

The Tahitians are sophisticated horticulturalists, considerably more so than groups like the Yanomama. They make very efficient use of the land for their gardens by terracing hillsides, diverting streams for irrigation, and enriching the soil in various ways. The primary horticultural tool is the simple digging stick. Since there are no metals, they have never developed the metal hoes characteristic of many other intensive horticulturalists. Tahiti's main domesticated plants were brought from Indonesia, and these include coconut palms, breadfruit trees, taro, yams, sweet potatoes, bananas and plantains, and sugar cane. The most important food is bread-fruit, a fruit that is plentiful and nutritious and stores well. The most versatile do-mesticated plant is the coconut palm. The coconut meat is a nourishing food and coconut milk is used for drinking. Palm leaves are used for thatch, and the fiber is used for the manufacture of mats and baskets. Fishing is also an important part of the Tahitian subsistence pattern, and the technology available for it is diversified and elaborate. This technology includes basketry traps, many forms of nets, fish poisons, harpoons, and many kinds of hooks and lines. Tahitians of both sexes are excellent swimmers. Women dive for crabs and other shellfish and even capture octopi. Men and boys dive to great depths for pearl oysters, the flesh of which is used for food and the shell for various implements and ornaments. Aside from seafood, the main source of protein is pork, and pigs are carefully fed and tended. Chickens are also raised.

## Economic Life and Stratification

What might be called **paramount ownership** is an evolutionary variation on the theme of lineage ownership. This type of ownership is ordinarily found among more intensive horticultural societies, although it has been known to exist in a few atypical hunter-gatherer societies and some simple horticultural societies. Paramount owner-ship prevails when a powerful individual—a chief—who is the head of a lineage, of an entire village, or of a vast network of integrated villages, claims personal owner-ship of the land within his realm and attempts to deprive those persons living on this land of full rights to its use. Actually, the ownership of all the land within a chief's realm is to a certain extent a fiction. The ownership rights of the chief are not as "real" as they are often made out to be. The Kpelle of Liberia in west Africa are inten-sive horticulturalists with a paramount mode of ownership, yet the ownership rights of the chief are quite limited. As James Gibbs explains (1965:200–201):

> Formally, land is said to be "owned" by the paramount chief, who divides it into portions for each town in the chiefdom, using for boundaries cottonwood and kola trees, creeks and hills. Each town chief divides the land for his town into segments for each quarter, using similar boundaries. These portions, in turn, are further split . . . into parcels for each of the "families" or unnamed lineages. . . .
> Because each man in the lineage is entitled to the use of a portion of the land, the lineage head cannot refuse to allot a piece of it to each household head in the lineage. Once land is parceled out, it stays within the lineage and reverts to the quar-ter elder or other original "owner" only when a lineage dies out or some other un-usual event occurs. Thus, although a town chief, a quarter elder, or a lineage head is, like a paramount chief, called "owner of the land," each is really a steward, holding the land for the group he represents.
> Actually, in everyday situations, the head of the household to whom lineage land has been allocated is spoken of as the owner of the land. He decides which bit of "his" land he will work during a given year and which portions he will allow to lie fallow. Most farms are individually owned by the heads of the households and

are worked with the help of the farmer's household group and cooperative work groups.

Thus, even though chiefs are the official owners of the land among the Kpelle, the powers of these chiefs appear to be significantly restricted. Since ordinary individuals make most of the daily decisions regarding the actual productive use of the land, these individuals are, in a sense, also its "owners."

Intensive horticulture and paramount ownership commonly imply partial redistribution. Marshall Sahlins (1963) highlights the important differences between pure and partial redistribution by comparing the distributional systems of Melanesian and Polynesian societies. As he notes, most Melanesian societies have had small-scale horticulture and big-man systems, whereas most Polynesian societies have been characterized by more intensive horticulture and partial redistribution.

Melanesian big men are persons who *seek prestige and renown* through the holding of elaborate feasts, but, as we have seen, their high status is relatively fragile and can quickly disappear when their elaborate feast giving declines. By contrast, Polynesian chiefs are *installed in office* through a system of hereditary succession and hold substantial economic leverage over the large mass of the population. One of their primary aims is the production and maintenance of a constant economic surplus, which they accomplish by compelling the people to relinquish a portion of their harvests. This leads to the formation of a "public treasury," a great storehouse over which the chief exercises control. The uses of this storehouse are plentiful. Chiefs support themselves and their families from it and also use it for providing lavish entertainment for visiting dignitaries, initiating major public projects such as irrigation works, building temples, sponsoring military campaigns, and supporting a vast range of political functionaries and administrative officials. In addition, portions of the storehouse are redistributed to the people as the need arises, and chiefs are expected to be generous with it. Those who are not sufficiently generous or who make excessive demands on the people's harvests are sometimes killed.

Polynesian partial redistributive systems are redistributive in the sense that they involve a continual flow of goods between the chiefs and the people. In this case, however, the flow of goods is an unequal flow: The people clearly give more than they receive in return. Although clearly similar in principle to the pure redistributive systems of small-scale horticulturalists, these intensified redistributive systems of more advanced horticulturalists are different in that they serve to promote a system of true social stratification. Three main social classes—consisting roughly of chiefs, subchiefs, and commoners—are a common pattern. These classes are distinguished by their differences in social rank, power, dress and ornamentation, patterns of consumption of luxury and other goods, direct involvement in economic production, availability of leisure time, and general styles of life.

Stratification systems of this type have been found among many of the intensive horticultural societies of sub-Saharan Africa as they existed in the eighteenth and nineteenth centuries. Here, the familiar three-class system of stratified life was frequently found (Lenski, 1966). The dominant class consisted of a small minority of powerful and privileged persons who lived off the economic surplus generated from those below. An intermediate class of officials and specialists served the fancies of the dominant class and carried out some of the lesser functions of political rule. The lowest class consisted of the large majority of ordinary people who were charged with producing enough economic goods to support the other two classes.

Chiefs or kings in some of these societies were treated with great respect and were often exalted and deified. In Dahomey, for instance, extreme acts of deference were shown the king. Even his ministers of state were expected to grovel in the dust in his presence, all the while throwing dirt over their heads and bodies (Lenski, 1966). Also, "no one could appear in his presence with his shoulders covered, or wearing sandals, shoes, or hat. No one could sit on a stool in his presence; if they sat, they were obliged to sit on the ground" (Lenski, 1966:154). Dahomean kings also possessed great wealth, both in the form of property and wives. They were nominally regarded as the owners of all property within the kingdom, were permitted to engage in incestuous marriages, controlled all appointments to public office, and approved the inheritance of property. Such exalted figures also possessed life-and-death power over their subjects, for persons who displeased the king could be (and often were) put to death.

Even though considerable stratification among African horticulturalists did exist, such societies, as is the case among intensive horticulturalists more generally, were characterized by what Lenski (1966) calls a "redistributive ethic." Among the southern Bantu, for example, a chief was expected to be generous and to take the common good into account, and a failure to do so led to a sharp decline in his popularity. As Lenski notes (1966:165):

> Though he is the wealthiest man in his tribe, he cannot use his wealth solely for the satisfaction of personal needs and desires. He is obliged to provide for the support of his ministers and courtiers. He must entertain all those who come to visit him. On great public occasions he is expected to slaughter many of his cattle and provide beer and porridge for all who gather at his village. He lends cattle, supports destitute widows and orphans, sends food to sick people and newly confined mothers, and in time of famine distributes corn from his own granaries or, if this is insufficient, purchases supplies from neighboring groups.

Similar systems of stratified life have also existed among many of the aboriginal societies of Polynesia. Hawaii, before the arrival of the Europeans, provides an excellent example from this region of the world. According to the description given by Sahlins (1958), Hawaii was divided into three main social strata: the "high chiefs" and their families, local stewards, and commoners. A paramount chief managed the use of lands throughout an entire island. He had the right to redistribute all lands upon his accession to office. In addition, he could alienate the land of any person of lower rank and transfer it to someone else. Commoners could be dispossessed from land for such reasons as hoarding surplus production, failing to contribute labor for the construction of irrigation works, and failing to make their household plots adequately productive. High chiefs and local stewards also controlled and supervised access to water used in irrigation.

Local stewards directly supervised household economic production, making sure that the land was being cultivated. In general, persons of high status could call on those of lower rank for the performance of various labor services; commoners, of course, were the major source of labor for communal projects. Refusal by a commoner to comply with a demand for labor could result in his death. It is clear that the major responsibilities of labor and economic production were carried out by the commoner class, and high chiefs and their families were freed from direct involvement in subsistence production. In this sense, chiefs constituted a kind of primitive "leisure class," putting others beneath them to work.

Hawaiian society also displayed class differences in consumption patterns. Although the redistributive ethic guaranteed an adequate food supply for all, and commoners have been described as "prosperous," certain choice foods were reserved for high chiefs. Moreover, luxury goods were often restricted to high-status persons and served as insignia of rank. The use of certain luxury items for dress and ornamentation was limited to high chiefs, and the quality of housing was closely associated with rank.

The Hawaiian paramount chief was considered divine. Because of the aura of sanctity that surrounded him, a series of elaborate taboos existed concerning contact with him, violation of which could result in death. For example, it was prohibited to let one's shadow fall on the paramount's house or possessions, to pass through his door ahead of him, or to put on his robe. Commoners were generally prohibited from touching anything used by the chief. In his presence, others were expected to prostrate themselves on the ground in a demonstration of extreme humility. When he traveled, people were warned of his coming so they could properly prepare themselves.

## Politics

Politically, intensive horticultural societies have quite often been organized into chiefdoms. In simple horticultural societies, the various villages of a tribe are usually politically autonomous, and politics is limited to the local level. The chiefdom, on the other hand, is marked by the integration of many separate villages into a centrally coordinated complex whole governed from the top down. In aboriginal Polynesia, chiefdoms were common, and the most advanced of these were found on the islands of Tonga, Tahiti, and Hawaii (Sahlins, 1963; Kirch, 1984). Here were sovereignties that included as many as tens of thousands of persons spread over areas as extensive as hundreds of square miles. The classical Polynesian chiefdom was a pyramidal arrangement of higher and lower chiefs. These chiefs were regular and official holders of offices and titles, and they claimed genuine authority over permanently established groups of followers. Authority resided in the office itself, and not merely in the person holding the position. Chiefs gained access to their positions through a line of hereditary succession. Chiefs used their large storehouses of food to support a permanent administrative apparatus created to carry out a variety of political functions. Such administrative officials as supervisors of the stores, talking chiefs, ceremonial attendants, and high priests, as well as specialized warrior corps, were supported from the chief's storehouse.

*A reconstruction of Tenochtitlán, the capital city of the Aztecs of ancient Mexico. The Aztecs were a very intensive horticultural society with an elaborate system of stratification and a state system of political organization.*

It is clear that a significant evolutionary gulf separates leaders in simple horticultural societies—big men and such—from genuine chiefs. Indeed, the chiefdom marks the beginning of the establishment of **power** and **authority** in social life. The real beginnings of power and authority emerge with the chiefdom because it is there that the necessary administrative machinery needed to compel compliance is created. Polynesian chiefs, for example, could not only issue commands, but could back them up as well. When that is possible, genuine power has become a significant social force.

The authority of chiefs is not without limit, however. Chiefs are still related to the common people through kinship ties, and they are expected to show concern for the common good. Chiefs who fail to meet these expectations frequently find themselves in the midst of a popular, and more than likely successful, revolt. In ancient Polynesia, for instance, many a chief who "ate the powers of government too much"—who made too many demands on the people—was dethroned and put to death (Sahlins, 1963). Thus, although chiefdoms have been able to create genuine power and authority, there are clear restraints on their coercive capacities. Lacking a genuine monopoly of force, primitive chiefs have not been allowed by their subjects to become true **tyrants**.

## FOR FURTHER READING

Richard Lee's *The !Kung San: Men, Women, and Work in a Foraging Society* (1979) is an excellent and highly detailed analysis of the best-known of all contemporary hunter-gatherer societies. Robert Kelly's *The Foraging Spectrum: Diversity in Hunter-Gatherer Lifeways* (1995) is an extremely valuable and unusually comprehensive analysis of the most important dimensions of hunter-gatherer lifeways. Burch and Ellanna (1994) provide a useful collection of essays on various aspects of hunter-gatherer societies, including territoriality, hunter affluence, culture contact, and government intervention. *Hunter-Gatherer Foraging Strategies: Ethnographic and Archaeological Analyses* (1981), edited by Winterhalder and Smith, is a collection of essays applying the approach known as optimal foraging theory to the analysis of hunter-gatherer subsistence practices. This approach assumes that hunter-gatherers adopt those foraging strategies that yield the highest caloric and nutritional outcomes for the least amount of time and energy invested. More recent works applying this perspective are Hawkes and O'Connell (1985), Winterhalder (1987), Kaplan and Hill (1992), and Kelly (1995).

Allen Johnson and Timothy Earle's *The Evolution of Human Societies: From Foraging Group to Agrarian State* (2000) provides excellent discussions of subsistence practices among the main types of preindustrial societies. Sutton and Anderson's *Introduction to Cultural Ecology* (2004) is a quite valuable discussion of the major types of preindustrial societies. The authors pay close attention to the ecological contexts in which these societies function, and also discuss optimization models of preindustrial subsistence practices, including optimal foraging theory. An article by Minge-Klevana (1980) contains extensive data on the workloads of preindustrial societies at different levels of technological development.

Marvin Harris's *Cows, Pigs, Wars, and Witches: The Riddles of Culture* (1974) and *Cannibals and Kings: The Origins of Cultures* (1977) contain interesting and highly readable accounts of subsistence and economic and political organization in preindustrial societies. Marshall Sahlins's *Stone Age Economics* (1972) is a famous work on precapitalist economic systems written from a perspective different in important respects from that of the present book. The edited collection by Stuart Plattner (1989) explores economic behavior throughout the whole range of preindustrial societies. Richard Wilk's *Economies and Cultures: Foundations of Economic Anthropology* (1996) is a very good discussion of important debates on the economic character of preindustrial societies.

Woodburn (1982) provides a valuable treatment of the most essential features of egalitarian societies. Morton Fried's *The Evolution of Political Society* (1967) is a classic work on preindustrial social evolution with special emphasis on the emergence of social stratification and the state. A classic work by Gerhard Lenski, *Power and Privilege: A Theory of Social Stratification* (1966), is must reading for anyone seriously interested in the evolution of social inequality and stratification. A classic article by Sahlins (1963) is an old but still very useful and insightful discussion of the contrast between tribes and chiefdoms using Melanesian and Polynesian societies as case studies. Upham (1990) provides valuable essays by specialists on political evolution in its early stages. Timothy Earle's *Chiefdoms: Power, Economy, and Ideology* (1991) is an excellent collection of essays on various aspects of chiefdoms, and his *How Chiefs Come to Power: The Political Economy in Prehistory* (1997) is an important recent work on chiefdoms. Patrick Kirch's *The Evolution of the Polynesian Chiefdoms* (1984) is an extremely thorough archaeological analysis of social and political evolution in Polynesia by a recognized expert. Service (1971) outlines the main stages of preindustrial political evolution.

Peter Bogucki's *The Origins of Human Society* (1999) sketches long-term social evolution from an archaeological perspective. Jared Diamond's *Guns, Germs, and Steel: The Fates of Human Societies* (1997) is a widely acclaimed popularized account of many aspects of human social evolution.

# CHAPTER

# 4

# Preindustrial Societies

## Agrarian and Pastoral Societies

This chapter continues the analysis of preindustrial social evolution begun in the last chapter by discussing agrarian and pastoral societies. It also examines various theories of the evolution of the entire range of preindustrial societies, and thus tries to explain the overall pattern of preindustrial technological, economic, and political evolution.

## Agrarian Societies

### Subsistence Technology

The first **agrarian societies** arose approximately 5,000 years ago in Egypt and Mesopotamia and slightly later in China and India. It was not long before agrarian societies were to be found over much of the globe. From the time when agrarian societies first emerged until the present day, the majority of people who have ever lived have done so according to the agrarian way of life. To the extent that this way of life remains today, it exists largely in substantially altered form in societies that are at least partially industrialized and are part of a worldwide capitalist economy. Hence, there are no true agrarian societies left in the world. But what were agrarian societies of the past like?

Agrarian societies rest upon true **agriculture.** Land is cleared of all vegetation and cultivated with the use of the plow and draft animals hitched to the plow. Fields are extensively fertilized, usually with animal manure. Land cultivated in this manner may be used more or less continually, and fallow periods are either very short or nonexistent. Farmers often crop a given plot of land annually, and in some cases several harvests may be reaped from the same plot of land in a single year.

A number of agrarian societies have existed in areas where rainfall was sufficient to nourish crops. Agrarian societies throughout Europe, for instance, were based on rainfall farming. But in many other agrarian societies, arid or semiarid climates have made rainfall farming impossible, and farmers have had to construct irrigation systems to water their crops. Farmers in ancient Egypt, Mesopotamia, China, and India, for example, practiced irrigation agriculture.

Agrarian farmers work much harder than do the members of earlier types of societies (Minge-Klevana, 1980). The tasks of clearing land, plowing, sowing and harvesting crops, tending animals, and so on require extensive labor inputs. Where irrigation systems must be constructed, people work even harder. Because of their efforts, agrarian farmers produce much more per unit of land than do horticulturalists, and they are able to produce large economic surpluses. But their greater efforts and larger surpluses do not yield for them a higher standard of living. Indeed, their standard of living is generally lower, and in some cases much lower, than that enjoyed by the members of horticultural societies. This apparent paradox will be resolved in due course.

Most members of agrarian societies are known as **peasants.** They are the primary producers—the persons who farm the land from day to day. Peasants differ from farmers in modern industrial societies, as well as from farmers in such preindustrial societies as colonial America, in their politically and economically servile condition to another class of persons, a landlord class, that owned or at least controlled the land and its products. But not all of the primary producers in agrarian societies have been peasants. Some have been slaves. Slaves differ from peasants primarily in that they are legally owned and can be bought and sold. In some agrarian societies—ancient Rome and Greece, for example—slaves actually outnumbered peasants.

Medieval England was characterized by an agrarian mode of economic production (Bennett, 1937). Between the twelfth and the fifteenth centuries, English peasants lived in an overwhelmingly rural society, one in which there were few, comparatively small cities. The peasants lived in small villages that commonly numbered about 100 persons. They spent most of their lives doing farm work, much of which was carried out by teams of peasants working cooperatively. Some peasants farmed the land in a "two-field" fashion. They would work on one field in one year while allowing the other one to remain fallow; then the next year they would reverse

*Scene from the Roman Senate. The Romans developed not only a complex state but also one of the largest empires the world has ever known.*

the process. Other peasants farmed the land using a "three-field" system. One field would be planted in the autumn with wheat or possibly rye; another would be planted with oats, vetches, or barley the following spring; and in the meantime, the third field would lie fallow. The next year the fallow field would be sown with wheat; the first field with oats, vetches, or barley; and the second field would remain fallow, and so on. Naturally, by rotating crops and fields in this manner the peasants were trying to keep the fertility of the soil as high as possible.

Peasants also applied animal manure to the soil to aid in its fertility, but getting enough manure was a constant struggle for a number of reasons. Peasants seldom had enough animals to produce all the manure they needed. Also, they did not have unrestricted use of their animals, for their landlords appropriated them on some occasions. Fodder to produce a sufficient quantity of manure was also in short supply. So the peasants did the best they could under difficult conditions, and this meant that they sometimes worked marl or lime into the ground as an additional fertilizer. Numerous animals were kept by peasants, both as means of working the farm and as sources of food. Oxen and cows were extremely important for farm work, and both were used for food and hides. Naturally, cows provided milk as a food product. Sheep were kept for their wool and for food. Pigs were also kept, and they were perhaps the most highly valued of all farm animals, at least as food sources. They had special significance as food sources because they could be economically fed, they put on weight quickly, and they could be efficiently prepared for slaughter.

Farm work for the average English peasant was extremely demanding, and peasants put in many long, hard hours in order to meet their subsistence needs and pay their taxes. The following description of peasant labor should convey just how demanding peasant life really was (Bennett, 1937:82–83):

> Once all this was finished the peasant's labours were not so pressing, and he could turn to the many other secondary jobs waiting to be done. If the land was heavy, draining operations were constantly necessary and worth while; ditches wanted digging out after the winter floods, and the good earth put on to the land again; hedges and enclosures round the little home or any private bit of enclosure required attention, and so on. Then . . . it was time for the first ploughing of the fallow field, and the busy activities in the garden where such vegetables and fruits as were then available were grown.
>
> So the days went by with plenty to occupy men till the end of May. The coming of June saw them making renewed efforts. The haymaking called for all their strength: first, there were the numerous compulsory days which they had to spend in getting in the lord's hay. . . .
>
> With the coming of August the peasant's activities reached their climax. Once again the demands made upon him by his lord were often very heavy. He had to appear in person again and again to gather in the lord's crops—and, although he usually worked one or two days more a week from August to Michaelmas than at other times in the year, this was not enough, and he had to give several extra days of his time as a boon or gift to his lord. And further, he had to come with all his family: everyone able to work, save perhaps the housewife, was pressed into service for so many days. This made the getting-in of his own crops a more difficult and anxious matter, and work during these crucial weeks must have been wellnigh unending.

Thus it was that the medieval English peasant toiled in his fields in a manner that the average hunter-gatherer or horticulturalist would have considered unthinkable.

## Economic Life

In agrarian societies the trend toward the privatization of economic ownership that was characteristic of the development of intensive horticultural societies continues and intensifies. Although paramount ownership represents a significant movement in the direction of private ownership, it has many of the characteristics of lineage ownership and is by no means a true mode of private property. True private ownership is reached with the evolution of **seigneurial ownership** in agrarian societies. Seigneurial ownership prevails when a small class of persons, generally known as *landlords* (*seigneurs* in French), claims private ownership of vast tracts of land on which there live and work peasants or slaves who pay rent and taxes and provide labor services to these lords. There is nothing fictitious about this type of ownership, since landlords have the power to deprive others of the unrestricted use of land, and these other persons frequently do *not* make the day-to-day decisions about how the land is to be productively used.

Seigneurial ownership was the prevailing mode of ownership in medieval Europe. Following Max Weber (1978; orig. 1923), Eric Wolf (1966) has called the type of seigneurial ownership characteristic of medieval Europe **patrimonial ownership.** In this type of ownership, land is privately owned by a class of landlords who inherit it through family lines and who personally oversee its cultivation. Patrimonial ownership contrasts with another type of seigneurial ownership that Weber called **prebendal ownership.** Prebendal ownership exists when land is owned by a powerful government that designates officials to supervise its cultivation and draw an income from it. As Wolf notes, prebendal ownership was "characteristically associated with strongly centralized bureaucratic states—such as the Sassanid Empire of Persia, the Ottoman Empire, the Mogul Empire in India, and traditional China. The political organization of these empires attempted to curtail heritable claims to land and tribute, and asserted instead the eminent domain of a sovereign, a despot, whose claims overrode all inferior claims to domain" (1966:51).

It is important to note that in different agrarian societies at different times peasants often owned the land they cultivated and on which they lived, at least in the sense that they had legal "title" to this land. Yet even these so-called free peasants were effectively deprived of full control over this land, since the landlord class (or the state) held the administrative right to levy taxes against these peasants and to extract labor services from them, as well as control them in other ways. This meant that the economic situation of free peasants was usually little different from those who had no legal title to land at all.

The distributive mode characteristic of agrarian societies is often called **surplus expropriation.** It occurs when a class of landlords compels another class of dependent economic producers to produce a surplus from their fields and relinquish it to them. The surplus is handed over in the form of rent, taxation of various sorts, and various types of labor services. There are several crucial differences between expropriation and partial redistribution, two worth noting here. First, landlords have considerably greater power than chiefs, and they use this power to place many more economic burdens on peasant producers than chiefs are capable of placing on their followers. Second, the flow of goods and services between peasants and lords is substantially more unequal than is the flow of valuables between chiefs and commoners. It is largely in one direction only—from peasants to lords—and lords are under no obligation to redistribute economic surpluses to the primary producers and usually do not do so. Although there may be in some situations a fine line between partial redistribution and expropriation, in most cases it is not difficult to tell whether redistribution or expropriation is operating within a society.

Under medieval European feudalism, surplus expropriation was the dominant distributive mode. Peasants owed landlords a specified rent for the use of the landlord's land that they paid either as a portion of their harvests (rent in kind), or by money (cash rent), or some combination of the two. In the earlier days of the feudal period, rent in kind was the standard form of rent payment, but as the feudal system evolved in the later Middle Ages, cash rent began to replace rent in kind. Since the peasant was thus producing both for himself and for his landlord, he had to increase his own toil as well as that of his family in order to meet these economic demands. Peasants also had economic burdens in the form of taxes. For instance, peasants had to pay a tax to grind their grain in the lord's mill, another tax to bake their bread in the lord's oven, and yet another to fish in the lord's fishpond. (Since peasants did not own these resources, they fell into this sort of dependence on their lords.) A third type of economic burden placed on medieval peasants was that of labor services. Peasants were required to spend so many days working on the lord's demesne (his home farm, or personal land on which he, and not his peasants, lived), tilling the soil and tending the animal herds. This burden often became very oppressive and left the peasant little time to provide for his own family's subsistence by working his own lands.

In ancient Rome a vast system of surplus expropriation also existed, but this system rested primarily on slave rather than peasant labor. The huge supply of slaves on which Rome relied was acquired by political conquest of foreign lands. Slave labor was much cheaper than peasant labor and therefore was the principal labor mode in Roman society (Cameron, 1973). There were many great Roman estates that had large slave gangs working on them; Pliny, for instance, mentions one estate that had 4,117 slaves (Cameron, 1973). Where slavery rather than serfdom is the principal labor mode, the system of surplus expropriation is more direct and obvious. For example, to calculate their economic gain, the Roman landowners essentially had to determine the amount of wealth their slaves produced for them and subtract from this the cost of acquiring and maintaining a slave labor force.

## Stratification

With the transition from intensive horticultural to agrarian societies, the limitations formerly placed on the stratification system were removed. The disappearance of the redistributive ethic and the removal of kinship ties between the members of different social classes were associated with the emergence of extreme forms of social stratification in which the majority of persons were frequently thrown into conditions of extreme poverty and degradation. One of the most striking characteristics of agrarian societies was the immense gap in power, privilege, and prestige that existed between the dominant and subordinate classes. Indeed, agrarian societies are by far the most highly stratified of all preindustrial societies. (Unless otherwise noted, the following discussion is based on the description of agrarian stratification provided by Lenski, 1966.)

Agrarian stratification systems generally contained the following social classes:

- A political-economic elite consisting of the ruler and his royal family and a landowning governing class
- The retainer class
- The merchant class
- The priestly class
- The peasantry
- Artisans
- Expendables

Although the first four of these strata may be considered privileged groups, the privileged segment of greatest significance in all agrarian societies was, of course, the political-economic elite: the ruler and the governing class. Likewise, although peasants, artisans, and expendables were all highly subordinate classes, the peasantry, since it constituted a majority of the population, was far and away the primary subjugated class.

The ruler in agrarian societies—monarch, king, emperor, or of whatever title—was that person who officially stood at the political head of society. The governing class consisted of those persons who were ordinarily the primary owners of land and who received the benefits that accompanied such ownership. But in fact both the ruler and the governing class tended to be both major landowners and major wielders of political power, and there were vital connections between these two segments of the elite. Taken together, they typically comprised no more than 1 or 2 percent of the population while appropriating approximately one-half to two-thirds of the total wealth. They typically enjoyed a considerable (and often enormous) amount of power, privilege, and prestige in comparison to other classes. A majority of the huge economic surplus generated within agrarian societies almost always found its way into the hands of the entire political-economic elite.

The rulers of agrarian societies have generally controlled great wealth. By the end of the fourteenth century, for example, English kings had an average income of approximately £135,000 a year, an amount that was equal to 85 percent of the combined incomes of the 2,200 members of the nobility and squirearchy. Rulers of some of the great agrarian bureaucratic empires have fared much better than this. Xerxes, emperor of Persia in pre-Christian times, is said to have had an annual income that would have totaled $35 million by modern standards. Similarly, the annual income of Suleiman the Magnificent of Turkey was judged to have equaled $421 million; the figures for Akbar the Great of India and his successor, Aurangzeb, are estimated at $120 million and $270 million, respectively. As for the wealth of the governing class, Lenski estimates that this class probably received on the average at least one-quarter of the total income of most agrarian societies. In late nineteenth-century China, for instance, the Chinese portion of the governing class (that is, excluding the Manchu segment of this class) received approximately 645 million *taels* per year in total income, a figure that amounted to 24 percent of the gross national product. Averaging out to about 450 *taels* per family head, the Chinese segment of the governing class had an annual income roughly 20 times that of the remainder of Chinese society.

Standing directly below the ruler and governing class in agrarian societies was the so-called retainer class. This class consisted of such functionaries as government officials, professional soldiers, household servants, and other persons who were directly employed to serve the ruler and governing class. Lenski estimates that the retainer class probably constituted around 5 percent of the population of most agrarian societies. A crucial role of this class was to mediate the relations between the elite and the common people. As Lenski notes, it was various officials of the retainer class who actually carried out the day-to-day work necessary for getting the economic surplus into the hands of the ruler and governing class. The actual privilege and social status of members of the retainer class varied considerably. Certain members of this class enjoyed greater privilege than some lower-ranking members of the governing class, while others of the class often enjoyed no special measure of privilege; their overall standing in society was perhaps only slightly better than that of the average peasant. On the average, however, members of the retainer class tended to share to a significant degree in the benefits of the wealth controlled by their employers. The retainer class was in effect a service class, but its general position in society was clearly nearer that of the privileged than of the disprivileged.

Also standing among the privileged segments of agrarian societies was the merchant class. Merchants, of course, engaged in commercial activity and were a vital part of the agrarian urban economy. The merchant class was often of great value to the ruler and governing class, since merchants dealt in many of the luxury goods that were purchased by the elite. Although many merchants remained poor, some amassed substantial wealth, and a few were wealthier than some members of the governing class. Yet, despite these material benefits, merchants were usually accorded very low prestige. In the traditional status-ranking system of China, for example, merchants were placed near the very bottom of the social scale, ranking even below peasants and artisans. Merchants in medieval Europe fared somewhat better, but they were still regarded as highly inferior to the governing class. Merchants appear to have been well aware of their low status, and many strove to raise their status to the level of the governing class by imitating its lifestyle.

Although the priestly class in agrarian societies was often internally stratified, in general it can be considered a privileged class. Indeed, priests have frequently commanded substantial wealth in many agrarian societies, and it has been a common pattern for them to be close allies of rulers and governing classes. In Egypt in the twelfth century BCE, for example, as well as in eighteenth-century France, priests owned 15 percent of the land. In pre-Reformation Sweden the Church owned 21 percent of the land, and in Ceylon, Buddhist monasteries are said to have been in control of about one-third of the land.

This privileged status of the priestly class as a whole no doubt resulted from the political alliances typically forged between priests and rulers and governing classes. The latter two groups have commonly sought priestly support for their oppressive and exploitative activities. Priests have therefore been properly rewarded for their aid to these dominant groups. However, the privilege of the priestly class was usually insecure. The holdings of this class were often confiscated by the political elite, and thus the economic alliance between the priesthood and the elite was often a shaky one. Moreover, not all priests were wealthy and of high status. In medieval Europe, for instance, priests were divided into an upper and lower clergy. The upper clergy lived in a privileged style consistent with its noble background, but members of the lower clergy—parish priests directly serving the common people— lived in a style resembling that of the common people themselves.

The peasant class in agrarian societies has occupied a distinctly inferior social, economic, and political status. Economically, the lot of peasants has generally been a miserable one, although the specific degree of their exploitation has varied from one society and one time to another. As noted earlier, a major burden placed on all peasants has been taxation, the principal means of separating the peasant from his surplus product. The oppressiveness of taxation has varied considerably. During the Tokugawa era in Japan, the rate of taxation of the peasantry varied from as little as 30 percent to as much as 70 percent of the crop. In China, approximately 40 to 50 percent of total peasant agricultural production was commonly claimed by landowners. In pre-British India, peasants apparently handed over from one-third to one-half of their crops to both Muslim and Hindu rulers. In Babylon during the time of Hammurabi, taxes ranged from one-third to one-half of the crop. In Ottoman Turkey, the tax rate varied from 10 to 50 percent. In sixteenth- and seventeenth-century Russia, the rate was 20 to 50 percent.

In a number of agrarian societies, multiple forms of taxation have existed. One of the most striking illustrations of a system of multiple taxation comes from the period of Ottoman rule in Bulgaria. Here, the Turks imposed nearly 80 different kinds of taxes and obligations on the peasantry. One such tax was known as the "tooth tax," a levy placed on a village by the Turks after they had eaten and drunk there. In official terms, the tax was said to compensate the Turks "for the wear and tear sustained by their teeth during the meal" (Lenski, 1966:269). Incredible as such a tax seems, it does indicate the lengths to which many agrarian elites have gone to benefit themselves at the expense of the bulk of the population.

In addition to the burdens of taxation, peasants were also subjected to other hardships. One of these was the **corvée,** or system of forced labor. Under this system, peasants were obligated to provide so many days of labor either for their lord or for the state. In medieval Europe, for example, peasants were obligated to work on their lord's land a specified number of days per week throughout the year. During the building of the Great Wall in China, some peasants were kept on forced labor projects nearly their entire adult lives. Peasant hardships did not end with the burdens of taxation and forced labor. If the peasant's lord operated a mill, oven, or wine press (and he frequently did), the peasant was under obligation to use them and to compensate the lord handsomely for such use. In some agrarian societies, the lord could take anything he desired from a peasant's personal property, and he could do so without payment. In medieval Europe, when a man died, his lord could claim his best beast. Furthermore, if a man's daughter married off the manor or without the lord's permission, the girl's father could be fined.

It should be obvious that the life of the average peasant was an extremely difficult one. By and large, life was lived with but the barest necessities for existence. The peasant diet was generally a poor one in terms of the quantity, variety, and nutritional adequacy of the food. Household furniture was extremely meager, and most peasants slept on straw-covered earthen floors. Sometimes conditions became so bad that a living was no longer possible and peasants had to abandon the land and attempt to sustain themselves by other means.

In addition to the severe economic deprivation typically suffered by peasants, the peasantry occupied a very low social status in all agrarian societies. A great gulf separated the lifestyles of peasants and the elite. The elite (and, to varying degrees, other classes as well) regarded peasants as extreme social inferiors, frequently conceiving of them as something less than fully human. In some agrarian societies, peasants were formally classified in various documents as belonging to essentially the same category as the livestock. Lacking all but the barest necessities of life, and deprived of any opportunity to pursue even such unremarkable amenities as an education or the cultivation of good manners, the peasantry stood in stark contrast to the privileged elite, where the social trappings of high status were a fundamental part of everyday life.

Standing below the peasantry in the agrarian stratified order were two other classes. One of these consisted of artisans, or trained craftsmen, a class that Lenski estimates probably represented about 3 to 7 percent of the population in most agrarian societies. Artisans were mainly recruited from among the ranks of the dispossessed peasantry. Although the incomes of peasants and artisans overlapped, artisans were generally worse off economically, many apparently living in destitute circumstances.

At the very bottom of virtually every agrarian society could be found a class of expendables. Constituting approximately 5 to 10 percent of most agrarian populations, these persons were found in urban areas. Their ranks were filled by beggars, petty thieves, outlaws, prostitutes, underemployed itinerant workers, and other persons who, as Lenski notes, were "forced to live solely by their wits or by charity" (1966:281). Members of this class suffered from extreme economic deprivation, malnutrition, and disease, and had a very high death rate. The sons and daughters of poor peasants who inherited nothing often fell into this extraordinarily hapless class.

One's class position in all agrarian societies was overwhelmingly determined by social heredity. Most persons died as members of the class into which they were born. Some social mobility did occur, however. Occasionally, a person rose in rank to one of the privileged classes. Nevertheless, such upward movement seldom occurred; downward mobility was much more common. As mentioned, children who inherited nothing from their poor peasant parents were often forced into either the artisan or expendable class in order to maintain any sort of existence at all. Thus, the possibility of improving one's disadvantaged position in an agrarian society was greatly limited.

## Politics

The chiefdom, containing only a limited capacity for compulsion, is inadequately backed by the administrative machinery necessary to overcome the most severe forms of resistance. When this administrative machinery is finally created, that form of political society known as the *state* has evolved. It is this type of political structure that prevails in nearly all agrarian societies.

The state not only continues the general evolutionary process of the increasing concentration of power but it also establishes a *monopoly of force* necessary to back that power up and ensure that the will of the power holders prevails. Indeed, this capture of a monopoly of force is essential to the very definition of a state. As Morton Fried notes (1967:230):

> Of great importance is the claim of the state to paramountcy in the application of naked force to social problems. Frequently this means that warfare and killing become monopolies of the state and may only be carried out at times, in places, and under the specific conditions set by the state.
>
> In the final analysis the power of a state can be manifested in a real physical force, an army, a militia, a police force, a constabulary, with specialized weaponry, drill, conscription, a hierarchy of command, and the other paraphernalia of structured control.

Although holding a monopoly of force is crucial to the nature of the state, other characteristics of states are also significant. First, the state emerges under conditions in which the significance of kinship ties is reduced. Kinship ties in chiefdoms serve to soften the use of coercive power. With the transition to the state, these ties between ruler and ruled are generally eliminated. Therefore, state-level rulers no longer subjugate their kinsmen, but dominate a great mass of unrelated individuals. Second, states promote elaborate legitimizing ideologies (van den Berghe, 1978). The naked use of force alone may be insufficient to guarantee compliance with the state's wishes, and rulers therefore commonly attempt to convince the people of their moral right to rule. The greater the psychological commitment of the people to the state, the less the likelihood of rebellion against it. Legitimizing ideologies have taken a variety of forms, but a very common tactic has been for state rulers to justify their rule in religious terms: to claim supernatural sanction of their role in society. Finally, unlike chiefdoms states have generally not been redistributive centers. The flow of the surplus to the state has been a one-way flow, and such surplus expropriation has resulted in substantial—indeed, often enormous—enrichment of the ruling powers.

The state in one form or another represents the outcome of a long process of political evolution in which democracy and equality were increasingly undermined and replaced with the domination of the many by the few. Although the evolution of the state was achieved in gradual rather than sudden fashion (Harris, 1977), its actual emergence represents a great watershed in human history. For it was here

*European peasants plowing in the mid-eighteenth century.*

that powerful leaders no longer needed to promise to be generous to their followers. They could and did promise their followers little or nothing, save continual subjugation and constant toil, and they had a sufficient monopoly of force to back up their rule.

## Pastoral Societies

### Subsistence Technology

**Pastoralism** (or pastoral nomadism) is a highly specialized subsistence adaptation found in arid regions of the world poorly suited to agriculture. It is based on the tending of animal herds rather than the growing of crops. Exactly when and how pastoralism first emerged is still debated. It may have arisen as early as 8,000 years ago in parts of the Middle East (Hole, 1977; Cribb, 1991), but this is by no means certain. There is evidence that early in prehistory a number of groups seemed to depend heavily on domesticated animals. However, true pastoralism—exclusive or near-exclusive dependence on animal herds, with little or no agriculture—may be a more recent phenomenon, dating only from approximately 3700 or 3500 BP (Sahlins, 1968; Cribb, 1991; Barfield, 1993). In any event, although classic pastoralism occurs later in history than cultivation, it is not evolutionarily "higher" or "more advanced" than agriculture. Rather, it is an alternative to agriculture in environments where aridity makes cultivation of the land difficult or impossible.

Pastoralists tend their animal herds year round and move seasonally with them in search of pasture (hence the name pastoral *nomadism*). Animals most frequently kept include sheep, goats, camels, cattle, and horses. Some pastoral groups depend on a single animal species, but most herd a number of different species. A few pastoralists practice no agriculture at all. These groups obtain agricultural products for their diet by trade relations with agricultural neighbors. Usually, however, pastoral groups engage in some agriculture in order to supplement the foods they obtain from their animal herds, but this is always distinctly secondary to their herding activities.

Pastoralists live and travel in relatively small groups that usually do not exceed 100 to 200 members. Population densities are quite low, usually fewer than 5 persons per square mile. Most of what pastoralists eat, of course, comes from their animal herds. They subsist principally on milk, meat, and blood. In eastern Africa, for instance, many pastoral groups have as their major dietary item a mixture of blood and milk obtained from their cattle. Although agricultural products generally supplement the diet, for some groups they do so only to a small extent.

Most pastoralists have been located in the dry regions of Asia and Africa: in southwest Asia, northern Africa, and the grasslands of eastern Africa. Pastoralism is also found in certain northern Eurasian forest regions, where reindeer herders predominate (Sahlins, 1968). Marshall Sahlins (1968:33) notes that the "classic locus of pastoral tribes is the transcontinental dry belt of Asia and Africa: Manchuria, Mongolia, Tibet, Turkestan, Iran, Arabia, the Sahara and its environs." Thomas Barfield (1993), a leading anthropological expert on pastoral nomads, categorizes the pastoral groups of the world into five zones:

1. *Africa just south of the Sahara, running from west to east, and from north to south in east Africa.* Here, cattle are the most prominent animal, although sheep and goats are also herded and donkeys are used for transport. Camels may be included in groups adjacent to the northern deserts. Some of the best studied groups in this region are the Dinka, Maasai, Nuer, and Turkana.
2. *The Saharan and Arabian deserts.* Pastoralists of this region usually specialize in just one animal, the dromedary (or one-humped) camel, which provides both food and transport. The people living in this region are Bedouin Arabs. This form of pastoralism is especially extreme not only because it relies on a single species but also because very large distances must be traveled in the cycle of annual migration.
3. *Central Eurasia, north of the Saharan and Arabian deserts, through the plateaus of Turkey and Iran and further east.* Pastoralists living in this region herd sheep, goats, camels, donkeys, and horses—virtually all of the animals known to pastoralists except cattle. Some of the best-known groups of this region are the Basseri and the Qashqa'i of Iran, the Turkmen, and the Central Asian Arabs of Afghanistan.
4. *The Asian steppe, running from the Black Sea to Mongolia.* Horse-riding pastoralists have predominated in this region. Horses are not only ridden but used

for food as well. Sheep, goats, cattle, and Bactrian (two-humped) camels are also herded. Today these groups are most commonly found in Kazakhstan, Uzbekistan, and Xinjiang, China. The most famous groups of this region are historical: the Hsiung-nu of the northern steppes of ancient China, the Scythians of southern Russia and the Ukraine, the Uighur of northwest Mongolia, and the Zunghar in the area where Russia, Mongolia, and China met. By far the most famous historical group, however, was the Mongols, who lived in the Mongolian steppe just north of China.

5. *The Tibetan Plateau and neighboring mountain regions.* Groups in this region live at extremely high altitudes unsuited for cultivation and where there are vast grasslands that are good for grazing animals. The animals that are herded are sheep, goats, and, most important, yaks. The yak is uniquely adapted to high altitudes and extreme cold, and is used for its hair, milk, meat, and also as a transport animal. Some groups also herd a yak/cattle hybrid known as a *dzo*, which can flourish at lower altitudes as well as high ones. The Drokba are a well-known group from this region.

The Hsiung-nu of the northern Chinese steppes were pastoralists who, beginning around 2200 BP, preyed upon Chinese civilization. Mounted on their horses, they regularly raided and looted it and wreaked all sorts of havoc (Barfield, 1989). They established an empire that was based on their extraction of an enormous amount of wealth by means of their raids. The Hsiung-nu were not interested in ruling China, but rather in escaping with their looted wealth back to the steppes. This was the key to their success. Because of their riding and military skills, Chinese civilization had great difficulty coping with them. (The Great Wall, in fact, was built as an effort to keep them out.) The Hsiung-nu were followed historically by the Hsien-pi and the Jou-jan (Barfield, 1993), and then, much later, by the Mongols, who engaged in the same raiding and looting strategy, only on a much larger scale. In the thirteenth century they were led by Chinggis Khan and his descendants and established the largest empire the world has ever known.

A well-known contemporary pastoral group is the Nuer, who numbered between 200,000 and 300,000 in 1930. They are pastoralists who live mostly in the Sudan in eastern Africa, but some of them live further east inside the borders of Ethiopia (Evans-Pritchard, 1940; Service, 1963; Mair, 1974). Most of their territory is open grassland through which travels the upper part of the Nile River and some of its tributaries. They experience two very different seasons, a dry one between December and June and then a very wet one between June and December. During the dry season there is not enough water, but during the wet season there is too much. Most of their economic activity centers on the herding of cattle, but they do grow some crops, such as millet and maize. Like most pastoralists, they disdain cultivation, regarding it as irksome, and think of herding and caring for their animals as the best way to live. Cattle are cherished possessions that constitute the main form of wealth. They are pampered animals—talked to, petted, their horns tied with ribbons, and so on. Milk is the Nuer's main food throughout an entire year. It is drunk fresh, combined with millet into a type of porridge, and made into cheese. Blood is either boiled to thicken or allowed to coagulate into a solid substance. It is then

Masai herdsmen of east Africa with some of their cattle. The Masai are one of the world's best-known pastoral societies.

roasted before it is eaten. Cattle are eaten when they are too old to breed or if they suffer serious injuries.

The Basseri are pastoralists who live in the dry steppes and mountains of southern Iran (Barth, 1961). Numbering about 16,000 in the entire tribe, they are tent dwellers who move about with their animal herds. Their habitat is hot and dry. Annual rainfall is generally 10 inches or less, and most of this falls in the winter. The Basseri keep a number of domesticated animals, the most important of which are sheep and goats. The products of these animals provide the major part of subsistence. Donkeys are kept for transport and for riding, horses for riding only. Camels are maintained for use in heavy transport, and their wool is also of value. Poultry is sometimes found as a source of meat.

The milk obtained from sheep and goats is a most important product. Sour milk is a staple and is processed for storage. Cheese is made, although seldom during the periods of daily migrations. The best cheese is allegedly made during the summer, when the Basseri maintain a stationary residence. Lambs are slaughtered for meat. The hides of slaughtered animals are sold in markets and also used as bags for storing water, sour milk, and buttermilk. Wool is also an important animal product. Felt is made out of lamb's wool, and sheep's wool and camel hair are sold and used in weaving and rope making. Goat hair is also of value and is spun and woven.

Many agricultural products are included in the typical diet of the Basseri. Some of these are produced by the Basseri themselves, the rest being obtained in trade. Cereal crops such as wheat are planted when the tribesmen first arrive in their summer camps, and these are harvested before the departure from the camps. The agriculture performed by the Basseri themselves is very rough, and, in general, disliked and disdained. Therefore, many of the Basseri are reluctant to engage in it. Many of the Basseri's necessities are obtained through trade. Flour, sugar, tea, dates, and fruits and vegetables are obtained exclusively or mainly by trade. Material for clothes, finished clothes and shoes, cooking utensils, and saddles are purchased in markets.

## Political Economy

Many pastoral societies are organized into uncentralized tribes that are highly egalitarian and in which political leadership is informal and leaders lack any real power or authority. The Nuer are a good example (Service, 1963; Mair, 1964, 1974). They do not have any permanent land rights and believe that land should be available for everyone. Cattle are owned by individuals, and some families may accumulate more cattle than others (and thus be somewhat richer), but unequal standards of living do not result, and thus there are no social class divisions. At the most, those who have more cattle may be given more prestige. Sharing and generosity are the norm in Nuer villages and even between villages.

The Nuer take exception to any form of behavior that might be interpreted as giving an order, and age is the only basis for deference (it is shown by younger to older people in a society famous for its finely graded age groups). Before they fell under the influence of European colonialism, fighting between Nuer tribes was regarded as a normal and even laudatory activity, but colonialism brought an end to this. At the time there were no individuals given special responsibility for the maintenance of order and settling of conflicts. After the fighting was stopped, such a role was created in the form of the famous "leopard-skin chief" (Mair, 1974). The leopard-skin chief, so called because he was the only person allowed to wear the skin of a leopard, had special responsibilities with respect to mediating decisions concerning acts of homicide and putting an end to feuds; however, he did not have any right to command the actions of others or to force obedience. As their principal ethnographer, E. E. Evans-Pritchard comments (1940:174–175):

> In taking the view that to regard the leopard-skin chief as a political agent or a judicial authority is to misunderstand the constitution of Nuer society and to be blind to its fundamental principles, we have to account for the part he plays in the settlement of feuds. We have stated that he has no judicial or executive authority. It is not his duty to decide on the merits of a case of homicide. It would never occur to Nuer that a judgement of any kind was required. Likewise he has no means of compelling people to pay or to accept blood-cattle. He has no powerful kinsmen or the backing of a populous community to support him. He is simply a mediator in a specific social situation and his mediation is only successful because community ties are acknowledged by both parties and because they wish to avoid, for the time being at any rate, further hostilities. Only if both parties want the affair settled can the chief intervene successfully. He is the machinery which enables groups to bring about a normal state of affairs when they desire to achieve this end.

By contrast with the Nuer, the Basseri constitute a stratified society that is politically organized as a chiefdom (Barth, 1961). The central leader is a chief who is granted considerable authority to command the actions of others. As Fredrik Barth (1961) notes, power is conceived as emanating from him, not delegated to him by his followers. The chief plays a major political role in settling disputes that the contending parties have been unable to settle informally. In this regard, Barth comments that the (1961:74) outstanding feature of the chief's position . . . is his power of decision and autocratic command over his subjects. . . . The right to command, to make decisions on behalf of persons in other tents than one's own, is a strictly chiefly prerogative. The monopolization by the chief of the right to command is a fundamental abstract principle of Basseri social structure.

Barth goes on to say that a Basseri chief "may give any person an order which the latter must obey without regard to any pre-established organizational pattern" (1961:75).

Not only does the chief have considerable power but he also has a great deal of material privilege and high status. He conducts himself in an imperial manner, lives in the largest tent, and maintains the highest level of consumption in his community. His high level of income derives both from inherited property and the right to collect various taxes from fellow tribesmen, the latter being collected in the form of so many sheep per hundred. This gives a contemporary Basseri chief an income of nearly 8,000 sheep. Taxes are also paid by followers in the form of clarified butter, and visitors to the chief's tent often bring livestock and other gifts. But chiefs are also redistributors in a manner highly reminiscent of chiefs in intensive horticultural societies. They are expected to be generous and often provide gifts of weapons and horses, at least to their more prominent subjects.

The chief is not the only wealthy or high-status man in the tribe. Other men can also accumulate wealth and rise in social rank. Some men are able, especially during a succession of economically successful years, to become wealthy herd owners, sometimes establishing flocks of sheep of 800 or even more. Nomads who accumulate large herds often invest some of the wealth in landed property and become part-time landlords. Barth comments (1961:105):

> The position of even a petty landowner is one of relative privilege. His title to land gives him entry into the local elite of his village and district, and in the case of wealthier landlords, also on a provincial or local level. In dealings with the local authorities, the man who owns land, however small the plot may be, is in an entirely different position from the ordinary villager.
>
> A transfer of capital from flocks into land holdings is thus economically advantageous to the wealthier herd-owner; it also offers striking social advantages within the framework of sedentary society. A number of Basseri choose to do this—frequently with no thoughts of future sedentarization. The land provides them with a secure store of wealth and a considerable annual income in the agricultural products needed in their normal pattern of consumption—it frees them from the necessity of purchasing these products and thus tends to increase the rate of growth of their herds. Unless disease strikes their herds severely, the process tends to become cumulative, with a steadily growing fraction of the nomad's wealth invested in land.

Thus, the Basseri have built a society considerably more developed than pastoral groups like the Nuer. They demonstrate the evolutionary possibilities that are contained within a pastoral economy.

Some pastoralists have even been able to create large-scale confederations and states. The classic example, of course, is the Mongol Empire. However, pastoral economies do not contain the internal conditions that will support such political structures. They are usually spread out over too large an area and are too economically unspecialized (Barfield, 1993). Therefore, the creation of states has depended on external relations. The Hsiung-nu of ancient north China could only create an empire by looting the wealth produced by Chinese peasants and expropriated by Chinese landlords and the Chinese state. When the Chinese state collapsed in 220 CE, the Hsiung-nu no longer had any rich provinces to loot or a government to terrorize, and their empire collapsed (Barfield, 1993). The same was true for the Mongols of later times. Barfield (1993:151) notes, "The foreign policies of all imperial confederacies of Mongolia had a single aim: to extract benefits from China directly by raiding or indirectly through subsidies, and to establish institutionalized border-trade agreements. Without such revenue the imperial confederacy would collapse."

# Causes of the Evolution of Preindustrial Societies

## The Evolution of Subsistence Technology

Table 4.1 summarizes the main characteristics of preindustrial societies. The question is, What accounts for the evolution of preindustrial societies from one stage to the next? We will begin by looking at the evolution of subsistence technology. Why did hunter-gatherers gradually give up food collection in favor of food production? Why did simple horticulturalists intensify their cultivation techniques, and why did intensive horticulturalists in various parts of the world begin to farm the land by using plows and draft animals? It was once widely believed by social scientists of all sorts that subsistence technology was a self-generating, independent force in its own right. It was thought that technological changes occurred as the cumulative result of the inventive powers of the human mind. It was also believed that whenever new forms of technology became available, people automatically adopted them because they saw the benefits they would bring.

Most social scientists have now abandoned this view of technological change, and a variety of theories have been developed to explain both the shift from hunting and gathering to agriculture and the intensification of agricultural production. One of the most widely embraced explanations of the evolution of subsistence technology is the population pressure argument proposed in the mid-1960s by Ester Boserup (1965, 1981; cf. R. Wilkinson, 1973). Boserup holds that people have no inherent desire to advance their level of technology. She postulates that people wish to make a living by the simplest and easiest means possible. Their natural inclinations are to meet their subsistence needs by expending the least amount of time and effort. Since adopting new technologies actually results in people having to work harder and longer, they will not switch to new methods unless special conditions compel them to do so.

Boserup believes that the principal condition compelling people to advance their technology is **population pressure**. Population pressure exists when population growth causes people to press against food resources. As the number of mouths to be fed increases, a point is eventually reached at which people begin to deplete their resources and suffer a significant drop in their standard of living. Boserup argues that it is at this point that people will start to intensify production. They adopt

**TABLE 4.1  The Main Trends of Preindustrial Social Evolution**

| Type of Society | Mode of Subsistence | Mode of Ownership |
| --- | --- | --- |
| *Hunter-gatherer* | Hunting of wild animals using spears, spear throwers, bows and arrows, nets, and traps. Gathering of wild plant food using a digging stick. Fishing often undertaken, and in some environments may be a principal subsistence activity. Small nomadic bands. | Normally some type of communal ownership. Vital resources that sustain life owned by the entire community, and no person may deprive others of the full right to use these resources. |
| *Simple horticultural* | Small-scale gardening, often using slash-and-burn cultivation. Men prepare garden sites, but women commonly the principal cultivators. Gardens moved frequently, and fallow periods generally long (e.g., 20 to 30 years). Sedentary villages. | Typically lineage ownership, which is a variation on primitive communism in which resources are communally owned, but owning group is a kinship group rather than entire community. |
| *Intensive horticultural* | Small-scale gardening, commonly using slash-and-burn techniques but with more frequent and intensive cultivation of plots and shorter fallow periods (e.g., 5 to 10 years). May also involve extension of technological inventory to include metal hoes and construction of irrigation systems, as well as more extensive fertilization of garden plots. Sedentary villages. | Usually paramount ownership. Powerful chiefs claim ownership of large tracts of land and exert considerable control over how land is used. However, primary producers who live on the land retain substantial decision-making power over day-to-day cultivation. |
| *Agrarian* | Large-scale intensive agriculture employing the plow and traction animals. Fields entirely cleared of vegetation and cultivated permanently or semipermanently. Extensive fertilization to maintain soil fertility. Peasant villages, towns, cities. | Typically some type of seigneurial ownership. Land owned and controlled by a private class of landlords, or by a powerful governmental apparatus. Landlords exert great power over the primary producers (peasants or slaves) who cultivate the land and impose severe penalties on them for its use. |
| *Pastoral* | Reliance on animal herds in arid environments not well suited for cultivation. Herds moved on a seasonal basis. Some cultivation practiced, or plant matter obtained through trade. Nomadic camps, some semipermanent villages. | Varies between collective rights to land and land held as private property. |

| Mode of Distribution | Social Inequality/Stratification | Political Organization |
|---|---|---|
| Generalized reciprocity. Sharing and generosity pervasive and compulsory social habits. | Typically no stratification. Inequalities of privilege generally absent. Mild inequalities based on age, sex, and personal characteristics (e.g., courage, hunting skill) but these are inequalities of prestige and influence only. General equality permeates entire society. | *Band*: Primary political role is that of headman, with informal leadership capacity and no power over others. |
| Pure or egalitarian redistribution. Goods funneled into the hands of a leader, who is responsible for reallocating them to the entire community in an essentially equal fashion. | Typically no stratification. Inequalities of privilege generally absent. Main form of inequality is personal prestige as, for example, achieved by redistributor big men. Frequently "rank" societies in Fried's sense. | *Tribe*: Political leaders with considerable prestige but no real power. Leadership typically limited to local village level. Villages largely autonomous politically (i.e., no political unification or centralization). |
| Partial or stratified redistribution. Goods funneled into the hands of a central social group that retains a large portion of these goods for its own subsistence and for building and maintaining a governmental administrative apparatus. Some reallocation. | Typically first emergence of genuine stratification. Common pattern is division of society into three social strata (chiefs, subchiefs, commoners). Power and privilege of chiefs limited by people's demands for their generosity. Redistributive ethic retained, preventing extreme stratification. | *Chiefdom*: Centralized political system organized into a hierarchy of powerful chiefs and subchiefs. Individual villages lose political autonomy and become subordinated to a centralized authority. |
| Surplus expropriation. A highly imbalanced and exploitative relationship between landlords and primary producers. Landlords extract surplus through rent, taxation, demands for labor services, and other mechanisms. | Typically extreme stratification. Bulk of population normally a subjugated and exploited peasantry. Rulers and governing classes possess great wealth and power. Serfdom and slavery most common forms of subordination of bulk of the population. Caste in some places. Poverty and suffering widespread. Placement of individuals in class structure largely by birth, but some mobility. | *State*: Political system having great concentration of power in the hands of a small elite, monopolization of the means of violence, expropriation of surplus production, and a legitimizing ideology. |
| Varies from pure redistribution to stratified redistribution. | Varies from highly egalitarian to rank to stratified societies. | Usually tribes, but some chiefdoms; confederations and even states occasionally established through interaction with other states. |

new forms of technology and work harder and longer in order to produce more food to feed more people. Simple horticulturalists, for example, may begin to adopt more intensive horticultural techniques. Likewise, intensive horticulturalists may switch to plow agriculture.

It is imperative to realize that Boserup's argument does not assume that the switch to more intensive technologies will lead to the resumption of old standards of living, let alone to any long-term improvement in the standard of living. Although this may occur in the short run (Conelly, 1992), the effect over the long haul is almost inevitably the continued deterioration of living standards. Her argument is simply that the adoption of more intensive modes of production is necessary in order to maintain as high a living standard as possible under the imposition of greater numbers.

Mark Cohen (1977, 1985) uses the logic of Boserup's argument to explain the origin of agriculture on a worldwide basis. Cohen notes that ancient hunter-gatherers had probably long understood how to domesticate plants and animals, but waited for perhaps tens of thousands of years before putting their knowledge to use. Apparently, they saw no benefits to the practice of agriculture, and they probably saw it as a less desirable way of making a living than collecting food from nature's storehouse. Indeed, when contemporary hunter-gatherers are asked by anthropologists why they do not practice agriculture, they usually respond with something like, "Why should we work harder in order to live no better than we're living now?" Richard Lee (1979), for example, asked a !Kung man named /Xashe why the !Kung did not adopt some of the practices of their agricultural neighbors, and /Xashe replied, "Why should we plant when there are so many mongongos in the world?"

As noted in the previous chapter, evidence from paleopathological studies indicates that all over the world hunter-gatherer societies of some 30,000 years ago show evidence of better nutrition and health than much more recent horticultural and agricultural societies (Cohen and Armelagos, 1984). Compared to later agricultural populations, ancient hunter-gatherers showed less evidence of infection and chronic malnutrition, less biological stress that would have disrupted childhood growth, and fewer dental cavities and less oral disease. Individuals in the ancient hunter-gatherer populations also seemed to live just as long, if not slightly longer, than the members of later agricultural communities. If, then, ancient hunter-gatherers were reasonably well nourished and knew how to plant crops but avoided doing so because that would mean more work for no improvement in their lives, what finally compelled some of them to cross the threshold to the agricultural way of life? Cohen argues that the reason was a "food crisis" due to growing population. He holds that hunter-gatherer groups in several regions of the world finally outgrew the capacity of their environments to sustain them at an acceptable standard of living. When this occurred, they were forced to start producing their own food in order to stave off the food crisis. They became willing to work harder because they now had something to gain from it.

Cohen's theory of the origin of agriculture is still widely debated by archaeologists, who are the social scientists best qualified to judge it. Some anthropologists and archaeologists feel that it is an "old" theory that is no longer "cutting edge." It is undeniable that the theory is, in terms of the current rate of scientific advance, a rather old one, but newer is not necessarily better. To think so is to commit what the sociologist Robert Merton has called "the fallacy of the latest word." We find Cohen's theory highly plausible for several reasons, especially in terms of what we know about the attitude of modern hunter-gatherers to the practice of agriculture, and a number of modern anthropologists and archaeologists have developed theories of agricultural origins that give population pressure a significant role (Binford, 1968; Harner, 1970; Flannery, 1973; M. Harris, 1977). Moreover, the leading current competitors to Cohen's theory, although "cutting edge," leave a great deal to be desired. These theories emphasize either *climate change* (Henry, 1989; McCorriston and Hole, 1991), *resource stress* (M. Harris, 1977; D. Harris, 1977; Hayden, 1981), or *particular patterns of social organization* (Hayden, 1992; Bogucki, 1999).

The most serious problem with the climate change and resource stress theories is that they are usually designed to explain the Neolithic in only one part (or at most a few parts) of the world. The theories of Henry and of McCorriston and Hole are intended to explain only the Middle Eastern (southwest Asian) Neolithic—in fact, these authors deny the possibility of any general theory of the worldwide transition to agriculture—and Marvin Harris's theory is unsatisfactory in explaining the Neolithic in southwest Asia, southeast Asia, or China (Fiedel, 1987). (Hayden's theory has other serious difficulties, but these are too complicated to discuss here.) It is precisely where these theories fail that Cohen's succeeds. His theory is predicated on the enormously important fact of the *worldwide* transition to agriculture, as well as on the fact that in at least four different regions of the world, agriculture was independently invented. As Cohen has argued, the worldwide character of the Neolithic at approximately the same time in world prehistory is of such striking significance that only a general theory that explains this whole process can hope to succeed.

Recent theories that emphasize certain patterns of social organization have their own difficulties. One type of theory has been developed by Brian Hayden (1992), who earlier (1981) favored a resource stress explanation. Hayden's later theory assumes that agriculture first arose in bountiful environments that allowed hunter-gatherers to produce economic surpluses and engage in competitive feasting. As this feasting escalated, people's increasingly competitive desires created the need for larger and larger surpluses, and food production arose in order to make larger surpluses possible. One problem with this theory is that food production did not always arise in bountiful environments conducive to competitive feasting. In fact, food production probably arose in most instances in environments of scarcity rather than abundance. To the best of our knowledge there is no real evidence that the origins of agriculture and competitive feasting are found together in the archaeological record. More than likely, Hayden has the relationship between agriculture and competitive feasting backwards. As we have seen earlier in this chapter, competitive feasting is most likely to be found in societies that have already adopted agricultural techniques.

Another social model of agricultural origins has been presented by Peter Bogucki (1999). Bogucki argues that in foraging societies strong sharing norms prevent people from being motivated to engage in food production because they would be required to give away a large amount of what they harvested. People will not become motivated to cultivate unless they can keep what they can produce, and this can only happen when the primary economic unit is something smaller than the band. In late hunter-gatherer times, foraging bands became atomized into what Bogucki calls "protohouseholds," which were kin groups that were economically self-sufficient. The formation of these groups is what led to the practice of agriculture because, with the obligation to share now lifted, these groups' members acquired the incentive to invest the greater time and energy it took to produce their own food. People now began to maximize their food production because they could store economic surpluses for later use.

This theory is unpersuasive for a variety of reasons, but especially because it makes the unwarranted assumption that prehistoric band societies would have continued to enforce their strong sharing norms even if people had started to farm the land and produce economic surpluses. This assumption is contradicted by what we know about food-storing hunter-gatherer societies. As noted earlier in this chapter, hunter-gatherers in bountiful environments have often been able to collect large economic surpluses and store them away for various uses, including such things as elaborate competitive feasting. Food-storing hunter-gatherers are usually highly stratified and have abandoned their strong norms emphasizing sharing. Food-sharing norms do not have a life of their own and are no longer necessary when individuals can produce what they need to survive, and more besides. Moreover, even in band societies that strongly enforce sharing norms, the household is still a relatively autonomous economic unit. When sharing occurs, people share more with their own kin than they do with the band as a whole.

Although there is still a good deal of disagreement concerning the causes of the early transition to agriculture, social scientists are more certain about the role of population pressure in leading to the **intensification of agricultural production.** Boserup (1981) herself presents considerable evidence that changes in the level of population density precede changes in the mode of economic production. For example, she points to the fact that the population increase in Japan from about 1600 to 1850 was closely followed by a shift in the intensity of production. As mentioned in Chapter 2, Boserup also notes that decreases in population density often seem to be followed by an actual *regression* in cultivation techniques. For example, in recent centuries some areas of South America experienced population reductions resulting from new diseases introduced by encroaching Europeans, and the indigenous societies of these regions regressed to less intensive cultivation techniques. Likewise, in the early twentieth century farmers in Tanzania, Vietnam, Ceylon, and India adopted less intensive agricultural methods when they were resettled by their governments to less populated regions and given more land to use. This was true even when the purpose of the resettlement was to spread more intensive methods to the areas of immigration.

Much additional research has supported the view that population pressure is the basic cause of preindustrial technological evolution. Increasingly intensive systems of agricultural production seem to have arisen as a response to growing numbers in such diverse regions of the world as South America, New Guinea, ancient Mesoamerica, and ancient Mesopotamia (Carneiro, 1968; Clarke, 1966; Sanders, 1972; Adams, 1972).

## The Evolution of Political Economy

Gerhard Lenski (1966) presents a well-known theory of the evolution of economic life and stratification. Because of its emphasis on the role of an economic surplus, we suggest calling it the *surplus theory*. Lenski's theory assumes that humans are essentially self-interested creatures who strive to maximize their own well-being. They behave largely according to a principle of enlightened self-interest, cooperating with each other when it can further their interests, and struggling with each other when that seems the avenue to the satisfaction of their interests. The theory also assumes that the objects individuals seek are always scarce relative to the desire for them, and that individuals are unequally endowed by nature to compete for the attainment of scarce objects.

Lenski (1966) argues that cooperation and sharing are strongly emphasized in small-scale hunter-gatherer and simple horticultural societies because these modes of behavior are essential to the satisfaction of individual interests. People will share with each other when such sharing is to their long-run benefit. When this condition is not met, however, people compete and contend and increasingly unequal economic and social arrangements will emerge. The crucial change that leads from cooperation to competition and conflict is a society's ability to produce an economic surplus. When a surplus becomes available, a struggle for control of it seems inevitably to arise, and the surplus ends up largely in the hands of the most powerful individuals and groups. As a society's level of economic productivity grows, the size of its surplus grows; growing surpluses produce ever more intense struggles to control them, and thus increasingly unequal societies. What, then, determines the size of the surplus? According to Lenski, it is a society's technological capacity. Technological advance is therefore the key to the evolution of political economy.

The empirical data discussed earlier on the evolution of stratification are highly consistent with Lenski's theory. However, there are some problems with the theory, and the close association between technological development and stratification pointed to by Lenski seems to mislead us theoretically. Although highly correlated with stratification, technological development may not be the actual causal factor. The major difficulty with Lenski's theory involves his assumption about the origin of an economic surplus. Lenski appears to assume that economic surpluses are more or less automatic results of technological advance. Yet this cannot really be the case. Technological advance makes surpluses possible, but, as Ester Boserup (1965) points out, people will not automatically desire to produce them because to do so involves more work for questionable results.

Boserup assumes, quite reasonably we think, that people generally follow a **Law of Least Effort**—they prefer to carry out subsistence activities (and many others for that matter) by expending a minimal amount of time and energy. If people are not naturally inclined to produce surpluses, then the question arises as to how they can originate at all. The answer would seem to involve political compulsion: People produce surpluses because other people are able to compel them to do so. And if this is the case, then stratification, at least in the sense of differential economic power, already exists. Surpluses, then, actually follow closely on the heels of the development of stratification (cf. Elster, 1985:169). To see how this can happen, and to see what is ultimately behind such a process, we propose an alternative theory that can be called the *scarcity theory.*

The scarcity theory, which is derived from suggestions made in the work of Michael Harner (1970, 1975), Morton Fried (1967), Richard Wilkinson (1973), and Rae Lesser Blumberg (1978), holds that the ultimate cause of the evolution of economic life and increasingly unequal social structures is population pressure. The following scenario may be imagined for purposes of illustrating the theory. Population pressure against resources has eventually led hunter-gatherers to begin adopting agricultural modes of subsistence, and agriculture eventually entirely displaces hunting and gathering. The "primitive communism" of hunter-gatherers gives way to the ownership of land by large kinship groups, but nonetheless ownership is still largely communal rather than private. However, further increases in population pressure cause horticulturalists to become more concerned about landownership.

Increasing scarcity in the availability of land suitable for cultivation leads some families to increased "selfishness" in landownership, and some families begin to own more land than others. Additional population pressure leads to still greater selfishness in landownership, and eventually private modes of property ownership emerge out of what was originally communal ownership. Since unequal access to crucial economic resources now exists, one segment of society is in a position to compel other segments to work harder in order to produce economic surpluses. The owning group lives off these resources and as a result is gradually able to withdraw from all direct economic production and become a kind of early or primitive "leisure class." Since technological advance has accompanied population pressure and declining standards of living, surpluses are now technologically as well as politically feasible. With additional advances in population pressure and technology, unequal access to resources becomes even more severe, and stratification intensifies under greater political compulsion by owning groups.

Of course, unequal landownership and political compulsion are not the only reasons that people will produce surpluses. Another good reason to produce them is to have food available in storage that can be used in lean times (M. Harris, 1977). This is one of the motives of chiefs in intensive horticultural societies. As we discussed earlier, African and Polynesian chiefs would often draw on their storehouses during times when harvests were insufficient to feed people adequately. However, this reason for surplus economic production cannot account for the development of significant economic inequalities. For those to develop, people have to be motivated to produce surpluses of a magnitude above and beyond what might be needed in reserve, and for that some type of compulsion is needed.

The scarcity theory holds that something probably very much like the process described above has happened in human history, and not just once, but many times. It is important to see that the scarcity theory and the surplus theory are similar in some ways—both are materialist and evolutionary theories. Whereas the surplus theory regards technological advance as the basic cause of the development of stratified political economies, the scarcity theory claims that the causal relationship between technology and stratification is illusory. It holds that both are results of population pressure and the scarcity of resources that this produces. The scarcity theory is favored here because the surplus theory seems to be contradicted by Boserup's interpretation of the causes of technological change and the data that support her interpretation, yet the scarcity theory fits Boserup's claim very nicely.

Humans seem to be creatures who need little prodding to compete for status, wealth, and power (Sanderson, 2001). The economic demands of small-scale band and tribal societies place strict limits on such competitive striving, but when these demands are lifted later in social evolution, competition begins to take center stage and economic and political inequalities emerge and increasingly widen. This means that stratification systems have, so to speak, a "life of their own"—they become to a large extent detached from their original causes. Lenski himself recognizes this and stresses it. Once groups with unequal access to the means of production emerge in society, advantaged groups are highly motivated to maintain their advantage, and enhance it if possible. Stratification systems therefore tend to be inherently self-perpetuating and self-enhancing.

# FOR FURTHER READING

Works by Harris (1974, 1977), Service (1971), Lenski (1966), Fried (1967), Johnson and Earle (2000), Minge-Klevana (1980), Plattner (1989), Wilk (1996), Diamond (1997), and Bogucki (1999), mentioned in the suggested reading list at the end of Chapter 3, are also highly relevant to the current chapter since they deal with the full range of preindustrial societies. Boserup's *The Conditions of Agricultural Growth* (1965) is the classic work on population pressure as the driving force in the intensification of economic production in preindustrial societies, and Mark Cohen's *The Food Crisis in Prehistory* (1977) is a detailed argument for population pressure as the primary cause of the emergence of agriculture. Patricia Crone's *Pre-Industrial Societies* (1989) is a valuable work that succinctly summarizes the basic features of agrarian societies. Eric Wolf's *Peasants* (1966) is a classic work on peasant society, and Samuel Popkin's *The Rational Peasant* (1979) is a well-known study of the rational foundations of economic life in peasant societies. Jonathan Haas, in *The Evolution of the Prehistoric State* (1982), provides an excellent discussion of archaeological evidence regarding the origin of the state with a particular focus on opposing theories of state origins.

The best work on pastoral societies that covers the entire pastoral world is Thomas Barfield's *The Nomadic Alternative* (1993). His *The Perilous Frontier* (1989) is a fascinating work on the Hsiung-nu, the Hsien-pi, the Mongols, and other historical horse-riding pastoral empires. See also Krader (1963) and Morgan (1987) on the Mongols. Fredrik Barth's *Nomads of South Persia* (1961) is a classic work on an Iranian pastoral society, the Basseri. Mair (1974) contains a discussion of several African pastoral societies. Lancaster (1981) discusses the Rwala Bedouin, and Goldstein and Beall (1989) provide an important work on Tibetan pastoralists.

Chapters 14, 15, and 16 of Sanderson's *The Evolution of Human Sociality: A Darwinian Conflict Perspective* (2001) contain extended discussions of economics, politics, and social stratification in preindustrial societies. These chapters cover some of the same issues discussed in this and the previous chapter of the present work, but also contain many additional discussions and take the analysis to a deeper theoretical level.

James Scott's *Domination and the Arts of Resistance* (1990) shows how, despite the invariable construction of systems of domination and inequality in large-scale societies, people dislike being dominated and develop various subtle (and often not-so-subtle) strategies of dealing with this domination.

# 5 The Rise of the Modern World

This chapter tells the story of the early beginnings of the modern world, which had as its centerpoint the rise of the capitalist mode of production as the dominant form of economic life. Closely associated with the rise of capitalism was the emergence of increasingly large-scale and powerful nation-states and the rise of an international system of states. In order to understand why these evolutionary events occurred, one needs to understand a long-term trend in the development of economic markets.

## The Emergence of Economic Markets

That economic institution known as "the market" exists when people offer goods and services for sale to others in some more or less systematic and organized way. It is important to distinguish between the terms *market* and *marketplace*. A **marketplace** is a physical site where goods and services are brought for sale and where buyers assemble to purchase these goods and services. In precapitalist societies, marketplaces are physical sites found at a small number of designated locations within the society. But in modern capitalism, the marketplace is "diffuse," meaning that it is spread pervasively throughout society. The **market,** by contrast, is not a physical place but a social institution, or a set of social relationships organized around the process of buying and selling valuables.

### Societies in Relation to the Market

Paul Bohannan and George Dalton (1962) have distinguished three kinds of societies with respect to their relationship to the market: marketless societies, peripheral market societies, and market-dominated societies.

**Marketless societies** have neither markets nor marketplaces. Although there may be a few economic transactions based on buying and selling, these are casual and few and far between. Since marketless societies have no markets, subsistence is not provided by market principles but by the mechanisms of reciprocity or redistribution. The !Kung, the Kaoka-speakers, and the Yanomama are marketless societies, as are indeed the vast majority of hunter-gatherer and horticultural groups.

**Peripheral market societies** have marketplaces but market principles clearly do not serve to organize economic life. In such societies, people may frequently be involved in marketplace activity, either as buyers or sellers, but this activity is a highly secondary economic phenomenon. People do not receive their subsistence through marketplace activities but through reciprocity, redistribution, and expropriation. In peripheral market societies, "most people are not engaged in producing for the market or selling in the market, or those who are so engaged are only part-time marketers" (Bohannan and Dalton, 1962:7).

Peripheral markets are found quite frequently among intensive horticulturalists, and almost universally in agrarian societies. The Aztecs, highly intensive horticulturalists who dominated Mexico during the fifteenth and sixteenth centuries, had peripheral markets of considerable scope and significance (Beals and Hoijer, 1971). In each city throughout the Aztec empire there existed large markets, and these markets were connected to each other and to the Aztec capital city of Tenochtitlán by a system of traveling merchants known as *pochtecah* (Hassig, 1985). A huge market located in a suburb of Tenochtitlán took place every fifth day. Potential buyers came to this market from miles around to buy the many and varied goods that were offered in it: gold, silver, jewels, clothing, chocolate, tobacco, hides, footwear, slaves, fruits and vegetables, salt, honey, tools, pottery, household furnishings, and many other items.

Peripheral markets were also significant in medieval Europe (Heilbroner, 1985). Markets in the small cities of medieval Europe were places where peasants would bring some of their harvests for sale. Merchants and artisans who lived in these cities, however, were more important to the life of the marketplace. These merchants and artisans manufactured goods to be sold in the markets and made their livings from such sale. Medieval Europe also had a special kind of marketplace activity known as a *fair*, which flourished in the thirteenth and fourteenth centuries (Abu-Lughod, 1989). This was a type of traveling market, held usually once a year, to which merchants from all over Europe came to sell their products. The fair combined social holiday, religious festival, and intense economic activity. At some of these fairs, merchants brought a considerable variety of products for sale, such as

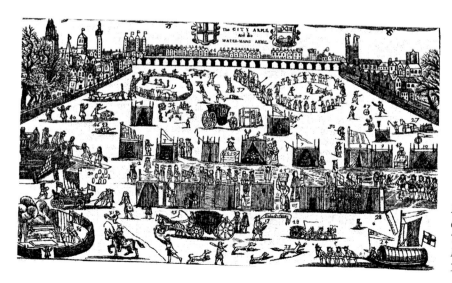

*Frost fair on the Thames, England, 1683.*

silks, horses, drugs, spices, books and parchments, and many other items (Heilbroner, 1985).

**Market-dominated societies** have both markets and marketplaces (i.e., "diffuse" marketplaces), and the market principle—the principle of buying and selling goods according to the forces of supply and demand—governs all important decisions concerning production, distribution, and exchange. In these societies, various types of reciprocity and redistribution may be found, but they are of very minor significance indeed. The only genuine market-dominated societies are those characterized by modern capitalism, whose emergence we shall begin to look at shortly.

## Aspects of the Market in Preindustrial Societies

In preindustrial (or *precapitalist*) societies in which manufacturing occurs as a substantial economic activity, it is usually a small-scale undertaking, generally confined to the homes of artisans or to a few small shops located in the marketplaces (Sjoberg, 1960). Even the largest workshops in **precapitalist societies** would be quite small by modern standards of manufacturing. With no mass market for goods, and thus strict limits on the formation of capital, productive units must necessarily remain small.

Precapitalist forms of specialization occur relative to the product rather than the production process. Each craftsman fashions an entire product, from beginning to end. As Sjoberg notes, "Specialization in product is often carried to the point that the craftsman devotes his full time to producing items made from a particular raw material; thus we have goldsmiths, coppersmiths, silversmiths, silk weavers, wool weavers, and so on, each with their own guild" (1960:197). In addition, the precapitalist craftsman typically functions as his own merchant in selling the final product.

In virtually all large-scale precapitalist societies with significant manufacturing sectors, craftsmen and merchants are organized into work organizations known as *guilds*. Guilds are specialized by occupation; they include as their members all persons who perform the same occupation or a highly specialized branch of an occupation. Sjoberg (1960), for instance, lists the following guilds in just one precapitalist city, Beijing in the 1920s: carpenters (Sacred Lu Pan Society), shoe fasteners (Sewers of Boots and Shoes Guild, or Double Thread Guild), tinkers (Clever Stove Guild), clock stores (Clock Watch Commercial Guild Association), leather stores (Five Sages Hide and Skins Guild), vegetable merchants (Green or Fresh Vegetable Guild), barbers (Beautify the Face Guild), and waiters (Tea Guild).

The most important function of guilds is creating and maintaining a monopoly over a specific type of economic activity: "The right to pursue almost any occupation concerned with manufacturing or trade, or even services, is possible only through membership in the guild that controls it" (Sjoberg, 1960:190). In exercising their monopolistic control over occupations, guilds engage in a variety of activities. As Sjoberg points out, they determine the selection of personnel for an occupation; train members for their work, usually through a master-apprentice relationship; set standards of workmanship for their members; control the output generated by their members; protect their members from excessive restrictions that might be placed on them by governmental or religious bodies; and assist their members in establishing shops or purchasing the raw materials they need to complete their work. Clearly, guilds play a crucial role in the lives of precapitalist craftsmen and merchants. Indeed, they are roughly comparable in their basic aims to today's labor unions and business and professional organizations.

What about price determination? In modern capitalism, prices for goods and services are determined by abstract supply and demand forces. Individuals may expect to go into stores and find fixed prices already attached to items. It has generally been understood that prices in precapitalist settings are usually not established in this way; rather, they are set by what is called *haggling*. Haggling occurs when a potential purchaser asks a merchant how much he wants for an item, the merchant replies, and then the purchaser offers a counterprice, which is usually much lower than that mentioned by the merchant. The seller and buyer then negotiate (haggle over) the price until eventually an agreement is reached or the buyer leaves in disgust. Haggling is often the typical mode of price determination in societies where mass markets do not exist and thus where sellers and buyers have little "knowledge of the market" for any given item. In addition, since haggling can take up large amounts of time, time must not be a valuable and scarce resource, as it is in modern capitalism. Therefore, haggling can occur only in settings in which people are seldom in a hurry to accomplish their everyday tasks (Sjoberg, 1960).

The question of the degree to which precapitalist economies are "rationally" organized is also a crucial one. Modern capitalism is a supremely rational type of economic system in the sense that there are a variety of sophisticated techniques used in the conduct of business—techniques designed to maximize economic productivity and growth. Thus, modern capitalists use advanced forms of accounting, finance, workplace organization, and marketing in the conduct of their business activity, and these procedures are crucial to their success. In precapitalist markets, however, such a rational organization of economic activity has generally been thought to be typically absent (Sjoberg, 1960). This nonrationality (not to be confused with "irrationality") of economic activity is expressed in numerous ways. For one thing, artisans and merchants commonly do not adhere to fixed work schedules closely regulated by the clock. On the contrary, they often start work at different hours in the morning and stop work at different times later in the day, according to the nature of other noneconomic activities in which they are engaged. In addition, precapitalist manufacturing is normally characterized by little synchronization of effort. Workers in one sector of manufacturing have little knowledge of what is happening in other sectors, and they make little if any effort to coordinate their activities with the activities being undertaken in these other sectors. Finally, the marketing of goods in precapitalist societies is generally subject to little standardization. For example, merchants seldom grade or sort their products, and there is little standardization of weights and measures. As Sjoberg notes, this lack of standardization is linked to the absence of a mass market and thus to the highly personalized nature of market activity.

## Some Qualifications: Precapitalist Commercialism and Its Growth

No sooner have we stated these traditional perspectives than we have to qualify them. Kajsa Ekholm and Jonathan Friedman (1982), for example, suggest that market activities have played a much greater role in earlier societies than has generally been recognized. They oppose the traditional division of "the world's history into distinctive market/nonmarket or capitalist/pre-capitalist systems," and maintain the "point of view that there exists a form of 'capitalism' in the ancient world" (1982:87–88). In other words, Ekholm and Friedman object to the very conceptualization of peripheral market societies, or at least claim that this conceptual category does not apply as broadly as ordinarily thought.

Ekholm and Friedman do not claim that there are no differences between ancient societies and modern capitalism; they argue simply that the differences are less great than people have been taught to believe. Other scholars go even further. Barry Gills and Andre Gunder Frank (1992), for example, suggest that there has been extensive commercial activity in many agrarian societies over the last 5,000 years, and that the shift to modern capitalism in the sixteenth century was less radical than is usually thought. They believe that the extent of markets and commercialism over the last few millennia has been greatly underestimated. Gills and Frank rely on studies of precapitalist markets by such social scientists as Morris Silver (1985), Philip Kohl (1978, 1989), and Joan Oates (1978). These scholars show that in ancient agrarian societies there frequently existed large-scale markets, including price-setting markets regulated by supply and demand; private warehouses stocked with goods; merchant middlemen; extensive investment in capital goods; large-scale trade networks; strong profit motives; and the accumulation of capital. Indeed, some societies—the Phoenicians of the late second and early first millennia BCE, for example, or the Italian city-states of the thirteenth and fourteenth centuries CE—were highly specialized for trade and overwhelmingly dependent on it.

Gills and Frank make an extremely important point, and it has become increasingly clear in recent years that the traditional view of the limited significance of markets in the precapitalist world must be strongly qualified. Market behavior and institutions were rarely if ever dominant in precapitalist societies, but in many of them, especially the more advanced agrarian ones, market activities played an important role. Indeed, since about 5000 BP there has been an important process of **expanding world commercialization** (Sanderson, 1994b). The existence of such a process is indicated by growth in the size and density of trade networks, as well as by increases in the number of large cities and the size of these cities.

In the first few centuries after 5000 BP, most trade networks were relatively small and a limited quantity of goods passed through them. Trade networks were either local or, at best, regional in scope. By about 2200 BP—in the early beginnings of the ancient Roman world—there had emerged a large-scale trade network stretching all the way from China through the Middle East to Mediterranean Europe (Curtin, 1984). This was a trade network obviously spread over a large portion of the world, and a much greater quantity of goods passed through this network than anything seen in the local or regional trade networks of earlier times. By about CE 1000, trade networks had become even more extensive and with a still greater volume of trade (McNeill, 1982; Wilkinson, 1992). The growth of cities tells the same story. In 4250 BP, only 8 cities in the world had populations greater than 30,000, but by 2430 BP, there were 51 cities of this size, together totalling 2,877,000 in population. After a decline in cities following the fall of Rome, the process of urbanization accelerated once again. By CE 1000, there were 70 cities having populations between 40,000 and 450,000 (totalling 5,629,000), and by CE 1500, there were over 75 cities with populations between 45,000 and 672,000 (totalling 7,454,000) (Wilkinson, 1992, 1993).

It is clear, then, that the traditional view of precapitalist market and commercial behavior cannot stand unchallenged. Commercialism was frequently of considerable importance in the precapitalist world, and it grew steadily in importance over a period of some 4,500 years. Moreover, the growth of world commercialization had major implications, for it contributed decisively to the massive takeoff into modern capitalism that began in sixteenth-century Europe. Indeed, without acknowledging this long-term process of world commercial expansion, it is not possible to explain the emergence of the modern capitalist world.

# The Origins of Modern Capitalism

Perhaps the greatest social transformation in world history was the European transition to the capitalist mode of production beginning in the sixteenth century. During this period there was also a relatively independent process of capitalist development in Japan. What kind of economic system preceded capitalism?

## European Feudalism

The system of economic life that prevailed in western Europe from approximately the collapse of the Roman Empire until the advent of modern capitalism was known as **feudalism.** Feudalism was especially characteristic of France, Germany, and the British Isles, although it existed in other parts of western Europe as well. The basic unit of economic production under feudalism was the **manor.** The manor was overseen by a powerful feudal landlord and cultivated by numerous peasants. The average peasant held perhaps as many as 30 acres of land on which he lived and that he cultivated for his own living. The land held directly by the lord for his own use was known as the **demesne.** As seen earlier, the relationship between lord and peasant was a highly unbalanced and exploitative one. The peasant owed the lord so many days of work on the demesne, and he also had to pay dues of various sorts. For instance, he often rendered certain food products and paid certain fees, such as those exacted by the lord when the peasant used the lord's winepress, oven, or grinding mill. Just how different the feudal system was from modern industrial society can be seen in the following remarks about feudalism by Douglass North and Robert Thomas (1973:11):

The customs of the manor became the unwritten "constitution," or the fundamental institutional arrangement of an essentially anarchic world, most properly viewed as small isolated settlements, frequently in the lee of a fortified place and surrounded by wilderness. The wooden or earth castle, the knight, and the relatively self-sufficient manor had emerged as the most viable response to the collapse of order and the recurrent invasions of Norsemen, Moslems, and Magyars. While the terror of foreign marauders had declined by the middle of the tenth century, the land seethed with continual warfare and brigandage as the power of local lords waxed and waned. Feudalism provided a measure of stability and order in this fragmented world. . . .

Commerce between different parts of Europe had always been potentially of mutual benefit, since the variety of resources and climatic conditions induced differentiation of crops and livestock. But trade had been sporadic because so many dangers within the wilderness beset the traveling merchant.

## Commercial Expansion and the Decline of Feudalism

As the feudal system wore on in the countryside, it was gradually confronted by the growth of towns. Sometime after CE 1000, and especially after 1100, parts of the continent of Europe began to undergo significant commercial expansion centered in the towns (Lopez, 1971; Cipolla, 1993). Existing towns grew, often quite rapidly, and new towns sprung up throughout Europe (Cipolla, 1993). Urban society was expanding at the expense of the countryside, and so much so that Cipolla (1993) remarks that the urban growth of the eleventh to thirteenth centuries marked a "turning point of world history." Cipolla goes on to note that the European towns of this period were different in some crucial respects from the towns of other civilizations, such as China, the Byzantine Empire, and the ancient Greek and Roman world. The merchants and craftsmen of these towns held a socially inferior position, as they have in almost all agrarian civilizations. The ideals of the landlord classes and of rural life dominated and submerged the ideas of the urban classes, and towns were simply organs within a larger overwhelmingly rural organism. The towns of late medieval Europe, on the other hand, enjoyed considerably more economic and social independence. In the words of Cipolla (1993:120–121),

> The medieval city was not just part of a larger organism, but an organism in itself, proudly autonomous and clearly separated from the surrounding countryside. Physically, the city was separated from the countryside by walls, moat, and gates. More important than that, the city was another world from a legal point of view, too. When a person passed through the gates of a city, he became subject to different laws, as when today we cross the border from one country to another. The contrast was as sharp in cultural as in economic terms. The merchants, the professionals, the craftsmen who lived in the towns did not acknowledge the control of the rural world or its cultural values; on the contrary, they evolved their own culture and their own values. The emergence of European towns in the eleventh to thirteenth centuries was not a spin-off of regional evolution. It was rather the expression of a cultural and social revolution which was based in the towns. The champions of the rural-feudal establishment were well aware of this, and they did not hide their indignation.

It was the growth in the number and size of these towns, and the growing conflict between the urban merchant classes and the rural landlord classes, that began to spell the end of the old feudal system and that paved the way for the emergence of a capitalist mode of production after the fifteenth century. But before we discuss the rise of capitalism and its eventual dominance of economic life, we need to consider what capitalism as a mode of economic life *is*.

## The Nature of Capitalism

There has been considerable debate concerning exactly when **capitalism** began; the answer given is usually a matter of how capitalism is defined, and here there is debate as well. History's most famous student of the capitalist system was Karl Marx. For Marx, capitalism was a type of economic system in which some individuals owned vital productive resources that they used in an effort to make the maximum profit. These individuals, whom Marx referred to as the **bourgeoisie** (or capitalists), employed another group of persons, whom Marx called the **proletariat** (or working class), who through their labor produced goods that the capitalists could exchange in the market for a profit. The capitalist was able to earn a profit because he paid the worker less than the full value of the goods that the worker produced. Marx argued that the profits of the capitalist did not arise through the simple process of the exchange of goods—through mere buying and selling. Rather, profits were generated through the process of production itself, and the act of selling goods only served to realize the profits that were already there in the creation of the product by the worker.

In Marx's view, then, capitalism required the existence of a class of workers who sold their labor power—their capacity to work—to capitalists for wages. Only through the exploitation of workers by capitalists in the wage relationship could profits be generated. Marx thus identified the beginnings of the capitalist mode of production with the Industrial Revolution in England in the middle of the eighteenth century, because it was not until this time that wage labor and the factory system became prominent economic phenomena.

Of course, Marx was well aware that the vigorous search for profits began in western Europe long before the Industrial Revolution. Beginning as early as the late fifteenth century, some European nations embarked on colonial expeditions in which the search for profits was of paramount significance. And during the seventeenth century, the search for profits was an obsession of governments throughout Europe. Yet Marx argued that the mode in which profits were realized in these centuries was fundamentally different from the mode in which they were obtained after the Industrial Revolution. Before the Industrial Revolution, profits were obtained through exchange rather than production relationships: through buying and selling rather than through the exploitation of a class of wage workers. A company could make profits by buying a product in one region of the world where its cost was low, and then selling it in another region in which a greater price could be asked. Marx identified this type of economic activity as a sort of capitalism, but he called it **merchant capitalism** in order to distinguish it from the **industrial capitalism** of a later era. Only industrial capitalism was a "true" system of capitalism for Marx.

Although some contemporary social scientists believe that Marx's distinction should be strictly maintained (e.g., Wolf, 1982), other social scientists, including many Marxists, hold a different view. Most notable among these is Immanuel Wallerstein (1974a, 1974b). Wallerstein rejects Marx's distinction between merchant and industrial capitalism and claims that capitalism is simply production in a market in which the aim of the producers is to realize the maximum profit. For Wallerstein, it does not matter whether there are wage workers or not. Indeed, for him several types of coercive, nonwage labor have existed within the capitalist mode of production. What is crucial about capitalism for Wallerstein is that the maximum accumulation of profits over time be the guiding aim of economic activity. Wallerstein believes that this requires the exploitation of workers, but that this exploitation may take a variety of forms, not just the exploitation of wage laborers. Given his conception of capitalism, Wallerstein sees it originating in the late fifteenth and early sixteenth centuries in conjunction with the rise of European colonialism.

This book is more sympathetic to Wallerstein's point of view but frankly recognizes that the Industrial Revolution of the eighteenth century dramatically changed the nature of capitalism. Indeed, the Industrial Revolution inaugurated a phase of capitalist development that was in certain crucial respects qualitatively different from anything that had previously existed. In siding with Wallerstein, we can scarcely overlook this important fact.

## Early Capitalism between the Thirteenth and Sixteenth Centuries

The most important commercial centers of Europe were in the northwest, primarily in what is now Belgium, and in southern Europe, especially the Italian city-states. The commercial expansion of this period contributed in a very significant way to the capitalist "great leap forward" that began in the sixteenth century.

In the northwest, the city of Bruges was an integral part of a growing center of merchant capitalism. It was part of a large trading area that covered the Mediterranean, Portugal, France, England, the Rhineland, and the Hanseatic League (Braudel, 1984). The Hanseatic League was a trading association of merchant capitalists who carried out their activities all the way from England to the Baltic Sea. In the south, a vigorous form of merchant capitalism developed in such Italian city-states as Florence, Pisa, Rome, Genoa, Venice, Siena, Prato, and Lucca (J. Cohen, 1980). The most important of these city-states were overwhelmingly specialized for trade. Banking became significantly developed, and merchants were highly admired and respected. The famous Medici, who were the richest Florentine bankers, merchants, and industrialists, were ensconced at the very top of the social and economic ladder (J. Cohen, 1980).

Jere Cohen (1980) argues that many of the capitalist methods and practices created in Italy during this time provided the basis for the spread of capitalism to other parts of Europe. As he notes, double-entry bookkeeping, marine insurance, and commercial law were invented by the Italians, who were the only ones to use them until the sixteenth century. The greatest of all the Italian city-states was Venice. This city-state was overwhelmingly devoted to foreign trade, the return on which has

*Scene from a Viennese market, approximately 1730.*

been estimated at an extraordinary 40 percent (Braudel, 1984). According to the great French historian Fernand Braudel (1984:123), Venice's "merchants firmly controlled all the major commodity trades in the Mediterranean—pepper, spices, Syrian cotton, grain, wine and salt." Venice's wealth and significance were also evident in the number of her galleys and cargo vessels.

While the capitalism of these centuries was for the most part merchant capitalism, a surprising amount of industry and manufacturing had developed. Some textile industries were highly mechanized, and manufacturing played an important part in the economies of several city-states, Venice included (J. Cohen, 1980). For example, "in Florence in 1338 there were said to be as many as 200 workshops engaged in cloth manufacture, employing a total of 30,000 workmen or about a quarter of the whole occupied population of the city" (Dobb, 1963:157).

## The Seventeenth Century and Mercantilism

By the sixteenth century, the center of capitalist activity in Europe had begun to shift from Italy to northwest Europe, first to Antwerp and then later to the Netherlands, England, and France. And, as Braudel (1984) notes, capitalism came to be associated with large territorial states rather than small city-states. In the seventeenth century, these large territorial states vigorously promoted capitalism in the form of **mercantilism.** Mercantilism involved governments' granting of monopolies to trading companies so that the companies could benefit from trade between the European nation and its colonies elsewhere. Monopolies for trading companies were not new to the mercantilist era, but the specific economic context in which these monopolies were granted—that of colonial trade—was (Beaud, 1983).

Mercantilist practices created an economic situation in which manufacturers in the European countries could receive extremely favorable terms of exchange for their products. Efforts were undertaken to prevent the colonies from manufacturing items that would compete with those being produced in the home country. More-over, every effort was made to encourage the import of raw materials from the colonies to the home country, the raw materials to be brought in at low prices, turned into manufactured goods, and then sold at very high profits (Beaud, 1983).

The great mercantilist trading companies of the seventeenth century were established in the Netherlands, England, and France. In 1602, the Dutch East India Company was formed. This company acquired a monopoly on trade with India, forbidding the English, the Portuguese, and the French to engage in such trade. The company had an army of nearly 12,000 men and a navy of between 40 and 60 ships. It brought into Europe each year between 10 and 12 million florins worth of goods. Between 1619 and 1663, the Dutch came to dominate the routes of the Far East. From 1648 to 1650, they imported from this area pepper and spices in quantities constituting 66 percent of all purchases and, in the same period, textiles totaling 14 percent of all purchases. They also began sugarcane production in Java. On the home front, the Netherlands established important processing industries, such as wool and linen processing; diamond cutting; and the dyeing, weaving, and spinning of silk. Other industries included sugar refining, brewing, distilling, tobacco and cocoa refining, and lead working (Beaud, 1983).

England became a major rival of the Netherlands during the seventeenth century. In 1600, the English East India Company was formed under a charter from Queen Elizabeth, and within 15 years the company had established more than 20 trading posts. These were located in India, certain islands in the Indian Ocean, Indonesia, and in Hiratsuka, Japan. Between 1610 and 1640, England's foreign trade increased by ten times. English kings "distributed privileges and monopolies, regulated and organized the control of manufacturers, prohibited the export of wool, and raised taxes on imported French and Dutch fabrics; Acts of Parliament went so far as to make obligatory the use of woolen cloth for mourning clothes" (Beaud, 1983:28–29). Moreover, especially vigorous mercantilist practices were carried out under the guidance of the statesman Oliver Cromwell. He issued a navigation act specifying that "European goods could be transported only on English ships or on ships belonging to their country of origin; products from Africa, Asia, or America could be imported only on ships of England or the colonies" (Beaud, 1983:29).

Mercantilist policies were also prominent in France. Cardinal Richelieu, Louis XIV, and Jean-Baptiste Colbert were the principal governmental personages associated with French mercantilism. Under Cardinal Richelieu, who was called on to handle royal finances in 1624, various protectionist measures were established. These involved such things as a protective tariff on textiles in 1644 and a 50-cent per ton tax on foreign ships in 1659. But mercantilism in France reached its apex between 1663 and 1685 under Louis XIV and his chief economic minister, Colbert. For these men, the trading companies were regarded as the armies of the king, the manufacturers of France as his reserves. Beaud (1983:39) states:

> [Colbert] watched over the establishment of more than 400 manufactures. There were "collective" works which brought together several artisan centers which benefited as a group from conferred privileges. . . . There were "private" works, individual enterprises (Van Robais in Abbeville), or large companies with branches in

several provinces, especially in mining and metallurgy . . . and woolen goods. Finally there were royal manufactures, which were the property of the sovereign. . . . The counterpart to the privileges (monopolies, of production or of sale, exemptions and financing) was strict controls (norms, quantity, quality). These policies developed luxury and export production (tapestries, porcelain, glassware, luxury fabrics) as well as basic production (iron working, paper making, armaments) and products for common consumption (woolen and linen fabrics, etc.). . . .

State policy extended to commerce as well as production. The French East Indies Company (1664) received a fifty-year monopoly on trade and navigation in the Indian Ocean and the Pacific Ocean.

## Capitalism as a World-System

An extremely influential perspective on the development of capitalism has been presented by Immanuel Wallerstein in his multivolumed *The Modern World-System* (1974a, 1980, 1989). Wallerstein regards capitalism as constituting, from the sixteenth century on, what he calls a **world-system.** Wallerstein defines a world-system as any relatively large social system having three principal characteristics:

1. A high degree of autonomy; that is, the system is self-contained in the sense that it does not depend for its existence on something outside it, although it will interact to some degree with other world regions
2. An extensive division of labor or specialization of roles within the system; this specialization is both geographical and economic, there being different kinds of economic activities devoted to different kinds of products in various geographical zones of the system
3. A multiplicity of societies and cultures, or the existence of different groups adhering to different traditions, speaking different languages, and so on

Wallerstein identifies two basic types of world-system: world-empires and world-economies. A **world-empire** is a world-system that is politically and militarily centralized and unified, every group within the empire being subordinate to one political center. Ancient Rome and classical China and India, for example, were organized according to this type of world-system. A **world-economy** is a world-system that lacks political and military centralization and unification. It therefore contains not only a multiplicity of societies and cultures but also a multiplicity of sovereign political units as well. In the past, there may have been numerous world-economies, but all of these either collapsed or quickly became converted into world-empires. In the modern world, however, there is only one world-economy: the capitalist world-economy, which has existed from the sixteenth century to the present day. Although Wallerstein notes that there have been attempts to turn this world-economy into a world-empire (most notably by Spain in the sixteenth century), these attempts have failed, and capitalism to this day has remained a politically decentralized system. Wallerstein holds that this political decentralization has greatly contributed to the long-term persistence of capitalism, inasmuch as empires tend to stifle innovation and individual creativity, factors that are basic to the capitalist organization of production.

But what exactly is a world-economy? What integrates it, or holds it together? Rather than being integrated by an overarching political structure, the capitalist world-economy is held together by a set of economic relationships involving the production and exchange of valued goods and services. In this sense the world-economy does not have the "tightness" of integration of a world-empire, but is a rather loosely structured network of economic relationships. These relationships involve extensive geographical and labor specialization. On the basis of such specialization, Wallerstein identifies three basic types of economic units that compose the world-economy: the core, the periphery, and the semiperiphery.

The **core** consists of those nation-states that dominate the capitalist world-economy and expropriate the bulk of the surplus produced within it. In the core are found those societies that are the most economically advanced or developed, that have the greatest degree of technological advancement, and that have the strongest governments and military structures. The wealthiest capitalists within the entire world-economy reside in the core, establishing economic enterprises there and in other parts of the world-system. Core societies specialize in the production of the most advanced goods—so-called *leading sector* goods. **Wage labor**—work performed by employees who bargain with employers in a labor market for the rate of compensation and the conditions of work—predominates as the mode of labor organization. Wallerstein suggests that wage labor is the predominant labor mode because work in the core is more highly skilled than work elsewhere, and more highly skilled work can be done more profitably when wage labor is employed.

The **periphery** is that segment of the world-economy that is most extensively subjected to surplus expropriation by the core. There is an intimate economic relationship between the core and the periphery, one in which the core dominates and exploits the periphery, which in turn becomes economically dependent on the core. The periphery has in most respects those characteristics that are the reverse of what one finds in the core. The societies and regions of the periphery are those that are least economically developed, that have the lowest levels of technological advancement, and that have the weakest governments and military units (or no sovereign governments or military units at all). The periphery specializes in the production of raw agricultural and mineral products for export, and **forced labor** rather than wage labor predominates here (or at least has done so historically). Forced labor is any system of labor in which workers are not legally free to sell their labor power in a market and are therefore politically compelled by members of some other group to work for them. The main historical types of forced labor have been slavery and serfdom. Under **slavery,** workers are owned outright and are under the complete political control of their owners. Under **serfdom,** workers are tied to specific parcels of land from which they have no freedom to move away. Wallerstein believes that since most work in the periphery is unskilled compared to work in the core, forced labor systems are more suitable because they are less costly.

The **semiperiphery** is that segment of the world-economy that operates between the core and the periphery. Wallerstein conceives of it as both an exploiter and as itself being exploited: It is an exploiter of the periphery, but it is exploited by the core. The societies of the semiperiphery are more technologically and economically advanced than those of the periphery, but less so than those of the core. They have stronger governments and military units than those found in the periphery, but weaker governments and military units than those possessed by core societies. Another way of characterizing the semiperiphery is to say that it contains features of both core and peripheral societies. Semiperipheral societies thus carry out certain economic activities that are typical of core societies—leading sector activities using wage labor—in conjunction with other economic activities characteristic of the periphery—export products using some type of coercive or semicoercive labor system.

For Wallerstein, capitalism is a vast system of surplus expropriation that goes on not only *within* regions but *between* them as well. Marx focused his attention on the surplus expropriation that went on within core societies, using England as a model. Wallerstein, though, has broadened the Marxian model of capitalism to a worldwide level. He recognizes with Marx that capitalists exploit workers within the developed European nations, but he goes a step further in asserting that there are crucial relations of economic exploitation that go on between nations, especially between core and periphery. Wallerstein views the periphery as having a vital role to play in the capitalist world-economy. Peripheral societies are organized by capitalists in the core to produce goods under conditions (e.g., cheap labor, abundant land and other resources) that yield extremely high rates of profit, and thus the periphery contributes substantially to the development and enrichment of core societies. (The relationship between core and periphery will become clearer in due course, especially in Chapter 9, where the problem of economic development and underdevelopment is discussed.)

Wallerstein's notion that capitalism has constituted a world-system from its very inception is a rather revolutionary idea. Before Wallerstein, all analysts of capitalism, including Marx himself, limited their analyses to individual nation-states. But Wallerstein believes that the proper unit for the analysis of capitalism is the world-system as a whole. He argues that one cannot comprehend what goes on in any single part of the world-system without understanding what is simultaneously going on in other parts of that system, indeed in the world-system as a whole. He believes that in order to understand the modern world from about 1500 on, societies can no longer be viewed as separate, independent units. Instead, they must be viewed in terms of their participation in or connection with a world-economy. This is a very bold idea, and the extent to which Wallerstein is correct is still hotly debated (cf. Skocpol, 1977; Brenner, 1977; Zolberg, 1981). Certainly one must be careful about pushing Wallerstein's world-system concept too far. However, despite its various limitations, the concept is a very useful one for understanding the modern world and its evolution over the past five centuries.

## The Capitalist World-Economy from the Sixteenth to the Eighteenth Centuries

Since its inception in the sixteenth century, the capitalist world-economy has been undergoing continual *expansion* and *evolution*. By saying that it has been expanding, we mean that it has been increasing its geographical range to cover ever wider areas of the globe. By saying that it has been an evolving system, we mean that its various components—core, periphery, and semiperiphery—have been changing their structure as parts of the whole. As we will see in the final two chapters, capitalism is now a vastly complex and immensely technologically sophisticated system that covers virtually the entire globe. But, as a world-system, what was it like during its early stages?

The first European nations to make a bid for core status in the sixteenth century were Spain and Portugal. These were the first European societies to engage in colonial expeditions in other regions of the world. Spain, in fact, attempted to turn the capitalist world-economy into its own world-empire. By the late sixteenth century, it was clear that these societies would no longer be at the head of the world-economy. Their places were taken by the Netherlands, England, and France, the main core societies from the late sixteenth century through the nineteenth century. Of these, the Netherlands was initially dominant. In these societies the principal economic activity was capitalist farming. Nobles increasingly leased their land out to tenants for a money rent and the land came to be farmed for profit. Many former nobles and peasants were converted into capitalist farmers. Much land was also turned over to the grazing of sheep, giving rise to an important wool industry in England. Industries of various types were also of growing significance in these core societies.

The periphery in the sixteenth century consisted of two major world regions: Iberian (Hispanic and Portuguese) America and eastern Europe. In Hispanic America, the Spaniards had established important colonies given over to large-scale agriculture and, more importantly, to gold and silver mining. Forced labor systems established by the Spaniards produced large quantities of gold and silver ore, which were exported back to Europe to be turned into coinage. The influx of these precious metals contributed in a major way to the expansion of the money supply in Europe and thus had a great impact on the world-economy. In Portuguese America (Brazil), sugar plantations were established and came to depend on extensive slave labor imported from Africa. Sugar became a commodity greatly valued in Europe for sweetening coffee and making chocolate.

In the other major peripheral region, eastern Europe, large-scale grain farming was the primary economic activity. This was carried out under a forced labor system that was essentially like the serfdom of earlier days. The peasant-landlord relation still prevailed, but peasants were producing for a world economic market, not simply for their lords. During the sixteenth century, eastern Europe, Poland especially, was a major exporter of grain to western Europe.

The semiperiphery in the sixteenth century was located in Mediterranean Europe, primarily in Italy and ultimately in Spain and Portugal. Sharecropping was the principal form of agricultural labor, and industry mainly involved the production of high-cost products, such as silks.

After the middle of the seventeenth century, England began to replace the Netherlands as the major core society, due in large part to the military defeats the English imposed on the Dutch. France also began to supersede the Netherlands, but the French did not attain the degree of success that the English did. During this time, several new societies entered the periphery. The most important of these were the U.S. South, a slave colony of England devoted to the production of numerous agricultural goods, and the slave societies of the West Indies, established primarily under the influence of the British and the French. The West Indian plantation societies were devoted heavily to sugar production. The semiperiphery at this time also expanded to include Sweden, Prussia, and the U.S. North.

## The Development of Capitalism in Japan

Traditionally, the rise of modern capitalism has been understood as a distinctly European phenomenon, and thus Europe has been viewed as containing a developmental dynamic that was largely absent in the rest of the world. This argument, though, can no longer be sustained, for at least one other society, Tokugawa Japan (1600–1868), also revealed a marked tendency toward capitalist economic development. Moreover, this capitalist development was a largely indigenous phenomenon and had little to do with any European influence. This must be so, for between 1639 and 1853, Japan adopted a policy of almost complete isolation from economic and political contact with Europe (Pearson, 1991).

Japan was the one society outside Europe to develop a genuinely feudal political-economic system (P. Anderson, 1974b). Feudalism emerged perhaps as early as 1185, but it is generally argued that the full development of the feudal system did not occur until 1338. The period from 1338 to 1600 has been called the classical age of Japanese feudalism, and the period from 1600 to 1868 (the Tokugawa era) has been called the period of late feudalism (Reischauer, 1956; J. W. Hall, 1970).

It used to be thought that the Tokugawa period was one of economic stagnation, but in the last several decades it has come to be recognized that this period was actually one of great economic vitality. Daniel Spencer (1958) claims that during this period Japan experienced the widespread commercialization of agriculture, an increasing flight of peasants into the towns and cities, large-scale urbanization, the worsening economic condition of the feudal nobility, increased monetization of the economy, and the beginnings of the factory system. Urbanization was so extensive that John Whitney Hall (1970) calls it "astounding." The growth of Edo (modern Tokyo) was truly remarkable; at the end of the sixteenth century it was only a small village, but by the early eighteenth century it had reached 500,000 inhabitants, and by the end of the eighteenth century it was well past one million in population. By the early nineteenth century, Japan was even more urbanized than Europe, and Edo had become the world's largest city.

Another striking feature of Japanese economic development during the Tokugawa epoch was the gradual *proletarianization* of the labor force (T. C. Smith, 1959; Leupp, 1992). Proletarianization is the process whereby workers are gradually converted from forced labor, such as serfdom, to wage labor, and it is an unmistakable sign of capitalist development. Proletarianization was most marked in urban areas, but it occurred in rural areas as well. By the end of the Tokugawa period, wage labor had become the dominant mode of compensating labor in the urban economy.

Recognition that modern Japan's capitalist roots extend back several centuries is a tremendously important accomplishment and a badly needed corrective to the old view of Tokugawa economic stagnation. Yet, focusing on the Tokugawa period may itself be starting too late, for the true roots of Japanese capitalism may be found several centuries earlier. It seems that important economic developments were occurring in Japan as early as the thirteenth century. At this time Japan was deeply enmeshed in a network of foreign trade with other parts of Asia, especially China. During the fifteenth and sixteenth centuries, foreign trade grew rapidly, and trade ventures were extended to more distant parts of the Far East. Japan was clearly a maritime economic power in these times (Sansom, 1961; Reischauer, 1956; J. W. Hall, 1970).

By the end of the Tokugawa period, Japan had become an essentially capitalist society in economic terms, even though it still retained old-fashioned feudal political and social institutions. By this time, the economy was clearly in the hands of the urban merchants rather than the feudal landlords (Spencer, 1958). As we shall see, this relatively independent trajectory of capitalist development in Japan holds major implications for understanding the rise of modern capitalism.

## Explaining the Transition from Feudalism to Capitalism

Explaining the transition from feudalism to capitalism has turned out to be one of the knottiest theoretical problems in contemporary social science. Numerous theories have been offered, but there has been little consensus about them. These theories contain weaknesses critical enough to preclude any of them offering a satisfactory explanation of the transition to capitalism. (An extended explication and critique of these theories may be found in Sanderson, 1994a, 1995, 1999b.) A serious weakness in nearly all of the theories is that they have been developed exclusively with respect to the European transition, ignoring the Japanese transition to capitalism altogether. The interpretation of the transition to modern capitalism set forth in this book, by contrast, has been explicitly developed to explain both the European and Japanese transitions, and thus is designed as a general theory. Our assumption is that any adequate social-scientific theory must apply to as many instances of a phenomenon as possible. Concerning the rise of capitalism, since there are only two cases, an adequate theory of this phenomenon should apply equally to both, and not merely to one alone.

The interpretation of the rise of capitalism set forth here contains two parts. First, there were several common characteristics of Europe and Japan that operated as important *preconditions* facilitating their transition from feudal to capitalist economies. Second, there was a *great historical trend*—expanding world commercialization—that provided the necessary context within which the preconditions operated to facilitate a capitalist transition. It was the interaction of these two kinds of factors—common preconditions on the one hand and a major historical trend on the other—that led to the transition to modern capitalism when and where it occurred. (A much more detailed presentation of this theory is found in Sanderson, 1994a, 1995, 1999b.)

Medieval Europe and medieval Japan shared at least five basic characteristics, each of which contributed in its own way to the emergence of modern capitalism. First, there was the factor of *size*. Japan and two of the three leading capitalist countries of early modern Europe, England and the Netherlands, were very small. Small geographical size minimizes the costs necessary to create systems of transportation and communication that help bring about economic development. Europe and Japan contrasted markedly with most of Asia, because most Asian societies, such as China and India, were bureaucratic empires spread out over large landmasses. The costs of maintaining large empires constitute a serious obstacle to capitalist development.

Second, there was *geography*. Japan and the leading capitalist countries of northwest Europe were located on large bodies of water that allowed them to give predominance to maritime rather than overland trade. Historically, in the long agrarian era those societies containing the greatest amount of commercialism—a kind of early capitalism or "protocapitalism"—have generally been ones in which maritime trade predominated (Amin, 1991). Maritime trade allows for a much more extensive and efficient development of networks of economic exchange than does overland trade.

A third factor was *climate*. Europe and Japan both had temperate climates, which is important when one recognizes that the greater part of the world colonized by Europe had tropical or subtropical climates. Japan's temperate climate, or perhaps its far northerly location, allowed it to escape European colonization, which meant that its economy never became subordinated to or dominated by some foreign economic power. In the modern world the least economically developed nation-states have generally been those exposed to many years of colonial domination by Europe. One of the reasons why Europe and Japan were the colonizers rather than the colonized was probably their temperate climate and northern latitudes.

Fourth, there was a demographic factor, *population growth*. Europe as a whole numbered about 30 million people in CE 1000 and grew rapidly from that point until about 1300. Population then underwent a dramatic decline until about 1450, largely due to the Black Death, but it began to grow again around 1450. It totalled some 67 million in 1500 and about 111 million by the mid-eighteenth century (Livi-Bacci, 1992). In Japan, population doubled from the twelfth to the sixteenth century (Taeuber, 1958), and by the beginning of the Tokugawa era, it had one of the world's densest populations (Janetta, 1987). Population continued to grow during the Tokugawa epoch, rapidly during the first half of the epoch but more slowly during the second half (Hanley and Yamamura, 1972). Population pressure on the land was clearly increasing in both Europe and Japan, and some scholars, such as Marvin Harris (1977), have seen this as contributing to the declining efficiency of feudalism and thus as necessitating a capitalist shift. Be this as it may, population growth in both regions led to extensive urbanization, larger pools of workers, expansion in the size of markets, and increased economic specialization (Boserup, 1981). All of these factors were critical for the growth of capitalism.

Finally, the *political structures* of Europe and Japan were similar in that they were the only true feudal regimes in world history (P. Anderson, 1974b). The key to feudalism is political decentralization or fragmentation. Great landlords divide their land into parcels known as **fiefs,** and grant these fiefs to lesser landlords, known as *vassals*, in return for military service and protection. Land may be even further subdivided, and the result is a hierarchy of lords whose political rule extends only so far as their ownership and control of land. It has been widely asserted that feudalism contributes to capitalist development because its politically decentralized nature gives an unusual amount of economic freedom to the merchant classes. Large centrally organized empires tend to stifle mercantile activity because it is a threat to the mode of surplus extraction used by rulers and governing classes. The freedom given to merchants under the feudal regimes of medieval Europe and Japan was probably the most important precondition that helped push these parts of the world forward as the first states to undergo a capitalist revolution.

These five preconditions did not operate in a vacuum, however, but occurred in the context of the great historical trend discussed at the beginning of this chapter—expanding world commercialization. The argument is that the rise of capitalism could only be a slow and gradual process because of the generalized hostility of landholding classes to merchants, the carriers of capitalism throughout history. As noted earlier, merchants generally occupied a very low position in the status-ranking systems of agrarian societies, despite the great wealth they sometimes accumulated. Therefore, mercantile activity could not expand rapidly because landlords would not allow it. Nevertheless, landlords were still dependent on merchants because they desired many of the goods merchants offered. Mercantile activity thus had to be preserved, and this gave merchants the opportunity to expand their activities slowly but surely. In due time, mercantile activity expanded to the point at which it could act as a kind of "critical mass" stimulating the huge leap in capitalist development after the sixteenth century.

Explaining the emergence of modern capitalism means explaining why capitalism arose when it did (why in the sixteenth century rather than in earlier or later periods), and also why it occurred first in particular regions (northwest Europe and Japan rather than other parts of Europe, Asia, or elsewhere). The theory offered here explains this "when" and "where" of capitalist development. Capitalism could not have occurred earlier (or at least much earlier) in world history because of the slow expansion of world commercialization and the need for a "critical mass" of mercantile activity to trigger a capitalist takeoff. That critical mass was not reached until sometime around CE 1000–1500. Numerous economic historians have thought that China during the time of the Sung Dynasty (CE 960–1275) was ready to take off into capitalism, but the tremendous economic advances it made during this time were eventually short-circuited (Elvin, 1973; E. L. Jones, 1988). The reason why this Chinese economic development petered out can be found in its unfavorable preconditions, especially the fact that China had a large landmass and a highly centralized and very powerful bureaucratic state. Northwest Europe and Japan had the most favorable preconditions for capitalist development at that time in world history during which a critical mass of commercialization had been achieved, and thus they were the world's first regions to experience the transition to the system that is now known as modern capitalism.

# The Political Sphere: The Formation of National States

What was happening in the political realm in the development of the modern world? In his pathbreaking work *Coercion, Capital, and European States* (1990), Charles Tilly identifies three major types of states that existed in Europe during the millennium from CE 990 to 1990: *large territorial states;* small states with extremely fragmented sovereignty, such as *city-states* and *urban federations;* and *national states.* Tilly shows that these states were not randomly situated in space and time; on the contrary, each type of state was found in a particular time and was associated with a particular form of economic organization.

The large territorial states were associated with regions where the landlord class was overwhelmingly dominant in the economy and where capitalism was weak and capitalists few. Russia, Poland, Hungary, and Brandenburg Prussia (now part of modern Germany) were states of this type. Here, there was an extremely strong alliance between the landlord class and the state. City-states and urban federations, by contrast, were found where there were many powerful capitalists who had concentrated large amounts of capital. As a result, there was a strong alliance between capitalists and the state, and the state was largely devoted to serving the economic interests of capitalists. City-states and urban federations were most characteristic of what Tilly has called the inner geographical core of Europe, especially the Italian city-states and the Dutch Republic.

These two different forms of the state were found in the first half of the millennium we are considering—from CE 990 to 1490. After the latter date, **national states** began to form. During the first half of the second millennium CE, there was nothing resembling a national state—that is, a large centrally coordinated state highly identified with a particular nationality, what today one calls, for example, England, France, or Germany. In fact, during these earlier times, England, France, and Germany did not yet exist as such. These regions and many others were divided into hundreds of smaller states. As Tilly (1990:39) states, there was an "enormous fragmentation of sovereignty then prevailing throughout the territory that would become Europe." There were perhaps as many as 500 states within the boundaries of Europe. In the Italian peninsula there were roughly 200 to 300 independent city-states, and in what is now southern Germany there were 69 free cities and numerous bishropics, duchies, and principalities. What a contrast with the present, where there are, or at least were before the eastern European nationalist movements of the early 1990s, only 25 to 28 sovereign European states (Tilly, 1990).

According to Tilly, the national states of Europe formed as a result of the strong concentration of both capital and military might. The new national states beginning to evolve in the sixteenth century were massive structures compared to most of their predecessors. Huge state bureaucracies were built, and these bureaucracies were devoted to both economic and military activities. They played a large role in managing and guiding the economy and in making war against other national states. Large standing armies were created to replace the relatively small private armies characteristic of feudalism. Historians have commonly referred to these new national states in their early years as forms of **absolutism** or **absolutist monarchy.** Perhaps the most important of the new monarchies were Spain, England, and France. In Spain, beginning in the late fifteenth century, the Hapsburg Dynasty came to power with the marriage of Ferdinand and Isabella. The Hapsburgs concentrated their attention on plundering the wealth of the New World through the establishment of colonies in the Americas. The treasure controlled by the Hapsburgs was greatly swelled by the precious metals shipped back to Spain from its overseas colonies. Absolutism in France was the result of a gradual development dating as far back as the fourteenth century (P. Anderson, 1974b), but it was in the late seventeenth century, under the reign of Louis XIV, that French absolutism achieved the zenith of its power. Louis XIV was the supreme symbol of absolute rule throughout all of Europe. He is reputed to have said "l'État, c'est moi" ("I am the state").

*Portrait of Louis XIV, the "Sun King." Louis was one of the great absolute monarchs of all of Europe in the seventeenth century.*

Although he may never have uttered those precise words, such language clearly expresses his view of his own power (Burns, 1973). The weakest and most short-lived of all the western European absolutisms was formed in England. Absolutism began there in the late fifteenth century with the rise to power of the Tudors, who were eventually replaced by the Stuarts at the beginning of the seventeenth century. English absolutism was not to survive past the end of the seventeenth century.

Thus it was that, after the sixteenth century, a system of interlocking yet highly competitive states was created, what is today called the **interstate system** (Wallerstein, 1974a, 1974b; Chase-Dunn, 1989a). This system was initially confined to Europe, but by the late twentieth century it had spread to encompass the entire world. The world is today divided into more than 180 sovereign states that engage in numerous economic, political, and military interactions with one another.

Within the interstate system, no single state has ever succeeded in achieving such a level of political control over all of the others that a world-empire would have resulted. There have been several efforts at such world-empire creation—most notably by the Hapsburgs in the sixteenth and seventeenth centuries, by Napoleonic France in the early nineteenth century, and by Germany in the twentieth century (Chase-Dunn, 1989a)—but each of these efforts failed. It would seem that the very logic of capitalism as an economic system makes it extremely difficult for a world-empire to emerge. As soon as any state begins to follow a path that it hopes will lead to world political domination, the other states start to gang up on it so as to prevent such an occurrence. Thus, capitalist economics and the interstate system go hand in hand. Indeed, had the capitalist world-system ever succumbed to world-imperial domination, it is doubtless the case that its essentially capitalist nature would have disintegrated (Wallerstein, 1974a, 1974b; Chase-Dunn, 1989a).

Much controversy has arisen over whether the capitalist world-economy and the interstate system are fused together as part of a single reality, or whether the interstate system is a substantially autonomous reality in its own right. Scholars such as Theda Skocpol (1977) and Randall Collins (1986) see the interstate system as largely autonomous (cf. Zolberg, 1981). They argue that capitalism and the interstate system are intertwined, but that the world political system must be studied as a reality in its own right. States are actors in a world political order in which political and military objectives cannot be understood simply in terms of capitalist economic interests. There is a great deal of truth in this assertion. It would be very difficult, for example, to explain such forms of contemporary political conflict as that between Israelis and Palestinian Arabs, between many Islamic states (e.g., Iraq) and the United States, or between Northern Irish Catholics and England simply in economic terms. Nonetheless, the position adopted in this book is that the political and military objectives of capitalist states cannot seriously depart from the capitalist economic interests that form the context in which these states operate. In Christopher Chase-Dunn's (1989a) words, there is only "one logic" within the capitalist world-system, a single logic in which economics and politics are essentially inseparable. The driving force behind this logic is, of course, that of ceaseless capital accumulation. It is the contemporary global force *par excellence*.

# FOR FURTHER READING

Classic works on European feudalism are Bloch's *Feudal Society* (1961; orig. 1930) and Georges Duby's *Rural Economy and Country Life in the Medieval West* (1968). See also Critchley (1978), Fossier (1988), and Le Goff (1988). Lynn White's *Medieval Technology and Social Change* (1962) is a famous analysis of some of the most important technological innovations of the feudal era.

Wallerstein's *The Modern World-System*, volumes 1 and 2 (1974b, 1980), is the classic statement of his world-system perspective and its application to European capitalist development until the mid-eighteenth century. Wallerstein (1979) contains some of his earliest essays developing the world-system perspective. Christopher Chase-Dunn's *Global Formation* (1989a; updated ed. 1998) is an excellent and highly comprehensive summary of world-system theory by another leading world-system theorist. See also Shannon (1996) and Sanderson (1999b:181–243). Fernand Braudel's *Civilization and Capitalism, 15th–18th Century* (3 vols., 1981, 1982, 1984) is a magisterial discussion of European capitalism from many angles. Eric Wolf's *Europe and the People Without History* (1982) is a classic work by an eminent anthropologist that examines preindustrial modes of production and the transition to European capitalism from a type of world-system perspective. Other good but much briefer overviews of the transition to modern capitalism can be found in Beaud (1983), A. K. Smith (1991), and Kriedte (1983).

Israel (1989) and de Vries and van der Woude (1997) provide good discussions of the emergence of Dutch capitalism between the sixteenth and nineteenth centuries. A much more detailed discussion of Sanderson's theory of the rise of capitalism in Europe and Japan is found in his *Social Transformations* (1999b:168–178). Alternative interpretations of the rise of modern capitalism can be found in Dobb (1963), Sweezy (1976; orig. 1950), Weber (1958; orig. 1904), Chirot (1985, 1986), J. A. Hall (1985), Mann (1986), Abu-Lughod (1989), North and Thomas (1973), E. L. Jones (1987, 1988), R. Wilkinson (1973), Harris (1977), and P. Anderson (1974a).

On Japanese feudalism and the Japanese transition to capitalism, see J. W. Hall (1970), Reischauer (1956), Spencer (1958), Sheldon (1958), Yamamura (1980), Leupp (1992), T. Smith (1959), P. Anderson (1974b), Hane (1992), Yoshihara (1986), and Halliday (1975).

Janet Abu-Lughod (1989) argues that there was already a world-system in place from the mid-thirteenth century to the mid-fourteenth centuries. Barry Gills and Andre Gunder Frank (1991; Frank, 1990, 1991; Frank and Gills, 1993) argue for the existence of a 5,000-year world-system of which the modern world-system is but a continuation. Christopher Chase-Dunn and Thomas Hall (1997) argue that world-systems are very general phenomena and the appropriate unit of analysis for studying the evolution of social life. They look at several different types of precapitalist world-systems, from the very simple to the highly complex.

Frank's *ReOrient: Global Economy in the Asian Age* (1998) and Kenneth Pomeranz's *The Great Divergence: China, Europe, and the Making of the Modern World Economy* (2000) are excellent scholarly works that challenge the received wisdom that Europe was the economically most advanced region of the world-economy in the sixteenth century. Frank claims that Asia (especially China) was the center of the world-economy in the centuries before and after 1500, and that Europe did not really spurt ahead of Asia until after 1800. At the present time, he claims, the center of the world-economy is shifting back to Asia. Pomeranz makes a similar argument, although he sees China as essentially economically even with Europe (rather than ahead of it) prior to 1800. He attributes Europe's (mainly England's) economic superiority after 1800 largely to the presence of coal deposits and the many benefits offered by the possession of overseas colonies in the New World. See also Blaut (1993) and Goody (1996).

Charles Tilly's *Coercion, Capital, and European States, AD 990–1990* (1990) is an excellent discussion of the rise of national states in Europe. See also Tilly and Blockmans (1994) and P. Anderson (1974b).

# CHAPTER

## 6 Industrialization and the Expansion of the World-System

Immanuel Wallerstein (1984) identifies three great trends in the evolution of the capitalist world-economy: increasing **mechanization** of production, increasing **commodification** of the factors of production, and increasing **proletarianization** of the labor force. Increasing mechanization involves the growing application of advanced technology, especially machinery, to production tasks. The level of commodification of the factors of production advances when land, labor, technology, and other productive forces increasingly come to be regulated by the market and by considerations of their profitability. Increasing proletarianization results when a larger percentage of the workforce is compensated in the form of wages. Taken together, these three trends mark what is known as a **deepening of capitalist development** (Shannon, 1996). This chapter explores the deepening of capitalism over the past two centuries. Of particular concern is what has been called the Industrial Revolution: what it was, when and why it occurred, and what its consequences were for the capitalist system. The chapter also explores the evolution and expansion of capitalism from the late nineteenth century to the present, as well as the rise and fall of great powers in the world-economy and the reasons why powerful states rise and fall.

## The Industrial Revolution and the Emergence of Industrial Capitalism

### The Industrial Revolution and Its Causes

The Industrial Revolution involved the transformation of a technology resting heavily on human and animal labor into a technology characterized by *machines* (Landes, 1969). Along with this came the transition from a heavy reliance on agricultural production to a reliance on the manufacture of goods for sale in the context of a factory system. The Industrial Revolution was, at bottom, a revolution in technology; it created, nevertheless, new and profound changes in the very economic structure of society, bringing new methods of production and exchange of goods, and profound changes in the organization of labor. Peter Stearns's (1993:11) definition of the

Industrial Revolution—or of *an* industrial revolution whenever and wherever it occurs—is an excellent one. He says that it involves "a massive set of changes that begin when radical innovations in technologies and organizational forms are extensively introduced in key manufacturing sectors and that end, in the truly revolutionary phase, when these innovations are widely, though not necessarily universally, established in the economy at large."

The Industrial Revolution began in England during the second half of the eighteenth century, its first phase typically being dated from about 1760 to 1830 (Landes, 1969). This initial phase of **industrialization** was characterized by the great expansion of the textile industry and by major developments in the manufacture of iron and the mining of coal. The textile industry, especially the manufacture of cotton cloth, was advanced through the invention of the spinning jenny, the water frame, the power loom, and the cotton gin. The growth of textile manufacture spurred the development of the factory system. The invention of the steam engine was also an important part of this process, as it was used to power the heavy machinery housed in the textile factories. Textiles formed a vital part of the English economy and were a major export in the international capitalist system.

The iron industry also underwent significant expansion in the first phase of industrial development. Iron was increasingly in demand for the manufacture of steam engines and machine tools; machine tool production itself became a significant feature of the English economy. The increasing manufacture of these products, in turn, caused an increase in the demand for coal and the expansion of the coal mining industry.

Industrial technology was soon to be found in several other parts of Europe during the nineteenth century, especially in Belgium, France, and Germany. France did not have the coal deposits of Britain or Belgium, and so its industrialization lagged behind theirs. However, it was still one of the world's earliest and leading industrializers. Cotton and wool production were important, as was metallurgy. Industrialization picked up speed in the 1840s with the development of the railroad system. German industrialization started somewhat later. Between the 1840s and the 1870s, coal production expanded greatly, and iron production started to expand in the 1850s. Railroads also began to develop at this time. German industrialization concentrated on capital-intensive heavy industry, and the state played a much larger role than it did in Britain, Belgium, or France (Stearns, 1993).

The United States began to emerge as a major **industrial society** in the 1830s. Textile factories emerged and spread across New England, the heartland of early industrialization. There were also important developments in machine building and printing. The development of railroads in the 1850s and 1860s was an extremely important part of American industrialization, especially as they expanded westward and allowed the opening up of the American frontier (Stearns, 1993).

By the late nineteenth century, both Russia and Japan had begun to industrialize. Between 1860 and 1900, Russia had increased its number of railroad miles from 700 to more than 36,000. Railroad expansion contributed importantly to the production of coal, iron, and wool. Japan's industrialization can be dated from the 1870s. Railroads were a major part of Japanese industrialization, as was mining, shipbuilding, textiles, construction goods, food processing, match production, and chemicals. As in Germany, the government played a critical role in financing and organizing the industrialization process (Stearns, 1993).

The Industrial Revolution created a new mode of economic production, *industrial capitalism*. As indicated in the last chapter, industrial capitalism differs from other forms of capitalism in that it involves the earning of profit through the employment of wage workers. The establishment of industrial capitalism on a major scale thus required the reorganization of the workforce into the factory system, and the factory became the basic social unit of capitalist production. Michel Beaud has said the following in regard to the emergence of industrial capitalism (1983:83):

> During the nineteenth century it was chiefly through the establishment of mechanized industry that the capitalist mode of production was extended. The "mills" which had begun to be built in England at the end of the eighteenth century became more widespread, not only in England itself, but in Belgium, France, Switzerland, Germany, and the United States. The development of these mills was particularly striking in the "driving" sectors of the time: textiles and metallurgy. Men who had previously been traders or merchants, as well as foremen and the sons of artisans, became manufacturers and availed themselves of a labor force that had become available through the transformation of the countryside or through immigration. These laborers were employed with the intention of extracting the maximum, and it was in conditions of misery and unbearable oppression that the original core of the modern working class was formed.

Obviously, industrialization did not end with these technological and economic developments. Rather than as an event or a series of events, industrialization is better thought of as a continual process that has existed down to the present time. In the middle of the nineteenth century, further technological innovations emerged

*Weaving cotton cloth in a British textile mill, 1835. The manufacture of cotton cloth was the spearhead of the English Industrial Revolution.*

and existing technologies were elaborated and applied to capitalist production on a wider scale. For example, the steam engine came to be applied to transportation. It was used to create the first steam railway and was applied as well to navigation with the invention of the steamboat. It was during this time that railroads began to emerge as an extremely significant aspect of capitalist investment (Dobb, 1963).

By the turn of the twentieth century, the automobile, electrical, and petroleum industries were becoming important features of life in industrial societies (Lenski, 1970). By World War II, the aviation, aluminum, and electronics industries were achieving major economic significance (Lenski, 1970). Recent years have witnessed such notable technological developments as the harnessing of nuclear energy and the manufacture of highly sophisticated computers on a major scale. It takes no particularly acute vision of the future to see that such developments are undoubtedly only the beginning of a series of enormous technological accomplishments.

This picture of the Industrial Revolution is highly schematic, but it should nonetheless serve to make clear just how significant were the technological changes that were taking place. These changes were to produce major changes in the structure of social life throughout virtually the entire world. But why did the Industrial Revolution occur when and where it did? Indeed, why did it occur at all?

Some scholars have seen the Industrial Revolution as rooted in population pressure (R. Wilkinson, 1973; Boserup, 1981). They see industrialization as simply another technological advance that, like earlier technological advances such as the emergence of agriculture or the invention of the plow, is rooted in the desire to stave off declining standards of living created by increasing numbers. It is unlikely, though, that industrialization can be explained by demographic growth. We are dealing here with a technological change far different from the technological changes of earlier eras.

A much better explanation is that the Industrial Revolution was the logical and predictable outcome of the evolving European world-economy (Wallerstein, 1989). By the middle of the eighteenth century, England had clearly emerged as the dominant power within this economy. England had expanded its import and export markets throughout the capitalist system and had concentrated within itself enormous quantities of wealth. This wealth became essential as capital to be used in financing factories and machinery, and thus England was in a uniquely favorable financial position to engage in industrial development. As Stearns notes, "Considerable investment funds were required—the new machines were expensive, far costlier than any manufacturing equipment previously devised, even in the very small factories that characterized much early industry" (1993:34).

But as Eric Hobsbawm (1968) points out, capitalism has no inherent bias toward technological innovation for its own sake. It only has a bias toward increased profitability and will innovate only when it is profitable to do so. With this insight, it is easy to see why England was strongly oriented toward major industrial development. Industrialization permitted increasing productivity and lowered costs, which in turn allowed for the expansion of England's existing domestic and foreign markets and for the creation of new ones. The result was the increasing accumulation of capital on a grand scale.

The Industrial Revolution was thus the historical product of the European capitalist world-economy, and it was initiated by the nation that was best suited economically to bring it about. This fact also helps explain why the Industrial Revolution occurred when it did rather than much earlier or later. It could not have occurred much earlier, since its emergence closely depended on the creation and substantial expansion of a capitalist world-economy. Its occurrence at some much later time was also unlikely, since industrial technology was an important—indeed, an essential—component of an expanding economic system fundamentally committed to unlimited growth.

So industrialization required a capitalist economy with a high level of commercialization and capitalists with a great deal of capital to invest in the new and very expensive machinery. But it also required critical raw materials, especially coal and iron. England, Belgium, and Germany possessed large coal deposits, and this helps to explain why industrialization occurred earliest in these regions of western Europe. There were also substantial deposits of iron ore in these regions, and these deposits were often located close to the coal sources. Because of the importance of textile manufacturing to the Industrial Revolution, fibers were also needed. Western Europe, Britain in particular, had a great deal of wool because of sheep farming, as well as access to cotton grown in the American South and in India and other parts of Asia (Stearns, 1993).

It is also important to see why the Industrial Revolution did not occur outside Europe. Of all the non-European societies, China was in one sense the most likely to have had an industrial revolution. As Wallerstein (1974a) has pointed out, in CE 1500 China was technologically at least as advanced, if not more so, as western Europe (cf. McNeill, 1982). But by 1800, western Europe had far surpassed China. This demonstrates that technological change is surely not an autonomous process, occurring for its own sake. Rather, it depends on particular conditions. Western Europe, and England especially, had precisely those conditions logically leading to major technological innovation. But what did China have (or not have) that impeded major technological advance? For one thing, it was not organized around a capitalist mode of production in the eighteenth century. In addition, it had an imperial bureaucratic state that did not depend on technological advance for its enrichment and that actively squashed many technological innovations because of their potential economic threat (Wallerstein, 1974a). Imperial China was therefore not well situated to experience the world's first industrial revolution.

## The Industrial Revolution in World-System Perspective

In the third volume of his *The Modern World-System* (1989), Wallerstein suggests that the notion of the Industrial Revolution is something of a myth, or at least that the way in which most scholars have spoken of these changes is highly misleading. Wallerstein is essentially making three closely related points: first, that the changes were not as dramatic or as revolutionary as commonly thought; second, that the so-called Industrial Revolution is not some sort of great dividing point between the past and the modern world; and finally, that what is called the Industrial Revolution was part and parcel of the evolution of the world-economy as a whole, not simply of individual societies within it.

As noted earlier, Wallerstein argues that one of the great evolutionary trends of the capitalist world-economy is increasing mechanization. This occurs throughout the entire system, but it is carried out faster and far more extensively in core societies. Increasing mechanization has gone on continually, even if not smoothly, throughout the history of capitalism. From this perspective, the Industrial Revolution of the eighteenth century was simply one phase in this evolutionary process, and therefore not really revolutionary at all. Considerable mechanization had occurred in earlier centuries, especially during the period between 1540 and 1640 (Nef, 1964; Tilly, 1983). All of this means that the "great divide" in world history is not the Industrial Revolution, as most social scientists have argued, but the transition to capitalism that began some three centuries earlier.

In addition, if the Industrial Revolution was part of the evolution of the capitalist world-economy as a whole, then one has to use the entire system as a reference point in understanding why it occurred. In this regard, Wallerstein insists that what is called the Industrial Revolution occurred in certain core societies during what he terms "the second era of great expansion of the capitalist world-economy" (Wallerstein, 1989). Capitalism was born in the fifteenth and sixteenth centuries and expanded throughout a significant portion of the globe during that time. Then, in the seventeenth century, it continued to expand, but at a much slower rate (Wallerstein, 1980). After about 1730, it entered a third phase, which was its second phase of rapid expansion. By the end of this phase—sometime during the middle of the nineteenth century—it had come to cover a large portion of the globe (most of it by the end of that century). And it was during this third phase that extensive industrialization occurred within the major core societies, and for reasons that have already been explained.

Wallerstein's overall position seems basically correct, but with the important qualification that he underestimates the extensiveness of the technological and economic changes after the middle of the eighteenth century. To be sure, increasing mechanization has been a continual process in the history of capitalism, but it has also been very sporadic and uneven. It is an exaggeration to imply that the technological changes before 1760 were on the same scale as those that occurred after that time. Therefore, while many scholars may overrate the significance of the Industrial Revolution, Wallerstein underrates its significance.

## Industrial Capitalism Since the Late Nineteenth Century

By the last quarter of the nineteenth century, the capitalist world-economy was dominated by four core societies: the United Kingdom, the United States, Germany, and France (Chirot, 1986). These four societies were the most highly industrialized and urbanized societies in the world. In 1900, they collectively produced approximately three-quarters of all the world's manufactured goods despite having only about one-eighth of the world's population (Chirot, 1977).

*Shinjuku skyscraper district of modern Tokyo, Japan. Japan is one of the most highly urbanized of the world's industrial societies.*

According to Daniel Chirot (1986), membership in the capitalist core was also held by five other societies: the Netherlands, Belgium, Switzerland, Sweden, and Denmark. The semiperiphery at this time consisted mainly of Spain, Austria-Hungary, Italy, Russia, and Japan (Chirot, 1986). The periphery consisted of Portugal, China, the Ottoman Empire, the eastern European countries, and all or nearly all of Latin America, Asia, and Africa.

World capitalism around the turn of the twentieth century had a number of crucial features that cannot be overlooked. One of these was the relative decline of Britain in the world economy and the relative rise of several other nations, especially the United States. As Beaud (1983) notes, Britain's share of world industrial production fell from 32 percent in 1870 to 14 percent just before World War I, and then to only 9 percent by 1930. At the same time, the U.S. share of world production was increasing. In 1870, the United States produced 23 percent of the world's goods; by the eve of World War I, it was producing 38 percent, and its share of world production had climbed to a full 42 percent by 1930. By the early twentieth century, the United States had clearly replaced Britain as the world's major core power.

Another crucial feature of world capitalism at this time was its entry into a new phase of capitalist development, what has often been termed **monopoly capitalism.** Under monopoly capitalism, the competitive character of capitalism was increasingly reduced as capitalist companies grew in size and in their concentration of capital. Large corporations began to dominate the market and to drive out smaller producers by ruining them economically and then swallowing them up. Eventually, a few giant corporations dominated the market for many industries. Beaud sums up the extent to which capital was being centralized in the hands of fewer and fewer companies during this time (1983:136–137):

Everywhere, the average size of business establishments and industrial companies increased. . . . In times of crisis mergers took place which benefited the most powerful companies; thus during the period 1880–1918 in Britain, 655 companies "disappeared" into 74 merger companies.

Above all, unprecedented concentrations of capital occurred, under the direction of a capitalist or of a family; trusts or groups very quickly came to dominate an entire industrial sector within a nation, especially in the United States and in Germany. In the United States in 1908, the seven largest trusts owned or controlled 1,638 companies. By 1900, the percentage represented by the trusts included 50 percent of textile production, 54 percent of the glassmaking industry, 60 percent of the book and paper industry, 62 percent of the food industry, 72 percent of the liquor industry, 77 percent of nonferrous metals, 81 percent of the chemical industries, and 84 percent of iron and steel. These included companies such as the United States Steel Corporation, founded by J. P. Morgan and E. H. Gary, which incorporated the Carnegie steel mills, and Standard Oil, founded in 1870 by J. D. Rockefeller, which in 1870 refined only 4 percent of American petroleum but by 1879 controlled 90 percent of the American refineries, and by 1904 controlled 85 percent of the domestic business and 90 percent of the export business as well.

In Germany the Krupp industrial empire employed 7,000 workers in 1873, and 78,000 in 1913; the AEG electrical industry, through an astonishing process of concentration, by 1911 controlled 175 to 200 companies, and employed more than 60,000 workers.

The emergence of monopoly capitalism was also characterized by a substantial increase in foreign investment by the core capitalist nations. Foreign investments quadrupled in Britain from the early 1890s to the early 1910s. In Germany, such investments doubled between 1883 and 1893, and then doubled again between 1893 and 1914. In France, they tripled between 1880 and 1914. About half of the foreign investments of the core powers were made outside Europe and North America. Latin America accounted for 19 percent, Asia for 16 percent, Africa for 9 percent, and Oceania for 5 percent (Beaud, 1983).

By the middle of the twentieth century, a new economic unit had become prominent in the capitalist world-economy: the **transnational corporation** (Barnet and Müller, 1974). The transnational corporation is today the central economic entity within world capitalism (Bornschier and Chase-Dunn, 1985). A transnational corporation is a company that has branches of production in more than one country. Long before the rise of such a corporation, capitalists *sold* their products in a world market, but the rise of the transnational corporation marked the emergence of international *production*.

The huge importance of the transnational corporations can be gleaned from a comparison of their sales revenues with the Gross National Products (GNPs) of some smaller European nations (Heilbroner, 1972). (*Gross National Product* is the total value of goods and services produced in a nation in a given year.) For example, in the late 1960s, General Motors had a sales level exceeding each of the GNPs of Belgium, Switzerland, Denmark, Austria, Norway, Greece, and Portugal. Similarly, the sales of Standard Oil of New Jersey exceeded the GNPs of all these countries except for Belgium and Switzerland. Today, the situation is similar. In 1997, General Motors had revenues exceeding the GNPs of Norway, Finland, Denmark, Poland, and Portugal, as well as such rich East Asian countries as Hong Kong and Singapore, and Ford Motor Company's 1997 revenues exceeded the GNPs of all of these except Denmark. Moreover, such Fortune-500 transnationals as Mitsui, Mitsubishi, Royal Dutch Shell, Exxon, Wal-Mart, Toyota, General Electric, IBM, Daewoo, and British Petroleum had 1997 revenues exceeding the GNPs of most of the world's countries outside the most highly developed ones (*Fortune*, 1998; Kiljunen, 2003).

The transnational corporation is only the latest in a series of strategies used by capitalists in the historic process of capital accumulation. By internationalizing production, capitalists are able to overcome certain barriers imposed on their accumulationist activities. One of these barriers is the existence of tariffs on imports. By locating a branch of their company in a foreign country, capitalists are able to produce and sell their products directly in that country and avoid costly tariffs and other restrictions.

In the capitalist world-system today, the great core powers are the United States, Germany, France, and Japan. Although the United States is still the leading core power, its dominance is not as great as it once was. Most of the other nations of western Europe, as well as Canada, Australia, and New Zealand, are also members of the core. The semiperiphery principally consists of poorer European nations, such as Portugal, Spain, and Greece; most of South America; and the better-off countries in Asia (e.g., Taiwan, South Korea, Singapore, and Hong Kong) and North Africa (e.g., Algeria, Morocco, and Egypt). The periphery consists of the rest of the less-developed world: almost all of sub-Saharan Africa, numerous Asian countries, and some countries in South and Central America. (Chapter 9 will provide a close look at these nations of the contemporary capitalist periphery and semiperiphery, with an eye to explaining their low levels of economic development.)

## The Japanese Transition to Industrial Capitalism

The discussion of industrial capitalism thus far has concentrated on Europe and North America, but it is well known that Japan has in recent decades emerged as a major industrial capitalist society and a world economic power. Many people, social scientists and laypersons alike, expect Japan to be the leading world economic power early in this century.

Japan was incorporated into the world-economy after 1853, when Western ships landed in its harbors and demanded that it end its two centuries of economic isolation from the West. Japan somewhat reluctantly accepted its inability to prevent Western contact and influence, but it took important steps to guarantee that Western contact would not do serious harm to its economy and society. In 1868, Japan underwent a major social and political transformation known as the Meiji Restoration, which not only changed the form of government but, more significant, initiated a major program of economic development and industrialization. It is important to recognize that Japan was incorporated into the capitalist world-economy as a semiperipheral rather than a peripheral country. It was economically strong at the time of incorporation, and thus it was able to resist being relegated to the production of raw materials for the benefit of core societies.

One of the first tasks of the modern national state that was created in Japan in 1868 was to make vigorous efforts to encourage large-scale industrialization, and the state came to play an extremely important role in the organization and development of the economy. Japanese industrialization involved direct government action to a degree far greater than was the case among the earlier European industrializing nations. Frances Moulder (1977) identifies three major ways in which the Japanese state involved itself in moving the economy forward:

1. It established pilot projects with its own funds and administered them.
2. It subsidized industries, especially heavy industry, railway construction, shipping, and mining; railways were a major government activity, as was mining; by the 1880s, six mines (devoted to the mining of iron, lead, gold, silver, copper, and coal) were being operated by the government, and these were virtually the only ones that were worked on a large scale with modern machinery; and the government also became heavily involved in manufacturing during the 1870s, especially in the textile industry.
3. It encouraged the formation of a system of national banks that would provide long-term loans at low interest rates to investors in modern industry.

The state continued to play a crucial role in Japanese economic development throughout the twentieth century, and plays such a role even today. The involvement of the Japanese government in the economy is so great that the country is sometimes jokingly referred to as "Japan, Inc." (Chirot, 1986).

It is mainly in the last 50 years that Japan has risen to the position of a leading world economic power. From the mid-1950s through the 1980s, the Japanese economy grew at a phenomenal rate. In 1989, Japan produced one-quarter of all the passenger cars manufactured throughout the world. By 1991, it produced about 30 percent of the passenger cars sold in the United States (this figure includes cars produced in Japanese factories in the United States). Japan has also outproduced other major industrial capitalist nations, or at least strongly challenged them, in the manufacture of such products as radios, quartz watches, televisions, calculators, video cassette recorders, stereophonics, computers, silicon memory chips, and robotics (Hane, 1992).

There are a number of important differences between Japanese capitalism and capitalism in the West (Yoshihara, 1986; Hane, 1992). One of these concerns the organizational structure of Japanese companies. Japanese companies usually guarantee lifetime employment to their workers. Workers generally spend their entire lives with the same company, and so they are totally committed to it and involved in it. Not only do they spend numerous hours working, but when they are not working they are commonly eating, drinking, or playing golf with coworkers or customers. How they are evaluated by the company is equivalent to the evaluation of their entire personality. Japanese workers at all levels therefore have enormous incentives to work hard. Labor-management relations are also different from those in Western capitalism. Workers in Japan are asked for their opinions much more than are Western workers, and emphasis is placed on group rather than individual decision making. Japanese companies lose very few days to labor disputes compared to the number of days lost by Western companies, and a mere 4 percent of the days lost by U.S. companies. Japanese companies also think more in terms of long-term rather than short-term profits.

Japanese companies are well known to collaborate very closely with each other, with firms forming conglomerates known as *keiretsu*. A *keiretsu* involves a giant producer at the top—Toyota, Nissan, or Sony, for example—and a number of satellite firms that supply the top company with the materials it requires to turn out its products. *Keiretsu* members confer closely with each other and engage in many forms of coordination of their activities. Each *keiretsu* is in essence a type of closed club whose members derive important economic benefits by keeping others out. In many ways, the Japanese economy is a network of closed systems within a larger closed system.

Japanese capitalism is also more collectivistic than Western, especially American, capitalism. This is largely a reflection of its much more collectivistic culture in which individuals are encouraged to subordinate their personal goals to group goals. Japanese collectivism is also reflected in the substantially greater role of the state in capitalist enterprises. As noted earlier, the state played a very strong role in the early development of industrial capitalism in Japan. Japanese capitalism proves that, although capitalism is usually associated with individualism, it does not require it.

Japanese culture is not only highly collectivistic but is also characterized by a marked asceticism. It emphasizes hard work, self-sacrifice, frugality, deferred

*Central Park section of modern New York City. Large-scale urbanization has been one of the most important consequences of industrialization.*

gratification, and planning for the future. Japanese asceticism is not the sole basis for the remarkable success of Japanese capitalism, but it can be regarded as an important "preadaptation" for Japanese economic development.

Some scholars have suggested that the phenomenal development of Japanese capitalism in the last half-century has resulted from its Confucian philosophy and religion (e.g., Berger, 1986). But, as Kunio Yoshihara (1986) has argued, this is very unlikely. The original homeland of Confucianism was China, and Confucianism arose over 2,000 years ago, but China has only very recently started on a path of significant economic development. If Confucianism has been a powerful factor in capitalist development, then China should be much more developed at the present time than it actually is.

## Hegemonic Rise and Fall in the World-System

Immanuel Wallerstein (1979, 1984) has introduced the concept of **hegemony** into the discussion of the world-economy and its evolution. A *hegemon* is a society so economically powerful that it dominates world production, trade, and finance, and can basically dominate all other economic actors. Economically, a hegemon is "number one," but a society can be number one without being truly hegemonic. Throughout much of the history of the world-economy, there has been no true hegemon.

To become a hegemon, a society needs not only an extremely efficient mode of capitalist production but also a very strong state and a strong military. According to Wallerstein, the first hegemonic power in the world-economy was Holland (the United Provinces), which was hegemonic between 1625 and 1675 (Israel, 1989). Dutch hegemony was rooted in a number of advantages. It had an extremely favorable geographical location on the North Sea, which facilitated its mercantile capitalism. It also possessed a special kind of ship, the *fluyt*, which was a trading ship that was built in such a way that it could save manpower, thus reducing labor costs, while not sacrificing economic productivity (Wallerstein, 1989; Israel, 1989). Dutch agriculture was also highly specialized and productive. This made possible a densely populated society—the densest in the Western world—that was highly urbanized; a large part of the Dutch population could be freed for work in nonagricultural production (Israel, 1989). Holland also enjoyed low freight charges and low interest rates. The Dutch had a very powerful state that was extremely capable of promoting Dutch production, finance, and trade. This state supervised a very broad range of economic activities and seemed to be uniquely suited to protecting and advancing trade (Israel, 1989). It also had a very powerful navy that consistently defeated its principal rivals—Britain and France—in war. The Dutch economy was so efficient that Britain and France could not dislodge it economically; they had to resort to constant war to try to gain the upper hand.

The Dutch "golden age" was over by 1675. Holland lost its hegemonic position, as all hegemons eventually do, but it continued to be a major economic power in the world-economy. When Holland slipped from its hegemonic position, Britain and France advanced. It was particularly Britain that gained from Holland's loss, and it became hegemonic by about 1815, maintaining this position for about 60 years (Wallerstein, 1979, 1989). It was, of course, the world leader in industrialization, producing approximately half of the world's goods in 1860, and more than half in such industries as iron and steel (Mann, 1988). It also carried a third of world trade and accounted for a quarter of the world's exports (Mann, 1988). Britain was known as "the workshop of the world." It had an extremely powerful state, and its navy ruled the seas. Its hegemony also became cultural in nature, as it transported its language and institutions throughout the world by way of the vast colonial empire it had created.

The loss of British hegemony can be dated from the early to mid-1870s. Most of Britain's subsequent economic decline took place by the beginning of World War I. From producing about one-third of the world's goods in 1870, it was producing only 14 percent by 1914, and this declined further to only 9 percent by 1930. Today, Britain is one of the most economically troubled of all industrial capitalist societies. In the 1970s and 1980s, the British picture was not a pretty one (although things improved somewhat in the 1990s). Unemployment reached 10 to 15 percent, domestic industry was in disastrous condition, the working class had become thoroughly demoralized, racial and ethnic strife were rampant, and Britain experienced a significant "brain drain," with many of its intellectuals and scientists leaving for other European countries and for the United States. Severe regional divisions emerged, with southeast England the most prosperous and the old industrial heartland of the north in the worst shape, with massive deindustrialization and unemployment. Things looked so bleak in the 1980s that British sociologist Michael Mann (1988:235) was led to remark that "by the year 2000 it will be as difficult to remember the greatness of Britain as it is now to remember the Empire of Spain."

Britain's main economic competitors were Germany and the United States, but it was the United States that became the next hegemon. The United States started out in the late eighteenth century as essentially two societies under one state. The U.S. North was a semiperipheral society of small farmers and artisans that later began to industrialize around the middle of the nineteenth century. The U.S. South was a peripheral society devoted to plantation agriculture based on slavery. The Civil War was essentially fought over these economic differences—over what type of society was going to control the expansion westward—and, of course, it was northern industrial capitalism that won. By the late nineteenth century, the United States had become a core society, although the South still lagged economically because of its heritage of slavery and corresponding low level of industrialization. From 1870 on, the ascent of the United States in the world-system was dramatic. In 1870, it produced 23 percent of the world's goods, but this had increased to 38 percent by 1914 and to 42 percent by 1930 (Beaud, 1983).

Why did the United States develop so dramatically? There have been many answers. Andre Gunder Frank (1979) calls attention to the unusually privileged position of the North, New England in particular, in the expanding system of mercantile capitalism centered on Britain. The United States was involved in a whole series of *triangular trades*, which were trade networks that linked New England, Britain, and the Caribbean in a variety of ways. As Frank puts it (1979:61), "This privileged position and role impinged on northern transport; mercantile and financial participation in southern and western export (and import) trade; the North-east's advantageous position in the West India trade, the slave trade and indeed world trade; north-eastern manufacturing development, largely for export; and in the associated capital accumulation and concentration in northern cities."

Graeme Donald Snooks (1997) agrees with Frank that the insertion of the New England colonies into the expanding system of British mercantile capitalism was a crucial factor, but this will only account for U.S. economic development up until about the American Revolution. What about the enormous development of the nineteenth century? Here, Snooks calls attention to the fact that the United States was the world's first *megastate*, a huge continent that was not, as in Europe, divided into a large number of competing nation-states. The United States had a huge amount of land to the west of its original colonies, and this appeared to be crucial to its massive economic development. Westward expansion began soon after American independence from Britain and was governed by a snowball effect (Snooks, 1997:372–373):

> Although the great westward movement began as a trickle in the 1780s, it soon reached a flood that grew exponentially. In 1800 there were 400,000 people west of the Appalachians—a considerable achievement in only a generation for a society with a population of just over 2 million at the time of the Revolution—and ten years later this had more than doubled to about one million. So rapid was this westward flow that the proportion of the total population settled in the new western states rose from 3 percent in 1790 to 15 percent in 1810, to 37 percent in 1840, and to 50 percent in 1860. . . .
>
> To accommodate the westward expansion the US government—which, unlike the British government, took a leading role in the new strategy—extended its borders by purchasing Louisiana from Napoleon Bonaparte (who had taken it from the Spanish) in 1803, by acquiring Florida from the Spanish in 1819, by taking Texas and the South-West from Mexico in 1845 and 1848 respectively, by acquiring Oregon Territory in 1846, and by purchasing southern Arizona from Mexico in 1853. But while the territorial basis for the world's first mega-state had been created by the early 1850s, it took a further forty years for the frontier to be closed.

This expansion, of course, required transportation technology, and prior to 1790 this was limited to ocean and river transport. Road building came later, but it could not facilitate more than intraregional trade. The use of steamboats carried things a step further, but according to Snooks it was the development of the railroad after 1850 that created a single market that stretched from the Atlantic to the Pacific. The railroad system was, Snooks argues, absolutely essential to the building of the U.S. megastate (Snooks, 1997:374–376; emphasis added):

> Railroad investment played a central role by creating, in response to strategic demand, an integrated mega-market in the second half of the nineteenth century that was to facilitate the unfolding of the American technological strategy—*an unfolding*

*that made it possible to achieve world dominance in the twentieth century.* As no system of canals and roads could have linked the east and the west across the Rocky Mountains into an integrated mega-market, the American technological strategy would have stalled in the absence of the railroad. In all probability this would have guaranteed the division of the continent into a number of nation-states rather than a single mega-state. These are the real benefits—dynamic benefits—of the railroad system.

With the creation of this megastate and megamarket, the United States was set on a path of massive economic development that was to lead it to a true hegemonic position by the end of the Second World War (but that was to last only until about 1967). The United States became a kind of "world policeman" during this period, which Daniel Chirot (1986) calls the "Pax Americana" ("American peace"). It also became the world's greatest dispenser of foreign aid. Between 1945 and 1966, nearly two-thirds of its foreign aid went to western European countries (mostly to Britain, France, and West Germany) to help them rebuild their economies, which soon became a major source of U.S. investment. Aid to the Third World was given for both **geopolitical** and economic reasons—to South Korea and Taiwan, for example, to help prevent the spread of Communism, and to Latin America to help maintain a favorable climate for American capitalist investment (Chirot, 1986).

By 1967 or perhaps slightly later, the United States had lost its hegemonic position, although it still remained, and remains today, the world's number one economy. Bergesen, Fernandez, and Sahoo (1987) present data showing very graphically the loss of hegemony. Looking at the world's largest 50 capitalist firms, they show that in 1956, 42 of these were located in the United States, but by 1980, only 23 were located there, and by 1998, the number had declined further to 16 (Bergesen and Sonnett, 2001). The U.S. loss was to the benefit of Europe and Japan. Europe went from 8 of the top 50 firms in 1956 to 20 in 1980 and 21 in 1998, and Japan went from none in 1956 to 6 in 1980 and 11 in 1998. Similarly, in 1956, the U.S. firms that were in the world's top 50 produced in 13 different industries, but by 1980, they were producing in only 7. The number of European top 50 firms produced in about 7 industries in both 1956 and 1980; since Japan had no top 50 firms in 1956, it obviously produced in no industries, but its top 50 firms were producing in 3 different industries in 1980. Between 1980 and 1998, things remained essentially the same in terms of the number of industries in which American, European, and Japanese top 50 firms were producing (Bergesen and Sonnett, 2001).

In a more recent study, Bergesen and Sonnett (2001) show that the loss of U.S. hegemony has been associated with the emergence of an essentially tripolar world-economy. In this study they examine *Fortune* magazine's top 500 firms—the global 500. During the period between 1994 and 1998, Europe was the headquarters for 34 percent of the global 500, the United States for 33 percent, and Asia (largely Japan) for 29 percent.

Why do hegemons always decline? A general theory of hegemonic decline can be stated approximately as follows (Hopkins and Wallerstein, 1982; Wallerstein, 1984; Mann, 1988; Goldfrank, 1983; Szymanski, 1981):

1. A hegemon favors a *free trade policy*, or an open world-economy. It wants unfettered trade because that way it can sell its goods throughout the world at maximum profit. However, this policy provides opportunities to a hegemon's competitors, which can quickly learn the secrets of the hegemon's success and imitate it.

2. Other economic powers—core powers primarily—can *gang up* on the hegemon and try to weaken it, either economically or militarily (or both).

3. There will inevitably arise *internal obstacles* to the maintenance of a hegemonic position. The secrets of the hegemon's success at its particular period of dominance in the world-economy eventually lose their effectiveness as conditions throughout the world change. What works at one time under one set of conditions will not work, or at least not work as well, at other times and under other conditions, and so on. One of these internal obstacles is *declining productive efficiency*. Industrial plants, for example, age and have to be replaced by new ones. Another internal obstacle involves *organizational structure*. Organizational forms that work at one time eventually lose their effectiveness and must give way to new forms.

4. The *high standard of living* created by a hegemon itself leads to inefficiencies for that hegemon. Wage costs, for example, may rise so high that they reduce competitiveness and lead to the export of jobs to other countries, especially Third World countries.

Michael Mann (1988) has applied these general principles to the case of British hegemonic decline. First, Britain's main rivals were Germany and the United States. They raised tariffs and emphasized protection for their goods, and thus Britain's free trade policy was weakened over time. Second, Britain was exhausted through two world wars. Finally, and perhaps most significantly, British hegemony depended on a global militarism and an unusually strong commitment to financial or commercial capitalism. Its commitment to militarism—Britain even today devotes more of its GNP to military spending than any other industrial capitalist society except the United States—was very economically costly, and its commitment to finance capitalism—using money to make money through banking, the stock market, and so on, rather than producing goods—led it to neglect industry (relatively speaking) and to fail to protect its domestic industry from foreign competition. It may seem odd that Britain was so committed to finance capitalism, given that it was the center of the Industrial Revolution, but it was in fact so. Even today, British wealth and investment is concentrated in the City of London (the name given to British financial and commercial capitalism)—government stocks, foreign exchange and money markets, the financing of trade, and banking. As Mann points out, the historical dominance of these forms of investment has left little capital for investment in British industry. He summarizes the situation thusly (1988:229):

> When German and American competition hit hard, from the 1880s, the response came from an essentially commercial political economy. Industry hit back through

its own resources, largely unaided by government. Mergers, at first cooperative, then often contested, attempted to find investment funds through concentration. Though British firms became proportionately the biggest in the world, this was not a very efficient route to greater productivity, as we saw. But industry's efforts were further harmed by government economic policy, dominated by commercial reasoning and actually implemented by the City/Treasury/Bank of England nexus. Industry has been left unprotected from either foreign competition or the vagaries of international currency movements. . . . Commerce prospers while industry decays.

The loss of hegemony by the United States has not been nearly as precipitous as the British decline. It has been slower and more gradual, and any further economic decline is also likely to be gradual. Some 40 years after its loss of hegemony, the United States is in much better shape than Britain was 40 years after its loss.

What were some of the factors that led to the loss of U.S. hegemony? One was aging technological infrastructure. Industrial plants got older and had to be replaced, and this was very costly. The United States was a world leader in steel production, for example, and by the 1970s the steel mills in Pittsburgh and elsewhere had become decrepit. Japan and Brazil were able to construct new mills and thus pick up the U.S. slack in steel production. Much the same can be said for automobile production. Also, the U.S. standard of living was extremely high, with wages very high. Wage costs rose to such a high level that they reduced U.S. competitiveness in the world market, which led to massive deindustrialization, especially in the old highly industrialized Northeast, where unions were strongest and wages highest (Bluestone and Harrison, 1982).

Cities such as Pittsburgh, Buffalo, Cleveland, and Baltimore saw thousands of their jobs exported to the Sun Belt in North Carolina and Texas, where unions were fewer in number and wages were lower; but even more of these jobs were exported to the much more low-wage Third World (Fröbel, Heinrichs, and Kreye, 1980). The case of Pittsburgh is very instructive. Highly specialized for steel production and other forms of heavy industry, Pittsburgh began losing jobs in the 1960s and the pace picked up in the 1970s and 1980s. Its population was nearly 700,000 in 1960, but by 2000, the population had declined to only about 320,000—less than half of what it was. Pittsburgh is still a major center for corporate capital, but many of the jobs have gone elsewhere. The United States has also suffered a decline in organizational efficiency. Its leading competitors, Germany and Japan, had shifted to new organizational forms that integrate large companies with state planning and banking agencies, but the United States resisted adopting these forms (Goldfrank, 1983).

In the 1980s and early 1990s, there was a great deal of speculation about whether Japan would become the next hegemon in the world-economy. In the United States, there developed a disdain for, and fear of, Japanese economic power, and "Japan bashing" abounded. However, with the onset of economic difficulties in Japan in the 1990s these fears seem to have abated and there is now little discussion of the Japanese threat. Can Japan achieve hegemonic status? Probably not. The U.S. share of world industrial production was still as high as 28 percent in 1984, over 15 years after its fall from grace, but in the same year Japan's share of world production was only 8 percent (Abu-Lughod, 1991). Japan's share of world industrial production increased to 21 percent by 1995 (World Bank, 1997), but then slipped to 14 percent in 2000 (World Bank, 2003). During their peak hegemonic years, Britain and the United States were producing on the order of 50 percent of the world's goods. Japan is obviously a far cry from this. Moreover, a hegemon requires a powerful military, and this Japan does not have. Although Japan should remain one of the world's leading economic powers for decades to come, it has little chance of becoming hegemonic; its neighbor, China, being a much larger society with a very powerful military, has a much better chance within the next half-century, its highly inferior economic position at the present time notwithstanding.

In his brilliant book *The Long Twentieth Century* (1994), Giovanni Arrighi has added a very interesting twist to the notion of hegemonic cycles of rise and fall. He argues that intertwined with the emergence of hegemons is a long economic cycle that he calls a **systemic cycle of accumulation** (SCA). The basic idea is this: Hegemons are initially associated with economic dominance in the areas of production and commerce, but over time these economic arenas become less and less profitable. The hegemon thus turns toward emphasizing the *financial* dimension of capitalism as a way of earning greater profits. Arrighi identifies four SCAs throughout the history of modern capitalism (note that each SCA lasts a shorter period of time than its predecessor):

1. SCA-1: *Genoa*—1450–1630 (180 years)
   Production/commerce phase—1450–1560 (110 years)
   Finance phase—1560–1630 (70 years)

2. SCA-2: *Holland*—1630–1785 (155 years)
   Production/commerce phase—1630–1740 (110 years)
   Finance phase—1740–1785 (45 years)

3. SCA-3: *Britain*—1785–1930 (145 years)
   Production/commerce phase—1785–1865 (80 years)
   Finance phase— 1865–1930 (65 years)

4. SCA-4: *United States*—1930–present (75 years so far)
   Production/commerce phase—1930–1970 (40 years)
   Finance phase—1970–present (35 years so far)

This formulation differs from Wallerstein's concept of hegemony in certain ways, but it is not altogether incompatible with it. The interesting thing about Arrighi's formulation is that it seems to apply so well to the contemporary United States. There has been much hand wringing since the early 1980s about how the United States has been concentrating on using money to make money without producing enough real goods. Many scholars and laypersons have been critical of this strategy, but what Arrighi shows is that this is the normal pattern for hegemons: Once production and commerce reach certain limits, the turn to finance capitalism seems inevitable. Of course, the turn to finance also signals a hegemonic decline and the eventual transition to a new hegemon.

## FOR FURTHER READING

Volume 3 of Wallerstein's *The Modern World-System* (1989) continues his discussion of the evolution of the capitalist world-economy through the early phases of industrialization. Daniel Chirot's *Social Change in the Modern Era* (1986) is a very good treatment of many of the social, economic, and political changes in capitalism since the early nineteenth century, and especially since 1900. Beaud (1983) contains some very informative material on the emergence and development of industrial capitalism. See also Davis and Scase (1985). Eric Hobsbawm's *Industry and Empire* (1968) is an older but still valuable work on the Industrial Revolution in England and the development of the English economy since that time. A very good recent work on the Industrial Revolution is Stearns (1993). Yoshihara (1986) discusses the development of industrial capitalism in Japan, and Hane (1992) is a very good source on modern Japan.

See Wallerstein (1984) on the three instances of hegemony in the history of the world-economy. Israel (1989) is an especially good source on Holland; see also Schama (1997). On the reasons for hegemonic decline, see Hopkins and Wallerstein (1982), Wallerstein (1984), Mann (1988), Goldfrank (1983), and Szymanski (1981). Mann (1988) is especially informative on the reasons for Britain's decline, as are Frank (1979) and Snooks (1997) on the reasons for the rise of the United States in the eighteenth and nineteenth centuries. Bergesen, Fernandez, and Sahoo (1987) nicely document the loss of the hegemonic position of the United States, and a recent article by Bergesen and Sonnett (2001) provides an update. Abu-Lughod (1991) has some interesting comments on why Japan will not likely gain a hegemonic position. Bluestone and Harrison (1982) analyze U.S. deindustrialization up close through a discussion of plant closings and the abandonment of entire communities. Fröbel, Heinrichs, and Kreye (1980) argue for the emergence of a "new international division of labor" in the 1960s and 1970s, which involved the shift of capital from the core to the semiperiphery and periphery and the creation of "free production zones," or special zones of a Third World country where wages are very low, working conditions poor, and the rights of workers virtually nonexistent. They are able to show how hegemonic decline, deindustrialization, and "reindustrialization" in less-developed countries are part of the same package.

Giovanni Arrighi's *The Long Twentieth Century* (1994) is a demanding but extremely important book on the history of hegemonic rise and fall and shifting capitalist economic strategies. It is a must for serious students of this subject. A related work is Arrighi and Beverly Silver's *Chaos and Governance in the Modern World System* (1999). This book focuses especially on the loss of U.S. hegemony and the shift of the center of the world-economy from North America to East Asia.

In addition to talking about cycles of hegemonic rise and fall, Wallerstein and his colleagues and followers have identified another type of cyclical dynamic in the world-system. This is the *Kondratieff wave*, or *K-wave*, which is based on the work of the Russian economist Nikolai Kondratieff (1984; orig. 1928). Kondratieff was imprisoned by the Soviets for this idea, which was considered "un-Marxist." A K-wave is an economic cycle lasting about 40 to 60 years. It consists of a period of economic boom lasting about 20 to 30 years, which is then followed by a downturn lasting another 20 to 30 years. Kondratieff himself, as well as the great economist Joseph Schumpeter (1947), thought that K-waves extended back to about

1800, but the contemporary political scientist Joshua Goldstein (1988) claims to have detected them all the way back to 1495. Goldstein identifies 10 K-waves up to the present time. According to this thinking, the world entered a downturn around 1970, which we are still in, although we should be pulling out of it very soon. Whether K-waves are truly genuine is much debated.

Political scientists tend to argue that Wallerstein's model of the world-system is too economic, and they suggest a more political model. In this regard, see Rasler and Thompson (1994) and Modelski and Thompson (1996).

# CHAPTER

# 7

# Industrial Capitalist Societies

This chapter continues the discussion of capitalism by looking at modern industrial capitalist societies. In particular, it explores several evolutionary transformations closely associated with the rise and expansion of industrial capitalism: the emergence of industrial stratification systems and welfare states, the rise of parliamentary democratic forms of government, the emergence of mass education, and the reduction in the size of families. The chapter concludes by asking whether industrial capitalist societies have made a transition to so-called postindustrial societies.

## Stratification in Industrial Capitalist Societies

As discussed in an earlier chapter, the movement of societies from the hunter-gatherer to the agrarian stage is closely associated with the development of increasingly complex and extreme forms of stratification. However, as Gerhard Lenski (1966) shows, with the passage from agrarian to industrial societies, a reversal of this trend seems to have occurred. In industrial societies the dominant economic class claims a smaller share of national income and wealth, and there has been a diffusion of income throughout the population to an extent unimaginable to the average members of agrarian societies.

Nonetheless, the inequalities of contemporary industrial societies are significant enough to permit analysis on their own terms, not just in terms of a broad comparison with the past (Rossides, 1976). What are these inequalities like?

### Income Inequalities

Data collected under the auspices of the U.S. government (U.S. Bureau of the Census, 1984) show that, for 1982, the highest-paid 5 percent of Americans received 16.0 percent of the total national income. When the data are divided into income quintiles (fifths) of the population, they show the following: The top income quintile received 42.7 percent of the total national income, the next quintile 24.3 percent, the middle quintile 17.1 percent, the next-to-lowest quintile 11.2 percent, and the bottom quintile a mere 4.7 percent of the total. Between this time and 1995, income inequality increased modestly (Kingston, 2000). The top 5 percent of the income distribution increased its share of income to 20 percent. In terms of income quintiles, the top quintile took 46.5 percent of the total income, the second quintile 23.2 percent, the third quintile 15.8 percent, the fourth quintile 10.1 percent, and the bottom quintile 4.4 percent.

The simplest way of measuring income inequality is through use of the Gini coefficient. This is a number varying from 0 to 1.0, with 0 indicating that everyone has exactly the same income and 1.0 indicating that one household has all of the income. Different Gini coefficients are reported for the United States for recent decades, but these usually average in the range of .40 to .45, indicating that income inequality is moderate to high. The United States has the greatest degree of income inequality for all advanced capitalist societies. Some other reported Gini coefficients (for the year 1999) are .368 for the United Kingdom, .352 for Australia, .327 for France, .300 for Germany, .273 for Italy, .250 for Sweden, .249 for Japan, and .247 for Denmark (World Bank, 2003).

These data, however, do not fully reveal the actual extent of income disparities. A more adequate picture of overall income distribution is obtained when income deciles (tenths), rather than quintiles, are used in the analysis. Gabriel Kolko (1962) has calculated the distribution of income in the United States from 1910 to 1959 using income deciles. The data he presents reveal a highly unequal distribution of income that did not change in any major way during this entire period. For example, in 1910 the top income decile received 33.9 percent of the total income, while the bottom decile received only 3.4 percent of the total. By 1959 the income share going to the top tenth had declined slightly, to 28.9 percent, but so had the share going to the bottom tenth, to 1.1 percent. The bottom 50 percent of the population received only 27 percent of the national personal income in 1910, and by 1959 the share of this poorer half had even declined slightly, to 23 percent. Thus, for both 1910 and 1959 the top 10 percent of the population received a greater total income than the bottom 50 percent. Throughout the entire period the only income groups to experience significant increases in income shares were the second- and third-richest income deciles, which experienced modest increases. As hardly needs saying, these groups were not among those in serious need of a greater share of the national income (Kolko, 1962). Some 40 years after Kolko did his research, we find that the income distribution has not changed all that much. In 1999 the top income decile received 30.5 percent of the total income, whereas the bottom decile received 1.8 percent (World Bank, 2003).

These data support two major conclusions: There are vast inequalities in the distribution of income in the United States, and this pattern of unequal distribution showed no significant trend toward greater equalization throughout the twentieth century. In fact, during the 1990s, income inequality actually increased somewhat. Although there have been major increases in the standard of living for a large part of the American population during the twentieth century, such increases should not be confused, as they often are, with any trend toward income equalization.

It is likely, however, that even these figures understate the real extent of income inequality in U.S. society, for there are forms of income that go unreflected in the figures. Many persons receive considerable amounts of *income in kind* rather than in direct cash payments, and such income is quite disproportionately concentrated among the already wealthy. Income in kind is especially prominent among the top income tenth, and especially among the top 5 percent (Kolko, 1962). It takes the form of expense accounts and many other types of executive benefits, and such benefits have long been an acknowledged form of the remuneration of many corporate executives (Kolko, 1962). Large-scale and often unlimited expense accounts have for many years been commonly extended to persons employed in or near the upper reaches of the corporate world. The top corporate elite also commonly receive such material benefits as a company car, a gas credit card, country club memberships, and even such luxuries as the use of yachts and private planes and company-paid jaunts to private retreats and exotic watering places (Kolko, 1962). Although all these benefits do not count as forms of reportable personal income, they constitute just as real forms of material privilege nonetheless.

The existing income distribution figures also fail to reflect income that goes unreported and dividend income from stock ownership that remains undisbursed to stock owners. Kolko believes that this unreported income, mainly in the form of dividends, interest, and so on, is largely confined to persons in the upper-income brackets. Not reporting such income is, of course, illegal, but it is apparently a widespread practice nevertheless. Were such income to be included in the income distribution figures, the pattern of income inequality would be even more extreme than it already is. In addition to such practices, there are legal ways in which actual income can go unreported. As Kolko notes, corporations often vote to retain dividend earnings on stock so that their wealthy, stock-owning directors will not be personally liable to pay taxes on the dividend income. The upshot of this practice is that "the corporations represent vast income reserves for the economic elite" (Kolko, 1962:23).

It is widely believed that taxation, through the allegedly "progressive" income tax, has served to reduce income inequalities and bring about a redistribution of income from wealthier to poorer individuals. This belief, however, is largely unjustified. Available studies show that taxation produces no notable equalization of income (Rossides, 1976). Actual rates of taxation of the U.S. public indicate a huge gap between theory and practice in the tax structure. Although the federal income tax is, in principle, progressive, the rich have built so many loopholes and safeguards into the tax laws that they are able to avoid any major redistribution of their huge incomes. Indeed, the rich have become so skilled at tax avoidance that they have placed the actual burden of taxation onto the shoulders of low- and middle-income groups (Kolko, 1962).

Britain displays similar inequalities in the distribution of income and wealth. Estimates show that in 1979 the top income tenth in the United Kingdom commanded 26.1 percent of the total income, while the bottom 30 percent received only 10.4 percent (Atkinson, 1983:63). This pattern changed little since 1954, when the top income tenth received 30.1 percent of the income and the bottom 30 percent received 10.3 percent (Atkinson, 1983:63). These are pretax figures, but calculations show that, for the United Kingdom just as for the United States, taxation has affected the income distribution only slightly (Atkinson, 1983:63). More recent data for Britain, available only for income quintiles, show that in 1991 the top quintile received 41 percent of the total income, the second quintile 23 percent, the third quintile 16 percent, the fourth quintile 12 percent, and the bottom quintile 8 percent (Deininger and Squire, 1996).

Yet, caution is called for in the interpretation of all these data. Despite the vast income inequalities in the United States and other advanced capitalist societies, the extent of social mobility (discussed later) in all of these countries shows that the richest and the poorest individuals are in many cases not the same people from one time period to another. Paul Kingston (2000:84) shows that in the short space of the seven years between 1971 and 1978 there was a striking movement of people between income quintiles: "More than half . . . of the top quintile in 1971 fell from this level by 1978, and more than a fifth had moved to the lower three quintiles. . . . Indeed, across the entire range of income levels, mobility was a common occurrence. Overall 60 percent moved to a different income quintile, and almost a quarter moved at least two quintiles." Thus, although the gap between the rich and the poor is vast, not all of the rich remain rich nor do all of the poor remain poor. Many of those in the bottom quintiles improve their income situation over time, and many of those in the top quintiles suffer appreciable income declines. This takes some of the edge off income inequality under modern capitalism.

## Wealth Inequalities

The distribution of total wealth (total assets minus liabilities) in the United States reveals much greater extremes than the distribution of income. Indeed, wealth is enormously concentrated at the top. Data collected by the federal government (Office of Management and the Budget, 1973) show the following pattern of distribution for 1962: The wealthiest quintile of the population owned 76 percent of the total wealth, the next quintile 15.5 percent, the middle quintile 6.2 percent, the next-to-poorest quintile only 2.1 percent, and the poorest fifth a minuscule 0.2 percent. Such figures reveal an enormous concentration of property, demonstrating that the wealthiest 20 percent of the population possesses more than three times the total wealth held by the remaining 80 percent.

Additional data on the concentration of wealth show essentially the same pattern. In 1972, the top 1 percent of the population held 56.5 percent of the total corporate stock, 60 percent of all bonds, and 89.9 percent of all trusts (U.S. Bureau of the Census, 1982). Closer scrutiny reveals that most of these assets are actually concentrated within the top 0.5 percent of the population. For the same year, the top 0.5 percent owned 49.3 percent of the corporate stock, 52.2 percent of the bonds, and 80.8 percent of the trusts (U.S. Bureau of the Census, 1982). It is true that in recent years there has been a large increase in the number of Americans who are stockowners, but stock ownership is still extremely unequal. In 1989, 46 percent of stock was owned by the "super rich," another 43 percent by the "rich," and the remainder of the population owned only about 11 percent of total stock (Wolff, 1995).

The most recent extensive research on wealth inequality in the United States has been carried out by Lisa Keister (2000a, 2004; Keister and Moller, 2000). Her research shows that the top wealth quintile owned nearly 85 percent of total wealth as of the early 1990s. However, this ownership was heavily concentrated within the upper segment of the top quintile, as the top 1 percent of wealth owners possessed almost 40 percent of total wealth and almost 50 percent of financial assets. In 1989, the Gini coefficient for wealth inequality was an extremely large .89, and in the late 1990s, the Gini coefficient for financial wealth was a huge .94 (Keister and Moller, 2000; Keister, 2004).

Keister's research also focuses on changes in wealth inequality between 1962 and the 1990s. There is a clear trend toward greater inequality in wealth. In 1962, the top 1 percent of wealth owners possessed 33.5 percent of the total wealth, but that had increased to 38.5 percent by 1995. The percentage of the U.S. population owning no wealth increased from 11 to 19 percent during the same period, and the Gini coefficient increased from .80 to .87. For a long period, the United States had less wealth inequality than several European countries, but during the 1990s, the United States gained the dubious distinction of being number one in wealth inequality.

Who are the wealthy and what do they own? In 1962, the average wealth of the top 1 percent of the wealth distribution was $3.2 million, and this had more than doubled in constant (inflation-adjusted) dollars, to $6.7 million, by 1995. This compares to a total wealth of only about $31,000 for the average household in 1962, a figure that had risen to $41,000 in constant dollars by 1995. In 1995, the extremely wealthy held about two-thirds of their wealth in business assets and stocks and bonds, whereas the largest item of wealth for the average household is their primary residence (amounting to about 30 percent of their wealth in 1995) (Keister, 2000a).

Keister argues that the stratified nature of U.S. society becomes more evident when wealth inequality is added to income inequality. Somewhat surprisingly, wealth inequality and income inequality are rather weakly correlated. Keister believes that wealth inequality is a truer measure of the real extent of economic inequality. As she puts it (2000a:9):

> When wealth (rather than income) is used as an indicator of family economic well-being, a different picture of advantage and disadvantage emerges; this suggests that our understanding of social inequality and social mobility has been limited by our nearly total focus on income. Moreover, because of the financial security and other advantages associated with wealth ownership, the control of wealth has been an important determinant of well-being throughout history, and the truly advantaged are still signaled by high net worth.

Keister goes on to remark that income is really a measure of short-term economic security, whereas wealth involves more permanent and long-run security. Since income and wealth inequality are weakly correlated, and since wealth inequality is substantially greater than income inequality, Keister argues that the United States is actually a more unequal society than it is usually considered to be, even by sociologists. Keister also presents evidence showing that wealth mobility is much more limited than mobility from one occupational and income group to another; this suggests to her not only a highly unequal society but also a very rigidly stratified one.

Regarding the distribution of wealth in Britain, Westergaard and Resler (1975) show that, in 1954, the richest 5 percent of the population owned 48 percent of all cash and bank deposits, 71 percent of all government and municipal securities, and 96 percent of corporate stock. More recent data for all wealth categories show that the richest 5 percent possessed 45 percent of the wealth in 1979 (Atkinson, 1983:161). Although the distribution of wealth is somewhat less unequal now than it once was (Atkinson, 1983:168), the concentration of wealth is still enormous. Britain remains, like the United States and all modern capitalist societies, a society permeated by deep economic inequalities (Westergaard and Resler, 1975). Unfortunately, we have yet to see research on wealth inequality in Britain that is comparable to Keister's research on the United States. However, if Keister is right about the greater importance of wealth inequality relative to income inequality in the United States, the same should be true of Britain and other advanced capitalist societies.

## The Class Structure of Industrial Capitalist Societies

There is no single way of conceptualizing the class structure of industrial capitalist societies. Daniel Rossides's (1990) analysis of the class structure of contemporary U.S. society is probably as good as any. Rossides identifies five major social classes in the contemporary United States: the upper class, the upper-middle class, the lower-middle class, the working class, and the lower class.

The upper class, no more than 1 or 2 percent of the population, consists of those families possessing great wealth and power, much of which is derived from inheritance. The members of this class occupy the key positions in corporations, banks, insurance companies, and so on. They enjoy very high prestige and are often strongly oriented toward the consumption of elite symbolic culture (e.g., fine art and music). In short, this class is an extraordinarily privileged, powerful, and prestigious segment of the nation's social structure. In Marxian language, this is the capitalist class.

The upper-middle class is composed primarily of successful business managers, members of the learned professions (e.g., law, medicine, architecture), and well-placed civil and military officials. Totalling approximately 10 percent of the population, its members generally earn high incomes and accumulate substantial wealth through savings and investment, and they typically enjoy high social prestige. The lower-middle class, consisting of approximately 30 percent of the population, mainly includes small businessmen, lower-level professionals (e.g., public school teachers, social workers, nurses), and sales and clerical workers. Most persons in this class receive moderate incomes and have but small amounts of savings and other personal wealth. Only fairly modest levels of prestige are accorded the members of this class.

The working class in U.S. society comprises roughly 40 percent of the population. The members of this class are employed as skilled, semiskilled, or unskilled manual and service workers. The class as a whole is subject to fairly high rates of unemployment, and its members frequently suffer under the burdens of no savings or investments and low social prestige. The incomes received by persons in this class are relatively low, on average, when compared to the incomes received by members of higher classes. The lower class, roughly 15 percent of the U.S. population, consists of those persons who may be regarded as living under conditions of poverty. Included in this class are "the chronically unemployed, underemployed, and underpaid, abandoned mothers, and the poor who are sick, disabled, or old" (Rossides, 1976:28). The members of this class suffer from greater or lesser degrees of acute economic distress, and have extremely low social prestige.

In Rossides's conceptualization, it is *occupation* that is the centerpoint for the identification of a person's class position, and most other class schemes developed by sociologists have also used occupation as the basis for the identification of classes (cf. Giddens, 1973; Goldthorpe, 1980; Gilbert and Kahl, 1993; Kingston, 2000). However, sociologist Erik Olin Wright (1985) has tried to map the class structure from a Marxian perspective. He uses three criteria for identifying a social class: *ownership or nonownership* of the means of production, possession of *credential assets*, and possession of *organizational assets*. This yields the following classes:

### *Owning Classes*
- Capitalists (owners of the means of production who employ 10 or more workers and who earn their incomes through the exploitation of workers)
- Small employers (owners who earn their incomes through the exploitation of workers but who employ fewer than 10 workers)
- Petty bourgeoisie (owners of small businesses who employ no workers)

### *Nonowning Classes*
- Expert managers (nonowners who have high educational credentials and high organizational authority)
- Expert supervisors (nonowners who have high educational credentials and moderate organizational authority)
- Expert nonmanagers (nonowners who have high educational credentials and no organizational authority)
- Semicredentialed managers (nonowners who have moderate educational credentials and high organizational authority)
- Semicredentialed supervisors (nonowners who have moderate educational credentials and moderate organizational authority)
- Semicredentialed workers (nonowners who have moderate educational credentials and no organizational authority)
- Uncredentialed managers (nonowners who have low educational credentials and high organizational authority)
- Uncredentialed supervisors (nonowners who have low educational credentials and moderate organizational authority)
- Proletarians (nonowning workers who possess no credential or authority assets)

Wright's scheme is a commendable effort to conceptualize class in terms of the possession of certain kinds of valuable resources, but it suffers from two serious flaws. One is that, in identifying 12 classes, it is somewhat unwieldly. Some of the classes are very small, comprising only about 2 or 3 percent of the population. The

*Wealthy capitalist Vincent Astor on board the* S.S. Mauretania, *1922.*

other problem, potentially more serious, is that Wright insists on seeing class as resting on some type of *exploitative* relationship. Classes are viewed as either exploiting other classes, as being exploited by other classes, or as being both exploited and an exploiter. There is a certain logic to this, at least in a technical Marxian sense, when one is dealing with capitalists, small employers, and proletarians, but it makes little sense to think of credentialed managers and supervisors as exploiting those classes that have fewer credential or organizational assets. Such groups are merely capitalizing on valuable resources to advance their own situation and are not intent on disadvantaging (and do not need to disadvantage) other groups in order to do so.

## Social Mobility within Modern Capitalism

A belief widespread among the members of modern capitalist societies is that one's class position need not be fixed at birth. It is thought that all individuals have good opportunities for moving up to a higher class—that is, for upward **social mobility.**

This idea has taken a particularly strong hold in the United States, where it tends to dominate thinking about the nature of stratification. Most Americans believe that the country's class system is highly "open," permitting a high degree of upward movement for persons who have the necessary motivation to get ahead. To what extent is this belief in the opportunity structure of modern capitalism justified?

When sociologists study mobility they distinguish between *intergenerational* and *intragenerational mobility*. **Intergenerational mobility** is movement up or down relative to the class position one was born into—that is, the class position of one's parents. If a woman is a lawyer and her father was a salesperson or ran his own business, then she has been intergenerationally upwardly mobile. But if a man's father was a salesperson and he himself is a semiskilled worker, then he has been downwardly intergenerationally mobile. **Intragenerational mobility** means movement from one's first job to the job one holds, say, in mid-career. Thus, if a man's first job was as a clerk in a company's mailroom but 20 years later he has become a leading manager in the same company, then he has been upwardly mobile in an intragenerational sense. Most studies of mobility are of intergenerational mobility.

Paul Kingston (2000) has summarized the results of a number of major studies of mobility in the United States, especially those of Blau and Duncan (1967), Featherman and Hauser (1978), and Erikson and Goldthorpe (1993). He shows that mobility is a pervasive feature of U.S. society. For example, in looking at the composition of the upper-middle class in 1973, Kingston shows that only 29 percent of its members were themselves upper-middle class in origin. The remaining 71 percent of the members of this class came from the lower-middle class (17 percent), the working class (42 percent), or the farming population (12 percent). Similarly, only 16 percent of the lower-middle class had themselves been born into that class. Fifteen percent came from the upper-middle class, 52 percent from the working class, and 18 percent from the farming population.

These findings concern what are called **mobility inflows**—the extent to which a social class is composed of people whose origins were in other social classes. We also need to look at **mobility outflows**—the extent to which people born into one social class end up in another. In the United States in 1973, we find, for example, that 59 percent of individuals whose origins were upper-middle class remained in that class, whereas the remainder were downwardly mobile into other classes. Of the lower-middle class, only 17 percent remained there. Forty-five percent moved up into the upper-middle class, and 38 percent moved down into the working class or the farming population. Similar patterns are found for the working class: Most people who start out in it end up elsewhere, with fully 27 percent moving all the way into the upper-middle class. Kingston shows that, overall, more than two-thirds of individuals end up in a social class that they did not start out in, with 51 percent being upwardly mobile and 17 percent moving down. This indicates a very high level of mobility indeed, a good deal of it being over moderate to long distances. Moreover, similarly high rates of mobility are found if we use other class schemes, such as Wright's Marxian scheme.

It is sometimes argued that the United States is unusual in its high mobility rates, but an examination of other industrial capitalist societies shows that this is not true. Mobility rates are very similar across all of these societies. Total mobility out-flow rates range from a low of 62 percent in West Germany, to a high of 73 percent in Sweden, Japan, and the United States (Erikson and Goldthorpe, 1993; Kingston, 2000), with the average being 69 percent. Even less-industrialized Ireland and Northern Ireland, as well as state socialist Hungary and Poland, have comparable rates.

Why is there so much mobility in industrial capitalist societies? The answer has little to do with an ideology of opportunity, as is so emphasized by Americans, and mostly to do with changes in the occupational structure that are induced by constant technological advancement. Throughout the twentieth century all industrial capitalist societies have, for example, greatly expanded the number of white-collar jobs available. Many of these jobs could be filled only by recruiting persons from lower social classes—manual workers and farmers. As Paul Kingston (2000:63) argues,

> Technological change, not some democratically opening up of the system, was the prime instigator of social mobility.
> . . . Americans can't congratulate themselves on creating much opportunity beyond what was systematically demanded by economic transformation. Were it not for the unintended consequences of technological change, social mobility—the sine qua non of opportunity—would be much lower than the actual rates that we experienced.

Most studies of mobility, especially the best-known ones, have considered only men for the simple reason that most full-time workers were men when these studies were conducted. Now that women are much more prominently represented in the full-time occupational structure, studies of mobility among women are beginning to be conducted. These show that mobility among women is just as common as mobility among men. However, more complexity is now introduced into the study of mobility patterns because husbands and wives often perform different kinds of work and thus, in essence, belong to different social classes. This makes it more difficult to identify the class origins of the sons and daughters of such couples, and thus more difficult to identify the extent of their mobility or even whether or not they are mobile. It is hoped that in time this new problem will be ironed out.

# The Origins of Parliamentary Democracy

Where one finds highly developed capitalist societies, one finds **parliamentary democracy** as the dominant form of political life. In fact, there is no real exception to this generalization. But what is meant by the term *democratic?* In its literal sense, democracy means "government by and for the people." This meaning implies the absence of a ruling elite that makes governmental decisions independently of the wishes of the populace as a whole. But it would be a distortion to restrict the concept to this literal meaning, since it is doubtful that any such form of government exists anywhere in the world above the tribal level of society. Rather, borrowing from Rueschemeyer, Stephens, and Stephens (1992), democracy shall be conceived as a system of government having the following four characteristics:

1. The existence of a parliamentary or congressional body having a power base separate from that of presidents or prime ministers
2. The regular, free, and fair election of government officials to office by means of universal suffrage (i.e., the entire adult population maintains the right to vote)
3. Responsibility of the remaining segments of government to the parliament or congress
4. The granting of individual rights and freedoms to the mass of the population and the general honoring of these liberties

A distinction should be drawn between *formal* and *substantive democracy,* as well as between *restricted* and *unrestricted democracy* (Rueschemeyer, Stephens, and Stephens, 1992). A **formal democracy** is a government that has officially declared itself to be a democracy, but whose actions are in fact inconsistent with its declarations. Formal democracies are governments that lack genuine democratic behavior and that are democratic in name only. Elections are held, but they are neither fair nor free, and political rights may be acknowledged in principle but are largely ignored in practice. Throughout the Third World today are many countries that fall into this category. **Substantive democracies,** on the other hand, are genuine democracies—those that are democratic in both name and deed.

A **restricted democracy** is one in which the four principles just mentioned prevail, but in which there is some restriction or limitation placed on them. For example, individual rights and freedoms may be limited in various ways, or the right to vote may be restricted to certain segments of the population by such criteria as property ownership, sex, or race. All of today's societies with full substantive democracy—**unrestricted democracies**—began as restricted democracies, and most of these have

*Session of the United States Congress. All modern democratic societies have legislative bodies whose members are brought to office through free, popular elections.*

had unrestricted democracy for only a surprisingly short length of time (not until 1920 or even later). For example, in the United States voting rights were originally extended only to free, white, adult men who owned property, and it was many years before blacks and women gained voting privileges. And in the early days of suffrage in Britain, property owners and other men of privilege were allowed two votes instead of one.

In the formation of modern parliamentary democracies, the parliamentary aspect emerged first and suffrage followed considerably later. It was not until the middle of the nineteenth century that universal (male) suffrage began to be established in governments that were already parliamentary in nature, and true universal suffrage—suffrage for both men and women—did not emerge until after about 1920. The first four governments to grant full voting rights to at least the male segment of the population were Switzerland (1848), France (1877), Norway (1898), and Denmark (1915). These four were followed fairly rapidly by four more: Sweden, Belgium, the Netherlands, and Great Britain. The earliest democracies to develop outside western Europe emerged in the United States, Canada, Australia, and New Zealand. All of these societies were settler colonies that originally hived off from Great Britain. There were several other European countries that made the transition to democracy but that were able to maintain democratic institutions only for a brief period: Austria-Hungary, Spain, Italy, and Germany. All four have since regained democratic institutions, but it is clear that their paths to democracy were strewn with severe obstacles (Rueschemeyer, Stephens, and Stephens, 1992).

How does one explain the evolution of parliamentary democratic modes of government? It will not escape attention that democracy has evolved in the West, and especially in connection with the development of modern capitalism. Indeed, every core capitalist society in the world today is, without exception, characterized by a genuinely democratic political system. Such a striking correlation cannot possibly have occurred by accident, and a causal connection is undoubtedly present. But what kind of connection? There is a Marxian explanation, which goes something like this: The form of government is a result of the form of economy and the social class that dominates the economy. Capitalist societies are dominated by a bourgeoisie, and parliamentary democracy is the form of government best suited to advancing the economic interests of the bourgeoisie. This is because parliamentary democracy gives capitalists the maximum economic freedom to maneuver, both locally and globally, in their search for profits. It interferes minimally with what capitalists want to do. Monarchy suited feudalism and early capitalism, but with the advance of capitalism the restrictions of monarchy were too great, and so it had to be destroyed and replaced by the form of government that we see in capitalist societies today.

This line of argument has been advanced by such scholars as Barrington Moore (1966) and Albert Szymanski (1978). Moore argues that the English Civil War of the 1640s marked parliament's gaining the upper hand in government (over the king) because of the rise to dominance of capitalist farmers in England. Parliamentary democracy became dominant because parliament represented the economic interests of capitalists. Szymanski makes essentially the same argument, contending that as capitalists became the dominant economic class, they established parliamentary forms of government because "these forms are best suited to articulate the diverse interests within this class and work out a common class will" (1978:147). A crucial consideration for capitalists is that they have freedom of economic maneuver, and a parliamentary form of government is the one best designed to protect this freedom. As Szymanski (1978:150) puts it, "Businesses must have assurances from the state that it will not arbitrarily interfere with the system of contracts and expectations. The best guarantee of moderation and lack of arbitrariness on the part of the state is the parliamentary form."

The Marxian argument does seem to be correct for the parliamentary dimension of democracy, but it does not hold up for that dimension of democracy that many regard as the most important—universal suffrage. This has been shown in an excellent study by Dietrich Rueschemeyer, Evelyne Huber Stephens, and John D. Stephens, *Capitalist Development and Democracy* (1992). In a detailed comparative and historical analysis, these authors have shown that in most cases, capitalists have been hostile to the political inclusion of the masses, largely because they fear the power that workers might acquire through the vote. There are almost no instances, they claim, in which the bourgeoisie has favored the development of genuine democracy in Western capitalist societies. Then why is there such a striking association between capitalism and democracy? Rueschemeyer, Stephens, and Stephens's answer is that capitalism has created large working classes that have organized themselves and pressed hard for citizenship rights, especially the right to vote. The authors show that democracy developed earliest and most fully in those capitalist societies that were in the forefront of industrial capitalist development and thus had the largest and best-organized working classes.

Democracy was most greatly resisted, on the other hand, in those societies where industrial capitalist development was retarded. In these societies, industrialization was slower and as a result the working classes remained small and politically anemic. Moreover, such societies were ones in which the landlord class still held considerable economic and political power, and this class is virtually always extremely hostile to democracy. Landlords are engaged in the exploitation of peasants through their direct submission and political subordination—what Rueschemeyer, Stephens, and Stephens call **labor-repressive agriculture**—and as long as landlords remain important in the economy democracy can advance but little. The authors point to Austria-Hungary, Spain, Italy, and Germany as the four western European societies in which democracy emerged late and with great difficulty, and indeed all four societies are those in which landlords maintained considerable economic power well into the twentieth century. Of these four, Spain was the last to develop democratic institutions and it was a society whose landed upper class was slow to disappear.

Rueschemeyer, Stephens, and Stephens argue that the route to democracy in the British settler colonies was somewhat different. These were societies that inherited the political achievements of Great Britain, which gave them a favorable and early start. In addition, the enormous availability of cheap land allowed for the development of a large class of independent farmers. Except for the slavery in the U.S. South, there was no system of labor-repressive agriculture, and (again with the exception of the U.S. South) the landed upper class did not control the state. And eventually the working classes in these societies did become strong and press for political inclusion. All of these conditions were highly favorable to the development of full substantive democracy. The authors also look at the failure of much substantive democracy to develop in Latin America, arguing that the great economic power of the landed upper classes in this region has been a severe barrier to democracy.

The theory of Rueschemeyer, Stephens, and Stephens is a non-Marxian materialist interpretation that seeks the explanation for the emergence and growth of democracy in the development of capitalism, but it is not because of the economic interests of capitalists that democracy advances. It advances *in spite of* these economic interests, and because of one of the fundamental *contradictions* of capitalism: the creation of large working classes that are able to use their strength in numbers and organization to advance their own interests against the interests of capitalists. Rueschemeyer, Stephens, and Stephens's work is an enormous intellectual advance, a tremendous achievement in the understanding of the evolution of modern democracy.

However, these authors may have missed an important part of the story. In the most extensive research on democracy ever undertaken using quantitative data, Tatu Vanhanen (1997, 2003) has looked at democratization in a large number of nation-states between 1850 and the present. Vanhanen's most basic argument is that governments in complex societies will be authoritarian or autocratic when the large mass of the population lacks resources that they can use to force states to become more democratic and sensitive to their needs and aims. Vanhanen proposes six types of resources that are useful to populations in struggling for more democratic governments: large nonagricultural populations, large urban populations, ownership of farms by independent families, high rates of literacy, high rates of university enrollments, and the deconcentration of nonagricultural economic resources. The first five of these are fairly obvious, the last less so. When nonagricultural economic resources are deconcentrated, their ownership and control are spread throughout many segments of a population, not being monopolized by a powerful state or by a small handful of extremely wealthy individuals. In the state socialist societies of eastern Europe the state controlled economic resources, and in capitalist societies of the nineteenth century economic resources were much more concentrated than they are today.

Vanhanen combined all of these factors into a large superfactor that he calls the *Index of Power Resources* (IPR). He then correlated the IPR with levels of democratization in 172 countries in the early 1990s and found an extremely close relationship. Further analyses of Vanhanen's data (Sanderson, 2004) reveal that the IPR is closely related to levels of democratization throughout the entire period between 1850 and 2000. Vanhanen's conclusion is that states will become democratic when the population gains power resources and remain authoritarian when people lack these resources. He thinks of democracy as not simply an either/or situation. Societies can have a wide range of levels of democracy, ranging from zero (no political rights, no suffrage) to very high levels (extensive political rights, universal adult suffrage). The greater the extent of people's power resources, the higher the level of democratization is likely to be in their society.

Unfortunately, Vanhanen makes an unwarranted assumption, which is that each of the six power resources are of equal significance in promoting democracy. Skeptical of this assumption, one of us (Sanderson, 2004) used Vanhanen's data to examine the separate effects of each of these resources. It was found that the single most important power resource was the level of literacy. This was true throughout the period between 1850 to the present. The deconcentration of nonagricultural economic resources turned out to be the second most important factor for the period between 1980 and 2000. (It may well have been important in early periods too, but there were no data on it available for these earlier periods to test for this possibility.) The question is, Why should literacy be so important for democracy? The answer seems to be that literacy is vital in providing people with both political knowledge and the possibility of communication and organization for political ends. Rueschemeyer, Stephens, and Stephens stress the growth of the working class as the key to democracy, but it would appear that it takes more than just a large working class to bring about democratization. The more literate that working class is, and the more its members are able to communicate with each other on political issues of vital concern to themselves, the greater the chances that they can put pressure on their governments to expand political rights and suffrage. A final question would then be, What is the main cause of literacy? The answer is undoubtedly the development and expansion of mass primary education, which we discuss later in this chapter.

## Capitalism and the Welfare State

In the twentieth century, all modern industrial capitalist societies created large-scale welfare states that, to one extent or another, were designed to improve the situation of various groups in society, in particular the working class. But there is no single type of welfare state, there being considerable variation in its nature. Gøsta Esping-Andersen (1990) has identified three different welfare state clusters. First, there is what he calls the *liberal welfare state*. This type of welfare state is a "minimalist" system in that the government provides citizens with meager to modest income support and a limited amount of other assistance. The clientele consists largely of the lowest-income segments of the working class. Strong work-ethic norms prevail, and entitlement rules are very strict. The United Kingdom, the United States, Canada, and Australia are the best examples of this type of welfare system.

*Conservative welfare states* are found in such European countries as Austria, France, Germany, and Italy. Here, social benefits are provided to the large mass of the population, but these are highly status differentiated. There are numerous social insurance schemes, each with its own particular rules, finances, and benefit structure. For example, in Germany, "Bismarck's pension for workers was not to be blended with that for miners and certainly not with the social policy for civil servants or for white-collar employees" (Esping-Andersen, 1990:60). Social insurance normally excludes nonworking wives, and family benefits are designed so as to encourage motherhood. Child-care services are poorly developed.

The final type of welfare state, the *social democratic state,* provides the greatest number and degree of benefits. This "maximalist" welfare state stands at the opposite extreme from the liberal welfare state. The social democratic welfare state aims to provide a high level of social and economic equality for all citizens, with the working class enjoying the same benefits as the members of higher social classes. As Esping-Andersen notes, everyone benefits and everyone feels obligated to pay for the benefits that all receive. This type of welfare state is most characteristic of Sweden, Denmark, Norway, and to some extent the Netherlands.

Esping-Andersen argues that the most critical feature of a welfare state is the *degree to which it has decommodified work.* Capitalism is the essence of **commodified work.** Work is commodified when its function is to provide the labor that will produce profits for capitalists, and when little or no provision has been made for the well-being of the worker. Work is decommodified to the extent that the debilitating effects of its profit-inducing capacities are counterbalanced by concerns for the quality of life of the worker. This means that workers enjoy extensive benefits in regard to such things as medical insurance and sick days, maternity or parental leave, educational leave, unemployment insurance, and retirement (early or otherwise). As Esping-Andersen (1990:23) puts it, work is decommodified when "citizens can freely, and without potential loss of job, income, or general welfare, opt out of work when they themselves consider it necessary." These are benefits that are normally enjoyed by civil servants and other white-collar workers, but in the most advanced welfare states they are extended as well to the working class. Thus, the social democratic welfare states are the most decommodified, and the liberal welfare states are the least decommodified. As Esping-Andersen (1990:141) explains, the most decommodified type of welfare state

> has deliberately abandoned the minimalist philosophy, and espouses entirely new principles with regard to its proper role in the life-cycle, now often committing itself to optimize people's capacities to work, to find work, and even to count on a good job with good pay and working environment. The goal is to allow individuals to harmonize working life with familyhood, to square the dilemmas of having children and working, and to combine productive activity with meaningful and rewarding leisure. In some countries, at least, this philosophy has buttressed recent decades of social-policy development; indeed, it often underpins the legitimacy and common understanding of many contemporary welfare states.

Why have different types of welfare states developed in different countries in the Western world? Esping-Andersen has carried out statistical analyses to answer this question. His analyses show that conservative welfare states have been most common in societies with a long history of authoritarian or highly autocratic states and with a very large Catholic population. Liberal welfare states have been the outcome in societies in which the power of left-wing political parties, especially parties representing the working class, has been relatively weak. Social democratic regimes have emerged under opposite circumstances from liberal welfare regimes: where left-wing or workers' parties have been well organized and politically powerful (cf. Moller et al., 2003).

If Esping-Andersen's findings are correct, they nonetheless leave open the question as to why the working class has been well organized and powerful in some societies but not in others. In a more recent work, John Kautsky (2002) provides an answer to this question by way of an analysis of the rise and development of so-called socialist labor parties (*not* Communist parties). Paralleling Esping-Andersen's analysis, Kautsky shows that socialist labor parties have been strong in a number of western European countries, especially Germany, Austria, Switzerland, Belgium, the Netherlands, Sweden, Norway, and Denmark. Since the 1920s, such parties have often received between 40 and 50 percent of the vote (and occasionally more than 50 percent) in Austria, Sweden, Denmark, Norway, and the United Kingdom. By contrast, in the United States and Canada, socialist labor parties have been weak (extremely weak in the case of the United States), seldom garnering more than a tiny fraction of the votes in major elections.

Kautsky argues that socialist labor parties became strong in those societies in which the political influence and social values of the nobility or aristocracy remained strong well into the twentieth century. The aristocracy was a social class that looked down on the rest of society, even the capitalist class for a long time, and that favored a rigidly class-divided and status-conscious society in which it was ensconced at the top. Aristocrats took a particularly dim view of the growing working class and wanted to keep it at the bottom of society, with no rights, material rewards, or respect. In societies in which aristocratic power and values remained strong, workers reacted extremely negatively and were led to form socialist labor parties to advance their social and economic position. As Kautsky notes, they were, of course, fighting against their capitalist employers, but in societies that remained rigidly hierarchical their fight also had to be against aristocratic groups. This was especially true where the aristocracy allied itself with capitalists, as was often the case.

Kautsky presents considerable evidence that socialist labor or working-class parties were indeed strong in societies with substantial aristocratic remnants. On the other hand, the two Western societies with the weakest socialist labor parties, the United States and Canada, were ones in which there had never been an aristocracy and where a social atmosphere of egalitarianism was present almost from the beginning. As in Europe, workers were not well off economically, but they were treated with much greater respect and thus reacted with much less hostility under these more socially egalitarian conditions. Kautsky also shows that a substantial socialist-labor movement developed in Japan, a society with a much different cultural tradition from the West. Socialist labor parties in Japan received approximately a third of the vote in many of the elections between 1955 and 1990. Japanese society was, like many European societies, rigidly hierarchical, with strong aristocratic elements persisting into the second half of the twentieth century.

What have been the main achievements of welfare states, especially those of the social democratic variety? Have they met their major goals? Upon their emergence in the late nineteenth century, one of the aims of the social democratic welfare states in Scandinavia was to create a more equal income distribution throughout the population. Various studies have suggested that the Scandinavian countries have been relatively unsuccessful in this endeavor, for their income distributions, even after taxation, do not differ all that much from the distributions found in other industrial capitalist societies (Parkin, 1971; Stevenson, 1974, 1982). However, as Esping-Andersen points out, looking at income distributions alone provides too narrow a framework for evaluating the achievements of this most advanced type of welfare state. For one thing, it has done a great deal to eliminate poverty. The percentage of the aged living in poverty in the United Kingdom and the United States is, for example, 29 percent and 24 percent, respectively, whereas in Sweden it is a mere 1 percent.

In addition, criteria for measuring the quality of life involve more than just the level of paid income. One has to look at such additional resources as health, housing, education, and social and political effectiveness, not to mention the extent of workplace decommodification. Esping-Andersen notes that periodic national surveys have been conducted in Sweden and Denmark since 1968 concerning the welfare state's equalizing effects. These studies show that, despite worsening economic conditions throughout the Western world during this time, living conditions have improved and there is a trend toward greater equality in the possession of economic resources. Thus, "for Scandinavia at least, the welfare state is a mighty opponent to the economy's inegalitarian thrust" (Esping-Andersen, 1990:57). The accomplishments of the social democratic welfare state are therefore much greater than a simple inspection of income distributions would suggest.

In their early days, socialist labor parties were fairly radical. They not only wanted a relatively egalitarian income distribution but they also actually wanted to replace capitalism with socialism. Throughout the twentieth century these radical aims were greatly tempered and toned down, such that labor parties began increasingly compromising with governments and capitalists and conceding more and more. They have come to live with capitalism and only wish to restrain its potentially negative impact. Moreover, these parties have broadened their constituency. They were originally parties of only the working class, but, as Kautsky points out, they have gradually evolved from "worker's parties" into "people's parties." This is because the size of the working class stopped increasing during the twentieth century (and actually shrunk in a few instances). Socialist labor parties originally expected the working class to continue to grow until it became a sizable majority of society. But, as this failed to occur, they had to adjust their political approach by looking to attract other segments of the population, such as the lower-middle class, which was a growing class.

## The Rise and Expansion of Mass Education

Another major feature of industrial societies is their large systems of **mass education.** Modern systems of formal education arose mainly during the nineteenth century and became consolidated in the twentieth; formal education of long duration is now the normal experience of youth in all industrial societies. Table 7.1 gives some idea of the size of enrollments at different educational levels. It is clear that both primary and secondary education are universal throughout the industrialized world. Tertiary education, which includes not only colleges and universities but also business schools and other postsecondary technical schools, has also become a major part of the educational systems of industrial societies. Tertiary enrollments are now extensive in industrial societies.

How did mass education get started and how has it expanded over time? The first Western society to introduce compulsory primary education was Germany (Prussia), which did so in 1763. Germany was followed by Denmark (1814), Sweden (1842), Norway (1848), Italy (1859), Switzerland (1874), England and Wales (1880), France (1882), the Netherlands (1900), and Belgium (1914) (Flora, 1983; Johansen, Collins, and Johnson, 1986). In the United States, the first state to establish compulsory education was Massachusetts, which did so in 1852, and by 1900, 32 states had established compulsory education (Flora, 1983). Japan first began compulsory education in 1872 (Hane, 1992). By the end of the nineteenth century, compulsory primary education had become well established throughout the Western world and enrollments were high (Benavot and Riddle, 1988).

Secondary education existed in the ninteenth century but did not experience significant expansion in most Western societies until the middle third of the twentieth century (Flora, 1983). Even as late as 1950, secondary education in most Western societies was still very limited, with less than 20 percent of the age group from 10 to

**TABLE 7.1  Educational Enrollments for Selected Industrial Societies**

| Society | Primary Education | Secondary Education | Tertiary Education | No. of Tertiary Students per 100,000 Population |
|---|---|---|---|---|
| United Kingdom | 100 | 92 | 52 | 3,135 |
| Netherlands | 100 | 100 | 47 | 3,176 |
| Belgium | 100 | 100 | 56 | 3,494 |
| Italy | 100 | 95 | 47 | 3,103 |
| France | 100 | 99 | 51 | 3,600 |
| Germany | 100 | 95 | 47 | 2,628 |
| Denmark | 100 | 95 | 48* | 3,189 |
| Sweden | 100 | 100 | 45* | 2,972 |
| Canada | 100 | 95 | 88 | 5,997 |
| United States | 100 | 96 | 81 | 5,339 |
| Australia | 100 | 96 | 80 | 5,401 |
| Japan | 100 | 100 | 41 | 3,139 |
| Russia | 100 | 88 | 43 | 2,998 |
| Czech Republic | 100 | 100 | 24 | 1,867 |
| Hungary | 98 | 97 | 24 | 1,926 |
| Poland | 99 | 87 | 25 | 1,884 |

*Note:* The first three sets of figures are enrollment ratios and are for 1997. The enrollment ratio is the number of students, of whatever age, enrolled at a given educational level divided by the total population in the age bracket normally representing that level. The figures for the number of tertiary students per 100,000 population are for 1994 or 1995.

Tertiary education is defined as all postsecondary education; it includes all students in colleges, universities, and various types of technical schools.

*Projections based on 1993 tertiary enrollment ratios.

*Sources:* World Bank (2001); UNESCO (1996, 1998); National Center for Education Statistics (2001).

19 attending a secondary school (Flora, 1983). Tertiary education, as would be expected, developed even later than secondary education. Enrollment levels in tertiary institutions were low even as late as 1965, including more than 18 percent of the relevant age group only in Canada and the United States. It was not until the 1960s that tertiary education began to expand on a major scale on its way to becoming the major social force that it is today.

What accounts for the building of mass educational systems? One line of argument sees mass education as an essential ingredient of *nation building* (Meyer, Ramirez, Rubinson, and Boli-Bennett, 1977; Meyer, Tyack, Nagel, and Gordon, 1979; Boli, Ramirez, and Meyer, 1985). The proponents of this theory argue that a good theory of mass education must be able to explain the following features of modern mass educational systems:

- Mass educational systems are intended to be universal, standardized, and highly rationalized. They apply to everyone in the same fashion, cutting across the class, ethnic, racial, religious, and gender cleavages of a society.
- Mass educational systems are highly institutionalized at a world level. They are extraordinarily similar in very different societies throughout the world, and have become increasingly similar over time.
- Mass educational systems are specifically directed toward the socialization of the individual as the primary social unit. This is seen, for example, in the extent to which educational rituals celebrate individual choice and responsibility rather than the imbeddedness of individuals in such corporate groups as social classes, castes, or extended families.

The nation-building theory proposes that mass education arose in the modern world specifically as a device for the intensive socialization of the individual into the values and aspirations of the modern, rational nation-state. To build such a state, citizens have to be loyal and committed to it, and they must be sufficiently knowledgeable of political life so as to participate in it and help maintain the political system.

This theory has much to recommend it and seems to make very good sense of those specific features of modern educational systems that the nation-building theorists see as most crucial. It can certainly help explain not only the origins of mass education but also the reasons why primary education, and to some extent secondary education, have become so prominent in so many societies around the world. However, the theory seems inadequate as a means of understanding many of the developments in higher education, especially why it has expanded so rapidly and so substantially in some societies. Most of what citizens "need to know" about the political life of their society is taught in primary and secondary schools. Moreover, the nation-building theory may not be fully adequate even in explaining a good deal of the expansion of secondary education. To explain these things we will draw on another theory: the credential inflation argument of Collins and Dore.

In his book *The Credential Society* (1979), Collins focuses on the U.S. educational system and why it has become one of the world's largest and most comprehensive systems, but an important part of Collins's overall theory can be extended to other modern educational systems. Collins views the character of U.S. education and its dramatic expansion throughout the past century as rooted in the great ethnic diversity of U.S. society. Such diversity has resulted in major struggles among ethnic groups for privilege and prestige. These struggles began mainly in the late nineteenth century and continued well into the twentieth. Education, Collins holds, became the major weapon used in such struggles. Dominant groups used the educational system as a means of maintaining their cultural and economic dominance. For them, it was a mechanism for transmitting their dominant cultural values to new immigrant groups of workers, as well as a resource to be used to reinforce their economic dominance. But subordinate groups also saw it as a resource they could use in their attempts to improve their economic status. The possession of a certain amount of education came to be viewed as establishing a set of *credentials* that would provide access to certain desired occupational positions. Education thus became an arena in which different groups competed for economic success. As this competition progressed, education began to increase in size and importance.

As more and more persons began to obtain educational credentials, however, an unexpected and unwanted thing happened: Their credentials declined in value. Drawing an analogy to monetary inflation, Collins calls this process **credential inflation.** Just as money inflates when there is more of it in circulation, educational credentials inflate when more people possess more of them. Credential inflation in the educational sphere means that the same amount of education no longer "purchases" what it once did. One must acquire more of it just to keep even in the struggle for economic success. Collins argues that this is exactly what has been happening in the U.S. educational system over the past century. The struggle over education has caused continual educational inflation, resulting in the massive expansion of the educational system (and educational requirements for jobs) over time. Since it now takes a college degree to obtain a job that could have been obtained with a high school diploma 40 years ago, a greater number of young people are going to college. Most of them go not because of a desire for learning, Collins insists, but because they seek credentials that they hope will pay off in economic success.

Collins also makes special note of the fact that, as U.S. education expanded, educational institutions were forced to make major changes in their curricula and in their overall character in order to appeal to an increasingly mass clientele. The most prominent changes involved the watering down of the classical liberal arts curriculum and the introduction of a host of extracurricular activities. The transformation of the high school into a mass institution, for instance, was accompanied by the so-called progressive movement in education. Two of progressivism's major innovations were the introduction of athletics and other extracurricular activities and the attempt "to substitute a rather vague 'life-adjustment' training for the classical curriculum" (Collins, 1979:115–116). Similar changes occurred when colleges and universities started to be attended by a larger clientele, most of whom were seeking educational credentials rather than intellectual stimulation.

Collins (1977) notes that there are significant differences among the educational systems of industrial societies. For example, England, Germany, and France have historically had educational systems that have been called **sponsored-mobility educational systems.** Here, students are placed into one or the other of two educational channels or tracks early in their educational careers. At approximately age 11,

*Could credential inflation
ever go this far?*

© United Media.

students take qualifying exams, and those who pass (usually only a small minority) are placed in the channel that leads to a university education and the occupational opportunities it affords. Those failing the exam (usually a large majority) end up in the track that terminates with a vocational education. By contrast, **contest-mobility educational systems** do no official channeling and there is a more open competition for the pursuit of advanced education. In this system, students do not take qualifying exams whose results determine their educational and occupational chances once and for all. Essentially, they can go as far as their abilities and inclinations will take them. The United States has the quintessential contest-mobility system, a system also found to some extent in Japan.

Collins argues that sponsored-mobility systems develop in societies where the level of class segregation is high. The class-segregated character of the educational system reflects the class-segregated character of the larger society. Competition for advanced education is strictly regulated, and as a result the system of tertiary education tends to remain relatively small, which means that these systems have been less inflationary, at least at the highest level. Contest-mobility systems, on the other hand, tend to emerge in societies in which the level of class segregation is low. Low class segregation is associated with a strong egalitarian ideology, and the educational system becomes the focus for the implementation of this ideology. As a result, a more open competition for advanced education occurs, which in turn leads to a larger and more rapidly inflating educational system at the tertiary level.

Collins's theory is a major contribution to the understanding of educational expansion, but there is one difficulty with it. This concerns his argument that ethnic diversity is at the root of educational expansion. The world's most ethnically heterogeneous society, for example, the old Soviet Union, has undergone less educational expansion than the world's most ethnically homogeneous society, Japan. Systematic empirical research seems to contradict the theory (Boli, Ramirez, and Meyer, 1985). Recent research by Sanderson using a large sample of contemporary nation-states found that ethnic heterogeneity is actually *negatively* rather than positively correlated with the expansion of educational enrollments. In other words, ethnic heterogeneity *inhibits* rather than promotes the growth of enrollments (cf. D. Brown, 1995:39–43). Fortunately, there is a simple way of explaining credential inflation and educational expansion that does not rely on the factor of ethnic heterogeneity, so the most important part of Collins's theory can be saved.

Ronald Dore (1976) has developed a similar argument that he has applied to several Western industrial societies, as well as to less-developed countries. What Collins calls **credentialism**—the process whereby educational systems come to be built around the pursuit of educational certificates for their occupational value rather than around learning as valuable for its own sake—Dore refers to by the term **qualificationism.** He suggests that it is a significant phenomenon in all or most major industrial societies. All (or at least most) contemporary nations have thus become infected with what Dore calls "the diploma disease." The diploma disease is a type of vicious circle in which individuals become obsessed with the acquisition of diplomas or degrees because employers increasingly emphasize such educational certificates in their statements of job qualifications. The two sides feed off each other, and educational certificates inflate as a result.

Although qualificationism seems to be a more prominent characteristic of the United States, Canada, and Australia than of other advanced industrial societies, it certainly became a significant feature of the educational systems of virtually all other industrial societies in the twentieth century. England, for example, experienced very significant growth of qualificationism throughout the century; in fact, it moved substantially away from a sponsored-mobility system and increasingly toward a contest-mobility system during the second half of the twentieth century. More recently, Germany and France, which have historically had very small systems of tertiary education with extremely rigorous standards for admission and graduation, have begun to expand their tertiary enrollments quite substantially.

Japan has created what is perhaps the most credentialized educational system in the industrialized world (Dore, 1976). As Dore remarks, almost from the very beginning of its industrialization Japan was building credentialism into its career preparation, and it underwent enormous educational expansion throughout the twentieth century. In 1918, private colleges in Japan were given the right to call themselves universities, and two decades later, 26 such universities had been established. At the same time, there were also 19 state universities and 2 municipal universities (Dore, 1976). By 1950, the total number of institutions of higher education had exploded to 350. The number swelled to 525 institutions (245 universities and 280 junior colleges) by 1960, to 861 (382 universities and 479 junior colleges) by 1971, and to 963 (446 universities and 517 junior colleges) by 1980. By 1987, there were over 2.3 million students enrolled in 474 universities and 561 junior colleges (Kitamura, 1991). This obviously represents an extremely high rate of educational expansion, with apparently no end in sight.

In conclusion, we suggest that the emergence of modern systems of mass education and their expansion in the twentieth century can be explained by combining the nation-building and credential inflation theories. However, since we have shorn Collins's theory of its ethnic heterogeneity argument, we need to provide a mechanism that will keep the process of credential inflation going. The process is, in essence, a quite simple one: the logic of the "market" for educational credentials causes continuous qualification expansion. As more people gain credentials, the worth of these credentials declines in terms of the kinds of jobs for which their holders can qualify. Therefore, unless people are willing to lower their occupational aspirations, they must stay in school longer in order to achieve a higher credential. Moreover, educational certificates that were once desirable as a basis for acquiring a certain job eventually end up becoming minimal requirements. If an educational certificate that was once held by few people later comes to be held by most or even all people, then employers will see it as meaning little and will have to start relying on the possession of a higher educational certificate as a way of sorting out applicants for jobs.

## The Demographic Transition

As is well known, in modern industrial societies relatively small families have become the norm, with most couples having two or three children, and population growth is relatively slow. This is in contrast to the very same societies prior to large-scale industrialization and urbanization, when couples tended to have more children (although population growth was still relatively slow); and it is especially in contrast to contemporary societies of the less-developed world, where large family size has long been the norm and population growth relatively rapid. The process whereby there has been a shift from large to small families is known as the **demographic transition** (Harris and Ross, 1987; cf. Handwerker, 1986). This major social transformation has occurred in three stages. In the first stage, characterized by societies prior to, or in the very early stages of, industrialization, both birthrates and death rates are high; population grows slowly because these two rates approximately cancel each other out. In stage two, which began in the nineteenth century, death rates begin to decline because of improvements in health care, sanitation, and the like; but since birthrates remain high, population begins to grow rapidly. With the transition to the third stage, birthrates begin to drop and once again remain only slightly higher than death rates, and thus population growth rates decline.

*Randall Collins is an eminent comparative and historical sociologist and sociological theorist. One of his most important contributions is his credential inflation theory of educational expansion.*

The big question is, Why have birthrates become so much lower in modern industrial societies? Why do couples have only two or three children rather than six, eight, or even more? One of the most common answers invokes the economic value of children's labor as the principal causal variable. Marvin Harris (1989; Harris and Ross, 1987) has been one of the foremost proponents of this view. Harris argues that in societies where agriculture remains the primary basis for subsistence, children perform many useful economic activities. They carry water, gather firewood, sweep floors, grind and pound grains, take food to adults in the fields, cook, work full time in the fields, fish and herd, and make pots, mats, and nets. Older children also perform the important task of looking after the younger ones much of the time, thus freeing their parents for other work. Where children perform these and other useful activities, it makes sense for childbearing rates to be high. Although children are costly to rear, the benefits they produce outweigh these costs. When a society shifts from an agricultural to an industrial economy, the economic value of children declines, and in direct proportion to the level of industrialization. In urban settings, children can no longer perform the valuable economic tasks that they undertake in rural settings, and the costs of rearing them far outweigh the value of any labor they might continue to perform. Under these circumstances, childbearing rates decline, families get smaller, and population grows more slowly.

A number of demographers—students of population—have made essentially the same type of argument (e.g., Caldwell, 1976; Boserup, 1986), and this argument is consistent with evidence from a variety of empirical studies. Benjamin White (1973, 1976, 1982), for example, found that Javanese peasant children performed almost half of all household work, and Nag, White, and Peet (1978) found a high correlation between the number of hours of children's household labor and that household's balance of income. Moreover, Ester Boserup (1986) examined the childbearing rates for people in various occupations in 28 less-developed countries. She found that, of people working in four different types of occupations, those working in agriculture had the highest rate of childbearing and those working in professional, managerial, technical, and clerical jobs had the lowest rate.

This view of the determinants of childbearing rates has not gone unchallenged. Bobbi Low (1991, 1993) and Paul Turke (1989) claim that the labor of children can never offset the costs of rearing them and that economic benefits in all settings flow from parents to children rather than the other way around. Hilliard Kaplan (1994) has examined data from three tribal societies in South America that combined hunting and gathering and horticulture. All three had very high childbearing rates, but children in each of these societies were consuming many more calories than they were producing. Kaplan concluded that these children were very costly to rear and hardly earned their keep in economic terms.

If children are economic costly to rear in all societies, then why do people have so many of them in most societies, and why has childbearing declined so markedly in modern industrial societies? Sanderson and Dubrow (2000) carried out a series of complex statistical analyses in which they attempted to answer this question. First, they looked at 63 contemporary societies at various levels of economic development during the period between 1960 and 1990 and examined the effects of six factors on the rate of childbearing: per capita GNP, the adult literacy rate, percentage of the population working in agriculture, percentage of the population living in urban areas, the level of female empowerment, and the infant mortality rate. Their results provided very weak support for the argument that childbearing is being adjusted primarily to the economic value of children's labor. The percentage of the labor force working in agriculture was not consistently related to the rate of childbearing, nor was the percentage of the population living in urban areas. And a simple increase in material wealth or the standard of living was not an important determinant of childbearing since the per capita GNP did not consistently relate to the childbearing rate. It was the infant mortality rate that emerged as the most important determinant of childbearing: As infant mortality declined, the number of children produced per woman declined as well. Childbearing rates were high in those societies with high infant mortality rates, and low in societies with low infant mortality rates. The second most important determinant was the level of female empowerment. Other things being equal, women had fewer children in those societies where they held more power relative to men.

In a second analysis, Sanderson and Dubrow looked at 27 now developed societies during the period between 1880 and 1940, which is the main period of the original demographic transition. This analysis also showed strong support for the causal role of infant mortality, which was easily the main determinant of the childbearing rate. However, the economic value of children's labor, as measured by the percentage of the population working in agriculture or manufacturing, did seem to have at least some effect, and so this factor may have been somewhat more important for the original demographic transition than for the 1960–1990 period.

Although childbearing rates do not appear to decline simply because societies develop economically and become wealthier, the shift of a society from a rural and agricultural base to an urban and industrial one may still be a significant part of the story. Hilliard Kaplan (1996) argues that modernization has caused people to reduce their number of offspring but to invest much more in each child—in essence, trading quantity for quality (cf. van den Berghe and Whitmeyer, 1990). Kaplan suggests that it is the development of skills-based competitive labor markets that is crucial to this process because such markets lead to an increase in the importance of parental investment in the well-being of each child. Kaplan's argument is supported by evidence showing that in modern societies, better-educated and wealthier parents tend to have fewer offspring than do couples who are less educated and earn lower incomes. However, what is missing in Kaplan's argument is any reference to reduced infant mortality. In order for parents to have only two or three children and invest heavily in each child, the rate of infant and child survivorship must be very high, and strong parent-child attachment is likely to be high only in those societies that have low rates of childbearing and infant mortality—that is, in postdemographic transition societies (Wiley and Carlin, 1999).

The discovery that female empowerment is an important determinant of lower rates of childbearing makes sense in terms of what has just been said. Female empowerment likely helps to reduce childbearing because women often regard having a large number of children as a serious burden; after all, they are the ones who assume most of the child-care duties in all societies. As women gain greater power, they become increasingly able to act on their desire to have fewer children (Penn, 1999). Moreover, Murthi, Guio, and Dreze (1995) show that female empowerment, especially when it results from greater education, leads women to have higher aspirations for each child, which in turn leads them to want to trade child quantity for child quality. Greater education also leads to a decline in infant mortality because it increases a mother's knowledge of nutrition and hygiene, and thus fewer births are needed to achieve a desired family size (Murthi, Guio, and Dreze, 1995).

In conclusion, Sanderson and Dubrow provide evidence to suggest that declining infant mortality and increasing female empowerment, rather than the declining economic value of children's labor, are the most important determinants of declining childbearing rates. However, their analysis also shows that these factors are not the whole story; much of the variation in childbearing rates is still unaccounted for. Sociologists and demographers still have more to learn about the causes of reproductive behavior and desired family size.

# The Rise of a Postindustrial Society?

One of the most influential sociological works of the past 30 years is Daniel Bell's *The Coming of Post-Industrial Society* (1973). Since Bell's work was published, the phrase **postindustrial society** has appeared frequently and approvingly in numerous sociological textbooks and other works. Bell argues that a new type of society, the postindustrial society, has in recent decades begun to emerge in the most economically advanced nations of the West, the United States in particular. The most fundamental feature of this type of society is its emphasis on the production of services rather than goods, and especially certain types of services. Whereas the industrial society delivers services in such areas as transportation, utilities, and telecommunications, the postindustrial society emphasizes services involving health, science, and education.

The emergence of a postindustrial society thus involves a major transformation in the very basis of society. An industrial society, Bell argues, is based on property; a postindustrial society, on the other hand, rests on knowledge, particularly theoretical knowledge. This change in the very basis of social life is also marked by a change in the class structure. The new dominant social class is no longer a capitalist class but a "social intelligentsia": a class of highly educated individuals whose social dominance rests on their possession of advanced forms of theoretical knowledge. The most important members of this class are teachers, physicians, lawyers, scientists, and engineers—people for whom work has become a "game between people" rather than a game between people and things.

For Bell, then, the postindustrial society is one whose overall character is vastly different from industrial or capitalist society. The desire for profit is no longer the driving force of economic and social life. Life becomes oriented around the accumulation of knowledge and its use for human betterment. Corporations come to be subordinated to what Bell calls the "sociologizing mode." This means that their emphasis shifts toward providing extensive benefits for their employees as well as toward their "social responsibility." In addition to and in conjunction with these changes, the postindustrial society gives a new emphasis to leisure. People acquire advanced forms of education not only for their important social uses but also for enjoyment and intellectual uplift. In general, a postindustrial society is far better educated than an industrial one.

Although Bell's ideas have gained widespread acceptance among many contemporary sociologists, there is cause to be highly skeptical of most of them. The basic difficulties with Bell's analysis have been insightfully delineated by a number of social scientists (Berger, 1974; Arriaga, 1985; Walker, 1985; Kumar, 1995). Stephen Berger (1974) suggests that many of the developments discussed by Bell do not represent the emergence of a new type of society that is opposed to capitalism, but rather of a new phase in the very development of capitalism. The expansion of government services, for example, may be understood as a necessary step in the political management of an advanced capitalist society. Moreover, Berger argues, the original motivation behind technological forecasting was military in nature, and most of the recent expansion of science has been due to government involvement in defense and space exploration. Berger's central argument against Bell is expressed as follows (1974:102):

> I would argue that these changes, if they are real, represent only the continued operation of the logic of industry. That logic, as analyzed by . . . Karl Marx, included the continuous enlargement of the areas of human work which were dominated by commodity production and the continuous use of scientists and engineers to create machines, techniques, and modes of organization to replace and control workers. . . .
> The shifts from goods to services and from manual to professional and technical workers make sense within an analysis of the dynamics of capitalism.

Similarly, Krishan Kumar (1995:32) argues that the new information technology "is being applied within a political and economic framework that confirms and accentuates existing patterns, rather than giving rise to new ones." "The instruments and techniques may change," Kumar notes, "but the overriding goals and purposes of capitalist industrial societies remain the same as before."

To Berger's and Kumar's remarks several critical comments may be added. One concerns Bell's notion that a propertyless intelligentsia has emerged as the dominant class within postindustrial society. A better interpretation, we believe, would hold that such a group, to the extent that it exists, lacks any real social power and is by and large in a service capacity to the capitalist system. After all, most teachers, scientists, and engineers are employed in large public bureaucracies. As Berger has noted, these public bureaucracies may be viewed from the perspective of the capitalist-induced expansion of government. A second comment involves Bell's treatment of the expansion of education. In this regard, Bell seems to confuse education with "schooling" (Berger, 1974). Although it is certainly true that schooling has been expanding on a vast scale in the contemporary United States, this should not be construed, as Bell seems to do, as resulting from the greater need and desire for knowledge. A more realistic interpretation, in our view, is that schooling has been expanding as a result of the inflation of educational credentials, as argued earlier. It is not the thirst for knowledge that leads people to stay in school for ever longer periods, but the desire for educational certificates that translate into better-paying and higher-prestige jobs.

In sum, then, modern industrial economies have increasingly become "service and information economies" (Harris, 1981), but this is not a process of the overturning of capitalism. Capitalism is alive and well, and the increased focus on service and information is simply another aspect of the commodification of economic and social life. Industrialism and capitalism have been extended rather than negated.

# FOR FURTHER READING

Anthony Giddens's *The Class Structure of the Advanced Societies* (1980) is a valuable theoretically informed analysis of many of the issues involved in the study of classes in modern industrial societies. See also Giddens and Held (1982). Erik Olin Wright's *Classes* (1985) is a heroic, if only partially successful, attempt to map the class structure of modern capitalist societies from a Marxian perspective. Frank Parkin's *Marxism and Class Theory: A Bourgeois Critique* (1979) presents a provocative critique of the Marxian approach to class in industrial capitalist societies and provides an important theoretical alternative. Raymond Murphy's *Social Closure: The Theory of Monopolization and Exclusion* (1988) extends Parkin's line of thinking. Charles Tilly's *Durable Inequality* (1998) presents a broadly similar argument. Paul Kingston's *The Classless Society* (2000) takes up the question as to whether classes in the United States and other industrial capitalist societies exist in the sense of being coherent and cohesive groups rather than mere categories. His highly controversial conclusion is that they do not. Lisa Keister's *Wealth in America: Trends in Wealth Inequality* (2000a) is probably the best study of wealth inequality in the United States in the last 40 years. Erikson and Goldthorpe's *The Constant Flux: A Study of Class Mobility in Industrial Societies* (1993) is an extremely comprehensive analysis of social mobility in a dozen industrial societies and is the best recent study of the subject.

Gøsta Esping-Andersen's *The Three Worlds of Welfare Capitalism* (1990), one of the best studies of the modern welfare state available, provides many useful insights into different types of welfare states, their origins, and their accomplishments. See also Huber and Stephens (2001) and Moller and associates (2003). Perhaps the best recent work on welfare states, and socialist labor movements more generally, is Kautsky's *Social Democracy and the Aristocracy* (2002).

Martin Carnoy (1984) presents an excellent overview of theories of the modern state, with a stress on classical and contemporary Marxian theories. Barrington Moore (1966) and Albert Szymanski (1978) present Marxian accounts of the emergence of democracy in the modern world. Rueschemeyer, Stephens, and Stephens's *Capitalist Development and Democracy* (1992) criticizes the Marxian explanation of democracy and offers a non-Marxian, but materialist, alternative that focuses on the balance of class forces and the role of working-class power. It is one of the best books ever written on the origins of democracy. Tatu Vanhanen's *Prospects of Democracy: A Study of 172 Countries* (1997) is a quantitative statistical analysis of the development of democracy in 172 countries between 1850 and 1990. It is an extremely valuable complement to the Rueschemeyer, Stephens, and Stephens (1992) book. He has updated this work in a more recent book (Vanhanen, 2003). These books are essential reading for serious students of democracy. Sanderson (2004) has reanalyzed Vanhanen's data and revised and extended his argument. Several books by William Domhoff (1970, 1978, 1983, 1990) take up the question of who has power in the United States.

The classic statement of the credential inflation theory of educational expansion is Collins's *The Credential Society: An Historical Sociology of Education and Stratification* (1979). Ronald Dore (1976) develops much the same argument for other industrial countries as well as for the less-developed world. David Brown (1995) has written an insightful book on the beginnings of credentialism and the early expansion of higher education in the United States that is critical of some aspects of Collins's argument; Brown develops a similar theory of the role of credentialism in the expansion of higher education. The argument that the origin and expansion of mass education are rooted in the building of modern nation-states is developed in Boli, Ramirez, and Meyer (1985) and related publications by the same authors. Beauchamp (1991) is a collection of valuable essays on the Japanese educational system, including its expansion.

Bowles and Gintis's *Schooling in Capitalist America* (1976) develops the Marxian thesis that the origin and expansion of U.S. education since the 1840s resulted from the desire of capitalists to socialize and discipline the working class and legitimate the capitalist system. This argument now seems to be largely discredited, even in the eyes of many fellow Marxists, and the authors themselves no longer defend it. A still popular, although rather dubious, explanation of the development of modern educational systems holds that education has expanded (especially at the secondary and tertiary levels) to provide people with the greater knowledge they need to do the increasingly specialized and demanding work characteristic of modern societies (Clark, 1962; Trow, 1966). This argument, which dates back to at least the 1950s and 1960s, is criticized in Collins (1979) and in Brown (1995).

A very useful work on the demographic transition and on birth and death rates in human societies more generally is Harris and Ross's *Sex, Death, and Fertility: Population Regulation in Preindustrial and Developing Societies* (1987). Sanderson and Dubrow (2000) overview various theories of reproductive behavior and the demographic transition and provide other useful references.

Daniel Bell's *The Coming of Post-Industrial Society* (1973) is the classic statement of the postindustrial society thesis. Krishan Kumar's *From Post-Industrial to Post-Modern Society: New Theories of the Contemporary World* (1995) critically evaluates this and related theses. See also Kumar (1988). Harry Braverman's *Labor and Monopoly Capital: The Degradation of Work in the Twentieth Century* (1974) is a well-known work that analyzes the transformation of the workplace in capitalist society since the late nineteenth century. Braverman advances the hotly contested thesis that there has been an overall deskilling of manual work during this period.

Harold Wilensky's *Rich Democracies* (2002) is an extraordinarily comprehensive work—nearly 900 pages with very small print—that looks in detail at many features of 19 industrial capitalist societies: variations in political and economic systems, welfare states, economic performance, higher education, stratification and mobility, political parties, work and jobs, mass media, family policy, crime, and health care. Wilensky also looks at the extent to which these societies are evolving along a convergent path and critically evaluates the postindustrial society thesis.

# CHAPTER

# 8

# The Rise and Demise of State Socialism

## The Origin and Nature of State Socialism

The world's first socialist society was born in 1917 when Russia underwent the Bolshevik revolution and became the Soviet Union. Elsewhere in Europe, other socialist societies began to emerge in the mid- to late 1940s, and in the less developed part of the world a number of socialist societies arose somewhat later, mostly in the 1970s. Table 8.1 lists the major socialist societies of the world as of 1989 and their current status. All of these societies were (or are) ones in which Marxism-Leninism (more accurately described simply as *Leninism*) was (or is) the dominant political ideology and the Communist party is in control of the state. (There are or have been a few other societies claiming to be socialist in a sense other than Marxist-Leninist. These are not included here.) These societies are perhaps best termed *state socialist* because of the strong role the state plays in the direction of the economy. To complicate matters, since 1989 in eastern Europe and 1991 in the Soviet Union, many of these societies abandoned state socialism (at least in its classical version) and shifted markedly toward a more capitalist, market-oriented economy. In these same societies the Communist party lost its monopoly of power, and substantial political liberalization was achieved. For the sake of terminological clarity, we propose to use the term **state socialism** (or **state socialist**) to refer to these societies as they were before 1989 (eastern Europe) or 1991 (Soviet Union), and to use the term **postsocialism** (or **postsocialist**) to refer to them from these dates forward (the term *postsocialist* was coined by the Hungarian economist János Kornai, an astute analyst of the state socialist economy and its postsocialist transition; see Kornai, 1992).

In analyzing these societies, we will first discuss their economic structure during their classical state socialist phase. At a later point we will look at the economic reforms they experienced in the 1970s and 1980s that led to the dramatic economic and political upheavals of 1989 and 1991. This will allow us to consider them as they are now—that is, as postsocialist societies. In this chapter we are concerned only with those state socialist societies that have undergone substantial industrialization: the former Soviet Union and the socialist societies of eastern Europe.

In the classical exemplar of state socialism, the Soviet Union, private property was almost completely eliminated, with the exception of consumer goods. Thus, one could own one's own house, car, or wardrobe privately (as items of personal property), but one could not privately own the means of economic production. Most of

**TABLE 8.1**    State Socialist (Leninist) Societies in 1989 and Their
Current Status

| Society | Year of Transition to State Socialism/Leninism | Current Status |
|---|---|---|
| Soviet Union | 1917 | Abandoned Leninism and fragmented into Russia and other successor states after 1991. |
| East Germany | 1949 | Abandoned Leninism in 1989 and reunified with West Germany in 1990. |
| Czechoslovakia | 1948 | Abandoned Leninism after 1989 and separated into the Czech Republic and Slovakia. |
| Hungary | 1948 | Abandoned Leninism after 1989. |
| Poland | 1948 | Abandoned Leninism after 1989. |
| Yugoslavia | 1945 | Abandoned Leninism after 1989 and fragmented into Bosnia-Herzegovina, Croatia, Macedonia, Slovenia, and Yugoslavia (Serbia and Montenegro). |
| Bulgaria | 1947 | Abandoned Leninism after 1989. |
| Romania | 1948 | Abandoned Leninism after 1989. |
| Albania | 1944 | Abandoned Leninism after 1989. |
| China | 1949 | Remains Leninist. |
| North Korea | 1948 | Remains Leninist. |
| Vietnam | 1954/1975* | Remains Leninist. |
| Mongolia | 1921 | Abandoned Leninism in 1990s. |
| Cuba | 1959 | Remains Leninist. |
| Congo | 1963 | Abandoned Leninism in 1990s. |
| Somalia | 1969 | No functioning government. |
| South Yemen | 1969 | Abandoned Leninism and reunified with North Yemen in 1990. |
| Benin | 1972 | Abandoned Leninism in 1990. |
| Ethiopia | 1974 | Officially a federal republic, but still dominated by the Ethiopian People's Revolutionary Democratic Front. |
| Angola | 1975 | Abandoned Leninism in 1990s. |
| Kampuchea | 1975 | Abandoned Leninism in 1990s and reestablished former name Cambodia. |
| Laos | 1975 | Remains Leninist. |
| Mozambique | 1975 | Abandoned Leninism after 1989. |
| Afghanistan | 1978 | No functioning government. |
| Nicaragua | 1979 | Abandoned Leninism in 1990. |
| Zimbabwe | 1980 | Abandoned Leninism in 1990. |
| Guinea-Bissau | 1980 | Abandoned Leninism in 1991. |
| Madagascar | 1972 | Abandoned Leninism in 1992. |

*The date 1954 refers to only the northern part of the country. The southern part became socialist in 1975, when Vietnam again became a unified state.

*Sources*: Kornai (1992); Ramsay (2001); Goldman (2001); Norton (2001); Collinwood (2001); Goodwin (2000); Spencer (2001); Central Intelligence Agency (1998).

the industrial sector and part of the agricultural sector were nationalized. Indeed, all sectors of the economy, except for small plots of land cultivated by collective farmers, were brought under the control of national economic planning. The very core of the Soviet economy was its state sector; all major industries were state owned and state operated in the areas of mining, heavy construction, railroads, communications, power production, urban retailing, large cooperative farms, and others. The major means of production were thus publicly owned, and all employees worked for the state. The private enterprise that did exist, such as small-scale artisans operating small farms in remote areas, was very limited (Lane, 1985; Kornai, 1992). The eastern European state socialist societies were based more or less on the Soviet model, but they had a tendency to be somewhat more open to capitalist or market-oriented economic activity, particularly after 1970 (Abonyi, 1982). This was especially true in Hungary and Yugoslavia. Yugoslavia was experimenting with market economics as early as the 1950s. It attempted to create a form of "market socialism," which involved retaining a basic state socialist economy but allowing considerable development of capitalist businesses alongside socialist operations.

However, the classical state socialist system, as represented best by the Soviet Union, kept market activity to an absolute minimum and gave overwhelming emphasis to state management and state economic planning. As János Kornai (1992:115) writes, in classical state socialism "the 'life or death' of a firm as a collective organization or organism is determined not by the 'natural selection' of market competition but by the bureaucracy. There is a complete absence of . . . entrepreneurs who introduce new products or new technologies, establish new organizations, and conquer new markets, while obsolete production and ossified organizations are squeezed out."

This absence of a market principle was perhaps nowhere more salient to the functioning of the economy than with respect to money and prices. Classical socialism was, according to Kornai (1992), not a fully monetized, but rather a *semimonetized* economy. Money existed, but it did not act as a universal means of exchange in the way that it does within capitalism, nor was it convertible into foreign currencies. Kornai also notes that prices were not set by market principles, but rather by bureaucratic decree. This means that they were not sensitive to the basic laws of supply and demand, and thus could not be used as indicators of how much of what products to produce. As we shall see, these economic characteristics had dramatic consequences for the functioning and evolution of the state socialist system.

Industrialization in the state socialist societies took place under the close control of the state (Gershenkron, 1962). In the Soviet Union, the major drive toward industrialization occurred from the late 1920s through World War II under the leadership of the Stalinist regime. In a very short time the Soviet Union was transformed from a largely agrarian society into one of the world's major industrial societies. The speed of industrialization in the Soviet Union, and the fervor with which the Soviet leaders carried it out, took a terrible human toll. Millions of peasants were either killed or sent to labor camps in order to make the transition from agriculture to industry. This was one of the sorriest sagas in human history.

By the second half of the twentieth century, the state socialist societies came to closely resemble the industrial capitalist societies in several important respects. To a large extent, industrialization created notable similarities in the basic social patterns of both types of society. However, the state socialist world, although it made considerable progress in this regard, was not able to achieve the truly high levels of economic prosperity characteristic of modern capitalism. By the late 1980s, the levels of per capita income of the state socialist societies were still only about one-third to one-half those of the industrial capitalist nations. Indeed, despite considerable economic progress, by the 1970s state socialism seemed to run up against severe constraints on further economic development. State socialist economies began to stagnate and suffer from a variety of ills. These ills led to various programs of economic reform that culminated in the postsocialist transition of the late 1980s and early 1990s.

## State Socialism and the Capitalist World-Economy

The relationship between the socialist states and the capitalist world-economy has been the subject of much debate, especially among Western Marxian social scientists. Christopher Chase-Dunn (1982), for instance, argues a position that has become popular among Wallersteinian world-system theorists. He holds not only that the state socialist nations had close economic ties with world capitalism, but, indeed, that the socialist states were integral parts of the capitalist world-economy. The position they occupy in the world-system is in the semiperiphery. The socialist states have this role, Chase-Dunn claims, because they engage in commodity production for a world market and have important dealings with the capitalist transnational corporations. It is thus Chase-Dunn's view that the socialist societies were not really socialist at all. Rather, they were essentially capitalist societies whose governments were led by socialist political parties.

At the opposite extreme from Chase-Dunn is Albert Szymanski (1982). Szymanski argues that the state socialist nations were thoroughly socialist. They had economies that involved no private ownership of the means of production and no production for profit. Moreover, Szymanski sees the state socialist economies as basically autonomous from Western capitalism, the economic exchanges between them and capitalist nations being mainly of a nonessential or luxury nature.

Szymanski offers several lines of evidence to support his position (his analysis is based almost entirely on the case of the Soviet Union). First, the agreements with Western capitalists that the Soviet Union entered into—agreements that involved various exchanges of goods or technology—were made on the Soviet Union's own terms. These agreements could not have significantly affected economic processes within the Soviet Union because they did not involve any direct investment or management rights for capitalists in Soviet enterprises. Second, although the state socialist societies invested in both core and peripheral capitalist societies, these investments were extremely small in comparison to those of the advanced capitalist nations. For example, in 1978, U.S. investments in the peripheral capitalist countries exceeded Soviet investments in those countries by a factor of 2,200. Third, the state socialist societies traded far more among themselves than with the advanced capitalist societies. For example, in 1978, about 60 percent of Soviet trade occurred with the other state socialist nations, but only 28 percent of its trade was with the core capitalist nations. Moreover, in the same year, only about 4 percent of the trade of the core capitalist societies was with the socialist states. Finally, if there were a close economic tie between the socialist and capitalist countries, the economic fluctuations so characteristic of capitalism should have been reflected in similar fluctuations in the socialist nations. However, the correlation between the capitalist and socialist societies in this regard was not strong. Indeed, "the period of the most rapid industrial growth in the USSR, 1928–1941, coincided with the period of the most protracted and deep depression in the modern history of capitalism" (Szymanski, 1982:75).

The disagreement between Chase-Dunn and Szymanski is a complex one that involves a wide range of issues, and it is therefore difficult to resolve in a definitive way. Indeed, this disagreement is only part of a much larger discussion about the nature of the economic systems in the Soviet Union and eastern Europe (cf. Sweezy, 1980; Lane, 1985). On Szymanski's side, it must be recognized that the state socialist societies did have economies that were different in important ways from Western capitalism. The state socialist societies had no private capitalist class engaged in profit maximization as an end in itself; they made use of centralized economic planning to a degree that is unheard of in Western capitalism; and they, the Soviet Union in particular, made relatively minimal use of market mechanisms to guide economic decisions. Thus, the state socialist societies obviously did have some important characteristics that one normally associates with a socialist mode of economic organization (Gorin, 1985; Davis and Scase, 1985).

On the other hand, Szymanski clearly errs in viewing the state socialist societies as having essentially fulfilled the expectations of Marx and Engels regarding the nature of socialist society. The plain and simple truth is that the Soviet Union and eastern Europe departed markedly from the classical Marxian conception of socialism. Although Marx did not spell out in any detail what he thought the future socialist society would look like, historians know some of the basic things he had in mind. For one, he was thinking of a society with a level of economic equality much greater than that which prevailed in the Soviet Union and eastern Europe. For another, he thought of socialism as being relatively democratic in nature, as giving everyone a strong voice in the whole process of social and economic planning. The politically repressive character of state socialism throughout most of its history shows that this expectation has not been even remotely realized. Finally, and in some ways most significantly, there is the fact that Marx conceived of genuine socialism as being built around producing goods in order to serve human needs rather than to earn a profit. State socialist societies did not live up to this expectation either inasmuch as their economies were devoted greatly to the production of commodities—goods that are designed to augment the value of their costs of production. In sum, it is a serious error to refer to the socialist states as Marxist states. Although these states have historically characterized themselves as Marxist, this is at best only a very partial truth.

This brings us back to Chase-Dunn's position. It is important to understand that he is not claiming that the state socialist societies were capitalist in the same way that Western capitalist societies are. He recognizes that the socialist societies have had unique forms of internal economic organization. His position springs from his world-system outlook. The state socialist societies were, he claims, important experiments in socialism that failed largely because the were greatly constrained by the existence of the capitalist world-economy (Chase-Dunn, 1989a). Socialist societies had great difficulty surviving within a capitalist world-system; they were compelled to interact to some extent with that system, and because of this they tended to be drawn back increasingly toward a capitalist mode of operation. Thus, the Soviet Union and eastern Europe became gradually reincorporated into the capitalist world-economy and lost most of whatever socialist content they once possessed. There is a good deal of evidence to show that this is precisely what happened over the past three decades, more rapidly and substantially in eastern Europe than in the Soviet Union itself (Frank, 1980; Abonyi, 1982; Rossides, 1990). Andre Gunder Frank (1980), for example, shows in considerable detail the extent to which the state socialist societies reinserted themselves into global capitalism. Since the early 1970s, they began to trade with Western capitalism much more vigorously, and many important financial and industrial agreements were established. Frank's analysis ends in 1979, but the process of reintegration he describes for the 1970s accelerated throughout the 1980s (Aganbegyan, 1989), and in the 1990s it grew by leaps and bounds.

In the end, then, Chase-Dunn's position turns out to be the more valid and enlightening one. The state socialist societies had only a limited Marxian socialist content to begin with and eventually lost most of what they had. This conclusion has implications for a final important question: Have the socialist countries ever had relations among themselves comparable to the relations among more- and less-developed capitalist countries? To the extent that there ever was a separate socialist world-system, it seems clear that this system never structurally resembled the capitalist world-system (Chase-Dunn, 1982; Chirot, 1986). In other words, the Soviet Union never acted like a socialist "core" that exploited its "semiperipheral" eastern European neighbors or "peripheral" socialist countries, such as Cuba. The Soviet Union did not depend on other socialist countries for its essential raw materials. In fact, it played an important role in exporting raw materials to other socialist countries (Chirot, 1986). Moreover, the Soviet Union historically acted in ways that were apparently designed to help less-developed socialist countries enhance their economic development. For example, it paid Cuba well above the world market price for Cuban sugar (Eckstein, 1986). Although it is true that the Soviet Union engaged in political and military domination over the eastern European states, as well as over many less-developed socialist countries, this domination was not comparable to the economic domination that some nations have exerted over others within the world capitalist system.

## Reform within State Socialism and the Transition to Postsocialism

As early as the 1970s, the socialist economies of eastern Europe began to combine state economic planning with considerable private ownership and market-oriented economic behavior. They were well ahead of the Soviet Union in making this move. Nevertheless, by the mid-1980s, the Soviet Union itself was spurred into the same basic kind of action. Economic reform in the Soviet Union began in earnest with the rise in 1985 of Mikhail Gorbachev to the position of General Secretary of the Communist party, the most powerful political office in all of Soviet society. Gorbachev pursued a strategy known as *perestroika*, or economic restructuring. The most fundamental aspects of this plan of economic reform were the following (Lapidus, 1988; Kushnirsky, 1988; Leggett, 1988; Zemtsov and Farrar, 1989):

- Whereas centralized economic planning was to be maintained as a guiding policy, individual firms were given increased responsibility to make decisions about their production activities. These firms were required to compete with each other, with the level of profitability being the main criterion for success. Firms that were not sufficiently profitable would be eliminated. Moreover, managers of firms were increasingly to be elected, rather than simply rising to power through the political patronage system traditionally in effect.
- The wage structure was to be overhauled in the direction of greater wage differentials. This was designed to serve as an incentive for workers to work harder and better. As a further incentive, workers could be fired for poor work and for excessive absenteeism. With this reform, unemployment would become a reality for the first time since the early years of Soviet society.
- New joint ventures with Western firms were to be undertaken. These ventures were designed primarily to attract Western capital and enhance the production of consumer goods.

What all of these changes had in common was obviously a recognition of the limitations of centralized economic planning, and thus an increased reliance on the market (Lapidus, 1988; Aganbegyan, 1988, 1989). The changes were designed to shift the Soviet economy in a more "capitalistic" direction, a move that would not surprise Wallerstein and the world-system theorists, since they see the Soviet Union as already substantially capitalist.

What lay behind these reforms? Why were they undertaken at this particular historical juncture? A large part of the answer obviously involves the deteriorating economic conditions that the Soviet Union began to face in the 1970s, conditions that had reached crisis proportions by 1985 (Leggett, 1988; Lapidus, 1988; Zemtsov and Farrar, 1989; Kaneda, 1988; Mandel, 1989). This was a crisis that was accompanied by a serious demoralization of many segments of Soviet society. Robert Leggett (1988) and Tatsuo Kaneda (1988) summarize the dimensions of the problem:

> Growth has been trending downward for several decades as the economy experienced repeated harvest failures, bottlenecks in industry, shortages of energy and labor, and chronically low productivity. GNP growth during the 11th Five-Year Plan (1981–85) had its worst showing of any five-year period since World War II.
>
> Meanwhile, improvements in living standards have tapered off as a result of the worsening performance of the economy, and popular discontent has grown. The latter has manifested itself in declining worker morale, more materialistic attitudes,

an increase in "deviant" and "delinquent" behavior by Soviet youth, rising crime rates, alcohol and drug abuse, and a rising anti-Russian nationalism among ethnic groups. (Leggett, 1988:23, 25)

Soviet leaders face the wastefulness of their entire economy; a decrease in the Soviet capacity for technological development; dependency on the technological progress of the West; a drop in international competitiveness; chronic shortages of basic necessities; the existence of black markets; widespread bribery and corruption; growing debt; feelings of alienation and habitual drinking among the people, who avoid work and whose rates of illness and mortality are increasing. (Kaneda, 1988:81)

But then if a severely deteriorating economic situation was the motivation for Gorbachev's economic reforms, what were the underlying causes of the economic problems? János Kornai (1992), one of the world's leading experts on the political economy of state socialism, has argued that these difficulties were inherent in the classical socialist system from the beginning, even if they took decades to fully manifest themselves. According to Kornai, bureaucratic economic planning in the absence of a market principle had especially severe consequences primarily because it failed to provide a rational pricing system that was sensitive to the basic laws of supply and demand. Because prices were not determined by consumer demand there was no way for economic planners to know how to adjust supply so that it was in harmony with demand. Indeed, the system worked so that whatever was produced would always be consumed, and therefore producers had no incentives to increase supply. This led inevitably to a situation of chronic shortage.

Moreover, Kornai argues, in contrast to capitalism, the state socialist system had always given priority to the production of means of production—those things, such as machinery, that are used for the production of goods—rather than to the production of consumer goods, which meant that the standard of living increased slowly. Two other features that Kornai sees as inherent in state socialism are, first, the existence of little incentive to create an indigenous technology and thus the need to borrow most of it from the West, a situation that severely reduced economic innovation; and, second, a strong emphasis on the quantity rather than the quality of goods produced, which led, of course, to severe problems with product quality.

A special point needs to be made with respect to the difficulty state socialism had in producing large amounts of high-quality consumer goods. In its first several decades, the Soviet economy worked reasonably well, and in fact was capable of producing industrialization on a scale sufficient to narrow the gap appreciably between itself and Western capitalism (Szelenyi, 1992; Chirot, 1991). However, the Soviet economy and state socialism in general seemed to run up against inherent limitations after a certain period. According to Daniel Chirot (1991), by the middle of the twentieth century the Soviet system was successful in creating an industrial economy based on steel, electrical machinery, and organic chemistry—a stage of industrialization that such economic powers as Germany and the United States had attained in the period between 1870 and World War I—but it became stagnant at that stage. It was never capable of moving into the next stage of industrial development, which in Western capitalism involved the production of such things as automobiles, consumer electrical goods, and services.

However, the problems inherent in state socialism as a mode of economic production may not have been the entire basis for the economic reforms. Certainly state socialism had some tremendous built-in limitations, but the crisis it began to suffer in the 1970s may have had other causes as well. In particular, one must consider the role of the capitalist world-system in imposing constraints on the functioning of state socialism. As noted earlier, in recent decades the Soviet Union began to reinsert its economy into the capitalist world-economy and to act more and more like a traditional capitalist state in the international economic arena. And why should this be? Christopher Chase-Dunn (1982, 1989a) points out that the capitalist world-economy exists as a hostile economic ocean within which state socialism must try to swim. Because of the external economic pressures the world-system creates, state socialist economies had serious obstacles put in the path of their economic functioning. These obstacles included the costs associated with needed military buildup and embargoes against trade. As a result of these obstacles, Chase-Dunn says, socialist states within the world-system tended either to be crushed by that system or to be pulled back into line as capitalist states. The impairment of their functioning by the capitalist world-system may have given them little choice but to play the game according to capitalist rules.

That the Soviet Union was in the process of being pulled back into line as a member of the capitalist system is strongly confirmed by Abel Aganbegyan's *Inside Perestroika* (1989). Aganbegyan, who was at one time Gorbachev's principal economic advisor, makes clear the extraordinary extent to which the Soviet Union desired for some time to compete in the capitalist world-economy using capitalist ground rules. According to Aganbegyan, a key feature of *perestroika* involved an economic shift toward export promotion. The Soviet Union was reorganizing itself so as to be able to manufacture and sell commodities competitively in the world market. For the world's most prominent socialist state, this was an extraordinary departure from traditional economic practices, and it surely indicates a pronounced shift in the economic outlook and interests of a sizable segment of the Soviet elite. It also suggests, as Aganbegyan is at pains to point out, that *perestroika* was no mere economic tinkering. Gorbachev and his supporters seemed to be doing much more than just repairing the flaws in the Soviet economy. They seemed to be attempting to complete the shift, begun some time before them (and, be it noted, *before* the full-scale economic crisis), of the Soviet Union toward full-fledged participation in the world capitalist system.

## Stratification within State Socialism

According to Marxian ideology, socialism was to produce a classless, if not totally egalitarian, society. In other words, even though there would not be complete equalization of income, the shift from private to state ownership of the means of production would eliminate fundamental class divisions and antagonisms. Unfortunately, what actually happened in state socialist societies was the creation of an alternative form of stratification rather than its elimination.

Frank Parkin (1971) provides a useful historical overview of the nature of stratification in the Soviet Union. As he notes, in the period immediately following the rise of the Communist party to power, there was a marked tendency toward the establishment of economic equality. Fundamental reforms were put into effect in order to equalize the distribution of incomes, and a drastic reduction of the wage differential between blue-collar and white-collar workers was achieved. (Similar income equalization policies were pursued as well after World War II in the other major eastern European Communist nations.) In addition to these measures, established privilege was attacked via major educational reforms, which were designed to bring large numbers of youth from subordinate classes into higher education.

Beginning in the early 1930s, however, this major egalitarian push was halted and even partially reversed through new policies established by Stalin. Stalin launched a major attack on all equalization programs, declaring himself steadfastly against *uravnilovka* ("equality-mongering"). It was argued that, in order to achieve full industrialization and the building of a modern society, greater material incentives had to be offered to persons engaged in more highly skilled forms of work. This policy was responsible for the reestablishment of sharp income differences between major occupational groups. Such new economic inequalities continued until approximately the mid-1950s. Around this time, a new attack on income inequality began and income differentials were reduced once again. Since the late 1980s, the implementation of *perestroika* included an attempt to increase income differentials. This was consistent with the Soviet Union's shift toward a more market-oriented, capitalist economy.

In recent times, it is clear that there were a number of social groupings that could be distinguished by different income levels and other forms of privilege. Whether or not these groups should be called "classes" is to some extent a matter of definition. Official Soviet ideology (at least prior to 1985 and the beginnings of *perestroika*) referred to them as "nonantagonistic strata," noting that the groups were not distinguished by the ownership of private property, which had been formally abolished in the Soviet Union. Thus so-called *nonegalitarian classlessness* was said to prevail under state socialism. That is, there were different social groups possessing unequal amounts of material privilege, but these groups were not considered classes because their level of privilege did not depend on their possession or lack of property. Since private ownership of property was absent, one group did not gain by holding other groups down, and the social relations between such groups were therefore not antagonistic ones.

From a classical Marxian viewpoint, which equates class with property ownership, the official Soviet view was not unreasonable. But as we saw in the last chapter, class cannot be defined simply in terms of ownership, because most of the population of all industrial societies does not own any means of production. Classes are more commonly defined by sociologists as groups that are built around particular kinds of occupations and that vary according to degrees of privilege and prestige.

From this perspective, it is perfectly sensible to regard the major socioeconomic groups within state socialist society as classes.

Parkin (1971) characterizes the class structure of state socialist society in the following manner (listing the classes from highest to lowest):

- The white-collar intelligentisa, consisting mainly of individuals in professional, managerial, and administrative positions
- Skilled manual workers
- Lower-level white-collar workers
- Unskilled workers
- Peasant farmers

The dominant and most privileged class within state socialism was the white-collar intelligentsia. Parkin suggests that the major class cleavage within state socialism was between this group and all the rest. Members of the intelligentsia not only received higher incomes than the rest but they also received bonuses and special wage supplements, as well as other less measurable rewards, such as high-quality accommodations, opportunities to travel abroad, and the use of official cars and state property. Furthermore, the social distinction between the intelligentsia and other classes was magnified by the fact that its members were more likely to be party members. Party membership in itself conferred additional benefits. These included the pulling of strings or the winning of favors, an opportunity to acquire the best theater tickets, or the ensuring of a place for one's children at good schools and universities.

Whereas Parkin sees the major class division within state socialism as between the intelligentsia and the rest of society, others would emphasize a line of demarcation between a tiny portion of the intelligentsia and everyone else. This group is what is most commonly called the *nomenklatura*. The intelligentsia made up perhaps as much as 20 percent of state socialist society, but the *nomenklatura* at most included 1 percent. It consisted of individuals at the very highest levels of the Communist party bureaucracy. Milovan Djilas (1957) regards the *nomenklatura* as a ruling elite broadly similar to the ruling classes of capitalist societies. He sees this elite, which he has referred to as a "new class," as a property-owning, highly privileged, and self-perpetuating class that dominated the rest of state socialist society. This argument has considerable merit, but it must be qualified. Anthony Giddens (1980), for example, although not disputing the existence of such an elite group, argues that it cannot be strictly compared to a capitalist ruling class. He observes that in state socialist society, the dominant class enjoyed rights only over the dispensation of collective property, and that this gave it a different character from capitalist classes, which have control over large supplies of private capital.

Victor Zaslavsky (1995) provides additional insight into the stratification system in the Soviet Union. He points out that this system consisted of "several interrelated subsystems of political, economic, territorial, and ethnic stratification, controlled by the state" (1995:118). He gives special attention to the most favored members of the intelligentsia, who were those working in the military sector of the economy. In their behalf, a whole system of "closed enterprises" and "closed cities" was created. Zaslavsky tells us more (1995:120–121):

> Having introduced the top-priority category of "closed cities," the redistributive state had taken a decisive step in the organization and administration of this territorial-based system of social stratification. Closed cities were considered the most important settlements in the country, with rights to permanent residence conferred only by birth or by special permission of the city administration. The hierarchy of population settlements in the redistributive state led to the establishment of a stable hierarchy of status and to the emergence of new social groups and categories whose members had different life chances and enjoyed very different levels of consumption. The closed cities also played an increasingly important role in structuring access to higher education and promoting the growth of the group of Soviet specialists traditionally known as the intelligentsia. Indeed, the major universities of the country were all located within these closed cities, as were the majority of specialists with a higher education. The proliferation of elite schools and specialized services such as private tutoring in closed cities gave their residents a decisive advantage in access to prestigious universities and other institutions of higher education. Membership in the Soviet elite and educated middle classes, thus, took on an increasingly hereditary character. . . .
>
> These and analogous policies of creating special "top priority" enterprises and entire industrial sectors, privileged geographic regions and settlements, and an accompanying system of most- and least-favored social and ethnic groups exemplify the enormous role the Soviet redistributive state played in creating and maintaining a hierarchical social structure. Using its position both as the sole employer for the entire labor force and as the primary agency of redistribution, the state established a political-administrative ascription for membership in major social groups and categories.

## The Modern Communist State: Leninist Regimes

One of the most striking characteristics of state socialist societies was the nature of their political regimes: In all instances, these societies had highly authoritarian and often brutally dictatorial states in which a single party, the Communist party, monopolized rule. A classic description of the contemporary Communist state was provided many years ago by Milovan Djilas in his book *The New Class* (1957). Djilas was a vice president of Yugoslavia who was expelled from the Communist party in 1954 after appealing for democratic reforms. In 1956, he was sentenced to a 10-year prison term for expressing the ideas contained in *The New Class*. Although released in 1961, he was reimprisoned in 1962 after the publication of his *Conversations with Stalin*.

As Djilas notes, "Everything happened differently in the U.S.S.R. and other Communist countries from what the leaders—even such prominent ones as Lenin, Stalin, Trotsky, and Bukharin—anticipated. They expected that the state would rapidly wither away, that democracy would be strengthened. The reverse happened" (1957:37). Djilas explains that the postrevolutionary Communist party had an extraordinarily high degree of ideological and organizational centralization. Remaining on the political scene long after victory, the party began strengthening and

*Lenin's Tomb in Red Square, Moscow.*

consolidating its power over the rest of society. It maintained an atmosphere of constant political vigilance; ideological unity within the party was demanded and great attention was paid to rooting out both real and potential opposition. Terrorist and oppressive methods were needed to achieve these goals. The result was the creation, in Djilas's words, of "a class whose power over men is the most complete known to history"—the Communist bureaucratic elite, or *nomenklatura*.

Until very recently, this bureaucratic elite maintained an administrative monopoly over the entire social order, including complete control over virtually all economic activity; tolerated no ideological deviation from the party line and swiftly used force to punish those who did deviate; and tyrannized the mind by suppressing all intellectual and artistic discoveries and creations that contradicted official party dogma. It is little wonder that Djilas has called the power of this class the "most complete known to history."

The Communist states of eastern Europe have often been referred to as *Marxist* or *Marxist-Leninist* states. Although there is some justification for this, the terminology is highly misleading and should either be avoided or used with great care. The

Soviet Union and its eastern European satellites adopted some of the ideas spelled out by Marx in the middle of the nineteenth century as essential elements of socialism. They socialized the means of production, eliminated the bourgeoisie, and reorganized the economy around centralized state planning. However, in many ways they were very un-Marxian. They produced an alternative version of capitalist commodity production, introduced the detailed division of labor into the workplace, failed utterly in abolishing alienated labor, failed to create a classless society, and failed miserably in producing a political system that Marx would have found acceptable. Marx argued that in their early stages, the first socialist societies would be forced to adopt what he called the "dictatorship of the proletariat" as a form of government. This would be a highly authoritarian government that would be necessary to restore social order and facilitate the transition to full communism. However, it would only be temporary and in due time would give way to an entirely new form of political order based on the "withering away of the state." The state would cease to have any ruling or dictatorial powers and would be reduced to the role of manager and coordinator of the economy. It would be a highly democratic state, with workers having direct input into political decision making.

Obviously, nothing like this developed in the first socialist societies, but it is important to set the record straight about what Marx really said and hoped for. And in setting that record straight, we would urge the abandonment of the terms *Marxist* and *Marxist-Leninist* to characterize Communist states. Although these states used those terms themselves, that is no justification for keeping them. They used these terms not out of a desire for social-scientific accuracy but as part of an overarching legitimizing ideology. As Kenneth Jowitt (1978) and Daniel Chirot (1986) suggest, it is more accurate to call them **Leninist societies** or **Leninist regimes.** These regimes have the following basic features (Chirot, 1986:265):

- The Communist party claims an absolute monopoly of political power.
- All key sectors of the economy are controlled and operated by the state.
- There is a formal commitment to creating an industrially advanced and highly egalitarian society.
- The regime legitimizes itself by appeal to Marxism-Leninism as an overarching political ideology.
- The Communist party regards itself as the ultimate interpreter of scientific and political truth, and its decisions and actions are not subject to doubt.
- There is close regulation of the daily lives of individuals and sharp limitations placed on their freedom of movement, of speech, of association, and of philosophical or ideological commitment.

A recent book by the French historian Stéphane Courtois and his colleagues, *The Black Book of Communism* (Courtois et al., 1999), shows that these features of Leninist regimes are only part of the story. Courtois and associates attempt to enumerate the human consequences of Leninist regimes in terms of the number of people who lost their lives as the direct or indirect results of the actions of these regimes. As the authors note, Leninist regimes virtually turned mass crime into the ordinary operation of the state. They estimate that approximately 100

million people died as the result of such things as executions, the slaughter of re-
bellious workers, and mass starvation of the peasantry. This, of course, ignores the
immense suffering of millions of others in forced labor camps and the like who did
not die. Courtois and colleagues break down the 100 million dead approximately as
follows:

- In the Soviet Union, 20 million died. Tens of thousands of hostages and prisoners who were never tried were executed, and hundreds of thousands of re-
  bellious workers and peasants were murdered in the period between 1918 and
  1922. Five million died as a result of the famine of 1922. Tens of thousands
  were murdered in concentration camps between 1918 and 1930. There were
  578,000 criminal convictions in 1926, 709,000 in 1927, 909,000 in 1928, and
  another 1,778,000 in 1929. And then the real horrors started when Stalin came
  to power and began the forced collectivization of agriculture. In the early
  1930s, two million peasants were deported, many of whom died as a result. Six
  million peasants died as a result of the great famine of 1932–33. These de-
  portations and deaths resulted from an ongoing struggle between peasants
  and the state. The peasantry wanted to retain enough of their harvest to provide for their own needs, but the state demanded that the peasants give up
  more. When the peasants refused, they were deliberately starved out. In 1937–
  38, some 700,000 people were executed for any type of political deviation from
  the Party line. Finally, the 1930s witnessed a dramatic expansion in the system
  of concentration camps. In 1935, there were nearly one million prisoners in the
  camps, a number that nearly doubled by 1941. These were mostly political
  prisoners.
- China subjected its population and its political dissidents to severe repression
  in the form of selective arrests, public humiliations, beatings, and imprison-
  ment in so-called reeducation camps. Between the rise of the Communists to
  power in 1949 and the death of Mao Zedong in 1976, perhaps as many as 65
  million people died. Between 1959 and 1961, China experienced the greatest
  famine in all of world history, with anywhere between 20 and 43 million estimated to have died from it. Courtois and colleagues blame this on total government incompetence in agriculture. The concentration camp system in China
  was huge. There were at least 1,000 camps and as many as 50 million people
  passed through them; some 20 million of these died in the camps. During the
  famous Cultural Revolution of 1966–76, the government engaged in extreme
  anti-intellectualism, persecuting teachers, scientists, and technicians in large
  numbers and killing many. There was an extreme emphasis on ideological
  conformity and, as in the Soviet Union, any kind of political deviation was severely punished, often with death.
- Cambodia's experience with Communism was horrendous. Renamed Kampuchea once Pol Pot came to power, an attempt was made to implement a type
  of socialist society overnight. Agriculture was collectivized in just two years.
  To accomplish this, the government inaugurated a campaign to move people
  out of the cities and back into the rural areas, and as a result they passed
  through a series of deportation camps. There were many purges and

massacres, and possibly one million executions. Courtois and associates describe Kampuchea as a nightmare world in which all human values had been destroyed and all human compassion and decency had been lost. People were reduced to cannibalism, eating human livers, stealing food from pigs, and eating rats, ants, and spiders.

- North Korea has been described as the "most closed state in the world." The people were subjected to the usual purges, executions, and prison camps. No Communist state has ever engaged in such total and consistent ideological indoctrination of the masses. As in other Communist states, North Korea has experienced severe famine, with possibly as many as two million people dying from starvation.

These are the most extreme examples of the dire human consequences of Leninist regimes, but all Communist or Leninist societies have been engaged in political repression, including the execution of real or perceived political dissidents. In eastern Europe as a whole, at least a million people died as a result of execution or death in labor camps, another million died in Vietnam, and nearly two million died in African countries that had adopted some variety of Leninism. Perhaps the most benign of all Leninist societies has been Cuba, but it too has not escaped political repression.

Why have the state socialist societies departed so greatly from Marx's hope for a highly democratic socialist state? Why have these states been so politically repressive, and why have their human consequences been so horrendous? In the case of eastern Europe, of course, **totalitarian dictatorships** were originally imposed, and to a large extent maintained, from the outside by the Soviet Union (Yugoslavia being an exception). But what, then, is the reason for the totalitarian character of the Soviet Union itself? One type of explanation has been offered by Immanuel Wallerstein (1998). He argues that Soviet totalitarianism resulted from the severe threat the Soviet Union experienced, both economically and militarily, from the Western capitalist world (cf. Chase-Dunn, 1982). In a genuine socialist society—the socialist world-government that will ultimately replace the capitalist world-economy—this threat will disappear, and the repressive state will then wither away (Wallerstein, 1984).

Although this argument initially appears to contain a strong air of special pleading—to be almost an apologia for Communist repression—there is some evidence consistent with it, or at least the first part of it. From about the late 1920s until sometime during the 1950s, the Soviet Union largely withdrew from the world capitalist system and followed an economic policy devoted to catching up with Western capitalism. It was precisely during this time that totalitarianism—indeed, Stalinist terrorism—was at its height (Nove, 1989). This terrorism substantially ceased after the death of Stalin in 1953, and with the shift to the new regime of Nikita Khrushchev, a bit of openness first started to appear (Nove, 1989). And, indeed, it was during the Khrushchev period that the Soviet Union starting showing signs of moving back toward greater participation in the world-economy. The fact that the last Soviet Union regime (that of Mikhail Gorbachev), with its strong orientation toward the world market, made such a dent in the totalitarian state suggests that totalitarianism is a political strategy associated with closure to a hostile world-economy.

However, this cannot be the whole story. A well-known competing explanation is at hand in the view of the state held by Max Weber. Weber thought that socialism would necessarily lead to extensive bureaucratic centralization of power in the hands of a ruling minority. Such centralization would be necessary as a means of managing a socialist economy. Thus, socialism would inevitably become much less democratic than capitalism. Bureaucracy encourages the concentration of power, and once such power has developed, it becomes self-perpetuating and its stranglehold is extremely difficult to break.

Along similar lines, Tatu Vanhanen (1997) argues quite persuasively that states will be authoritarian when the mass of the population lack resources that they can use to force them to be less repressive and more democratic. His Index of Power Resources, referred to in the last chapter, shows extremely low values for Leninist states and very high values for Western democracies. The average IPR for 12 major Leninist societies in 1980 was 1.53 (the highest was for Yugoslavia, at 15.7; if we exclude Yugoslavia, the average was only 0.35). By contrast, the average for 18 liberal democracies was 42.1 (the highest was for the United States, at 52.2). So it seems clear that a major reason Leninist societies are so repressive is that the vast majority of the population has few or no power resources to prevent that from happening. Albert Somit and Steven Peterson (1997) note that virtually all states throughout human history have been authoritarian, and that this seems to be endemic to the human condition when the governed lack political resources. Leninist regimes, sad to say, are therefore much closer to the norm of human history than are democratic regimes.

Nonetheless, modern Leninist regimes have been repressive and brutal on a scale never seen before in the world, and this extremity must be explained. Does it have to do with the modern military and communication technology available to Leninist regimes, thus making severe repression and brutality all the easier? Is it the result of the extreme measures deemed necessary to catch up with Western capitalism in a short time, as seemed to be the case with Stalin's forced industrialization of the 1930s? These factors may well play a role, but a full understanding still eludes us. One thing, though, is crystal clear: Strong state control over the economy has not produced, and seemingly cannot produce, a democratic state because of its negative effect on the power resources of the masses.

## The Collapse of Communism

Major political changes began in the Soviet Union in the mid-1980s and in eastern Europe in the late 1980s. Mikhail Gorbachev's introduction of *perestroika* was accompanied by the political reforms known as *glasnost*. *Glasnost* was essentially devoted to greater "openness" in political and social life. The mass media were given more freedom to report events accurately and thoroughly; there was more toleration of intellectual and artistic freedom of expression; some elections of public officials were held; and some political prisoners were released. *Glasnost* cannot be understood, as some might think, as simply being some sort of philosophical or intellectual sea change based on a sudden awareness of the humanistic implications of democracy. It seems much more appropriate to think of it as the political counterpart of *perestroika:* It was the political expression of the Soviet Union's shift toward full reintegration into the capitalist world-economy. Gorbachev and other Soviet leaders seemed to think that the return to free-market capitalism required a much greater degree of political openness than had previously been the case—that a more liberal economy required a more liberal state (Kumar, 1992).

However, *glasnost* was only the beginning of the political changes. In the autumn of 1989, Poland, East Germany, Czechoslovakia, and Romania experienced major transformations in their authoritarian regimes. The political monopoly of the Communist party was broken and significant steps were taken in the direction of much greater democracy and openness. Then, in 1991, after a right-wing attempt to overthrow Gorbachev failed miserably, the Soviet Union was publicly delegitimated, the Communist party lost its monopoly of power, and Gorbachev was removed from office and replaced by his chief ultraliberal opponent, Boris Yeltsin. What happened in eastern Europe in 1989 and the Soviet Union in 1991 was, quite literally, the collapse of Communism as a political and social movement and a state ideology. This collapse was complicated and exacerbated by intense waves of nationalism all over the former Communist world. The Soviet Union disintegrated as a

*Mikhail Gorbachev, former leader of the old Soviet Union. Gorbachev set in motion a number of economic and political reforms that ultimately led to the demise of the Soviet Union and its replacement by Russia and a number of newly independent former Soviet republics.*

single state as a result of many of the old Soviet republics claiming political sovereignty (the largest and most politically significant of these new sovereign states is, of course, Russia). Czechoslovakia separated into two states, Slovakia and the Czech Republic. And, in the most horrendous fashion, the state once known as Yugoslavia was entirely broken apart, succumbing to some of the most virulent nationalist movements the modern world has ever seen.

The collapse of Communism beginning in the fall of 1989 took almost everyone—social scientists, journalists, political commentators, and ordinary citizens—by great surprise. No one expected that a political party with the level of political and military control that the Communist party had achieved could be so swiftly and decisively thrown out of power. How do we account for such a profound and surprising political transformation? One well-known explanation has been advanced by Randall Collins and David Waller (1992; Collins, 1986). They view the collapse of the Soviet Union as the latest historical instance of the phenomenon that has been called a **state breakdown.** This is a severe crisis within a state that leads to widespread political conflict and the collapse of a state's capacity to rule (Goldstone, 1991). Collins and Waller's theory is a kind of Weberian geopolitical argument. They root the breakdown of the Soviet state in the overextension of its "empire"—the incorporation of many different nationalities into the U.S.S.R. after 1917 and again during World War II, and the military domination of its eastern European satellites. This overextension created severe economic costs, especially in military buildup, which simply became unbearable over time. The system was ultimately unsustainable. Collins and Waller are saying, in essence, that the immediate causes of Soviet state breakdown were economic, but that these economic problems resulted from the **geopolitics** of the Soviet empire rather than from any inherent feature of state socialism as an economic system.

Collins and Waller's argument has a good deal to recommend it, but it is doubtless not the whole story. One of the things the theory clearly does help to explain is the wave of nationalist movements that have erupted all over eastern Europe. It also provides one of the pieces to the puzzle of the Soviet Union's severe economic problems. However, the economic difficulties of state socialism cannot simply be laid at the door of the Soviet Union's geopolitical arrangements. As noted earlier, there do seem to be serious problems inherent in state socialism as an economic system. As Kornai (1992) has shown, the intrinsic nature of state socialism turns it into a permanent shortage economy and produces economic difficulties that feed on themselves and worsen over time. State socialism was reasonably successful for a time in generating a great deal of industrialization and improvement in living standards in eastern Europe, and especially in the Soviet Union. It has not been the abject failure that it has often been portrayed to be (Szelenyi and Szelenyi, 1992). Nevertheless, by the mid-1970s, it began to stagnate, and its economic problems have only worsened since that time. State socialism was not an economy well suited to making the move into the production of mass consumer goods and services, and thus it began to fall ever farther behind Western capitalism after about 1975. And, as pointed out earlier in this chapter, one cannot ignore the role of the surrounding capitalist world-economy in creating all kinds of pressures designed either to destroy socialism or cause it to want to relink itself with the world-capitalist system. This has been a source of economic difficulties quite apart from geopolitics.

We conclude that the causes of the recent state breakdowns in the Soviet Union and eastern Europe have been primarily economic. It was the economic problems created within state socialism, and from a variety of sources, that led to *perestroika* and *glasnost*. However, important political factors were involved as well in determining the specific outcomes that these reforms eventually led to (Hahn, 2002). In essence, Gorbachev and his allies unleashed political forces they could not control. Once reforms were initiated, political infighting began within the Soviet political elite, and it was this infighting that was the immediate cause of the collapse of the Soviet Union (Hahn, 2002). As for eastern Europe, by 1989, it had become obvious to many members of these societies that the Soviet Union was no longer willing to intervene militarily to quell popular discontent. And, with the Soviet Union's military control over eastern Europe removed, people no longer had to fear that popular protest would be extremely dangerous, as it had been in the past. They took to the streets and demanded an end to the long-hated regimes, regimes that even many members of the Communist elites in eastern European countries wanted to see ended. Things had been brewing under the surface for many years, and when they all came together in one explosive push it seemed as if it all simply happened overnight. But, as we have seen, these events had been developing for a long time.

Were these state breakdowns "people's revolutions"? That the collapse of Communism was due in large part to popular rebellions by the masses has been a widespread interpretation among both intellectuals and journalists (Chirot, 1991). However, despite all the popular discontent throughout eastern Europe, it is doubtful that this played more than a small role in bringing Communist regimes down. The movements against the Communist regimes, to the degree that they can be called revolutions at all, were not people's revolutions but rather what are known as "revolutions from above"—revolutions initiated by one segment of the political elite against another (Hahn, 2002). These revolutions occurred both because of the shifting economic (and hence political) interests and outlook of an elite segment, and because the Soviet Union had greatly relaxed its military and political domination of eastern Europe. A look at the past makes the point. In 1956, there was a people's uprising against the Hungarian Communist regime, and in 1968, an attempt at liberalization of the Communist regime in Czechoslovakia was made. Both movements were quickly crushed by Soviet military force. What had changed between 1968 and 1989? The answer is, the Soviet elite, or at least a significant segment of it, had come to view things in an entirely new way. Indeed, it has been shown in some detail that Gorbachev and his supporters either desired or easily tolerated the regime transformations that occurred in eastern Europe in 1989 (Kumar, 1992:345–349). Popular discontent figured in the downfall of these regimes only at the very end, when everything had basically been decided, and then more as show than as real substance. Krishan Kumar has captured the situation almost perfectly (1992:320–321):

> Is it not the case rather that it is only when the upper classes cannot maintain the old order that we find the clear evidence of the determination of the lower classes to end it? Does this not suggest that causal priority has to be assigned to the problems of the

existing power structure and the existing power holders in society—that is, to the distemper at the top rather than at the bottom of society? Discontent, latent or manifest, among the lower classes can be taken as the more or less given of most stratified social orders. Regimes can be peppered with popular rebellions without succumbing to them, despite these expressions of manifest disaffection on the part of the people. This has been the case with the majority of the agrarian empires of the pre-industrial world.

It is only when the ruling structures of society are in a clear state of decay or dissolution that popular discontent can express itself in a confident way. Then we usually find spokesmen from the upper classes urging on popular feeling against the regime. Revolutionaries, often released from prison or returned from exile abroad, busy themselves with organizing the mass discontent. After the success of the revolution, the idea of a popular uprising against a hated tyranny becomes the official myth of the new regime. This conceals the fact that the old regime has died, often by its own hand, rather than been overthrown in a popular outburst of indignation.

# Postsocialism: Achievements, Failures, Prospects

With the collapse of Communism and the transition to postsocialism in the old Soviet Union and eastern Europe, where are the postsocialist societies headed? Let us attempt to answer this question with respect to the three main social sectors we have been discussing: the economy, the stratification system, and politics.

## The Economy

The economic situation in some eastern European postsocialist countries seems to be improving, or at least holding steady, but in Russia it has continued to deteriorate (Ericson, 1995; Castells, 1996; Kagarlitsky, 2002; Stiglitz, 2003). Between 1991 and 1992, GDP declined by 29 percent, and by another 12 percent by 1993. Total economic investment fell by 40 percent in 1992 and by another 16 percent in 1993. The rate of economic accumulation fell by 34 percent in 1989, by another 32 percent in 1992, and by yet another 26 percent in 1993. In 1993, Russian foreign debt amounted to 64 percent of GDP and a huge 262 percent of annual exports. Between 1991 and 1998, total agricultural and industrial production declined by about 50 percent, and capital investment in 1996 was only some 24 percent of its 1990 level. There was a huge flight of capital amounting to more than $150 billion between 1992 and 1999. Moreover, science and technology decayed badly; the production of oil and gas, a crucial part of the Russian economy, was in a state of disorganization and decline; and the infrastructures of telecommunications and transportation badly needed repair and suffered from a lack of equipment. In sum, "By the mid-1990s the military-industrial sector, the heart of Soviet industry, was essentially wrecked" (Castells, 1996:139).

And there were major consequences for the quality of life of the average Russian citizen, as indicated by falling birthrates and increased mortality, including infant mortality. In some sectors of the economy, incomes declined markedly, and often people had to wait many months before they even received paychecks. Housing and transportation increased in price; standard items of consumption became luxuries; the consumption of meat, fish, and milk declined by 25 percent or more; the health care system collapsed; diseases such as cholera, typhoid fever, and diptheria reappeared; purchasing power fell to levels approximating those of the 1950s; and inflation destroyed the life savings of many Russian citizens. As Boris Kagarlitsky (2002:98) puts it, "Russia was flung back decades, losing almost all of the achievements of the post-Stalin period."

According to Kagarlitsky (2002), a Russian social scientist who was a political prisoner during the Breshnev regime, this economic deterioration resulted from the unique political and economic situation that arose during *perestroika* and that intensified with the collapse of Communism and the transition from Gorbachev to Yeltsin. A new economic oligarchy formed that was not a true capitalist class and that was wholly unprepared to promote economic development. This oligarchy was inextricably intertwined with a Russian state that, despite *glasnost*, became anything but democratic. The state perpetuated and greatly intensified the old Soviet pattern of corruption; it rigged elections and engaged in actions that were purely designed to maintain itself in power and to benefit economically from the changed situation.

Despite the privatization of industry, the state continued to perform most of the functions of ownership; a good deal of privatized property actually became renationalized beginning as early as 1995. Russia actually resembled a feudal-bureaucratic society more than a capitalist society, Kagarlitsky claims, one in which parasitic politicians who work through bribes are much more important than entrepreneurs. Entrepreneurs benefit more from exporting their capital than using it for domestic investment and economic development, and perhaps as much as half of the Russian economy has fallen into criminal hands (Remnick, 1997). In the words of Kagarlitsky (2002:32–33):

> To the degree that Russia is now part of the world system, included in the processes of globalization, it is a capitalist country. But neither the production that is occurring in Russia's internal market, nor the labour relations and other social relationships that exist with the domestic economy, can be described as capitalist. . . .
>
> The present day "success stories" of Russian exporters have not been based on copying Western methods of enterprise management. The largest corporations have retained all the features of traditional Soviet enterprises. The elite that has chosen such a model of "integration into the world system," however, is not able to modernize the country. On the contrary, the elite has a vital interest in maintaining Russia's backwardness and its archaic social structures, albeit with "European" stage scenery.

Kagarlitsky argues that this archaic and extremely corrupt state structure must be overthrown before serious economic development and modernization can begin in Russia. The oligarchs and the Russian state have led the country to a dead end, he says, and the only way out is through a new revolution that will destroy the oligarchs and create an entirely new type of state. Kagarlitsky may well be right, but doing this will be extremely difficult, and as a result the situation looks quite bleak in Russia for the forseeable future.

The causes of these disastrous consequences in Russia must be sought both inside and outside the country. As Joseph Stiglitz (2003:133–134) puts it, "While those in Russia must bear much of the blame for what has happened, the Western advisers, especially from the United States and the IMF [International Monetary Fund], who marched in so quickly to preach the gospel of the market economy, must also take some of the blame." Western advisers preached the "neoliberal" ideology that the market is the key to success and that it can virtually do no wrong, and they wanted to privatize the economy as quickly as possible.

One recommendation was that most prices should be completely freed from their previous governmental restraints, but this led very quickly to massive inflation, which wiped out the savings of much of the population. But some prices were kept artificially low, especially those for natural resources. This led new private entrepreneurs to buy oil and other resources at very low prices and sell them for much higher prices in the West. They made billions of dollars in the process, but this did nothing to stimulate the Russian economy because the money was invested in the U.S. stock market or kept in offshore bank accounts. This and other policy recommendations were intended to increase foreign investment in Russia, but nothing of the sort happened. New oligarchs got rich quickly and took their money out of the country. Had privatization of the Russian economy proceeded more slowly, carefully, and thoughtfully, then the crises that emerged would have been much less severe, and a real transition to a market economy that had real growth potential might have gotten a foothold (Stiglitz, 2003).

Many of the other postsocialist states, especially those that were former Soviet satellites, have experienced similarly dramatic economic declines, and misguided Western policies have played a major role here too. As Stiglitz (2003:151) points out,

> Only a few of the former Communist countries—such as Poland, Hungary, Slovenia, and Slovakia—have a GDP equal to that of a decade ago. For the rest, the magnitudes of the declines in incomes are so large that they are hard to fathom. . . . Moldova's decline is the most dramatic, with output today less than a third of what it was a decade ago. Ukraine's 2000 GDP is just a third of what it was ten years ago.

Stiglitz notes that the most successful postsocialist societies, such as Poland, have been the ones that have not succumbed to the pressure of the IMF's radical privatization policies.

## Stratification

Because of the uncertainties of postsocialist economies, it is difficult to tell just what forms new postsocialist stratification systems will eventually take. However, as these societies become more capitalistic it is almost a certainty that inequalities of income and wealth will become increasingly prominent. There is clear evidence of this already. In Russia, the *nomenklatura* has lost its complete monopoly on political power, and as a result the careers of many members of that group have been destroyed (Zaslavsky, 1995). At the same time, as already noted, many members of this group have benefitted enormously from the new privatization. They have been able to strike deals with new private firms, often becoming co-owners, and are in the process of forming a fast-growing class of property owners. Some have already become extremely rich and flaunt their wealth in the most garish ways (Zaslavsky, 1995).

According to Kagarlitsky (2002), the new Russian class structure looks approximately as follows. At the top are the "oligarchs," a tiny group of about 40 superrich persons with close ties to the Russian state (or whose members overlap with the state). The oligarchs wield enormous economic and political power. Next are the merely very rich "New Russians," consisting of capitalists and state bureaucrats who lack any real political power. They constitute only about 1 percent of the population. Then there is a small middle class constituting about 8 percent of the population, a very large working class comprising some 66 percent of the population, and a class of people living in real poverty, who make up about 26 percent of the population.

## Politics

Given the political changes thus far, what are the prospects for genuine democracy in eastern Europe, Russia, and the newly independent former Soviet republics? Some evidence suggests good reasons for optimism. Table 8.2 shows democracy and political rights scores for Russia, eastern Europe, and newly autonomous states that were former Soviet republics. By 1993, all of these societies had achieved at least some small amount of formal democracy in terms of political participation and popular elections, and many had established a substantial amount. Many established high levels of formal political liberties and rights. Moreover, most of these societies (17 of 23) were able to sustain or even enhance their formal democratic institutions by the end of the millennium. Based on these statistics, the political future would appear to be rosy.

However, considerable caution is called for. In the early 1990s, a number of social scientists expressed pessimism, at least about the near future (Hobsbawm, 1991; Jowitt, 1992; Steel, 1992). Ken Jowitt (1992), a leading specialist on Soviet and eastern European politics, has argued that the Leninist legacy of corrupt authoritarian regimes is likely to remain for some time and constitutes a very inadequate foundation for constructing a genuinely democratic polity. Jowitt suggests that postsocialist countries in the future will more likely resemble the Latin America of the past than the western Europe of the present—that is, that they will experience the constant breakdown of attempts to establish democracy. The most one might hope for in the near future, he argues, is a kind of "liberal authoritarianism," or the type of highly restricted democracy that characterized the western European states before the mid- to late-nineteenth century. Jowitt's pessimism has been echoed by Ronald Steel (1992:170–171), and for largely the same reasons:

**TABLE 8.2   Democracy and Political Rights in Postsocialist and
Newly Autonomous States, 1977–2003**

| Country | Democracy Score | | | Political Rights Score | | |
|---|---|---|---|---|---|---|
| | 1980 | 1993 | 2000 | 1977 | 1988 | 2003 |
| Albania | 0.0 | 7.7 | 12.0 | 1 | 1 | 5 |
| Azerbaijan | — | 3.1 | 11.8 | — | — | 2 |
| Belarus | — | 6.5 | 7.2 | — | — | 2 |
| Bosnia-Herzegovina | — | 16.2 | 24.8 | — | — | 4 |
| Bulgaria | 0.0 | 35.4 | 24.1 | 1 | 1 | 7 |
| Czech Republic | 0.0 | 40.3 | 39.3 | 1 | 1 | 7 |
| Estonia | — | 17.7 | 24.1 | — | — | 7 |
| Georgia | — | 19.8 | 14.8 | — | — | 4 |
| Hungary | 0.0 | 27.4 | 25.4 | 2 | 3 | 7 |
| Kazakhstan | — | 1.5 | 8.2 | — | — | 2 |
| Kyrgyzstan | — | 2.4 | 11.0 | — | — | 2 |
| Latvia | — | 19.5 | 27.7 | — | — | 7 |
| Lithuania | — | 23.5 | 28.2 | — | — | 7 |
| Macedonia | — | 12.2 | 20.2 | — | — | 5 |
| Moldova | — | 8.0 | 22.0 | — | — | 5 |
| Poland | 0.0 | 19.6 | 22.3 | 2 | 3 | 7 |
| Romania | 1.1 | 27.5 | 20.7 | 1 | 1 | 6 |
| Russia | — | 27.0 | 20.7 | 1 | 2 | 3 |
| Slovakia | — | 38.4 | 36.8 | — | — | 7 |
| Slovenia | — | 33.0 | 29.1 | — | — | 7 |
| Tajikistan | — | 3.0 | 9.2 | — | — | 2 |
| Ukraine | — | 21.7 | 32.7 | — | — | 4 |
| Yugoslavia | 0.0 | 20.7 | 20.7 | 2 | 3 | 5 |

*Note:* Democracy scores are calculated as the rate of voter participation multiplied by the extent of political party competition, which is then divided by 100. A political rights score of 7 indicates the greatest recognition of political rights, a score of 1 the least recognition (these scores have been reversed from the original coding).

*Sources:* Vanhanen (2003); Gastil (1989); Freedom House Survey Team (2003).

For all the justifiable euphoria that has greeted the downfall of Stalinist dictatorships in most of the region, the fact remains that the states of this region are, for the most part, without a democratic tradition or modern economy. Some are quite likely to revert to previous forms of militarism and authoritarianism. All will probably be plagued by unemployment, inequality, and the consequent social unrest. The states of this traditionally unstable region have been frozen in an authoritarian mold for at least four decades, and some for many more. They have been cut off from the forces of democratization and modernization that have transformed Western Europe. They have a long history of anarchy, ethnic violence, endemic hatreds, regional warfare, and authoritarianism. The fact that they have been liberated from communist dictators does not mean that they will be pacific or democratic.

*Vladimir Putin, current president of Russia. Many scholars see Putin as the head of a political and economic oligarchy that must be radically reformed before Russia can be truly modernized.*

Kagarlitsky's (2002) recent analysis of the corrupt and authoritarian political scene in Russia suggests that the pessimism of these observers is well justified. It is abundantly clear that democracy in Russia is purely nominal or formal. Despite its democracy and political rights scores, there is no real democracy there at all. The same is true, although often to a lesser extent, of many of the other eastern European states and former Soviet republics. Gordon Hahn's (2002) perspective is quite similar to Kagarlitsky's. As he notes, Russia's revolution left many of the old ruling party bureaucrats in power rather than replacing them with an entirely new set of political leaders, and this has prevented Russia from creating a genuine democracy. In Hahn's words, the Russian government (2002:505)

> convenes elections regularly and has achieved significant democratization in rela-
> tions among elites. It has not developed, however, a truly liberal order where human
> rights are wholly secured and political institutions of a mature civil society, such as
> political parties and other associations, bring societal interests into politics by plac-
> ing their representatives in decisionmaking positions and thereby intermediating
> state and societal interests. Instead of the domination of formal institutions function-
> ing according to the rule of law, informal institutions leave leaders and bureaucrats
> unaccountable. Arbitrary rule wrestles with the rule of law in a fairly even contest. . . .
> There is little separation and balance between the executive, legislative, and judicial
> branches or effective civilian control, particularly parliamentary oversight, over the
> military.

Thus, Russia still has a long way to go before it establishes genuine democracy; it is very difficult to predict when that might become truly possible. Much work also remains to be done for many of the other "new democracies" of this part of the world.

# The Future of Socialism

With the collapse of Communism in its twentieth-century form, what is the future of socialism as a political philosophy and worldwide sociopolitical movement? Is it dead once and for all, as many observers have been claiming? Clearly, the answer is no. Many Western Marxists and other leftist intellectuals remain committed to a socialist future, but one that is much more humane and democratic than the old decayed socialism. Immanuel Wallerstein (1998), for example, argues that capitalism has only perhaps 50 or so years left in it, and that we are heading toward a great historical transition. Capitalism will encounter insurmountable problems that will bring it crashing down. In Wallerstein's view, it will in all likelihood be replaced by a type of global socialist system, which may or may not be an improvement on capitalism (although Wallerstein clearly hopes, and no doubt privately believes, that it will be better). Wallerstein envisions a new world-system in which all economic structures are nonprofit enterprises, some controlled by the state and some by other means. He argues that since nonprofit hospitals, for example, have operated under this kind of system and remained efficient, there is no reason in principle why other economic enterprises could not. These economic structures would not need to be internally autocratic or authoritarian in organization, could provide for worker participation in high-level decision making, and could build in safeguards against sloth and incompetence—one of the major undoings of the old state socialism—by penalizing it.

Similarly, Terry Boswell and Christopher Chase-Dunn (2000) see capitalism as unsustainable in the long run, but, unlike Wallerstein, they have mapped out a fairly detailed plan for constructing a global form of socialism that will retain many of the market principles of capitalism. All of these scholars, and many others like them, view the old state socialism as a perversion of socialist ideals that failed for a variety of reasons, chief among them the pressures of the surrounding capitalist world-economy. They remain optimistic that socialism can still work, and be a substantial improvement on capitalism, if it is constructed with an eye to learning from the errors of the past.

It remains to be seen whether any form of genuine socialism can ever be workable and a feasible alternative to capitalism. It may be that there really is no viable alternative to capitalism, and that the best we can do is "capitalism with a human face," as in the northern European social democracies of the present-day world. The big problem that seems to stand in the way of constructing a viable socialism is the "human nature" problem. The evidence from all over the world is that people, or at the very least a large number of them, seek power, status, and wealth. In small-scale hunter-gatherer and horticultural societies, those who strongly seek these things are not allowed to pursue their ambitions, and they lack the means to prevail against the will of the majority. But in societies of larger scale—agrarian and industrial societies—this is no longer possible, and significant inequalities become universal. If a socialist system along the lines imagined by Wallerstein or by Boswell and Chase-Dunn were to be established along relatively egalitarian lines, it is difficult to imagine it remaining that way for long. And it is much more difficult to eliminate sloth,

incompetence, and bureaucratic centralization than Wallerstein imagines. One can
be a socialist by philosophical principle but at the same time recognize that it is extremely difficult, if not impossible, to make it work in practice. This is why there may
be no viable alternative to some form of capitalism.

## FOR FURTHER READING

Chirot (1986) and Davis and Scase (1985) contain very good and easily understood treatments
of state socialism. See also Lane (1985). János Kornai's *The Socialist System: The Political
Economy of Communism* (1992) is a definitive work outlining the basic principles undergirding
the functioning and evolution of state socialism from the perspective of an economist. Christopher Chase-Dunn's edited collection, *Socialist States in the World-System* (1982), is a provocative set of essays in which a number of contemporary Marxian scholars debate the nature of
state socialism and its relationship to the capitalist world. Older but still useful works on state
socialism are Djilas (1957) and Parkin (1971).

Kumar (1992) is an extremely insightful article on the 1989 revolutions in eastern Europe. See also Kumar (2001). Gordon Hahn's *Russia's Revolution from Above* (2002) is a highly
detailed analysis of the collapse of the Soviet Union from the beginnings of its economic and
political reforms in 1985 through the seizure of power by Yeltsin. Hahn shows in meticulous
detail how the collapse was brought about by complex infighting among four different segments of the Soviet political elite. Two good collections of essays on the Soviet collapse and
the situation since then are Lapidus (1995) and Dallin and Lapidus (1995). See also Jowitt
(1992). Remnick (1997) is a journalistic account of post-Soviet Russia. Eyal (2003) discusses
state socialism in Czechoslovakia and its postsocialist breakup in the early 1990s.

*The Black Book of Communism* (1999), by Stéphane Courtois and five other historians, is
an attempt to assess the human consequences of Communism. The book was originally published in French and caused quite a stir when it first appeared in 1997. It is must reading for
those who want a frank assessment of the realities of Communism.

An important set of essays put together by Daniel Chirot (1989) shows how eastern Europe has been less developed than western Europe since the early Middle Ages. Western
Europe was not really responsible for "underdeveloping" it after the sixteenth century, as argued by Wallerstein. This lower level of eastern European development provided fertile
ground for its political and military takeover by the Soviet Union after World War II.

Boris Kagarlitsky's *Russia Under Yeltsin and Putin* (2002) is an extremely vivid depiction
of the failures of Russia in the postsocialist period. Kagarlitsky shows how the economic situation deteriorated in the 1990s and how Russia is still ruled by an undemocratic elite that has
little prospect of modernizing the country.

Immanuel Wallerstein's *Utopistics: Or Historical Changes of the Twenty-First Century*
(1998) argues that we are in the midst of a major worldwide transition from capitalism to
something else, probably a type of socialism. By "utopistics," Wallerstein means careful consideration of the historical alternatives we currently face, not the creation of some sort of uto-
pia, which is an impossible task. Wallerstein makes brief suggestions as to what alternative he
would choose. Terry Boswell and Christopher Chase-Dunn's *The Spiral of Capitalism and Socialism* (2000) discusses both capitalism and state socialism from a world-system perspective
and provides a thoughtfully worked-out strategy for a new version of socialism. Like
Wallerstein, the authors are committed socialists, but are fully aware of the failures of former
state socialist societies and their negative human consequences. They favor a democratic socialism that gives an important role to markets along with centralized planning and build on
the socialist rethinking of Roemer (1994).

# 9 Economic Development and Underdevelopment

Sometime after the end of World War II, social scientists began to speak of three "worlds." These worlds represented social, economic, and political categories into which contemporary societies could be placed. The First World consisted of the industrially advanced capitalist nations, which had parliamentary democratic forms of government: the United States, Canada, England, France, the Netherlands, Sweden, most of the rest of western and northern Europe, and also Australia and Japan. The Second World was industrially advanced, or at least on the path toward industrial development, but the societies of this category had socialist economies and totalitarian forms of government. Included in this category were the Soviet Union and the eastern European socialist states. The rest of the world, not counting primitive or preliterate societies, was the Third World. This world consisted of the poor, technologically backward, economically underdeveloped societies constituting most of Latin America, Africa, and Asia.

Having conceptualized something called a Third World, social scientists proceeded vigorously to study it. Many kinds of social scientists became involved in investigations focusing on different aspects of life in the Third World. Yet the overriding question for most investigators was why the societies of the Third World had failed to achieve the levels of technological and economic development, as well as the social patterns, so characteristic of the First World, and to some degree of the Second. They asked, putting it more simply, Why are poor countries poor? This question is the principal focus of the current chapter. After discussing the nature of underdevelopment, the chapter will examine the major theories that social scientists have proposed to explain underdevelopment. Then it turns to look at regional patterns of development and underdevelopment in East Asia, Latin America, and sub-Saharan Africa. The chapter also looks at the relationship between a country's position in the capitalist world-system and the nature of its state structure, paying particular attention to its level of democracy.

## The Nature of Underdevelopment

Social scientists first called the societies of the Third World "backward nations," but later abandoned this expression as derogatory, adopting instead the expressions "underdeveloped societies," "less-developed societies," and "developing nations."

Although these terms have also been criticized and others proposed, they have stuck and continue to be used by most social scientists. To understand exactly what is meant by underdevelopment, or by an underdeveloped nation, a useful first step is to distinguish between *under*development and *un*development (Frank, 1966). *Undeveloped societies* may be regarded as those outside the framework of a capitalist world-economy that rely on preindustrial technology in the context of a precapitalist economy. Societies surviving by hunting and gathering, horticultural, pastoral, or agrarian methods of production, and having some sort of premarket economy are referred to as *undeveloped*. The term *underdevelopment* is reserved for societies incorporated into a capitalist world-economy and functioning within it in some way. **Underdeveloped societies** may thus be regarded as the least technologically and economically advanced members of the modern world-system.

There are a number of reasons why the underdeveloped world became an object of intense social-scientific scrutiny after World War II. For one, the Third World was seen (by antagonists on both sides) as a major battle ground in the so-called Cold War between the First and Second Worlds. Another reason concerns the sheer size of the gulf that separated the First and Third Worlds. It is difficult to overstate the degree to which the lives led by average people in the First World differ from those led by the majority of the population of the Third World. A good place to start, then, is with the basic facts regarding underdevelopment.

The most commonly used measure of economic development is a nation's per capita Gross Domestic Product (GDP), which is the total value of goods and services it produces per person in a given year (a similar measure that is often used is the Gross National Product, or GNP, which is now sometimes called Gross National Income, or GNI). It can be seen that most of the underdeveloped nations have per capita GDPs that are quite low when compared to those of the developed nations. The average per capita GDP of the underdeveloped nations shown in Table 9.1 is $4,580, obviously much lower than the average for the developed capitalist nations, which is $26,073. There are significant differences between different regions of the less-developed world. Latin America is best off, with an average per capita GDP of $6,540; Asia is next, with an average of $5,136, and Africa lags far behind at $2,065. Actually, this figure for Africa is misleading, for there are major differences in geography and culture between Africa north of the Sahara and sub-Saharan Africa. North Africa is dry, inhabited largely by Arab populations with a history of agriculture and pastoralism, and largely Islamic in religion; sub-Saharan Africa, by contrast, is tropical or subtropical and inhabited by a wide range of societies with mostly horticultural economies (although pastoral economies have been found throughout the drier parts of East Africa). These two parts of Africa belong to essentially different worlds, and their levels of economic development reflect it: North Africa's per capita GDP is $4,163, whereas sub-Saharan Africa's is a dramatically lower $1,165.

We have separated out four Asian societies that once belonged to the underdeveloped world but that have experienced so much economic development that they essentially have become recent members of the developed world: South Korea, Taiwan, Hong Kong, and Singapore. Their average GDP per capita is $20,497, obviously much closer to the rest of the developed world than to the less-developed world.

**TABLE 9.1  Social, Demographic, and Economic Characteristics of Selected Contemporary Nations at Different Levels of Economic Development**

| Country | POP | RNI | CHM | LFA | GDP | POV | GIN | KWH |
|---|---|---|---|---|---|---|---|---|
| **Developed Countries** | | | | | | | | |
| Denmark | 5.4 | 0.4 | 6 | 4 | 27,627 | — | 0.247 | 6,030 |
| Sweden | 8.9 | 0.3 | 4 | 3 | 24,277 | 6 | 0.250 | 14,138 |
| Norway | 4.5 | 0.6 | 5 | 4 | 29,918 | 4 | 0.258 | 24,248 |
| United Kingdom | 59.9 | 0.4 | 6 | 2 | 23,509 | 16 | 0.368 | 5,384 |
| France | 59.2 | 0.4 | 6 | 2 | 24,223 | 10 | 0.327 | 6,392 |
| Germany | 82.2 | 0.3 | 6 | 3 | 25,103 | 7 | 0.300 | 5,690 |
| Netherlands | 16.0 | 0.6 | 7 | 3 | 25,657 | 7 | 0.326 | 5,993 |
| Belgium | 10.3 | 0.3 | 7 | 3 | 27,178 | — | 0.287 | 7,286 |
| Italy | 57.7 | 0.2 | 7 | 5 | 23,626 | — | 0.273 | 4,535 |
| Spain | 39.5 | 0.2 | 6 | 7 | 19,472 | — | 0.325 | 4,497 |
| Canada | 31.0 | 1.0 | 7 | 4 | 27,840 | 7 | 0.315 | 15,260 |
| United States | 284.0 | 1.2 | 9 | 3 | 34,142 | 14 | 0.408 | 11,994 |
| Australia | 19.4 | 1.2 | 7 | 5 | 25,693 | 18 | 0.352 | 8,884 |
| Japan | 127.1 | 0.3 | 5 | 6 | 26,755 | — | 0.249 | 7,443 |
| **Postsocialist Countries** | | | | | | | | |
| Russia | 144.8 | −0.2 | 19 | 12 | 8,377 | 25 | 0.487 | 4,050 |
| Czech Republic | 10.3 | −0.1 | 7 | 5 | 13,991 | 2 | 0.254 | 4,682 |
| Poland | 38.7 | 0.1 | 11 | 19 | 9,051 | 2 | 0.316 | 2,388 |
| Bulgaria | 8.1 | −0.6 | 16 | — | 5,710 | 22 | 0.264 | 2,899 |
| Hungary | 10.2 | −0.2 | 11 | 7 | 12,416 | 7 | 0.244 | 2,874 |
| Romania | 22.4 | −0.3 | 23 | 42 | 6,423 | 28 | 0.311 | 1,511 |
| **Newly Developed Countries** | | | | | | | | |
| South Korea | 47.6 | 1.0 | 10 | 11 | 17,380 | 2 | 0.316 | 5,160 |
| Taiwan | 22.2 | 0.8 | 7 | — | 16,100 | — | — | — |
| Hong Kong | 6.9 | 1.7 | — | 0 | 25,153 | — | — | 5,178 |
| Singapore | 4.1 | 2.7 | 6 | 0 | 23,356 | — | — | 6,641 |
| **Underdeveloped Countries** | | | | | | | | |
| *Latin America* | | | | | | | | |
| Mexico | 99.4 | 1.6 | 36 | 15 | 9,023 | 16 | 0.531 | 1,570 |
| Brazil | 172.6 | 1.4 | 39 | 23 | 7,625 | 12 | 0.607 | 1,811 |
| Venezuela | 24.6 | 2.1 | 24 | 9 | 5,794 | 23 | 0.495 | 2,493 |
| Peru | 26.1 | 1.7 | 41 | 36* | 4,799 | 16 | 0.462 | 654 |
| Bolivia | 8.5 | 2.4 | 79 | 47* | 2,424 | 14 | 0.447 | 390 |
| Argentina | 37.5 | 1.3 | 22 | 1 | 12,377 | — | — | 1,938 |
| Uruguay | 3.4 | 0.7 | 17 | 4 | 9,035 | 2 | 0.423 | 1,871 |
| El Salvador | 6.4 | 2.0 | 35 | 22 | 4,497 | 21 | 0.522 | 568 |
| Guatemala | 11.7 | 2.6 | 49 | 25 | 3,821 | 10 | 0.558 | 341 |
| Panama | 2.9 | 1.7 | 24 | 14 | 6,000 | 14 | 0.485 | 1,310 |

**TABLE 9.1** *(Continued)*

| Country | POP | RNI | CHM | LFA | GDP | POV | GIN | KWH |
|---|---|---|---|---|---|---|---|---|
| **Underdeveloped Countries** *(continued)* | | | | | | | | |
| *Asia* | | | | | | | | |
| Saudi Arabia | 21.4 | 2.8 | 23 | 19* | 11,367 | — | — | 4,710 |
| Iran | 64.7 | 1.6 | 41 | — | 5,884 | — | — | 1,407 |
| Jordan | 5.0 | 4.2 | 30 | 15* | 3,966 | 2 | 0.364 | 1,207 |
| India | 1033.4 | 1.8 | 88 | 64* | 2,358 | 44 | 0.378 | 379 |
| Nepal | 23.6 | 2.4 | 105 | — | 1,327 | 38 | 0.367 | 47 |
| China | 1271.9 | 1.0 | 39 | 72* | 3,976 | 19 | 0.403 | 758 |
| Indonesia | 213.6 | 1.6 | 51 | 42 | 3,043 | 13 | 0.317 | 345 |
| Thailand | 61.2 | 0.9 | 33 | 44 | 6,402 | 2 | 0.414 | 1,352 |
| Malaysia | 23.8 | 2.4 | 11 | 17 | 9,068 | — | 0.492 | 2,474 |
| Philippines | 77.0 | 2.1 | 39 | 37 | 3,971 | — | 0.462 | 454 |
| *Africa* | | | | | | | | |
| Egypt | 65.2 | 2.0 | 52 | 32 | 3,635 | 3 | 0.289 | 900 |
| Algeria | 30.9 | 1.9 | 39 | — | 5,308 | 2 | 0.353 | 581 |
| Morocco | 29.2 | 1.8 | 60 | — | 3,546 | 2 | 0.395 | 430 |
| Senegal | 9.8 | 2.6 | 129 | 77* | 1,510 | 26 | 0.413 | 114 |
| Kenya | 30.7 | 2.5 | 120 | 80* | 1,022 | 27 | 0.449 | 126 |
| Tanzania | 34.5 | 2.7 | 149 | 84* | 523 | 20 | 0.382 | 55 |
| Ghana | 19.7 | 2.4 | 112 | 59* | 1,964 | 45 | 0.407 | 204 |
| Ethiopia | 65.8 | 2.3 | 179 | 89 | 668 | 31 | 0.400 | 21 |
| Madagascar | 16.0 | 2.9 | 144 | — | 840 | 49 | 0.381 | — |
| Ivory Coast | 16.4 | 3.0 | 180 | — | 1,630 | 12 | 0.367 | — |

*Legend:* POP = total population in millions (2001); RNI = annual percentage of population increase (1990–2001); CHM = child mortality rate, calculated as the annual number of deaths to children from birth to age 5 per 1,000 children of that age group (2000); LFA = percentage of the labor force employed in agriculture (1995–2001); GDP = Gross Domestic Product per capita calculated in U.S. dollars (2000); POV = percentage of the population living in poverty, defined as an income of $1 or less per day for the less-developed countries, $2 or less per day for the postsocialist countries, and $11 or less per day for the developed countries (years vary between 1994 and 1998); GIN = the Gini coefficient, a measure of income inequality that varies from 0 to 1.0 (the higher the coefficient, the greater the inequality) (2001); KWH = kilowatt hours of electricity consumed per capita per year (1999).

*These data come from the World Bank (1997) and are for 1990.

*Sources:* The data for POP, RNI, CHM, and GIN come from the World Bank (2003). Data for LFA, GDP, and KWH come from the United Nations (2002). POV data for underdeveloped and postsocialist countries are from the World Bank (2003), whereas POV data for developed countries are from the United Nations (2001). Data for Taiwan come from Collinwood (2001).

The general measure of technological advancement used in Table 9.1 is the number of kilowatt hours (KWH) of electricity consumed per person per year, long considered perhaps the best indicator of the level of industrialization. The developed capitalist countries and the postsocialist countries in Table 9.1 average 9,127 kilowatt hours consumed per year. By contrast, the underdeveloped nations average just 1,018 hours consumed (1,295 in Latin America, 1,313 in Asia, and only 304 in Africa).

In much of the underdeveloped world today, agriculture remains an extremely important economic activity, and, in some countries, peasants still outnumber workers of any other type. Most of these peasants farm small plots of land using techniques inherited from their ancestors thousands of years ago. Although industrialization and the formation of working classes has proceeded to some extent in all underdeveloped nations, in many it has not gone very far. In the underdeveloped nations shown in Table 9.1, approximately 39 percent of the labor force is engaged in agriculture (LFA); the figure is lowest in Latin America (20 percent), highest in Africa (70 percent), and in between in Asia (39 percent). By contrast, only some 5 percent of the labor force is engaged in agriculture in the industrial capitalist societies.

Underdevelopment involves considerably more than low levels of technological and economic development. It also has important social dimensions. Social and economic inequality is an especially important characteristic of underdeveloped societies. In most underdeveloped societies, wealth is enormously concentrated in the hands of a few, and tiny elites generally dominate the manufacturing and agricultural sectors of the economy. Throughout the Third World, the bulk of the land is normally owned by a tiny fraction of the population. What is true of the inequality of wealth also holds for income inequality. As the data for the Gini coefficient (GIN) in Table 9.1 reveal, income inequality in underdeveloped nations is notably higher than in developed countries. In the developed countries, the Gini coefficient averages 0.306, whereas it averages 0.428 in the underdeveloped countries (0.503 in Latin America, 0.400 in Asia, and 0.384 in Africa).

Table 9.2 presents another look at income inequality, comparing the shares of the income "pie" received by the top and bottom 10 percent of the population, and the ratio between the two. In the developed countries in Table 9.2, the top 10 percent receives on average slightly more than 8 times the income of the bottom 10 percent. In the underdeveloped countries, the top 10 percent receives an average of nearly 25 times the income of the bottom 10 percent (36 times in Latin America, 13 times in Asia, and 21 times in Africa). So, not only is the income pie considerably *smaller* in the underdeveloped countries owing to their lower per capita GDPs, but it is divided up far more *unequally.*

What of the standard of living of everyday people in such societies? Per capita GDP is the mostly commonly used indicator of the standard of living in a country. By that metric, we have seen that the standard of living in the developed countries in Table 9.1 is on average nearly 6 times higher than it is in the underdeveloped countries. However, we have to be careful in using GDP as an indicator of the standard of living, because it does not take into account the very different levels of inequality in the two groups of countries, and especially the proportion of the population living in poverty.

Table 9.3 presents the percentage of the population living in poverty in selected societies in the less-developed world. It is common practice to set poverty levels in the Third World at either less than $1 a day or less than $2 a day. As can clearly be seen, the standard of living in most underdeveloped nations is very low. On average, about 26 percent of the population in these countries lives on less than $1 a day

TABLE 9.2    Income Inequality in Developed and Underdeveloped Nations

| Country | Income Share of Bottom 10%* | Income Share of Top 10%[†] | Ratio of Top 10% to Bottom 10% |
|---|---|---|---|
| **Developed Nations** | | | |
| Denmark | 3.6 | 20.5 | 5.7:1 |
| Sweden | 3.7 | 20.1 | 5.4:1 |
| United Kingdom | 2.3 | 27.7 | 12.0:1 |
| France | 2.8 | 25.1 | 9.0:1 |
| Germany | 3.3 | 23.7 | 7.2:1 |
| Netherlands | 2.8 | 25.1 | 9.0:1 |
| Canada | 2.8 | 23.8 | 8.5:1 |
| United States | 1.8 | 30.5 | 16.9:1 |
| Australia | 2.0 | 25.4 | 12.7:1 |
| Japan | 4.8 | 21.7 | 4.5:1 |
| **Latin America** | | | |
| Mexico | 1.3 | 41.7 | 32.0:1 |
| Brazil | 0.7 | 48.0 | 68.6:1 |
| Venezuela | 0.8 | 36.5 | 45.6:1 |
| Peru | 1.6 | 35.4 | 22.1:1 |
| Bolivia | 1.3 | 32.0 | 24.6:1 |
| El Salvador | 1.2 | 39.5 | 32.9:1 |
| Guatemala | 1.6 | 46.0 | 28.8:1 |
| **Asia** | | | |
| Philippines | 2.3 | 36.6 | 15.9:1 |
| Jordan | 3.3 | 29.8 | 9.0:1 |
| India | 3.5 | 33.5 | 9.6:1 |
| China | 2.4 | 30.4 | 12.7:1 |
| Indonesia | 4.0 | 26.7 | 6.7:1 |
| Cambodia | 2.9 | 33.8 | 11.7:1 |
| Malaysia | 1.7 | 38.4 | 22.6:1 |
| **Africa** | | | |
| Egypt | 4.4 | 25.0 | 5.7:1 |
| Nigeria | 1.6 | 40.8 | 25.5:1 |
| Senegal | 2.6 | 33.5 | 12.9:1 |
| Kenya | 2.4 | 36.1 | 15.0:1 |
| Tanzania | 2.8 | 30.1 | 10.8:1 |
| Cent. African Rep. | 0.7 | 47.7 | 68.1:1 |
| Zambia | 1.1 | 41.0 | 37.3:1 |

*Proportion of total national income received by the bottom 10% of the population

[†]Proportion of total national income received by the top 10% of the population

*Source:* World Bank (2003). The data are for varying years between 1993 and 1999.

**TABLE 9.3   International Poverty Lines: Percentage of the Population Below $1 and $2 a Day in Selected Underdeveloped Countries**

| Country | Population Below $1 a Day | Population Below $2 a Day |
|---|---|---|
| **Latin America** | | |
| Mexico | 15.9 | 37.7 |
| Brazil | 11.6 | 26.5 |
| Venezuela | 23.0 | 47.0 |
| Peru | 15.5 | 41.4 |
| Bolivia | 14.4 | 34.3 |
| El Salvador | 21.0 | 44.5 |
| Guatemala | 10.0 | 33.8 |
| **Asia** | | |
| Bangladesh | 29.1 | 77.8 |
| Jordan | 2.0 | 7.4 |
| India | 44.2 | 86.2 |
| China | 18.8 | 52.6 |
| Indonesia | 12.9 | 65.5 |
| Nepal | 37.7 | 82.5 |
| Pakistan | 31.0 | 84.7 |
| **Africa** | | |
| Egypt | 3.1 | 52.7 |
| Nigeria | 70.2 | 90.8 |
| Senegal | 26.3 | 67.8 |
| Kenya | 26.5 | 62.3 |
| Mozambique | 37.9 | 78.4 |
| Cameroon | 33.4 | 64.4 |
| Zambia | 63.7 | 87.4 |

*Source:* World Bank (2003). The data are for varying years between 1994 and 1999.

(16 percent in Latin America, 25 percent in Asia, and 37 percent in Africa), and 58 percent lives on less than $2 a day (38 percent in Latin America, 65 percent in Asia, and 72 percent in Africa).

Far fewer people are living in poverty in the developed world (Table 9.1). Here, the average is only about 10 percent, but it is actually much less than that if we use the poverty standards applied to the Third World. This 10 percent represents the proportion of the population living on less than $11 a day, obviously a much higher level than the poverty levels set for the Third World. By Third World poverty standards, virtually no one in the developed world is living in poverty.

Underdeveloped societies also stand out because of their demographic features. They are growing at a rate some four times faster than the developed nations (RNI). The developed countries are growing at about 0.5 percent a year, whereas the

*Slum in Lagos, Nigeria, with the skyline of Lagos in the background. Poverty often reaches extreme proportions in Third World countries.*

less-developed countries are growing at a rate of about 2.1 percent (1.8 percent in Latin America, 2.1 percent in Asia, and 2.4 percent in Africa). This greater rate of growth is attributable to the fact that much of the underdeveloped world is still in the second stage of the demographic transition: death rates have fallen in recent decades owing to improvements in sanitation, health care, and the like, but birth-rates remain high. The underdeveloped nations currently constitute about three-fourths of the world's population, but because of their rapid growth rates, an ever greater percentage of the world's population will live in these nations in the years ahead. Many scholars argue that rapid population growth is creating increasingly severe problems in the underdeveloped world, and for some Asian and African nations, population growth has created problems of crisis proportions.

A final characteristic of the underdeveloped world involves general standards of nutrition and health. One of the most useful measures of a nation's overall nutritional and health status is its child mortality rate (CHM). As can be seen from Table 9.1, child mortality rates are much higher in underdeveloped countries. Whereas the developed capitalist nations have child mortality rates of approximately 6 per 1,000 children, the underdeveloped nations in Table 9.1 have an average rate of just over

66—eleven times higher. (The rates by continent are 37 in Latin America, 46 in Asia, and a huge 116 in Africa.)

# Why Underdevelopment?

How can we explain not only the historical problem of underdevelopment but also the marked failure of most of the underdeveloped world to move toward the status of the developed nations? Social scientists have developed three principal theoretical approaches to the problem of underdevelopment: *modernization theory, dependency theory,* and *world-system theory.* In many ways, world-system theory is a more flexible version of dependency theory, and so these two approaches are very similar. They stand sharply opposed, however, to modernization theory, and in fact originally emerged as alternatives to that approach.

### Modernization Theory

**Modernization theory** is a broad theoretical strategy that includes a variety of complementary, but also competing, theories. The diverse theories that coexist within the modernization approach are united by two fundamental assumptions. First, underdevelopment tends to be seen as an *original state,* as a condition of society that has always existed in some form or another. Modernization theorists tend to conceive underdevelopment as a social and economic process that long predates the emergence of modern capitalism. Indeed, they suggest that it was only with the rise of modern capitalist societies that underdevelopment was first overcome, despite the fact that many contemporary nations have not yet been able to reach this developmental stage. For the modernization theorists, then, such societies as the Yanomama, the Aztecs, and medieval England were or are underdeveloped in much the same way that contemporary Brazil, Thailand, and Nigeria are. This view is in sharp contrast to the point made earlier about development and underdevelopment being meaningful concepts only when they are applied to nations incorporated into a capitalist world-economy.

Second, modernization theory also assumes that underdevelopment results from the *internal deficiencies* of a society. This notion is the counterpart to the claim that development results from certain special qualities of those societies having achieved it, qualities that set them apart from the rest. Three broad kinds of internal deficiencies are proposed by modernization theorists as causes of underdevelopment. One of these is *insufficient capital formation.* Many economists argue that underdeveloped societies have been unable to generate an amount of capital sufficient to get them to a "takeoff point": a point at which they could begin rapid economic growth.

Other modernization theorists have mentioned *outdated business techniques and practices* as factors preventing economic development. They suggest that underdeveloped societies commonly do not have the modern rational techniques of marketing, accounting, finance, sales, and so on, that are so common in the developed nations. The failure of such societies to adopt these modern rational business practices keeps their productivity and profit rates low and prevents significant development within them.

Finally, more sociologically oriented modernization theorists stress that underdeveloped societies generally lack the kind of *consciousness or mentality*—the kind of outlook on the world—that promotes development. Development is said to occur when people adopt rational, future-oriented value and ethical systems, and religions or philosophies that embody these kinds of values and ethics. It is alleged that most people in underdeveloped countries are governed by attitudes and values stressing the past and the importance of custom and tradition. Moreover, they are often caught up in religions that emphasize that human suffering can only be changed in the afterlife and that attempting to change the secular world is futile. Thus, people are rendered fatalistic and generally accept their situation in life and do not make rational efforts to change it. When people remain passive in regard to changing their situation, their underdeveloped state is perpetuated.

Perhaps the best-known of all modernization theories is that developed by economist W. W. Rostow (1960). According to Rostow, economic development involves the passage of a society through five evolutionary stages: the stage of traditional society, the stage of the preconditions for takeoff, the takeoff stage, the drive to maturity, and the age of high mass consumption.

All underdeveloped societies are in the stage that Rostow calls *traditional society*. This is a type of society that in Rostow's view has been little touched by modern capitalism and by modern science and technology. In this kind of society, people are attached to the land, their families, and the forces of custom and tradition. Societies begin the transition out of this stage of social and economic life when they acquire the *preconditions for takeoff*. The idea spreads that economic progress is both possible and desirable. Education broadens, banks and other capital-mobilizing institutions appear, as do modern manufacturing enterprises using the latest technology. The *takeoff* is achieved when a society has reached the point at which it can carry on sustained economic growth. The *drive to maturity* involves a long period of sustained economic progress during which a society attempts to apply its new technological capacity to a wider and more diverse range of economic activities. Finally, a society becomes ready to enter the *stage of high mass consumption*. At this point, the economy is capable of producing a wide range of consumer goods, and individuals are capable of consuming at a level that is beyond their basic needs for food, shelter, and clothing.

Although Rostow's analysis focuses more on development than on underdevelopment, there is clearly implied in his work a theoretical conception of underdevelopment. Underdeveloped societies are those that have not passed beyond the stage of traditional society. They have yet to experience those crucial stimuli that prompt people to want to reorganize their society so that self-sustaining economic growth can be realized. Underdeveloped societies lack the social patterns, political structures, and values that promote economic progress. Instead, the traditional features of these societies lead to a perpetuation of historically low levels of economic productivity.

Despite its considerable fame, Rostow's analysis of development and underdevelopment is not particularly impressive. The vast majority of his discussion is taken up with detailed descriptions of his stages, especially the last four. This sort of detailed description is of limited use. As Baran and Hobsbawm (1973) point out, once a takeoff stage has been posited, the stages that precede and follow it are logically implied by it. Thus, the identification of these stages reveals little that we do not already know. Moreover, simply "pigeonholing [an underdeveloped society] in one of Rostow's 'stages' does not bring us any closer to an understanding of the country's economic and social condition or give us a clue to the country's developmental possibilities and prospects" (Baran and Hobsbawm, 1973:51). In other words, it gives us no insight into what the actual causes of development and underdevelopment are.

One of the most recent formulations of modernization theory is that of David Landes, an eminent Harvard historian. In his book *The Wealth and Poverty of Nations* (1998), Landes emphasizes ideas as the critical factor in development, as well as forms of property and government. Development is largely a matter of knowledge and know-how, of having new, innovative ideas. Britain led the way in capitalist development because it had not only a systematic method for finding new knowledge but also secure private property, personal liberty, reliable contracts, and honest, ungreedy, and responsive government. China lagged because it lacked institutions for learning and finding new knowledge (despite its world leadership in technology centuries earlier). It remained, Landes says, mired in metaphysical skepticism and speculation. A key to Japan's success was a work ethic similar to Calvinism. South Korea and Taiwan have been successful because Japan was a good colonial master.

Landes's book is recent, but his ideas are very old and have been repeated many times. Although he is by no means totally off the mark, he seems to place far too much emphasis on science and knowledge and on other kinds of ideas. Moreover, he fails to ask why some societies have these things in the first place and others do not. The critical stance toward Rostow and Landes may be extended to modernization theory in general. By and large, it has failed to produce an acceptable interpretation of the conditions that stimulate development and of those that establish obstacles to it. One major failing of the modernization theorists lies in the concept of "traditional society." A major difficulty with this concept is its extremely general character. Traditional societies include not only ancient Rome, medieval Europe, and classical China, but also contemporary Kenya, Chile, and India. These societies differ dramatically in terms of a whole range of social, technological, economic, and political patterns, yet the concept of traditional society is used to cover them all. Can a concept that is applied so broadly, and that ignores crucial differences among societies, really be a useful one?

There is another crucial difference among the societies mentioned above: their relationship to world capitalism. Ancient Rome, medieval Europe, and classical China were all historic civilizations that existed before the development of European capitalism; but contemporary Kenya, Chile, and India are all nations that have been subjected, at one time or another and in one form or another, to European colonialism. This suggests another major weakness of modernization theory: its virtual neglect of the economic and political relations that have historically existed between contemporary underdeveloped nations and the nations of the developed world (Frank, 1967). It is difficult to see how social scientists can justify paying little or no attention to these relations when formulating theories of underdevelopment.

As important as these weaknesses are, the real failing of modernization theory has been its inability to predict successfully the way development can be produced. Various modernization theorists have served as advisors to governments in developed nations and have made numerous recommendations regarding methods by which development in the Third World can be stimulated. In general, they recommend closer contact between the developed and the underdeveloped countries. Greater capital investment in the Third World, or large amounts of foreign aid to poor countries, are among the most frequent recommendations that have been made. Also, sociologically sensitive modernization theorists commonly recommend that underdeveloped countries should seek to imitate the social patterns of the advanced industrial nations. Yet, despite the implementation of these recommendations, in some cases on a grand scale, many of the underdeveloped nations have not been developing all that much, at least in relation to the developed capitalist countries. The economic gap between countries is actually larger today than it was a few decades ago (Firebaugh, 1999). Although many poor countries have been getting richer, most have not been getting rich fast enough to close the gap between rich and poor countries (i.e., the rich countries have been getting richer as well). Such facts scarcely speak well for modernization theory.

Despite the severe criticism that it has received, modernization theory has never died out. Not only does it survive but it probably is still the most widely embraced of the theoretical approaches to underdevelopment. For instance, it is precisely the type of thinking that informs the actions of those who set world development policy in important international organizations, such as the International Monetary Fund, the World Bank, and the World Trade Organization. Nevertheless, it must share theoretical attention with the approaches that came to challenge it in the 1960s, the first of which was dependency theory.

## Dependency Theory

**Dependency theory** was first developed in Latin America and came to the attention of North American and European social scientists largely through the writings of the American-educated economist Andre Gunder Frank (1966, 1967, 1969, 1979). By the mid-1970s, this approach had become very popular, especially among sociologists. In many ways, dependency theory is a specialized offshoot of the Marxian theory of capitalism.

The basic underlying assumptions of the dependency approach stand in stark contrast to those of modernization theory. Rather than conceiving underdevelopment as an "original state," as something characteristic of a "traditional society," underdevelopment is viewed as something created within a precapitalist society that begins to experience certain forms of economic and political relations with one or more capitalist societies. Underdevelopment is not a product of certain internal deficiencies, as modernization theory holds. It results not from the absence of something, but from the *presence* of something. Thus, dependency theory would not regard India in 1700 as an underdeveloped society. At that time it was an agrarian, precapitalist empire. But by 1850 it was well on the road to becoming underdeveloped due to its relationship to British capitalism.

The root cause of underdevelopment in the dependency perspective is **economic dependency.** Economic dependency exists when one society falls under the sway of some foreign society's economic system, and when the first society's economy is organized by persons in the foreign society so as to benefit primarily the foreign economy. Economic dependency implies that there are relations of economic domination and subordination between two or more societies.

The concept of dependency as an explanation for economic underdevelopment has been developed most prominently by Frank (1966, 1979) and Samir Amin (1974). For Frank, the concepts of development and underdevelopment have meaning only when applied to nations within the capitalist world-economy. Frank envisions this world-economy as being divided into two major components: *metropolis* and *satellite.* (These concepts are basically equivalent to Wallerstein's concepts of core and periphery.) The flow of economic surplus in the world-economy is from the satellite (or periphery) to the metropolis (or core), and the world-economy is organized to make this happen. The underdeveloped nations therefore have become and remain underdeveloped because they are economically dominated by developed capitalist nations that have continually been extracting wealth from them. Frank (1966) has called this process the *development of underdevelopment.* In this view, the development of the rich nations and the underdevelopment of the poor ones are but two sides of the same coin; underdevelopment of some nations has made development for others possible. The primary victims of this process are the vast majority of peasants and urban workers of the underdeveloped world itself. And who benefits from such a system? The members of developed nations do, since, it is claimed, their standard of living is raised substantially. But the greatest benefits go to capitalists in the metropolitan countries, as well as to the agricultural and industrial elites of the satellite countries. The latter have close economic and political ties to the metropolitan elite and play a crucial role in maintaining the situation of economic dependency.

Samir Amin's (1974) contributions to dependency theory center on his concepts of **articulated** and **disarticulated economies.** According to Amin, the developed nations have highly articulated economies, or ones whose multiple sectors closely interrelate such that development in any one sector stimulates development in the other sectors. Underdeveloped societies, by contrast, have disarticulated economies. These are economies whose various sectors do not closely interrelate. As a result, development in any one sector is commonly unable to stimulate development in the other sectors. Those sectors that are most developed in disarticulated economies involve the production of raw materials for export to the developed countries. What is the cause of economic disarticulation? According to Amin, it is foreign control of the economy. Capitalists in the developed world have important connections with those peripheral capitalists who control the production of raw materials.

What disarticulation really means, Amin argues, is that the kind of development characteristic of the advanced industrial societies cannot occur. When a society's economy becomes disarticulated due to foreign economic control, attention is directed to the development of those economic activities that benefit core capitalists. Those activities that would involve production for the overall benefit of the domestic economy are consequently neglected.

The concept of dependency can be understood more thoroughly by examining its various forms. Theotonio Dos Santos (1970) suggests three historical forms of dependency through which the now-underdeveloped nations have passed. The first of these he calls *colonial dependency*. Under this form of dependency, which began as early as the sixteenth century in some parts of the world, European capitalist powers colonized precapitalist regions and established a monopoly over land, mines, and labor. Surplus wealth was extracted from these regions by means of European control over trade relations. The economic character of these colonized regions was powerfully shaped by their subordination to European nations.

A second historical form of dependency identified by Dos Santos is *financial-industrial dependency*. This form of dependence began in the late nineteenth century. It was characterized by the expansion of European industrial capital (as opposed to the earlier merchant capital) into the backward regions of the world. This form of dependency was part and parcel of the monopoly phase of capitalist development. Financial-industrial dependency involved heavy investment of big capitalists in the world's backward regions mainly for the purpose of producing raw materials to be exported back to the core nations.

The most recent form of dependency is termed by Dos Santos the *new dependency*. This kind of dependency is a post–World War II phenomenon and involves the emergence of transnational corporations that engage in extensive economic investment in Third World countries.

In addition to this concern about the forms of dependency, there is the question of how economic dependency creates and sustains underdevelopment. Dependency theorists often disagree with respect to the particular mechanisms whereby this occurs. Several different mechanisms through which dependency induces underdevelopment have been proposed by various theoreticians, and more than one is sometimes proposed even by the same theorist. Four possible dependency mechanisms are most frequently suggested in the current dependency literature (Chase-Dunn, 1975; Delacroix and Ragin, 1981; Barrett and Whyte, 1982):

- *Exploitation through repatriation.* It is often suggested in dependency writings that foreign firms reinvest only a portion of their profits derived from Third World investments in the Third World itself. The bulk of these profits is shipped home (repatriated) for the benefit of the investing nation.
- *Elite complicity.* A common theme in dependency writings is the claim that the rich capitalists of Third World countries enter into various types of agreements with rich core capitalists to maintain the status quo of the underdeveloped country. This occurs because the elites of both countries benefit from the prevailing economic situation.

- *Structural distortion.* Some dependency theorists argue that economic dependency leads to a distortion of the economy in the underdeveloped nation. This distortion then creates severe barriers to economic development. This argument, for example, is the kind made by Amin when he speaks of the disarticulation of the economy that results from the dependence of Third World countries on the capitalist core.
- *Market vulnerability.* It is sometimes argued that the peripheral nations are especially harmed by world market conditions. World demand for the primary products of peripheral countries tends to decline over time, and this decline is aggravated by price fluctuations for primary products.

These four ways in which dependency can induce underdevelopment should not be thought of as mutually exclusive. It is entirely possible that underdevelopment could result from more than one mechanism operating at the same time, or even from the simultaneous operation of all of them.

In recent years, numerous sociologists and other social scientists have conducted empirical investigations designed to test the basic claims of dependency theory. These studies generally examine a large number of the world's nations and employ the most advanced and sophisticated statistical procedures. An early review of this work by Volker Bornschier, Christopher Chase-Dunn, and Richard Rubinson (1978) examined the results of 16 such studies (cf. Rubinson and Holtzman, 1981). Most of the studies reviewed by Bornschier and coauthors examine economic growth from about 1960 until the early 1970s. Initial examination of the studies indicated that some found that dependency promoted economic growth, whereas others found that dependency retarded economic growth. Bornschier and colleagues went on to scrutinize these studies to determine what would have produced such apparently contradictory findings. They showed that the findings of each study were closely linked to the way dependency was conceptualized and measured. By and large, the studies that showed that foreign investment promoted economic growth conceptualized and measured investment in terms of *recent flows of investment capital.* By contrast, those studies demonstrating that foreign investment retarded growth conceptualized and measured investment in terms of *long-term stocks of foreign investment.* The authors held this finding to be of great substantive significance. On the basis of it, they concluded that "the immediate effect of inflows of foreign capital and aid is to increase the rate of economic growth, while the long-run cumulative effects operate to reduce the rate of economic growth" (1978:667). Moreover, they went on to say (1978:667–668):

> These results tend to confirm the hypothesis that current inflows of investment capital and aid cause short-term increases in growth due to the contribution to capital formation and demand as foreign corporations purchase land, labor, and materials and start production, while the long-run structural distortions of the national economy produced by foreign investment and the exporting of profits tend to produce negative effects over time. We conclude, then, that the effect of short-term flows of investment and aid has positive effects on growth, but that their cumulative

effect over time is negative. Many of the seemingly contradictory findings of these studies can be reconciled under this proposition.

In more recent work, Bornschier and Chase-Dunn (1985) have expanded this line of inquiry to include a greater number of studies (36 rather than 16), and have reached the same basic conclusions. Moreover, using a sample of 103 nations, they have gone on to conduct new original research on the developmental effects of short-term capital flows versus long-term stocks of capital. They regard this original research as eliminating some of the flaws of the earlier studies. Once again, the same basic conclusions are forthcoming, the most important of which is that long-term penetration by foreign capital hinders a country's chances of economic development.

Unfortunately, despite Bornschier and colleagues' seemingly elegant solution to confusion, things cannot be resolved quite so easily. Their conclusions have been challenged by Glenn Firebaugh (1992). Firebaugh's challenge is methodologically complex and subtle, but his main claim is that dependency researchers have misinterpreted the results of their studies. Although underdeveloped countries highly dependent on foreign investment may experience slower economic growth than countries that are less dependent, this does not necessarily mean that foreign investment dependence is the *cause* of slower growth.

Firebuagh's analysis suggests that the most important question to ask about investment dependence is, What would happen to underdeveloped societies if they did not receive foreign investment? Dependency theorists argue that foreign investment is associated with a range of conditions (e.g., Amin's disarticulation) that have the effect of crowding out or displacing domestic investment that would otherwise occur (Dixon and Boswell, 1996a, 1996b). Without foreign investment, dependency theorists assume that domestic investment will replace foreign investment and that underdeveloped countries will start down a path of self-sustaining articulated development. However, what if the alternative to foreign investment is no investment (or, more realistically, substantially less investment)? In that case, countries will grow slower without foreign investment than with it.

Foreign investment may not be as beneficial for economic growth as domestic investment, but Firebaugh's research indicates that it may be better than no investment at all. Interestingly, the resolution of this debate hinges on the answers to some of the questions posed by early dependency thinkers: Do transnational corporations destroy local business and industry? Do they absorb local entrepreneurial talent into pursuits that are not optimal for the economic development of their own countries? Do they foster consumption patterns that lower domestic savings rates?

In summary, to establish that foreign investment has a negative effect on economic growth in the Third World, dependency researchers will have to demonstrate more directly that investment dependence leads to the sort of erosion of domestic investment postulated by early dependency theorists. For underdeveloped countries, this debate suggests that, while there may be costs to foreign investment, there are benefits as well, and underdeveloped countries have to weigh each carefully.

## World-System Theory

Despite its superiority to modernization theory, dependency theory has certain weaknesses that cannot be overlooked. By the late 1970s, these weaknesses had begun to be noticed even by many of this approach's most enthusiastic supporters, and today dependency theory is regarded as a flawed, if still highly useful, perspective. Of the objections that have been raised against it, the most important are essentially as follows (Roxborough, 1979; Hoogvelt, 1982; Leys, 1982; Blomstrom and Hettne, 1984):

- In spite of its severe criticism of modernization theory's failure to place contemporary underdeveloped societies in their historical context, in its own peculiar way dependency theory is also ahistorical. Although it gives great attention to the historical relationship of underdeveloped societies to the capitalist core, it tends to ignore the precapitalist history of these societies. This history is very important, however, in conditioning the way in which a particular precapitalist society will be incorporated into the capitalist system and the results of that incorporation (Chase-Dunn, 1989a; Lenski and Nolan, 1984).
- Dependency theory tends to overgeneralize about contemporary underdeveloped nations. It assumes that their dependent status renders them all essentially alike. Yet, there are important differences between these nations with respect to such things as class structure, political system, and geographical and population size, and these differences play a role in shaping a nation's current development level and future developmental prospects. Another way of putting this is to say that dependency theory concentrates too much attention on the external relations between an underdeveloped society and the capitalist core, and not enough attention on the underdeveloped society's internal characteristics.
- The poverty and misery of contemporary Third World countries cannot simply be blamed on the economic intrusion of the more advanced capitalist countries (Chirot, 1977, 1986). Most of the countries and regions that fell under the economic control of the more advanced countries already had extensive poverty before they came to be dominated by these countries. Although in some instances this poverty and misery may have become worse as a result of foreign influence, by and large that poverty and misery were already there from the beginning.
- Dependency theory usually asserts that the high levels of economic development found in the core have been made possible by their exploitation of the semiperiphery and periphery. But this is very unlikely. Core societies have developed largely because of their own internal economic organization, and the possession of semiperipheral or peripheral zones has probably contributed only modestly. In fact, the world's most developed society, the United States, never had any colonies at all.
- Dependency theory is too pessimistic in asserting that economic dependency makes economic development impossible. This is contradicted by the

experience of a number of countries in recent decades. For example, Brazil underwent substantial economic growth between the mid-1960s and the mid-
1970s, and east Asian countries such as Taiwan, South Korea, Hong Kong, and
Singapore have experienced dramatic growth since the 1950s.

- Dependency theory's main policy recommendation for the underdeveloped
countries—breaking out of the capitalist system by socialist revolution—has
failed badly. Just as modernization theory can be criticized for its failures in
practice, dependency theory can as well. The vast majority of the Third World
countries that have opted for socialism in recent decades have failed to generate any real developmental impetus; in fact, their record is inferior to that of
numerous countries that have remained capitalist.

These criticisms have considerable force, but they apply more to some dependency theorists than to others. We need to distinguish two rather different strands of
dependency theory (Bornschier and Chase-Dunn, 1985), what might be called
"hard" and "soft" dependency theories. The hard version of dependency theory is
associated primarily with the works of Frank and Amin discussed earlier. It sees economic dependency as always generating the development of underdevelopment,
and thus as rendering development impossible (or at least extremely difficult) so
long as it continues. The soft version is associated mainly with Fernando Henrique
Cardoso (1982; Cardoso and Faletto, 1979) and Peter Evans (1979; cf. Bornschier and
Chase-Dunn, 1985). It does not assume that dependency must always lead to the development of underdevelopment. Under some circumstances, there can occur what
Cardoso has called "associated dependent development," or simply "dependent development." This is a type of economic growth that occurs primarily as the result of
extensive investment in manufacturing industries by transnational corporations.
Soft dependency theorists insist that in recent decades a new form of dependency
has grown up alongside the old form. In the older, or "classical," dependency, core
countries use peripheral countries as sources of investment in raw agricultural and
mineral products. But in the newer dependency, investment occurs within the industrial sector. And this form of dependency, it is argued, is not incompatible with
certain amounts of economic development.

It is obvious that the soft version of dependency theory is much more flexible
than the hard version, and thus largely free from the criticisms cited earlier, especially the third. Dependency and development can coexist. To the extent that a dependency perspective is an appropriate guide for our thinking, it should clearly be
the softer version. Indeed, it is noteworthy that one of the two major developers of
the hard dependency theory, Andre Gunder Frank, has now abandoned his original
hard position and moved toward a much more flexible one. He no longer thinks that
dependency is a necessary obstacle to development, and he has also come to reject
the notion that the adoption of a socialist alternative to capitalism can produce anything better.

It is but a short step from the softer dependency theory to a full-blown **world-
system theory** of underdevelopment. Wallerstein has claimed that it is the capitalist
world-system as a whole that develops, not particular societies. He acknowledges

*Immanuel Wallerstein, the founder of the world-system perspective on long-term social change. The first three volumes of his work* The Modern World-System, *along with other important works, have profoundly influenced the understanding of patterns of economic development and underdevelopment in recent centuries.*

that internal characteristics of societies matter, but they exert their effects only in the context of a society's position within the world-system at a particular time in history. As the world-system evolves, there is increasing polarization between core and periphery, and it is difficult for less-developed nations to improve their status, or at least improve it very much. However, at particular historical junctures opportunities are created for some countries to move up. Wallerstein (1979) proposes three basic strategies that nations can adopt to accomplish this: seizing the chance, development by invitation, and self-reliance.

During periods of contraction of the world-economy, core countries may be in a weakened economic position. If so, peripheral or semiperipheral countries may be able to use aggressive state action to improve their position. This is the strategy of *seizing the chance*. Wallerstein suggests that Russia adopted this strategy in the late nineteenth century, and that it was employed by Brazil and Mexico during the 1930s.

*Development by invitation*, by contrast, occurs during periods of expansion of the world-economy. During these periods, "space" or "room" is created for some countries to move up because there is an increased level of demand for commodities on a world scale. Underdeveloped countries with just the right internal characteristics (especially geopolitical circumstances) may be treated unusually favorably by core countries. As a result they may be able to use the resulting economic advantages to inaugurate a developmental surge. Wallerstein suggests that Scotland followed this developmental strategy in the late eighteenth century. Perhaps the best recent exemplars of the strategy are the East Asian countries of Taiwan and South Korea.

Some countries, though, may see their best chance for economic development resting on withdrawal from the world-system and adoption of some version of socialism. The most successful employment of this strategy—*self-reliance*—has been by Russia (the Soviet Union), beginning in 1917. The rapid industrialization of the Soviet Union, however, came at an enormous human cost.

Despite the differences between world-system theory and classical dependency theory, it is clear that the former is only a version of the latter. Wallerstein stresses what he calls "limited possibilities" for transformation of underdeveloped countries within the world-economy. Most countries don't move up, and those that do don't move very far. They move from the periphery into the semiperiphery, or from a lower to a higher semiperipheral position. Since most nations continue to stagnate rather than move up, and since there is increasing polarization within the system, Wallerstein is not optimistic about the fate of the underdeveloped countries within a capitalist context. For him, the only real solution to the problems of the underdeveloped world is a long-term one: the ultimate worldwide collapse of capitalism and its replacement by a socialist world-government.

## Explaining Underdevelopment: Some Conclusions

World-system theory is an improvement on dependency theory, especially its harder version, but it is still not quite the theory we need. Like dependency theory, it tends to overstress external relations and underplay the internal characteristics of societies. It is also too negative about the possibilities of capitalist development in the less-developed world.

Our grand conclusion is thus that none of these theories works as well as we would like, especially for the current era in which we live. Dependency and world-system theories work fairly well in explaining patterns of world inequality and unequal development over the past several hundred years, but they work less well for the current era—the last 40 to 50 years. There has been and continues to be more development going on in the less-developed world than both dependency and world-system theory allow for. Glenn Firebaugh's (1992, 1996) research suggests that foreign investment since the 1960s stimulates more than inhibits development, and his research also suggests that polarization basically stopped in the early 1960s. Moreover, much of the periphery seems to be gradually disappearing, having moved up into the semiperiphery. Sub-Saharan Africa is the only major region of the world that is still peripheral. These findings call into question three of the most basic principles of world-system theory: (1) foreign investment leads to underdevelopment in most of the Third World, (2) polarization is an ongoing process within the system, and (3) the core needs a periphery in order to develop to high levels. And yet, modernization theory does not really work either. It is much too simplistic in assuming that all societies can develop equally by garnering enough foreign investment, building the right technology, and acquiring the right values and attitudes. Therefore, we still lack a solid unified theory of underdevelopment that applies to the current period as well as to the past. The construction of such a theory should be one of the major goals of development scholars in the years ahead.

# Development in East Asia

Let us now turn away from theory to look at a number of actual regions and societies in the less-developed world. The greatest development is occurring in East Asia, and this region of the world is likely the harbinger of the future of the less-developed world, so let us start with it.

## The Biggest Success Stories: The East Asian Tigers

Since about the mid-1950s, a startling degree of economic development has occurred in the East Asian societies of Taiwan, South Korea, Hong Kong, and Singapore. Before 1950, these societies were very poor peripheral countries. According to the sorts of economic and social indicators that we have just reviewed, East Asia was roughly similar to present-day sub-Saharan Africa, the poorest region of the world. Today, it is among the most prosperous regions outside the capitalist core. South Korea and Taiwan have per capita GDPs in the $16,000–18,000 range (see Table 9.1), and Hong Kong and Singapore's per capita GDPs are much higher ($25,153 for Hong Kong and $23,356 for Singapore). All of these societies have extremely low infant mortality rates for non-core nations, as well as rates of population growth more similar to core than to non-core societies. Moreover, at least in Taiwan and South Korea, this development has occurred without producing the extremely sharp income inequalities so characteristic of other rapidly growing less-developed countries. These countries today have income distributions that resemble those of core nations, or that are even more egalitarian.

Collectively, these four East Asian countries are frequently known as the "Asian Tigers." It has frequently been asserted that the economic development of these countries is a fatal blow to dependency theory (Barrett and Whyte, 1982; Berger, 1986). Certainly, if one is talking about the strong version of dependency theory, it is impossible to deny that assertion (Bienefeld, 1981). However, this East Asian development is not inconsistent with the soft dependency theory or with world-system theory. Indeed, it would seem that world-system theory is well suited to explain what has been happening in recent decades in East Asia. In order to show that this is so, we shall confine ourselves to Taiwan and South Korea. Hong Kong and Singapore are really city-states rather than countries, and they have only a tiny agricultural sector. Because of their unique nature, they are not particularly good test cases for any theory of underdevelopment.

Taiwan and South Korea seem to be exceptionally good examples of Wallerstein's strategy of development by invitation (Bienefeld, 1981; Cumings, 1984), and their accomplishments result from a unique combination of five circumstances. Some of these circumstances involve internal characteristics of the societies themselves, whereas others involve the larger world-economy (Cumings, 1984; Crane, 1982; Koo, 1987; Evans, 1987; Aseniero, 1994).

First, it is true that both Taiwan and South Korea have a history of economic dependency, but the dependency they experienced was unique. Around the turn of the twentieth century, Taiwan (then known as Formosa) and Korea (which, of course, had not yet been divided into South Korea and North Korea) became colonies of Japan. But Japan was no ordinary colonizer, for it engaged in practices not found among European colonizers. The Japanese built up in these colonies a large infrastructure of transportation and communication, and even established heavy industries, especially in steel, chemicals, and hydroelectric power. Thus, although

Taiwan and Korea became dependent, they nonetheless acquired certain technological and economic resources generally absent in other dependent countries. These resources helped establish a foundation for developmental efforts once Japanese colonialism ended.

Second, both Taiwan and South Korea undertook major land reforms after World War II. These reforms produced a much more egalitarian distribution of land. It is well known that land reform efforts have failed, or not even been attempted, in most other less-developed countries. In most of these countries land is enormously concentrated in the hands of a few rich landowners, and this uneven distribution is a major obstacle to development. But land reform in Taiwan and South Korea led to major increases in agricultural output, and industrialization efforts could therefore begin to succeed.

Third, the unique geopolitical situation that Taiwan and South Korea were in was critical to their developmental successes. During the 1950s, the United States became the world's leading economic power, and it perceived a severe threat to its economic position from the Soviet Union and China, the latter having just had a revolution (in 1949) and become part of the socialist world. There was great fear that both Taiwan and South Korea would become part of this world, and so the United States pumped huge amounts of money, in the form of both aid and loans, into both countries. Although the United States had given aid and loans to many other countries, the amounts going into Taiwan and South Korea were unparalleled. There is no doubt that this economic assistance played a crucial role in helping launch these countries' developmental efforts.

Fourth, all of this was happening during a period in which the world-economy was undergoing major expansion. Thus, the increase in world economic demand made "room" or "space" available for some countries to improve their position. Moreover, the United States directly encouraged the upward mobility of Taiwan and South Korea by opening its own domestic markets to the products of these countries. This occurred primarily after 1960. In the 1950s, the industrialization of Taiwan and South Korea was oriented mainly to producing for their domestic markets, but after 1960, it shifted toward an emphasis on selling competitively in the world market. This kind of industrialization, known generally as **export-oriented industrialization,** is a common developmental strategy of less-developed countries. Whether it works or not is another question. That it has worked so well for these two countries depended significantly on the protected markets that the United States carved out for them in its own territory.

Finally, the largest single investor and the largest director of economic growth in both countries was the state. This, too, was the legacy of Japanese colonialism. Both Taiwan and South Korea had structured their state apparatuses on the Japanese model and had developed the kind of highly efficient state that could, in the context of the other four conditions, lead them into significant economic development. Specifically, the state in these two countries played a major role in keeping the wages of workers down, which is essential for export-oriented industrialization because it makes products cheaper and thus more competitive on the world market. It also built up military-style discipline in the factories, thus contributing to high productivity.

Because of the success of Taiwan and South Korea, the question has naturally arisen as to whether they constitute models for economic development that other countries can imitate. Some social scientists who are especially enthusiastic about East Asian development believe that they do (cf. Berger, 1986). Yet, there are reasons to question the exportability of the East Asian model. As Bruce Cumings argues, "The developmental 'successes' of Taiwan and Korea are historically and regionally specific, and therefore provide no readily adaptable models for other developing countries interested in emulation" (1984:38). Certainly, the Asian financial crisis of 1997–2000 has taken some of the glow off the East Asian model. The role of the state in guiding development and the relationship-based financial systems of these countries, once lauded by many analysts, are now often derided as "crony capitalism." On the other hand, the emergence of "new tigers" such as Thailand, Malaysia, and Indonesia lends some support to the optimists. As was the case with the original four tigers, these countries have experienced very rapid economic development in recent years. For instance, GDP per capita increased by more than 100 percent in all three countries over the period from 1975 to 1999. (For reference, GDP per capita in the United States grew by 48 percent over the same period.)

In summary, some extremely important things have happened in Taiwan, South Korea, Singapore, and Hong Kong since the end of the Second World War. These events are compatible with some of the claims of soft dependency and world-system theories of underdevelopment, especially world-system theory. However, some aspects of development in these countries make sense within a modernization framework as well. Therefore it would appear that no single perspective can explain their developmental dynamics over the past half-century.

## The Rise of China

After the death of Mao Zedong in 1976, China spurned state socialism and embarked on a capitalist path of development, introducing market mechanisms and opening itself to foreign economic investment (Aseniero, 1996; So and Chiu, 1995; Weil, 1996; Castells, 1996, 1998). Major economic reforms began officially in 1978. Between 1980 and 1995, China was the fastest growing economy in the world, averaging approximately 10 percent growth per year in GDP. In 1995, China's GDP grew 10.2 percent, compared to only 2.0 percent for the industrialized countries and 2.6 percent for the world as a whole (Keister, 2000b). Since 1995, GDP growth has slowed slightly but is still extremely high: 8.8 percent in 1997, 8.0 percent in 2000, and 7.3 percent in 2001 (http://www.worldbank.org). Chinese development has concentrated on export-oriented industrialization, and exports have grown dramatically. They were 9.2 percent of GDP in 1990, 18.1 percent in 1992, and 23.0 percent in 1995 (Keister, 2000b). Foreign investment in China has also grown enormously. In 1990, China attracted about 2 billion U.S. dollars in foreign investment, but this increased markedly to about 20 billion in 1992, to over 30 billion in 1994, and to more than 40 billion in 1998 (*The Economist*, 2000). Since then, it has remained at about the same level. Throughout the 1990s, China was second only to the United States as a recipient of foreign investment (Weil, 1996). By far the biggest investor has been

Hong Kong, which in the late 1990s was investing over 20 billion U.S. dollars a year. The other major investors are Japan, the United States, Singapore, South Korea, and Taiwan (*The Economist*, 2000).

Most of the economic development that has been occurring in China has been in Shanghai, Hainan Island, Guangdong, Fujian, Zhejiang, and other cities and provinces along China's southern and eastern coastline. There has emerged a whole megaregion adjoining Hong Kong and composed of Shenzhen, Canton, the Pearl River Delta, Macau, and Zhuhai, and it has become a huge metropolitan area (Castells, 1996). In 1995, it covered a space of more than 50,000 square kilometers and had a population in the range of 40 to 50 million people. In the words of Manuel Castells (1996:409), it "is likely to become the most representative urban face of the twenty-first century."

China's per capita GDP was only $890 a year in 2001, but this figure is very misleading because the majority of Chinese are still peasant farmers and most remain untouched by the capitalist development that is occurring. China is a huge country with great regional variation, and most of the capitalist development, as already noted, is occurring along the southern and eastern coastlines. Here, per capita GDP is much higher than in the rest of China.

Since economic reforms began in China in 1978, an enormous amount of privatization of state-owned companies has occurred. In 1978, consumer goods produced by privately owned firms amounted to less than 1 percent of consumer goods produced by state-owned firms. This increased to 48 percent by 1990, to 89 percent by 1994, and to a full 179 percent by 1998. This means that by 1998, almost twice as many consumer goods were being produced by private firms as by state-owned firms (http://sinowisdom.com). China has also adopted the characteristic type of large business group found in other highly successful parts of Asia. We refer to the

*Skyline of Guangzhou, Guangdong Province, People's Republic of China. Extraordinarily rapid capitalist development has been occurring in this and adjacent regions of China since the 1980s.*

Japanese *keiretsu,* the South Korean *chaebol,* and the Taiwanese *guanxi qiye.* These are uniquely East Asian economic networks dominated by a large firm and consisting of many firms who coordinate their activities closely with each other. China began to form such business groups, known as *qiye jituan,* in the 1980s and they have become extremely numerous and greatly increased the efficiency and profitability of Chinese firms (Keister, 2000b).

Much closer economic ties began to develop in the 1990s between the "three Chinas": Mainland China, Taiwan, and Hong Kong. These ties were strengthened after July 1997 when the British returned Hong Kong to Mainland China. So and Chiu (1995) suggest that this increasing economic integration makes the three Chinas, as a single unit, a core nation in the world-economy that can draw on the assets of each of its parts: China's abundant and cheap labor and raw materials, Taiwan's capital and technology-intensive industries, and Hong Kong's worldwide financial and trading network. This is probably overstating the case, but the point is made nonetheless. In all likelihood, these three Chinas will eventually become politically unified, and it can be expected that this unified Chinese superstate will develop even more rapidly after this point and will probably become the dominant world economic power within 50 years.

## Development in Latin America

Latin America is that region of the less-developed world that has the highest level of economic development. Mexico, Argentina, and Brazil have the highest per capita GDPs of Latin American countries; they also have relatively low percentages of the labor force working in agriculture (15, 1, and 23 percent, respectively).

Latin American incorporation into the world-economy has progressed through six major stages (Skidmore and Smith, 2001):

1. *Colonialism, early 1500s to 1830.* Latin America was incorporated into the world-economy as a peripheral region devoted to the production of raw agricultural and mineral products. Most of it was colonized by the Spaniards, but the Portuguese had a major colony in Brazil. The Portuguese imported slaves from West Africa and put them to work on sugar plantations and in gold and silver mines; nearly 40 percent of all of the Africans imported into the New World as slaves came to Brazil. Some of the sugar plantations were huge and were often referred to as "factories in the field." Some of these plantations contained as many as 500 slaves. The Spaniards in Latin America made limited use of slavery, relying instead on other methods of forced labor (Harris, 1964). They began with the *encomienda,* which gave some of the *conquistadores* the right to tax and collect tribute from the native Indian population, as well as the right to draft labor. The *encomienda* was later replaced by the *repartimiento.* This was a similar system of forced labor but the right to tax, collect tribute, and draft labor was given to officials of the Spanish Crown and their heirs rather than to private *encomenderos.* Both of these systems were replaced by the famous *hacienda* system,

which emerged after political independence in the nineteenth century. The *hacienda* was a system of debt peonage. Private landlords provided Indian peasants supplies of food and clothing, which threw them into debt, but their wages were set so low that the debt could never be repaid. Since the Indians had no choice but to continue working for their *haciendados* for life, the landlords were guaranteed a permanent supply of extremely cheap labor.

2. *Early postindependence, 1830–1880.* Political independence had essentially come to Latin America by 1830 with the granting of independence to Brazil. After this point, Latin American countries were gradually pulled increasingly into the world-economy as exporters of raw materials and importers of consumer goods. Britain was the hegemonic power in the world-system during this time, and as such had replaced Spain and Portugal as the European country most extensively involved in Latin America.

3. *Initiation and expansion of export-import growth, 1880–1930.* Near the end of the nineteenth century, economic activity expanded considerably in Latin America, and there was great prosperity for the upper classes. However, Latin American countries were still largely raw materials exporters and most of their consumer goods came from Europe. Another major feature of this period was extensive immigration from Europe.

4. *Import-substitution industrialization, 1930s–1960s.* After about 1930, Latin American countries made their first real move to industrialize and to develop more diversified economies less dependent on exports. Their aim was to produce their own consumer goods and stimulate internal economic growth. To do this, they adopted the strategy known as **import-substitution industrialization** (ISI). This strategy uses high tariffs to discourage imported goods and to raise their price in domestic markets. With imported goods kept to a minimum or too expensive, domestic industry can be developed to a much greater extent and can stimulate economic growth. Relatively speaking, ISI was a success, especially for some of the most important Latin American countries, but economic growth had stagnated by the 1960s. This is because the ISI strategy has certain inherent limitations. First, it must rely on the importation of capital goods, such as machine tools, because producing such goods domestically is very difficult in the early stages of industrialization. This helps to maintain the dependency of the local economy on the core. Second, there are natural limitations on local demand because of the limiting spending powers of not only the masses, but even the middle classes. Only so many refrigerators or cars, for example, can be sold in a highly underdeveloped country. Third, because ISI is capital-intensive rather than labor-intensive, it is very limited in its ability to create jobs for workers. As the ISI strategy in Latin America reached these limits, a new developmental strategy was put into place.

5. *Stagnation of ISI growth and a turn toward export-oriented industrialization, 1960s–1980s.* The new developmental strategy was export-oriented industrialization, or EOI, which we described earlier for South Korea and Taiwan. As stated then, EOI involves producing for the world market rather than domestic mar-

kets. Such a strategy depends on keeping wages low so that prices can be low and thus exported industrial goods can be competitive in the world market. To make this strategy work, what Guillermo O'Donnell (1973) has called *bureaucratic-authoritarian* states emerged throughout Latin America. These states—which emerged in Brazil in 1964, Argentina in 1966, and Chile in 1973—crushed the working classes in order to keep wages down. As part of the EOI strategy, Latin American countries, Brazil in particular, engaged in close relationships with core transnational corporations, especially American transnationals. Export-oriented industrialization produced a substantial amount of economic development in Latin America, but it was mostly dependent development.

6. *Crisis, debt, and democracy, 1980s–1990s.* By the mid-1980s, EOI had begun to peter out. Large foreign debts were accumulated because of the huge sums of money that were borrowed from world financial institutions to finance the export-oriented strategy. Between 1980 and 1990, foreign debt nearly doubled; much more had to be borrowed just to pay the interest on existing loans. Economic stagnation ensued, and GDP per capita declined by nearly 10 percent. Strict economic reform policies were imposed by the World Bank and International Monetary Fund, and as a result Latin America began to pull out of its economic doldrums to some extent. Skyrocketing inflation declined, investment from the capitalist core increased, and economic growth reached 3.5 percent per year by the mid-1990s. Developmental strategies were rethought along new lines. Politically, the bureaucratic-authoritarian states collapsed and a process of "redemocratization" began.

Brazil exemplifies very well all of these stages (Skidmore and Smith, 2001). During the colonial era, as already noted, Brazil used slave labor for the mines and sugar plantations. In the 1820s, sugar accounted for about 30 percent of Brazilian exports. After this time it began a long decline, accounting for only 5 percent of total exports by 1900. Sugar was replaced by coffee, and in 1900, Brazil was producing nearly 75 percent of the world's coffee. Coffee declined dramatically in the last century, accounting for only 18 percent of the world's coffee by 1978.

During the period of ISI, there was a large-scale expansion of Brazil's industrial sector. At this time, Brazil began to develop such heavy industries as steel and automobiles, and industrial production constituted nearly 30 percent of total GDP by 1975. However, there still remained a large rural proletariat eking out a bare living, especially in the coffee fields. After the ISI period was over, Brazil went through some 20 years of rule by several bureaucratic-authoritarian regimes, all of which were led by the military. During this EOI period, economic growth was phenomenal—approximately 10 percent a year between 1968 and 1974—and many economists referred to this as "the Brazilian miracle." By the late 1970s, EOI-produced growth had substantially faded and serious economic problems developed. One was inflation, which exceeded 100 percent in 1980. There was also a huge foreign debt, which in 1986 was $82.5 billion, the world's largest. Income inequality also increased during the EOI period. The proportion of national income going to the top income decile was 39.6 percent in 1960 but had grown to 50.9 percent by 1980. Likewise, the proportion going to the bottom income half of the population declined from 17.4 percent in 1960 to 12.6 percent in 1980.

In 1993, none other than Fernando Henrique Cardoso, the father of the "soft" school of dependency theory, became finance minister, and then acceded to the presidency in 1995. By this time, Cardoso had toned down his leftist political views considerably, and began implementing more moderate economic policies. Inflation was brought under control and the economy stabilized. However, many social problems remained and economic crises eventually returned in the second half of the 1990s. Throughout the 1990s, Brazil, like all major Latin American countries, tried to restructure its relationship to the larger world-economy, with uncertain and inconsistent results. Some segments of Brazilian society became better off, but others became increasingly marginalized.

In an important recent study, James Mahoney (2003) shows that differential levels of social and economic development in Latin American countries have been closely related to the degree of Spanish colonial penetration a country experienced in earlier times. The most socially and economically developed countries in Latin America over the past century, such as Argentina, Costa Rica, and Uruguay, have tended to be those that experienced little colonial penetration. By contrast, the least socially and economically developed countries of the twentieth century, such as Bolivia, Honduras, and Nicaragua, have generally been those where the greatest degree of colonial activity was present. As Mahoney points out, these results confirm the dependency hypothesis of Andre Gunder Frank (1978, 1979) that the regions of the Americas that became most developed were the ones subject to "benign neglect." In this sense, dependency theory applies well to the history of Latin America. However, as pointed out earlier in this chapter, because many Latin American countries have undergone a surprising amount of economic and social development in recent decades, dependency theory applies less well to its current and possible future state.

Why is Latin America as a whole the most developed region of the Third World? It may be due to the fact that Latin America was the region first colonized by Europe and the first region to gain political independence (Sanderson, 1995, 1999b). Most Latin American countries became independent in the early nineteenth century, whereas independence was not gained throughout Asia and Africa until the middle of the twentieth century—a century to a century and a half later. Latin America has therefore had a longer period of time in which to develop, and this may have made the difference. Mahoney (2003) shows, for example, that a necessary condition for social and economic development in Latin America has been the presence of an indigenous capitalist class. Other things being equal, Spanish Latin American countries that had large and vigorous capitalist classes (e.g., Mexico, Venezuela, and Argentina) developed earlier and farther than countries that had small and anemic ones (e.g., Bolivia, Peru, and Paraguay). Since the most successful Latin American countries had these classes earlier and longer than Asian and African countries, it stands to reason that the Latin American countries would have become more developed than their counterparts in the other two continents.

# Sub-Saharan Africa: A Failure of Development

Before 1500, Africa was a vast continent consisting of many different societies at different levels of social evolution: hunter-gatherers, simple and intensive horticulturalists, and pastoralists in east and north Africa. Some of these societies had reached the level of civilization and the state, but, except for Egypt, they arrived at this point later and had less-developed and less-complex civilizations than found in other parts of the world. There was for many centuries a vigorous trade between parts of north Africa and parts of sub-Saharan Africa. Many sub-Saharan African societies had slave systems long before the Europeans arrived to carry off Africans for their own form of slavery.

North Africa and sub-Saharan Africa are really quite different. North Africans are predominantly Arabs and adherents of Islam, and pastoralism was the predominant mode of production prior to European penetration (and still is in some places). North Africa, although geographically African, really belongs to the cultural region of the Middle East. Most sub-Saharan Africans have been hunter-gatherers and horticulturalists and have had their own indigenous and quite varied religious and cultural traditions. This discussion focuses entirely on sub-Saharan Africa.

Samir Amin (1972) has distinguished five stages in the incorporation of Africa into the capitalist world-system:

1. *The New World-African Slave Trade, 1500–1860.* Some 40 million Africans were put on slave ships destined for the New World and the slave systems of the United States, the Caribbean, and Brazil. Only about 10 million of these actually arrived, most having perished in the horrendous conditions aboard the ships, especially during the famed "Middle Passage." Why was it Africans, especially west Africans, who provided the labor force for the New World plantations? Wallerstein (1979) says that the slaves had to be drawn from a region outside the world-economy whose workers were not being used in that region for peripheral forms of production. Since slaveowners were rational capitalists, cost considerations were paramount. Africa seemed to fill the bill best because its populations had not been peripheralized, and because Africa was geographically close to the New World. Presumably Asians—Indians and Chinese mainly—could have been enslaved, but the costs of transporting them the much greater distances from Asia to the New World would have been much higher. Some scholars have suggested that Africans were enslaved because of European racism; Africans were thought to make the best slaves because they were allegedly lower in intelligence and physically stronger. Racism might have played some role, but it is doubtful that it was more than a minor one.

2. *Gradual abandonment of the slave trade and the emergence of Africa as a peripheral region, 1800–1880.* Britain abolished its role in the slave trade in 1807, but there was a great deal of slave trading that occurred after that time nevertheless. During this time, Africa was slowly but surely being converted into a region designed for the production of agricultural goods for export.

3. *Colonization and full peripheralization, 1880–1960.* Around 1880, the famous "scramble for Africa" among the European powers began. This was the only major world region that had so far not been colonized. Britain and France were the main colonizers, but Belgium, Portugal, and even a few other European countries were involved as well.
4. *Decolonization and attempts at ISI development, 1950s–1975.* The first African society to be decolonized was Ghana in 1957, and the last was Mozambique in 1974. Therefore all of African decolonization took place within a period of 17 years.
5. *Stagnation and crisis, 1975–present.* Despite the efforts at import-substitution industrialization, little headway was made. Rather than developing, most sub-Saharan African societies declined economically, and began to experience other serious problems as well, such as severe ethnic hostilities and the emergence of brutally repressive states.

Sub-Saharan Africa's economies have deteriorated alarmingly since decolonization. Its proportion of the world's export products declined from more than 3 percent in 1950 to only 1 percent in 1990, and its external debt rose from just over 30 percent of GNP in 1980 to nearly 80 percent in 1994. The World Bank reports that, of the $231 billion in foreign investment that went into the Third World in 1995, only 1 percent went to Africa. In 1991, there was only one telephone line for every 100 people in comparison to 2.3 lines for the Third World as a whole land and 37.2 for the industrial countries. By the early to mid-1990s, real income had declined by almost 15 percent from its level in 1965. Food production has declined markedly, to the point where many African countries cannot feed themselves. Taxes are high, inflation is rampant, and currencies are unstable. Technological infrastructure has decayed everywhere: Roads have become paths and ruts, bridges are collapsing and do not get repaired, railways are in a state of decay, phones do not work, and universities have deteriorated. Hospitals are in such a poor state that patients often need to bring their own blankets and bandages (Castells, 1998; Ayittey, 1998).

In the last 20 years, the contintent has experienced severe ethnic hostilities, civil wars, political chaos, and massive government corruption (Castells, 1998; Ayittey, 1998). Ethnic groups engage in genocidal actions against each each other, and governments often conspire in this. For example, in 1994, ethnic conflict in Burundi and Rwanda between Tutsis and Hutus resulted in some 700,000 Tutsis being killed, and hundreds of thousands of Hutus were slain as well. This genocidal civil war led to over a million Hutu refugees fleeing into neighboring Zaire. Many countries seem to have almost completely distintegrated. As Ayittey (1998:54) comments, "For much of 1992 Somalia lay in ruins—effectively destroyed. It had no government, no police force, no basic essential services. Armed thugs and bandits roamed the country, pillaging and plundering, and murderous warlords battled savagely for control of Mogadishu."

Dependency and world-system theories blame exploitation by the core for Africa's current problems. In the words of Andre Gunder Frank, "the lemon was sqeezed dry and then discarded." But this is very dubious. George Ayittey (1998) places most of the blame on sub-Saharan Africa's internal problems, as does Manuel Castells (1998). Both trace Africa's massive problems to what they call the "predatory" or "vampire" state characteristic of so many African societies. Dishonesty, thievery, embezzlement, and the like are everywhere. African political leaders can be compared to gangsters and crooks who have seized political power merely to advance their own interests. In fact, states as they are usually thought of really do not exist in Africa. The political institutions that are crucial parts of states—for example, the military, police forces, the civil service, parliaments, and judiciaries—have suffered a kind of debauchery. Parliaments either do not exist or are little but charades. Political dictators have staffed each of these institutions with their own tribesmen who will be completely at their beck and call. There is little or no professionalism and accountability in any of these institutions. However, Ayittey argues that, although Africa's problems are mostly of internal origin, the West has magnified them. Western leaders, he says, have been seduced by despots. They have often supported procapitalist African dictators and supplied them with economic and military aid. Ayittey also notes that American blacks have often praised African leaders and failed to realize the horrendous actions these leaders were engaged in.

If the predatory state is the principal source of Africa's horrendous economic and social problems, then the obvious solution would be to destroy this type of state and replace it with a more democratic type. But that is much more easily said than done. As Ayittey points out, the commitment to reform has been weak in African countries. African despots have been extremely reluctant to give up power and would rather destroy their economies instead. And it is likely that the African state is not the real source of the problem, but simply another dimension of the problem. The real question is, Why do sub-Saharan African societies have such states in the first place? This is what must be explained.

# World-System Position and the Form of the State

So far we have focused on the economics of less-developed countries and said little or nothing about their politics. What is the nature of political life in the Third World? Or, putting it somewhat more precisely, How does a nation-state's political structure relate to its position within the capitalist world-system? Table 9.4 shows democratization levels and the extent of political rights for core, semiperipheral, and peripheral societies. It is obvious that core societies have by far the highest levels of democratization and respect for political rights. As discussed in Chapter 7, in this zone highly stable democratic governments are the norm. It was in the core, of course, that parliamentary democracy first arose, and today every core state is democratic. We have already seen why this is the case. Democracy was favored in core societies because these societies had the largest and most literate working classes, and the struggles of the working classes in the nineteenth and twentieth centuries for political inclusion were vital to the development of full substantive

TABLE 9.4    **Democracy and Political Rights in Core, Semiperipheral, and Peripheral Societies**

| Society | Democracy Score 2000 | Political Rights Score 2003 |
|---|---|---|
| **Core Societies** | | |
| Australia | 35.3 | 7 |
| Belgium | 42.7 | 7 |
| Canada | 24.2 | 7 |
| Denmark | 41.2 | 7 |
| France | 35.5 | 7 |
| Germany | 35.5 | 7 |
| Italy | 45.6 | 7 |
| Japan | 24.9 | 7 |
| Netherlands | 38.4 | 7 |
| Sweden | 37.7 | 7 |
| Switzerland | 40.0 | 7 |
| United Kingdom | 30.2 | 7 |
| United States | 34.5 | 7 |
| **Semiperipheral Societies** | | |
| Algeria | 15.6 | 2 |
| Brazil | 27.4 | 6 |
| Costa Rica | 22.0 | 7 |
| Ecuador | 14.2 | 5 |
| Egypt | 3.0 | 2 |
| Greece | 35.9 | 7 |
| Indonesia | 13.4 | 5 |
| Iran | 5.2 | 2 |
| South Korea | 29.1 | 6 |
| Mexico | 20.8 | 6 |
| Oman | 0.0 | 2 |
| Peru | 8.4 | 6 |
| Saudia Arabia | 0.0 | 1 |
| Singapore | 8.5 | 3 |
| Trinidad and Tobago | 18.9 | 5 |
| Turkey | 33.1 | 5 |
| Venezuela | 16.5 | 5 |
| **Peripheral Societies** | | |
| Afghanistan | 0.0 | 2 |
| Angola | 0.0 | 2 |
| Bangladesh | 17.3 | 4 |
| Benin | 12.8 | 5 |
| Bolivia | 20.7 | 6 |
| Burma/Myanmar | 0.0 | 1 |
| Congo | 0.0 | 2 |
| El Salvador | 9.7 | 6 |
| Ghana | 16.6 | 6 |
| Guatemala | 5.5 | 4 |

TABLE 9.4   *(Continued)*

| Society | Democracy Score 2000 | Political Rights Score 2003 |
|---|---|---|
| **Peripheral Societies** *(continued)* | | |
| Haiti | 2.9 | 2 |
| Honduras | 15.2 | 5 |
| Kampuchea/Cambodia | 5.5 | 2 |
| Kenya | 8.4 | 4 |
| Laos | 0.4 | 1 |
| Malawi | 22.2 | 4 |
| Nigeria | 9.7 | 4 |
| Rwanda | 0.0 | 1 |
| Sudan | 1.5 | 1 |
| Uganda | 9.1 | 2 |

*Notes:* Democracy scores are calculated as the rate of voter participation multiplied by the extent of political party competition, which is then divided by 100. A political rights score of 7 indicates the greatest recognition of political rights, a score of 1 the least recognition (these scores have been reversed from the original coding).

*Sources:* Vanhanen (2003); Freedom House Survey Team (2003).

democracy (Rueschemeyer, Stephens, and Stephens, 1992). By and large, the tradition of democratic government has become so strongly entrenched in the advanced capitalist societies that it has come to constitute an independent force in its own right. Democratic philosophies pervade the whole fabric of life in these societies.

In the capitalist periphery, democracy and respect for political freedom has been very much the exception, and those peripheral societies that do have some type of democracy usually have a fairly low level of it. Political regimes based on military dictatorship are widespread throughout the peripheral capitalist world. In peripheral societies the industrial working class is usually small and politically weak and literacy rates are often low. The predominant ruling class consists of landlords incorporating a large and often illiterate peasantry into the process of labor-repressive agriculture. As Rueschemeyer, Stephens, and Stephens (1992) point out, democracy is not possible in societies with such a balance of class forces. In addition, extreme forms of authoritarianism may be necessary to maintain sheer order under conditions of severe exploitation and abject human misery and suffering. Under such conditions democracy is, in a way, a "luxury" that peripheral societies (or, more accurately, their ruling elites) cannot "afford."

In semiperipheral societies, the levels of democratization and the extent of political rights are intermediate between those in core and peripheral societies. As in the case of the periphery, many societies have formal rather than true substantive democracies. Moreover, these societies have often been vulnerable to political crises in which formal democracy has collapsed back into authoritarianism. Latin America is a region of the world that can be strongly characterized in these ways. The relative

TABLE 9.5 Democracy and Political Rights in Newly Democratizing
Less-Developed Countries, 1977–2003

| | Democracy Score | | | Political Rights Score | | |
|---|---|---|---|---|---|---|
| Country | 1980 | 1993 | 2000 | 1977 | 1988 | 2003 |
| **Latin America** | | | | | | |
| Argentina | 0.0 | 27.0 | 26.1 | 2 | 6 | 5 |
| Bolivia | 0.0 | 10.5 | 20.7 | 2 | 6 | 6 |
| Brazil | 3.8 | 20.5 | 27.4 | 4 | 6 | 6 |
| Chile | 0.0 | 20.2 | 23.1 | 1 | 3 | 6 |
| Ecuador | 6.0 | 21.1 | 14.2 | 2 | 6 | 5 |
| El Salvador | 0.0 | 10.2 | 9.7 | 4 | 5 | 6 |
| Honduras | 0.0 | 14.1 | 15.2 | 2 | 6 | 5 |
| Mexico | 1.7 | 10.6 | 20.8 | 4 | 5 | 5 |
| Nicaragua | 0.0 | 16.6 | 18.5 | 3 | 3 | 5 |
| Panama | 0.0 | 21.6 | 25.3 | 2 | 2 | 7 |
| Suriname | 0.0 | 6.5 | 22.1 | 2 | 5 | 7 |
| Uruguay | 0.0 | 39.7 | 31.9 | 2 | 6 | 7 |
| **Asia** | | | | | | |
| Bangladesh | 5.4 | 13.7 | 17.3 | 2 | 4 | 4 |
| Cambodia | 0.0 | 5.9 | 5.5 | 1 | 1 | 2 |
| Indonesia | 1.1 | 4.0 | 13.4 | 3 | 3 | 5 |
| South Korea | 1.7 | 30.0 | 29.1 | 3 | 6 | 6 |
| Lebanon | 9.5 | 11.7 | 25.9 | 4 | 2 | 2 |
| Philippines | 0.0 | 23.4 | 21.5 | 3 | 6 | 6 |
| Sri Lanka | 5.3 | 15.7 | 20.2 | 6 | 5 | 5 |
| Taiwan | — | 4.6 | 29.4 | — | — | 6 |
| Turkey | 0.0 | 12.2 | 33.1 | 6 | 6 | 5 |
| **Africa** | | | | | | |
| Cape Verde | 2.4 | 8.4 | 12.1 | 2 | 3 | 7 |
| Central African Rep. | 0.0 | 12.2 | 11.3 | 1 | 2 | 3 |
| Chad | 0.0 | 0.0 | 9.2 | 1 | 2 | 2 |
| Ivory Coast | 0.0 | 2.3 | 7.6 | 2 | 2 | 2 |
| Guinea-Bissau | 0.0 | 0.0 | 10.0 | 2 | 2 | 4 |
| Kenya | 0.0 | 11.5 | 8.4 | 3 | 2 | 4 |
| Liberia | 0.0 | 0.0 | 5.3 | 2 | 3 | 2 |
| Madagascar | 2.3 | 11.0 | 9.9 | 3 | 3 | 5 |
| Mozambique | 0.0 | 0.0 | 10.5 | 1 | 2 | 5 |
| South Africa | 1.3 | 3.1 | 12.4 | 3 | 3 | 7 |
| Togo | 0.0 | 0.6 | 7.6 | 1 | 2 | 2 |

*Note:* Democracy scores are calculated as the rate of voter participation multiplied by the extent of political party competition, which is then divided by 100. A political rights score of 7 indicates the greatest recognition of political rights, a score of 1 the least recognition (these scores have been reversed from the original coding).

*Sources:* Vanhanen (2003); Gastil (1989); Freedom House Survey Team (2003).

absence of substantive democracy in semiperipheral societies can be explained in much the same way that we explained democracy's relative absence in the periphery: Landlords continue to play a strong role in the economy, the working class remains small and politically anemic, levels of literacy are often low, and there is often much discontent stemming from very high levels of human misery. Because of the political weakness of the industrial working class, the limited democratic inroads that have been made have generally required a political coalition between the working class and the middle class (Rueschemeyer, Stephens, and Stephens, 1992).

However, since the early 1980s there has been a fairly dramatic wave of democratization occurring in parts of the periphery and semiperiphery, especially in Latin America (Green, 1999; Doorenspleet, 2000; Schaeffer, 1997). Table 9.5 presents democratization scores for 32 "new democracies." Does this latest wave of democratization signal a resumption of the long-term evolutionary trend toward greater democratization? Perhaps, but caution must still be exercised.

Throughout the twentieth century, politics in many Latin American countries showed something of a cyclical alternation between more and less repressive regimes (Skidmore and Smith, 2001; E. Stephens, 1989). Given this pattern, the prediction of a long-term directional trend toward democracy may be premature. We will have to wait and see if the new democracies can sustain themselves and avoid collapsing back into some kind of authoritarianism. Undoubtedly, some of them will collapse, but it is also likely that others will sustain democracy and perhaps even move toward real substantive democracy. The same prediction seems reasonable with respect to new Asian democracies. In the case of Africa, prospects are probably not as good. As we saw, many of the societies of this region are governed by extremely repressive and brutal states, and most democracy is a sham (Ayittey, 1998). African societies still are overwhelmingly dominated by agriculture and have very little industrialization and very small working classes. Literacy rates are generally quite low. Thus, the conditions for continued democratization, even of the purely formal sort, are much less favorable in Africa than they are in Latin America and Asia.

# FOR FURTHER READING

Each year the World Bank publishes the *World Development Report*, which contains extensive data on development indicators in all of the world's countries. A similar document is the United Nations's *Human Development Report*, also published every year. Good introductions to the whole problem of underdevelopment are Bradshaw and Wallace (1996) and McMichael (2004).

Rostow's *The Stages of Economic Growth: A Non-Communist Manifesto* (1960) is the classic statement of modernization theory. More recent statements are found in Berger (1986), Apter (1987), and Landes (1998). The classic formulations of dependency theory are Frank (1966, 1979) and Amin (1974). See also the edited collection of commentaries on Frank's work by Chew and Denemark (1996). The more recent softer version of dependency theory can be found in Evans (1979) and Cardoso and Faletto (1979). See also Cardoso (2001). The classic world-system statement on underdevelopment is Wallerstein (1974b); see also Bornschier and Chase-Dunn (1985). Bill Warren (1980) returns to the classical Marxian view that colonialist and imperialist domination of the less-developed world will eventually produce development there. An article by Firebaugh (1992) poses a severe methodological challenge to dependency and world-system theory; see also the replies to this article by Dixon and Boswell (1996a, 1996b). Good overviews of the major theories of underdevelopment are found in Roxborough (1979), Hoogvelt (1982), Larrain (1989), and So (1990).

Skidmore and Smith's *Modern Latin America* (2001) is an extremely good historical analysis of Latin America's involvement in the world capitalist system and its current status. Peter Evans's *Dependent Development: The Alliance of Multinational, State, and Local Capital in Brazil* (1979), written from the point of view of soft dependency theory, is a classic. See also Evans (1987), Gereffi and Wyman (1990), and Haggard (1990). On east Asia, see So and Chiu (1995), Weil (1996), Cumings (1984), Koo (1987), Gereffi and Wyman (1990), Haggard (1990), Aseniero (1994, 1996), Hornik (1994), Keister (2000b), Arrighi, Hamashita, and Selden (2003), and Ciccantell and Bunker (2003). The website http://sinowisdom.com provides up-to-date information on economic activity in China.

George Ayittey's *Africa in Chaos* (1998) is a very detailed analysis of the massive economic and political problems in contemporary Africa and an attempt to explain them. Castells (1996, 1998) provides insightful analyses of all three major regions of the less-developed world and their relationship to global capitalism in the current era.

An important recent work on democratization in the Third World is Schaeffer's *Power to the People: Democratization Around the World* (1997). See also Kurzman (1998), Green (1999), Markoff (1996), and Doorenspleet (2000). Robinson's *Promoting Polyarchy: Globalization, U.S. Intervention, and Hegemony* (1996) is a pessimistic analysis of the prospects for genuine democratization in the Third World.

# CHAPTER

# 10 Globalization

$A$ word that seems to be on almost everyone's lips these days is **globalization,** by which is generally meant a process of the "compression of the world" and of a growing "consciousness of the world as a whole," a phenomenon having economic, political, social, and cultural dimensions (Robertson, 1992). It has become commonplace in recent years, for instance, for people to talk of how what happens in far-off places, such as Shanghai or Baghdad, matters for how we live our lives on the other side of the globe, and matters in a way in which it never had before. For example, a decision made by a board of directors in Japan determines the fate of auto workers in Ohio. The use of aerosols in Europe contributes to an increase in skin cancer in South America. AIDS emerges in Africa and rapidly spreads around the world. Likewise, our consciousness of such events has grown appreciably. Students protest against the production of university merchandise in sweatshops thousands of miles away and prepare themselves for their role in the "global economy." People talk about environmental problems in terms of "saving the planet" and worry about "world peace." Political conservatives agonize over a "new world order" and liberals fret about the regulation of "global corporations." All people, it would seem, have a stake in this thing called globalization.

Interestingly, the term *globalization* is of very recent vintage. In the major dictionaries of English, French, Spanish, and German of the 1980s or the first half of the 1990s, the word is not listed (Therborn, 2000a). In sociology, the term is barely more than 20 years old. Since the early 1990s, there has been an explosion of social-scientific research on the topic. A review of this literature reveals multiple uses of the term. Some scholars emphasize economic processes in defining globalization, while others focus on political, social, or cultural processes. One good definition of globalization is that of the Swedish sociologist Göran Therborn (2000b:154), who defines it as "the tendency to a world-wide reach, impact, or connectedness of social phenomena or to a world-encompassing awareness among social actors." An equally serviceable definition is provided by Held, McGrew, Goldblatt, and Perraton (1999). For them, globalization involves "the widening, deepening, and speeding up of worldwide interconnectedness in all aspects of contemporary social life" (1999:2).

There are a number of reasons why globalization has become an object of such intense interest in recent years. The collapse of Communism, the "disappearance" of some of the periphery, and the economic boom of the 1990s all gave special impetus to the concept of globalization and to the practice of "thinking globally." In addition, it is worth noting that talk of globalization is sometimes simply a way of putting a contemporary gloss on the very basic, enduring questions that preoccupied modernization and dependency theorists from the 1950s to the 1970s: Is the widening and deepening of the capitalist world-economy "good" or "bad"? If good, is it good for all or good for only some? If bad, is it bad for all or bad for only some? However, the main reason for the great interest in globalization has to do with the basic facts. While a minor academic industry emerged in the 1990s that was devoted to debating whether or not globalization was actually occurring, it is now clear that the world has changed in recent years, and in precisely the direction described by Therborn and by Held and colleagues—the increasing worldwide interconnectedness of social life and world-encompassing awareness among people all over the globe.

After discussing the nature of globalization, this chapter proceeds to review the debate over the consequences of one form of globalization. We examine the views of some of the leading critics of globalization and try to assess globalization's costs and benefits. We also extensively review arguments and evidence regarding the impact of globalization on the state of the global environment. The chapter concludes by asking whether or not globalization is in fact the novel phenomenon it is usually claimed to be.

## The Nature of Globalization

Since globalization refers to a variety of processes, it is best to think in terms of several "globalizations." There is **economic globalization,** a process involving the increasing integration of the world-economy through international production, trade, finance, investment, and migration. There is also **political globalization,** which involves the emergence of a "world polity" as nation-states have increasingly joined together in a growing number of international agreements, accords, and alliances, and as people around the world have established a variety of international nongovernmental organizations. Finally, there is **sociocultural globalization,** or the evolution of a "world society" and "world culture" through processes involving the harmonization of institutions, tastes, preferences, norms, and values, and the tendency for a growing proportion of the world's population to consume the same cultural products. While all three variants of globalization are related, they are distinct enough to merit independent examination.

### Economic Globalization

The extent of international trade, capital flows, and migration are the main elements of economic globalization. A key indictor of economic globalization is the *ratio of world trade to world output.* If the world-economy is in fact becoming increasingly global, then interconnectedness via trade should be growing faster than the world-economy itself. Data indicate that this is in fact occurring. In 1990, the ratio of world trade in goods and services to world GDP was 19 percent. In 2000, just 10 years later, it had increased to 29 percent. This means that the ratio of trade to output grew by 52 percent in the decade of the 1990s (World Trade Organization, 2001). The rate of growth in trade relative to output across the 1990s was more than three times that observed in the 1970s and twice that observed in the 1980s.

Another important indicator of economic globalization is *change in the ratio of cross-border capital flows to world output*. The reasoning behind the use of this indicator is similar to that just described: If the world-economy is truly becoming more global, then the amount of capital flowing across international borders should be growing faster than the world-economy itself. Again, data indicate that this is the case. In 1990, gross private capital flows (i.e., commercial bank lending, bonds, foreign direct investment, and other private credits and investments) amounted to 10 percent of world GDP. By the year 2000, the ratio of gross private capital flows to world GDP had grown to 29 percent (World Bank, 2002). Cross-border capital flows relative to world output thus grew by 190 percent in the 1990s.

A third indicator of economic globalization is the *increasing flow of people across international borders*. Data indicate that the number of international migrants is growing considerably faster than world population itself. In 1990, the world's stock of international migrants—people born in one country but residents in another—stood at nearly 120 million people, or about 2.3 percent of the world's population. By 2000, the world's stock of international migrants had risen to 175 million people, or about 2.9 percent of the world's population (National Research Council, 2000; International Organization for Migration, 2003). International migrants relative to world population therefore grew by 26 percent in the decade of the 1990s. Whereas 1 of every 44 persons in the world was an international migrant in 1990, 1 of every 34 was by 2000. The rate of increase in the ratio of growth in migrants relative to world population in the 1990s was roughly three times that experienced in the period between 1975 and 1990.

In their book *Global Capitalism: The New Leviathan*, Robert Ross and Kent Trachte (1990) see the process of economic globalization as having created a new form of capitalism, what they call *global capitalism*, that is highly distinctive from earlier forms of capitalism (competitive and monopoly capitalism). In addition to the extensive migration of capital from society to society and region to region, global capitalism is distinguished by the existence of a world market in sites for manufacturing production and a spatial division of production tasks throughout the world. Although the periphery has traditionally been associated with raw materials production, under global capitalism a significant segment of it has been increasingly reoriented to the production of manufactured goods. Similarly, Manuel Castells (1996) argues that we are now making the transition from a world-economy to a truly *global economy*. A world-economy is one in which capital accumulation goes on throughout the world, but a global economy is *one that has the capacity to work as a single unit on a planetary scale*. In a global economy (Castells, 1996:93–95),

> Capital is managed around the clock in globally integrated financial markets working in real time for the first time in history: billion dollars-worth of transactions take place in seconds in the electronic circuits throughout the globe. . . . New technologies allow capital to be shuttled back and forth between economies in very short time, so

that capital, and therefore savings and investment, are interconnected worldwide, from banks to pension funds, stock exchange markets, and currency exchange. Since currencies are interdependent, so are economies everywhere. . . .

Labor markets are not truly global, except for a small but growing segment of professionals and scientists . . . , but labor is a global resource in at least three ways: firms may choose to locate in a variety of places worldwide to find the labor supply they need, be it in terms of skills, costs, or social control; firms everywhere may also solicit highly skilled labor from everywhere, and they will obtain it provided they offer the right remuneration and working conditions; and labor will enter any market on its own initiative, coming from anywhere, when human beings are pushed from their homes by poverty and war or pulled towards a new life by hope for their children. . . .

Science, technology, and information are also organized in global flows, albeit in an asymmetical structure. Proprietary technological information plays a major role in creating competitive advantage . . . the characteristics of new productive knowledge favor its diffusion. Innovation centers cannot live in secrecy without drying up their innovative capacity. . . .

In spite of the persistence of protectionism and restrictions to free trade, markets for goods and services are becoming increasingly global. This does not mean that all firms sell worldwide. But it does mean that the strategic aim of firms, large and small, is to sell wherever they can throughout the world, either directly or via their linkage with networks that operate in the world market . . . the *dominant segments and firms, the strategic cores* of all economies are deeply connected to the world market, and their fate is a function of their performance in such a market.

## Political Globalization

Although there are a number of dimensions of political globalization that we could usefully explore, perhaps the most tangible and well-researched concerns the emergence of a "world polity" (Meyer, Boli, Thomas, and Ramirez, 1997; Beckfield, 2003). Here, political globalization is conceived of as involving not only a growing interconnectedness between nation-states in the interstate system, but also an increasing connectedness between supra-, sub-, and non-state actors. Very simply put, recent years have witnessed the emergence of a denser and increasingly global network of decision making and debate in which *global* policies have been forged (e.g., the Kyoto Protocol on global climate change). There has been a multiplication of the occasions for "global gatherings" of all sorts, such as the yearly World Trade Organization meeting, which brings together representatives of most of the world's governments, and the yearly countermeeting protesting the WTO's actions, which brings together many of the world's other stakeholders in trade and development issues.

The best way to measure the growth of a world polity is to examine increases in the number of ties that countries, and nonstate actors within countries, have to international organizations. Consider first the *growth of intergovernmental organizations (IGOs).* IGOs are international organizations that have national governments as their members. In joining IGOs, governments cede varying degrees of their sovereignty to such organizations to make collective decisions and manage global problems. Well-known examples of IGOs are the United Nations (UN), the European

Union (EU), the North Atlantic Treaty Organization (NATO), and the North American Free Trade Agreement (NAFTA). In 1960, the average country was a member of 18 such organizations, but by 2000, the average country belonged to 52 such organizations (Beckfield, 2003)—an increase of 189 percent.

Consider also the *growth of international nongovernmental organizations* (INGOs). INGOs are international organizations that have nongovernmental actors as their members. Well-known examples of INGOs are the International Red Cross, Greenpeace, Rotary International, and the International Chamber of Commerce. Such organizations are not formed by governments; rather, they have private individuals or organizations as their members. In 1960, the average country had within it private individuals or organizations who were members of 141 INGOs. By 2000, however, the average country was tied to 984 INGOs (Beckfield, 2003). The average nation-state was thus 598 percent more integrated into the global polity through INGOs in 2000 than it was in 1960, indicating again that decision making in recent decades has indeed grown increasingly global.

## Sociocultural Globalization

Sociocultural globalization involves the emergence of a "world society" or "world culture." This is evidenced in processes of cultural and institutional consolidation and in the increasingly cosmopolitan character of cultural consumption, as cultural products, knowledge, and lifestyles diffuse across national boundaries. For instance:

- As a criterion for membership, signatories to the WTO treaty agreed to alter their national environmental, health, and safety policies in order to make them as unrestrictive of trade as possible—implying that, over time, environmental, health, and safety policies (among others) will look increasingly alike from country to country.
- McDonald's has over 31,000 restaurants in 118 countries, and famously strives to have its french fries in the country of Peru taste *exactly* like its french fries in Peru, Indiana.
- All of the world's 20 biggest grossing films of 2002 were produced by a Hollywood studio.
- CNN is everywhere, being available in just about every country with a cable or satellite television system.
- Some of the best 1960s-style "garage rock" today comes from Japan.

Of the three forms of globalization under consideration, sociocultural globalization is probably the most difficult to measure. However, in addition to the above we can point to three indicators of sociocultural globalization. First, recent years have witnessed a dramatic upswing in *international tourism*. In 1990, the average country experienced tourist arrivals and departures equivalent to 60 percent of its population. By 2001, tourist arrivals and departures had increased to 86 percent of population in the average country (World Bank, 2002). As a result, more people have direct, face-to-face experience with the world outside their home countries than ever

*A McDonald's restaurant in Dhahran, Saudi Arabia. The spread of McDonald's and other American fast-food restaurants all over the world is a leading example of sociocultural globalization.*

before, and thus more experience with different cultures, languages, cuisines, and so on.

Second, the last decade witnessed a sharp upswing in *international telephone traffic*. In 1990, the total incoming and outgoing international telephone traffic in the average country amounted to 34 minutes per person. By 2001, the volume of international telephone traffic had risen to 125 minutes per person in the average country (International Telecommunications Union, 2002). The time that individuals spend in telephone communication with people in other countries thus grew by 268 percent during the 1990s—a volume of international communication that is historically unprecedented.

Finally, consider the *growth of the Internet*, which has knit hundreds of millions of people together in various forms of international communication and exchange. In 1990, there were only about 45,000 people worldwide using the Internet, but by 2001, the number of Internet users had ballooned to an estimated 483,056,000, more than a thousand-fold increase (International Telecommunications Union, 2002). In per capita terms, the change looks just as impressive. In 1990, Internet users made up just 0.01 percent of the population in the average country. In 2001, they made up 18 percent. Again, people are connected across international boundaries today in ways that would have been unimaginable just a few decades ago.

### What Drives the Globalization Process?

Although globalization is a multidimensional process, are the economic, political, social, and cultural dimensions of globalization equal as causal evolutionary dynamics, or can pride of place be given to one of these dimensions as essentially driving the others? The view that none of these dimensions is of greater causal significance than the others—that globalization is, on a causal level, a truly multidimensional process—has been taken by a number of scholars, most notably Anthony Giddens (1990) and David Held and his colleagues (1999). Giddens identifies four dimensions of globalization—the world-capitalist economy, the nation-state system, the world military order, and the international division of labor—and refuses to give priority to any of them in shaping the globalization process. It seems odd that Giddens separates the capitalist world-economy and the international division of labor. The latter is, for him, the divide between the advanced industrial and the less-developed countries. In our view, the world-economy and the international division of labor are inextricably intertwined, two parts of one and the same thing. But the fact that Giddens separates them shows just how multidimensional his causal perspective on globalization is.

World-system theorists, on the other hand, tend to give priority to the evolution of the capitalist world-economy as the driving force of globalization. It is especially capitalist evolution that is behind sociocultural globalization. The spread of common tastes and common patterns of cultural consumption would never have been possible without the increasing globalization of capitalism. They acknowledge that the emergence of a world polity has to some degree an evolutionary logic of its own, as Meyer and his colleagues (1997) suggest. However, it is also the case that a large proportion of the IGOs and INGOs that now exist have come into existence primarily to facilitate or regulate economic activity. Our own view is in agreement with the world-system perspective on this issue, which is not surprising, given the overall theoretical framework of this book: evolutionary materialism and infrastructural determinism.

## Globalization and Its Critics

Whether looked at in economic, political, or sociocultural terms, globalization is a fact of contemporary life. What are we to make of it? How should we evaluate it and its consequences? Opinions differ sharply. Some view globalization as an unambiguously positive development that promises to create a world of unparalleled peace and prosperity. Others take a much more negative view. In fact, globalization, especially its economic form, has come under severe attack in the last decade by a range of critics both inside and outside the academic world. In Seattle in December 1999, as the WTO prepared to hold an important meeting, a variety of individuals and groups engaged in a number of protests, some of them involving smashing windows of corporate buildings, that eventually led the WTO to reschedule its meeting. Along with the WTO, the International Monetary Fund (IMF) and the World Bank are the major global economic organizations directing the process of globalization and the primary targets of antiglobalization sentiment and activity. The hostility to them is expressed well by Joseph Stiglitz (2003:3):

> The protests at the Seattle meeting of the World Trade Organization in 1999 were a shock. Since then, the movement has grown stronger and the fury has spread. Virtually every major meeting of the International Monetary Fund, the World Bank, and the World Trade Organization is now the scene of conflict and turmoil. The death of a protestor in Genoa in 2001 was just the beginning of what may be many more casualties in the war against globalization.

In May 2003, an international conference with a strong antiglobalization theme was held at the University of California at Santa Barbara. Several dozen speakers—mostly academicians, journalists, and political organizers—were invited to tell perhaps as many as a thousand conference attendees what was wrong with globalization and what to do about it. For three days speakers lectured those in attendance about how globalization was having mostly harmful effects, especially on populations in the Third World. Scarcely a single positive thing was said about the globalization process. Toward the end of the conference's final session, which was devoted to a summing up of the views of the leading speakers, one attendee asked the panelists whether they thought there was anything good about the globalization process. This led four of the panelists to seize the opportunity to attack globalization even more severely than they had already. One panelist, a Russian who had been a political prisoner under the old Soviet regime, said that the one good thing about globalization was that it would ultimately destroy capitalism, which in turn would lead to

*Opening session of the World Trade Organization (WTO) conference in Doha, Qatar, November 9, 2001. The WTO is a major indicator of political globalization and plays a major role in economic globalization.*

a better economic system: socialism! The profound irony of this remark seemed to be totally lost on the speaker.

The WTO is the primary target of the antiglobalization forces. It was created in 1995, and by 2002, 144 nations, accounting for some 97 percent of world trade, belonged to it (Singer, 2002). The WTO's philosophy is that free trade is the key to economic growth throughout the world and improves the economic situation of all countries. It is an enormously powerful organization, having the authority to enforce some 30,000 pages of rules and agreements relating to world trade (Singer, 2002). Peter Singer (2002) delineates the main charges that have been made by the antiglobalization forces against the WTO: (1) it places economic concerns—profits—ahead of environmental concerns, animal welfare, and human well-being; (2) it undermines the sovereignty of nations; (3) it is undemocratic in its operations and procedures; and (4) it increases world inequality, or even makes the poorest populations of the world worse off than they otherwise would have been.

Singer examines a good deal of evidence relating to each of these charges. He concludes that the first three are basically true. The WTO does generally act in ways that demonstrate its elevation of maximum profits over environmental concerns and animal and human well-being. Singer shows that when disputes have arisen requiring the WTO to choose between permitting free trade and supporting a national policy designed to protect the environment, it has always chosen free trade. The WTO also does tend to undermine national sovereignty. Once nations join the WTO, they are under strong pressure to remain in it and to adjust their own national policies to be in accord with what the WTO wants. As for the third charge, the WTO is formally democratic and in fact claims that it has a special kind of democracy because a complete consensus is required before a decision can be declared. The WTO therefore considers itself as having an even better form of democracy than simple majority rule. However, this is very misleading and in practice not really very democratic at all. Since a complete consensus is required to reach a decision, a single state can veto an issue because of its own special interests. This happens frequently, and it is the most powerful states with the largest economic consequences at stake that are most likely to engage in a veto. And different countries end up having very unequal bargaining power. As Singer puts it (2002:75–76):

> In practice, the agenda is set by informal meetings of the major trading powers, especially, up to now, the United States, the European Union, Japan, and Canada. On major issues, once these powers have reached agreement, the results are presented to the formal meeting, but by then they often are a fait accompli. Moreover, the poorer nations often lack the resources to participate fully in the innumerable WTO meetings.

The fourth charge against the WTO—that it contributes to widening the gap between the richest and poorest segments of the world's population, or that its policies even contribute to an absolute reduction in the level of economic and physical well-being of the poorest populations—requires considerably more attention to resolve. Critics of globalization point to the fact that about 1.2 billion people—some one-fifth of the world's population—currently live on less than $1 a day and approximately 2.8 billion live on less than $2 a day (Singer, 2002; Lomborg, 2001). This certainly looks bad, and clearly indicates that much work remains to be done to improve conditions for the poorest people in the less-developed world. However, in assessing the effects of globalization, the most important question is whether those living in the underdeveloped world have become worse off or better off in the era of globalization. Whereas the critics suggest they have become worse off, a good deal of evidence seems to suggest otherwise.

Much of this evidence has been summarized by Singer (2002) and by Bjørn Lomborg (2001). In 1960, life expectancy in the less-developed world was about 46 years (World Bank, 1984), but by 1997, it had climbed to 65 years (Lomborg, 2001). If we omit Africa, which is a special case with a much lower average life span (about 49 in the year 2000), it was nearly 70 years. This is extremely significant when one realizes that in the United States in 1900 life expectancy was only 49 years. Thus, the average person in Latin America and Asia today is living almost 21 years longer than the average American a century ago! Life expectancy has increased primarily because infant and child mortality rates have plummeted throughout the Third World in recent decades, and also because calorie intake has increased and nutrition improved. Infant mortality in the less-developed world in 1960 was approximately 150 (World Bank, 1984), whereas by 2000 it had declined to about 57 (and to 35 if sub-Saharan Africa is excluded) (United Nations, 2002). In the United States in the mid-nineteenth century, infant mortality was approximately 160. Only three underdeveloped countries in the world today have a rate that high (all of them in Africa), and the average, as we have seen, is much lower. In 1970, about 35 percent of people in the less-developed world were considered to be starving, but this declined to 18 percent by 1997. And there has actually been a decline in the *absolute number* of people starving even though world population has increased substantially, with approximately 920 million people starving in 1971 but declining to 792 million in 1997. As for calorie intake in the less-developed world, it rose from slightly more than 1,900 calories a day in 1961 to over 2,650 calories a day in 1998—a 38 percent increase.

Moreover, the United Nations has constructed a Human Development Index (HDI) to measure the quality of life in all of the world's countries. The HDI is a weighted average of life expectancy, educational attainment, and per capita GDP; it can vary from 0 to 1.0. The HDI for the United States in 1999 was .934, and for Italy, one of the least developed of the core countries, it was .909 (United Nations, 2001). In the Third World, HDI scores have risen considerably since 1970. For example, the HDI in South Korea in 1970 was .589 but rose to .875 by 1999. For Indonesia the corresponding numbers are .316 and .677, for Brazil .569 and .750, for Mexico .675 and .790, for Turkey .492 and .735, for Ecuador .542 and .726, for Iran .464 and .714, for Guatemala .416 and .626, for India .258 and .571, for Egypt .286 and .635, and for Zambia .320 and .431 (United Nations, 1992, 2001). In the vast majority of Third World countries the HDI has been continually increasing in the last half-century, and in only a handful has it declined (and then only slightly).

Based on these figures, it would seem difficult to conclude that globalization has been making life worse for the average person in the less-developed world.

Things seem to be improving rather than deteriorating. Yet, critics of globalization insist that, even if there has been some sort of absolute improvement for the world's worst-off populations, globalization has nonetheless led to an increase in global inequality—a growing gap between the world's rich and poor. This is a very difficult issue to assess, and for two fundamental reasons.

First, there is major disagreement among the leading scholars studying this problem as to whether global inequality actually has been increasing. A statistic frequently cited by those who say it has comes from the United Nations' 1999 *Human Development Report*. In 1960, the ratio of the richest quintile of the world's population to the poorest quintile was approximately 30:1. By 1990, this had increased to 60:1, and by 1997, to 74:1. And a very well known study by Korzeniewicz and Moran (1997), using more statistically sophisticated procedures, found that inequality was increasing. However, this study has been criticized for how it measured income inequality: It failed to take into account the differences in prices and consumer purchasing power between countries.

Glenn Firebaugh (1999, 2000, 2003) measures income inequality between countries by using what are called PPP, or Purchasing Power Parity, income estimates, which adjust incomes so that they take into consideration these between-country differences in purchasing power. Using such a measure, Firebaugh has found that global income inequality remained essentially stable between 1960 and 1989 (with the global Gini coefficient changing from .540 to only .543 during this period). Schultz (1998) and Lomborg (2001) have reached similar conclusions using PPP income measures. In Lomborg's research it was found that the ratio of the richest fifth of the world's population to the poorest fifth declined slightly between 1960 and 1997, from about 13:1 to about 12:1. Focusing on a more recent period, Goesling (2001) finds an actual decline in between-nation inequality between 1980 and 1995. During this period, the Thiel index (similar to the Gini coefficient) declined from .65 to .53. However, there is major disagreement on whether PPP measures of national income or more traditional measures are more appropriate. There is also disagreement on other technical statistical matters that affect the results any particular researcher obtains. At this point it is hazardous to draw any firm conclusion as to whether global inequality is increasing, decreasing, or remaining essentially the same.

Second, to complicate matters, there is also disagreement over the meaning and importance of inequality. Some argue that the critical issue is not inequality and its current trajectory, but whether those at the bottom of the world's income distribution are improving their position in absolute terms (Singer, 2002). Even if the gap between the world's rich and the world's poor is growing, if the poor are better off now than they were 10, 20, or 30 years ago as the result of globalization, then globalization is a good thing. However, sociologists have long known that people tend to evaluate their own situation in life relative to what others around them have rather than with respect to their own absolute situation. If some people have less than others they observe around them, then they tend to *feel* deprived regardless of other circumstances, a phenomenon known as *relative deprivation*. Thus, if global inequality is increasing, then the world's poor subjectively feel more deprived even if their absolute circumstances are improving in objective terms. But which way should we assess well-being? Should we pay more attention to people's subjective experiences or to their objective reality? Moreover, it is well known that inequalities are associated with social tensions that frequently lead to conflict and violence, and no one thinks these are good things. If there is more global inequality and more conflict and violence resulting from it, then globalization appears in a more unfavorable light.

It is also clear that, despite improvements in living conditions in the Third World in the era of globalization, these are *average* improvements. There are still many people whose lives have not been improved, or may actually have gotten worse, as the result of globalization. As Joseph Stiglitz (2003:248) puts it, although globalization has been beneficial for hundreds of millions of people, "for millions of people globalization has not worked. Many have actually been made worse off, as they have seen their jobs destroyed and their lives made more insecure. They have felt increasingly powerless against forces beyond their control. They have seen their democracies undermined, their cultures eroded." There are still some segments of many underdeveloped societies that lead an extremely marginal and unpleasant—in some cases, wretched—existence. Tens of millions of people are still living in crowded shantytowns in extremely flimsy makeshift housing, areas that contain open sewers and that are disease infested. Democracy is still the exception rather than the rule throughout the Third World, and most so-called democracies are formal rather than substantive democracies. In many Third World countries brutal authoritarian states oppress the citizenry and send out "death squads" to deal with dissenters (Petras, 1987).

Moreover, in the era of globalization many Third World countries have established special forms of economic production concentrated in what are known as *free production zones*. These are geographical areas of countries that are often zoned off from the rest of the society by special fences and other devices and within which economic activities are carried on with few restrictions on the use of labor (Fröbel, Heinrichs, and Kreye, 1980). Within these zones, sometimes called *world market factories* because production is destined for the world market, wages are often extremely low and working hours very long, work involves intense levels of concentration, work is often of short duration and thus workers can be subject to sudden unemployment, labor unions are banned, workers have few or no rights, and much work may be dangerous and result in physical harm. The governments of many Third World countries have created these zones at the request of capitalists in the core because they wish to attract foreign investment, hoping that it will lead to higher levels of development. Core capitalists want these zones because they can make superprofits in them. In order to attract foreign investment to these zones, Third World governments offer additional incentives to core capitalists: income tax exemptions of 5 to 10 years; reductions of rates on taxes, surtaxes, and surcharges; freedom of foreign exchange control; preferential financing facilities; preferential tariff rates on transportation costs; and possibilities of renting or buying preconstructed factories and office buildings (Fröbel, Heinrichs, and Kreye, 1980).

In the face of this large mass of often contradictory and inconsistent evidence, it is difficult to know just what to conclude. Not only do sociologists disagree, often dramatically, among themselves, but when other social scientists (e.g., economists, political scientists, and anthropologists) are brought into the picture, then matters get even more complicated. However, one thing is abundantly clear. The recommendation of the opponents of globalization that the globalization project be abandoned is, in Stiglitz's words, neither feasible nor desirable. As the most fundamental economic reality of our times, globalization is scarcely going to go away. The solution is to manage and regulate it in order to make it work as well as possible for a majority of the world's population. Globalization has already produced many good consequences. To make it work even better, we need to regulate or reform some of the key economic institutions of the advanced industrial world, such as the WTO and the IMF, and perhaps create new institutions to help guide the process. Stiglitz puts it extremely well (2003:222): "We cannot go back on globalization; it is here to stay. The issue is how we can make it work. And if it is to work, there have to be global public institutions to help set the rules."

Reforming and regulating globalization, Stiglitz argues, means, for one thing, making the WTO into a more democratic organization that is more accountable. The WTO overwhelmingly represents the economic interests of capitalists in the core countries, but pressure needs to be put on it to make it more sensitive to policies that also benefit people in the Third World, including those at the very bottom of those populations. Within the framework of the WTO, the rich countries have often imposed strong trade barriers to goods from Third World countries while pressuring those countries to limit trade barriers to the rich countries' own goods. And "rich countries impose tariffs on manufactured goods from poor countries that are, according to one study, four times as high as those they impose on imports from other rich countries" (Singer, 2002:95). There are some signs that the WTO is becoming responsive to criticism, but it remains to be seen how far it will go in modifying its policies (Singer, 2002).

But the problem lies not only with the WTO. Two other global organizations that need reform are the World Bank and the IMF. These organizations play a major role in lending money to Third World countries, but the money comes with strings attached. In order to qualify for loans, Third World countries must follow strict policies that the World Bank and IMF dictate. For the past 25 years, these organizations, the IMF in particular, have dictated "neoliberal" economic policies devoted to extreme commitment to free markets. The IMF has consistently acted in high-handed and imperialistic ways to impose these and other policies, and the result has frequently been one economic disaster and crisis after another in the Third World (and even in more developed Asian countries and postsocialist societies trying to make the transition to capitalism). So reform in the IMF and the World Bank is also needed if the benefits of globalization are to be more fully shared by all of the world's peoples.

In the end, perhaps the best conclusion at this time is that globalization has done more good than harm but can still be made to work better. However, there is still the question as to the effects of sociocultural globalization, which has led to the spread of largely U.S. culture all over the globe. Whether or not this is a good thing depends on one's view of U.S. culture and one's level of appreciation of cultural diversity and indigenous cultural traditions. It is therefore largely a question of values rather than of any strictly scientific evidence. For example, on a visit to the Nether-lands a few years ago, one of us expressed to his Dutch host a desire to eat at a res-taurant that served *pannekoeken*. These are very light Dutch pancakes with various fillings that are dusted with powdered sugar. A restaurant was found and the *pannekoeken* consumed, but the Dutch host explained that it was becoming harder and harder to find these restaurants since they were being increasingly replaced by McDonald's and other American fast-food chains. The author bemoaned this fact since he relishes *pannekoeken*, studiously avoids fast food when in Europe, and favors the continuation of indigenous culinary and other cultural traditions. In this sense, sociocultural globalization is a bad thing—at least for him. But even in a scientific sense one can identify a down side to this form of globalization. It is now well known that U.S. fast-food restaurants have contributed to a serious obesity problem in the United States. As fast-food restaurants continue to spread throughout the world, world eating habits may change, and the largely U.S. obesity problem may become more of a world problem. Since obesity is bad for health, and since good health is universally valued, then in a real scientific sense globalization may be a bad thing. Of course, the issue is more complicated than this simple example can convey, but the point is made nonetheless.

## Globalization and the Environment

Since the 1970s, a great deal of discussion has focused on the impact of world popu-lation growth and high levels of industrialization on the environment. This discus-sion has corresponded closely to the emergence of the current era of globalization. Although environmental problems certainly existed prior to this era, the three pro-cesses of economic, political, and sociocultural globalization have rapidly and simul-taneously (1) integrated nearly all parts of the world into a capitalist world-economy that depends on economic growth, and thus greater resource use and output, for its functioning; (2) transformed national environmental problems and their regulation into global problems regulated by a world polity; and (3) given rise to a world soci-ety whose members increasingly have a world-encompassing awareness of environ-mental issues.

For these reasons, the debate over the state of the global environment, and over the role of globalization in environmental problems, has preoccupied scientists and policymakers as never before. The main concerns have been that we will sooner or later create severe pollution problems; experience serious land erosion, declining ag-ricultural yields, and deforestation; and run out of vital sources of energy, especially fossil fuels. In the last 15 years, the concern has shifted heavily to global warming and the depletion of the ozone layer. There have been real fears that the climate changes associated with these phenomena will produce a host of negative conse-quences, such as rising sea levels and the inundation of coastal areas and cities. At current rates of demographic and economic growth and industrial output, how sus-tainable are the world's natural environments in the absence of major technological breakthroughs? Is it possible that much of the world could experience ecological and economic collapse in the near- or mid-term future?

The pessimists seem to outnumber the optimists, or at least to have captured much more public attention. Perhaps the most famous statement by the pessimists was the Club of Rome Report issued in the early 1970s under the title *The Limits to Growth* (Meadows, Meadows, Randers, and Behrens, 1972). Put together by a distinguished international group of scientists, the report predicted ecological catastrophe within 20 years or so if major changes in population growth and resource use were not made very soon. A few years later, the eminent economist Robert Heilbroner (1980) assessed the current demographic and ecological situation and concluded on a very pessimistic note, saying that "the outlook for man, I believe, is painful, difficult, perhaps desperate, and the hope that can be held out for his future prospect seems to be very slim indeed" (1980:20).

Heilbroner saw three reasons why the future looked so grim, the first of which was continuing rapid population growth in the Third World. He predicted that at the then-current rate of growth, the Third World would have to support some 40 billion people by the end of the twenty-first century. The only way to bring population growth under control would be by installing highly authoritarian governments that would establish extremely strict birth control policies. Heilbroner also thought that the world was using up natural resources at such a rate that its inhabitants were rapidly approaching the finite limits of the earth's ability to support the industrial form of technology. An ecological catastrophe could be avoided, once again, only by the introduction of extremely authoritarian governments, because capitalists would never voluntarily restrict their industrial output. Finally, Heibroner argued that if these first two problems did not get us then a third one would: heat pollution. Industrial output generates heat as a natural by-product, and the ever-greater amounts of heat produced by continually increasing industrial output will have calamitous effects on the environment and human health and well-being. Unless we can find a way to solve the problem of heat pollution, the future for the human species, Heilbroner said, was one of extinction. Heilbroner continued to update his arguments in later editions of his original book, but they did not change in any essential way.

The original Club of Rome report was severely and widely criticized, and the authors later admitted that they made various mistakes of calculation and overstated the matter. However, 20 years later, a second report was issued that was allegedly based on more careful calculations and greater caution. This was published in the book *Beyond the Limits*, by Donella Meadows, Dennis Meadows, and Jørgen Randers (1992). The authors performed a series of 13 computer simulations designed to determine what controls would have to be placed on resource use and population growth in order to allow for a sustainable world through the twenty-first century. Of their 13 simulations, only 2 produced a sustainable world. All of the others led to ecological collapse. The authors claimed to show that a sustainable world was possible only if all of the following conditions were implemented simultaneously:

- Pollution controls
- Land yield enhancement
- Land erosion protection
- The development of more resource-efficient technology

- Faster development of new technology
- Every couple in the world limiting itself to two children
- Every nation in the world limiting its industrial output to the level of contemporary South Korea

Moreover, all of these conditions must be implemented very soon, they said, probably within 20 years (that means 20 years from the time their book was published in 1992, which will be the year 2012—only a few years from now!).

The pessimistic view has also been put forward by the Worldwatch Institute, an environmentalist organization led by Lester Brown. Each year since 1984, this organization has published a *State of the World* report. Each new report provides an update on population growth and world resource use, and the message is usually that people are continuing to undermine the natural environment through their actions and that major changes need to be introduced. Changes that have occurred have not been extensive enough to prevent an eventual ecological collapse (Worldwatch Institute, 2003; cf. Lomborg, 2001).

An early and major critic of the pessimistic view was another economist, the Nobel Prize winner Julian Simon (1981). Simon argued that not only is the world not running out of crucial resources, but that the extent of these resources is not even known. He maintained that the doomsaying forecasters went wrong in a fundamental methodological way by basing their forecasts on the concept of "known reserves" of natural resources. Simon claimed that this concept is essentially worthless as a basis for predictions, since the known reserves of any resource are limited by how diligently it has been searched for. According to Simon, the earth's natural resources

*Ecological degradation. Strip mining for nickel in Sudbury, Ontario.*

probably exist in much greater abundance than forecasters imagine. Moreover, since the prices of these resources have been falling over time, this means that the resources are actually less scarce now than they once were. Simon also argued that population growth is not likely to produce dire future consequences because growth rates have been falling and will continue to fall; eventually, less-developed countries will achieve the low growth rates of the highly developed countries.

In a recent, highly detailed analysis of the problem, Bjørn Lomborg (2001) sides with Simon but goes much further. Interestingly, Lomborg was a member of Greenpeace, the radical environmentalist organization, and started his research in order to prove Simon wrong. To his great surprise, once he carefully examined the relevant data, he concluded that Simon was indeed correct. Lomborg's general conclusion is that the environment is in relatively good shape and can sustain a technologically intensive, industrial capitalist economy for many years to come. We still need to improve, Lomborg admits, but we are doing much better than the pessimists argue and we are nowhere near ecological collapse.

Lomborg points out that the Worldwatch Institute predicted in the early 1970s that the world was running out of food; food production would go down and prices would go up. Even though this did not happen, the institute made the same prediction again in 1996, but it has not happened since then either. Lomborg says that food has become cheaper than ever and prices continue to decline. The Food and Agriculture Organization (FAO) predicts that there will actually be more food in the near future, not less. With respect to deforestation, Lomborg shows that, although quite a bit of tropical forest has been disappearing, the rate of deforestation has actually been dropping. The FAO puts the rate of net deforestation at 0.8 percent a year for the 1980s, at 0.7 percent a year in the 1990s, and at an even lower 0.46 percent a year as of 2001. Over 80 percent of tropical forests are still in existence, and only about 14 percent of the Amazonian rain forest has been deforested since the very beginnings of forest cutting. Lomborg claims that only 5 percent of the world's forests are needed in order to permanently satisfy the world's demand for paper.

A critical concern of the environmentalist movement is that the world is running out of fossil fuels—its most important energy source. The original Club of Rome report predicted oil would run out by 1992; this did not happen. *Beyond the Limits* (1992) revised the original forecast and made the new prediction that oil would run out by 2031 and gas by 2050. Lomborg seriously doubts that this will happen either, because oil and gas reserves, although finite, keep expanding (gas reserves have doubled and then some in the last 30 years). How can these reserves be getting larger rather than smaller? The answer is that as the demand for oil and gas increases, companies search more vigorously for new supplies and keep finding them. Moreover, the technology of oil and gas exploration has improved, and this has made it easier not only to find new sources but also to exploit them. Methane gas in coal beds is now being exploited, and more attention is being given to tar sands and shale oil as the costs of extracting oil from these sources have declined. This is extremely significant when one realizes that the ratio of the availability of shale oil to ordinary petroleum resources is approximately 242:1.

Another major worry has been air pollution. Here again, things seem to be much better than we have tended to think. A sense of historical perspective can be extremely helpful. One of the major air pollutants, sulfur dioxide, reached its peak level in London, for example, in the mid-nineteenth century. Since then it has declined markedly, and so much so that its concentration in the air is now lower than it was in the late sixteenth century. A similar pattern holds true for smoke particles; since 1957, smoke pollution has declined by 62 percent in the United States and by a huge 95 percent in the United Kingdom. Pittsburgh, once the world center of steel production, was so smoky in the first half of the twentieth century that at 9:00 o'clock in the morning on a sunny day it was often dark. Some 360 days during the year were classified as smoky days. Today, however, there are virtually never any smoky days in Pittsburgh. Air quality has improved, in most cases dramatically, in all major cities in the developed world. Air pollution is still a problem in many large cities in the less-developed world, and much work remains to be done there. However, there is every reason to expect that it will be. In the highly industrialized world, large manufacturing cities became more polluted as industrialization proceeded, but once a certain level of wealth was achieved, the increasing affluence made it possible to pay to clean up the air. As cities in the now less-developed world eventually reach this level of affluence, they should start bringing about major reductions in air pollution.

The one problem we have not yet addressed is global warming, the current number one environmental concern. A working group of the United Nations known as the Intergovernmental Panel on Climate Change (IPCC) released its *Third Assessment Report* in 2001 (summarized in Singer, 2002). The report can be considered highly authoritative; it had 122 lead authors and was reviewed by another 337 experts. The *Report* looked at weather records for the past 140 years and found that the 1990s was the hottest decade during that time and 1998 the hottest year. Global temperature is rising three times as fast as it was a century ago, and sea levels have risen by some 4 to 8 inches. The *Report* attributes these changes to an increase in the emission of greenhouse gases, especially carbon dioxide, methane, and nitrous oxide. It predicts a rise in global temperature by 2100 of between 1.4° C and 5.8° C. If this occurs, there will be major worldwide consequences: Sea levels will rise as much as 35 inches in some places; food production will increase in some places but fall in others; tropical diseases will become more widespread; and hurricanes and tropical storms will occur over a wider area and hit more large urban areas. The developed countries may be able to cope with these problems, although at considerable cost, but it will be much more difficult and costly for the less-developed societies to deal with them.

Lomborg (2001) raises some serious questions regarding the IPCC's report. Some global warming is occurring, he acknowledges, but it is by no means clear how much is likely to occur within the next century. The IPCC's predictions are based on very complex computer models that rely on numerous assumptions. Even changing one assumption can affect the long-term outcome dramatically. Without going into the details of Lomborg's discussion, suffice it to say that there is a great deal of uncertainty built into the models used by the IPCC, and so it is very difficult to know the extent of global warming over such a long period of time. Lomborg estimates that, because of certain countervailing factors, global warming is likely to be less than the IPCC predicts. Moreover, it is not certain that all global warming is due to greenhouse gas emissions. It is entirely possible that other factors, such as an increase in direct solar irradiation in recent decades, are contributing as well.

The IPCC's predictions also fail to consider likely technological and economic changes. Lomborg estimates that by around 2030–40, solar energy will have become much cheaper and thus highly competitive with fossil fuels, and a marked reduction in the use of fossil fuel energy will significantly decrease carbon dioxide emissions, which represent the majority of greenhouse gas emissions. By the end of the twenty-first century, it is reasonable to expect that fossil fuels will not be used at all. Lomborg's calculations suggest that, when all of the above-mentioned considerations are taken into account, the global temperature is likely to increase only some 2.0–2.5° C, rather than the 4.5–5.5° C that many pessimists are predicting, within the next century. Lomborg's conclusion is that global warming will not be an ever-worsening problem and that the amount of warming that does occur can be dealt with by making technological changes to cope with environmental changes, such as building sophisticated sea walls to deal with higher shoreline water levels, and will actually be far cheaper in the long run. In his words (2001:317):

> There is no doubt that mankind has influenced and is still increasing atmospheric concentrations of $CO_2$ and that this will influence temperature. Yet, we need to separate hyperbole from realities in order to choose our future optimally. . . . We still do not know whether we live in a world where the doubling of $CO_2$ concentrations will mean a rather small (1.5° C) or a dramatic (4.5° C) temperature increase.

Moreover, the consequences of global warming are not likely to be nearly as serious as many have predicted (2001:317–318):

> Global warming will not decrease food production, it will probably not increase storminess or the frequency of hurricanes, it will not increase the impact of malaria or indeed cause more deaths. It is even unlikely that it will cause more flood victims, because a much richer world will protect itself better. However, global warming will have serious costs—the total cost is about $5 trillion. Moreover, the consequences of global warming will hit the developing countries hardest, whereas the industrialized countries may actually benefit from a warming lower than 2–3° C. The developing countries are harder hit primarily because they are poor—giving them less adaptive capacity.

What, then, should we do? Since some amount of global warming is certainly a reality, and since it will have some negative consequences, some action must be taken now. But what action? The usual recommendation is that the highly industrialized countries need to start cutting emissions from fossil fuel usage dramatically in the coming years. This has been the recommendation of various international agreements, the latest of which was the Kyoto Protocol in 2001. The United States was the only nation not to agree to this Protocol, arguing that it placed undue demands on the industrialized countries, itself in particular, and exempted the less-developed countries entirely from the need to reduce emissions. Lomborg argues that the Kyoto

Protocol is too drastic a solution, will be inconsequential anyway, and will be more expensive in the long run. As he puts it, "Despite our intuition that we naturally need to do something drastic about such a costly global warming, economic analyses clearly show that it will be far more expensive to cut $CO_2$ emissions radically than to pay the costs of adaptation to the increased temperatures" (2001:318). In sum, we need to reduce emissions, but only modestly, and to use the new technology and increased wealth being produced in the years ahead to implement changes that will allow us to adapt to the consequences of climate changes.

It is not really possible to say with any certainty who is right: the environmentalists or Lomborg. This is an extremely difficult matter to settle, as all matters regarding the future are. But Lomborg's arguments should caution us against being highly alarmist concerning the human impact on the environment. Things do not appear to be as bad as many have imagined, and numerous dire predictions have failed again and again. For example, we obviously did not run out of oil in 1992, as the original Club of Rome report predicted, and it is already obvious that Heilbroner's prediction of a world population of 40 billion people by the year 2100 will be wildly incorrect (current estimates are in the vicinity of 10 to 11 billion). Moreover, the major new technological breakthroughs that are very likely to be made in coming decades will make existing problems easier to solve (although, if historical experience is any guide, they are likely to generate new problems of their own). We should be seeing a cleaner, cheaper, more efficient technology that will greatly lessen the human environmental impact. We will return to this point in the final chapter.

## Is Globalization Something New?

Given the breathless language with which globalization is often discussed in the popular press, one could easily be forgiven for concluding that today's globalized world is a truly novel and unprecedented phenomenon. Ross and Trachte as well as Castells certainly see it in that way. But there are notable dissenters. World-system theorists generally take the position that, although the current form of globalization has unique features, globalization itself is not something new. Capitalist production has always been global, they insist. In this light, Chase-Dunn, Kawano, and Brewer (2000) document the existence of several periods of trade globalization prior to the current period. And consider the following description of the daily life of an inhabitant of London:

> The inhabitant of London could order by telephone, sipping his morning tea in bed, various products of the whole earth, in such quantity as he might see fit, and reasonably expect their early delivery upon his doorstep; he could at the same moment and by the same means adventure his wealth in the natural resources and new enterprises of any quarter of the world, and share, without exertion or even trouble, in their prospective fruits and advantages; or he could decide to couple the security of his fortunes with the good faith of the townspeople of any substantial municipality

in any continent that fancy or information might recommend. He could secure . . . cheap and comfortable means of transit to any country or climate without passport or other formality . . . and could then proceed abroad to foreign quarters, without knowledge of their religion, language, or customs, bearing coined wealth upon his person, and would consider himself greatly aggrieved and much surprised at the least interference. But, most important of all, he regarded this state of affairs as normal, certain, and permanent, except in the direction of further improvement, and any deviation from it as aberrant, scandalous, and avoidable.

The world that is described in this quotation must surely represent something new, unlike anything seen before. The words, however, are not from the latest bestseller on globalization, but are the (now famous) words of the British economist John Maynard Keynes (1920), who was describing *the world that existed in the years before World War I!* The period from 1870 to 1914, as Keynes's description indicates, was in many ways strikingly similar to the world of today. Then, too, economic globalization in the form of international trade, investment, and mass migration was knitting the world together in a truly global world-economy. Improvements in transportation and communication were also dramatically "shrinking" the world, generating a world polity and world society. And, as is so often the case today, our "inhabitant of London" found this all "normal, certain, and permanent," and found it difficult even to imagine that the future might hold in store anything other than more of the same.

That is all well and good, you might think, but surely the world is more globalized today than it was in the late nineteenth or early twentieth centuries? But this is not indisputably clear. Consider a few key facts about the period from 1870 to 1914:

- The ratio of world trade to world output—described earlier as a key indicator of economic globalization—was nearly as high in the 1870s and 1880s as it was in the 1970s and 1980s (O'Rourke and Williamson, 1999). Indeed, by one estimate, the ratio of world trade to world output was higher in 1879 than it would be in any year after World War I until 1974 (Chase-Dunn, Kawano, and Brewer, 2000).
- Cross-border capital flows were also very extensive around the turn of the twentieth century. The world's foreign capital stock amounted to nearly 20 percent of world output across the 1900–1914 period. This represents a ratio of foreign investment to output that the world would not surpass until the 1980s (Obstfeld and Taylor, 2003). As they do today, international financial markets facilitated such cross-border capital flows. According to the economists Maurice Obstfeld and Alan Taylor (2003), such markets were, in some respects, actually *more globalized* in the period preceding World War I than is the case today.
- Tens of millions of people migrated across international borders over the 1870–1914 period (Chiswick and Hatton, 2003). Some estimates suggest that as many as one in ten people moved from one country to another in the decades surrounding the turn of the twentieth century. Although exact data for the world

as a whole are difficult to come by, we do know that the flow of international migrants was greater in this period than ever before or since. For instance, take one of the major destinations for such migrants—the United States. In 1890, 14.8 percent of the U.S. population was foreign-born (Gibson and Lennon, 1999). After World War I, the foreign-born population of the United States would never again be so large. In 2000, it reached a post–World War I high of 10 percent of the population (Lollock, 2001).

If today's globalized world is not as distinctive as it is often portrayed, does this mean that talk of globalization is misguided? Might it simply be a case of commentators, activists, and scholars being swayed by a fashionable buzzword or blinded by a "presentist" bias in which today's swirl of rapid social change is understood in relation to an (imaginary) past populated with stable or slowly changing *national* economies, polities, and societies? To be sure, there is a sense in which this is the case. Compare, for instance, the latest page-turner on globalization or, indeed, the business page of today's newspaper with Karl Marx and Friedrich Engels's description, written in the mid-nineteenth century, of the consequences of capitalism's first 100 years on the world scene (Marx and Engels, 1848; in Tucker, 1978:476–477):

> Constant revolutionising of production, uninterrupted disturbance of all social conditions, everlasting uncertainty and agitation, distinguish the bourgeois epoch from all earlier ones. All fixed, fast-frozen relations, with their train of ancient and venerable prejudices and opinions, are swept away, all new-formed ones become antiquated before they can ossify. All that is solid melts into air. . . .
>
> The need of a constantly expanding market for its products chases the bourgeoisie over the whole surface of the globe. It must nestle everywhere, settle everywhere, establish connexions everywhere. . . .
>
> The bourgeoisie has through its exploitation of the world-market given a cosmopolitan character to production and consumption in every country. . . . All old-established national industries have been destroyed or are daily being destroyed. They are dislodged by new industries, whose introduction becomes a life and death question for all civilized nations, by industries that no longer work up indigenous raw materials, but raw material drawn from the remotest zones; industries whose products are consumed, not only at home, but in every quarter of the globe. In place of the old wants, satisfied by the productions of the country, we find new wants, requiring for their satisfaction the products of distant lands and climes. In place of the old local and national seclusion and self-sufficiency, we have intercourse in every direction, universal inter-dependence of nations. And as in material, so also in intellectual production. The intellectual creations of individual nations become common property. National one-sidedness and narrow-mindedness become more and more impossible, and from the numerous national and local literatures, there arises a world literature.

As is so vividly illustrated in this quotation, much of what we tend to think of as distinctive of contemporary life, and attribute to a novel process of globalization, is in fact not all that distinctive. It has been a feature of societies within the capitalist world-economy for hundreds of years. So, there is a sense in which talk of globalization today is overblown. However, that is not all there is to the story. Although contemporary globalization may not exactly represent the epochal transformation that some theorists claim, the data that we examined earlier regarding contemporary economic, political, and cultural globalization indicate that it nonetheless represents a profound change *relative to the period that immediately preceded it*.

The world described by Keynes was significantly "deglobalized" after the beginning of World War I. The globalization trend of 1870 to 1914, expressed in rapidly expanding international trade, investment, and migration, was reversed after World War I into a pattern of isolationism marked by rising barriers to trade, investment, and immigration. This retrenchment of globalization was so significant and so profound that the world would not experience similar levels of globalization again until the 1970s or 1980s (i.e., not until 50 years later).

Why was the globalization trend of the 1870–1914 period reversed? The causes are fairly clear: World War I, the Great Depression, and World War II effectively shattered the world experienced by Keynes's Londoner. Beginning with World War I, policy in Britain and the other leading industrial capitalist societies turned in the direction of increasing national self-sufficiency. Even before World War I, problems were brewing and agitation by the end of the century was essentially equivalent to today's antiglobalization protests. Indeed, a genuine political backlash against globalization was well under way by the beginning of the war. As Jeffrey Williamson and his colleagues have shown (Hatton and Williamson, 1998; O'Rourke and Williamson, 1999), mass migration from people-exporting countries in Europe meant that landowners in such countries no longer had an abundant supply of cheap agricultural labor. As the mass migration proceeded, the cost of labor rose, and the returns to landowners declined. Simultaneously, in the people-importing countries of the period—most significantly the United States, Canada, Australia, and Argentina—income inequality grew rapidly as millions of unskilled immigrants flooded the labor market and began to compete with established workers for jobs, driving down the price that all workers could demand for their labor.

These changes set off a political reaction in both areas of the globalizing world-economy. In people-exporting countries, landowners successfully agitated for higher tariffs on their agricultural goods to cut their losses. The idea of "free trade" came under increasing attack. In people-importing countries, opposition to further immigration, often spearheaded by indigenous workers, grew intense. The door to immigrants was progressively closed. The case of the United States is typical of that of the major people-importing countries of the time. Immigration to the United States from China was banned in 1882 and from Japan in 1908. In 1917, *all* Asians were excluded. This was followed by the introduction of a literacy test for immigrants and, in 1921 and 1924, a quota system was instituted that drastically restricted immigration from southern and eastern Europe (Chiswick and Hatton, 2003). Some observers have noted that this nationalistic and nativistic reaction to globalization may, in turn, have helped pave the way for World War I.

The Great Depression deepened the reaction to globalization (James, 2001). In response to the intense domestic political pressures that this crisis generated, governments in all of the leading industrial capitalist societies turned further inward, raising tariffs on imported goods, establishing import quotas, and clamping down further on immigration. Cross-border capital flows slowed to a trickle. As Obstfeld and Taylor (2003) describe it, international investment came to be regarded with suspicion, and international prices and interest rates, which had moved in tandem in the context of the globalized international financial market of the turn of the century, fell "completely out of synch." And globalization was demonized, often being described as the main cause of the Great Depression. In this way, Obstfeld and Taylor remark (2003: 75), "The world economy went from globalized to almost autarkic in the space of a few decades."

The story of this earlier episode of globalization and of its demise is important for several reasons. First, and most obviously, it allows us to get some perspective on contemporary globalization. Today's globalization is typically judged or assessed relative to the period of retrenchment that preceded it (the 1914–1973 period). Relative to that period, globalization does indeed represent a profound change. But, as we have seen, relative to the era of globalization of the late nineteenth and early twentieth centuries, it looks considerably less extraordinary.

Second, the fact that the globalization trend of 1870 to 1914 was reversed so quickly and fundamentally should serve as a cautionary tale. Those who talk about globalization as an inevitable force would do well to ponder the fate of the world of Keynes's Londoner. It is at least conceivable that the world of today could experience a similar reversal. Those who welcome globalization and see it as a progressive force that produces more "winners" than "losers" should pay heed to just how powerful the losers can become. If their concerns are not effectively addressed, it is not out of the question that the twenty-first century equivalents of our Old World landowners and New World workers might band together to reverse the tide of globalization once again. (We may see signs of this already in an antiglobalization movement that is a remarkable coalition of [1] labor groups concerned about job loss owing to international trade and investment; [2] environmental groups concerned about the impact of globalization on the environment; [3] the representatives of protected industries and sectors—such as agriculture—concerned to keep in place the government subsidies and trade barriers that keep them afloat; [4] nativist groups opposed to immigration; and [5] nationalist groups concerned about the loss of national sovereignty.) Finally, the fact that this earlier episode of globalization ended so tragically, with two world wars and a Great Depression, makes Joseph Stiglitz's (2003) call for a wise, rational, and equitable mechanism for the management and regulation of globalization all the more pressing.

# FOR FURTHER READING

The single most comprehensive work on globalization is Held, McGrew, Goldblatt, and Perraton's *Global Transformations: Politics, Economics, and Culture* (1999). They discuss in considerable detail economic, political, and cultural globalization, and also devote chapters to global migration, military globalization, and the impact of globalization on the environment. If one were to read only a single source on globalization, this would be the one. Anthony Giddens's *Runaway World: How Globalization Is Reshaping Our Lives* (2002) is a short, provocative work on globalization and some of its most important implications. Robertson (1992) provides a perspective on globalization that emphasizes its cultural side. See also Therborn (2000a, 2000b). Meyer, Boli, Thomas, and Ramirez (1997) and Beckfield (2003) discuss the evolution of a world polity. Altman (2001) illustrates both economic and cultural globalization by way of discussing the globalization of the sex industry.

Critical perspectives on globalization can be found in Amin (1997), Hoogvelt (1997), and Kohler and Chaves (2003). Peter Singer's *One World: The Ethics of Globalization* (2002), Held and McGrew's *Globalization/Anti-Globalization* (2002), and Joseph Stiglitz's *Globalization and its Discontents* (2003) are extremely useful for understanding the main objections to globalization and provide balanced accounts of globalization's pros and cons. A largely favorable view of globalization, along with supporting evidence, is provided by Lomborg (2001). The best studies of the question whether global inequality is increasing or decreasing are Korzeniewicz and Moran (1997), Firebaugh (1999, 2000, 2003), and Goesling (2001).

Robert Heilbroner's *An Inquiry into the Human Prospect* (1980) was one of the best-known and earliest of the spate of books taking a deeply pessimistic view of the human future. A new edition "updated for the 1990s" is available, but it is little changed and Heilbroner's pessimism remains. Kennedy (1993) takes a similar pessimistic view. Meadows, Meadows, and Randers (1992) use computer simulations to argue that major changes in population growth, resource use, and industrial output must be made very soon if the world is to be ecologically and economically sustainable throughout the twenty-first century. Sing Chew (2001) discusses ecological degradation, especially deforestation, from a long-term historical perspective. Bjørn Lomborg's *The Skeptical Environmentalist: Measuring the Real State of the World* (2001) is an important critique of the environmental pessimists written by a former pessimist and one of the most important books on the environment written in several decades.

That globalization is not something entirely new is demonstrated in O'Rourke and Williamson (1999), Obstfeld and Taylor (2003), and Chase-Dunn, Kawano, and Brewer (2000). Clark (2000) shows that globalization in the broadest sense is a process that extends thousands of years into the past. Ever since the Neolithic Revolution, and especially since the rise of civilization and the state, the world has become more globalized.

# CHAPTER

# 11 Retrospect and Prospect

## The Past 10,000 Years and the Next 100

In this final chapter we take a long look backward and a short look forward. Our look backward attempts to summarize the broadest changes in human societies over the past 10,000 years and their significance for the human condition and the quality of human life. The key question concerns the extent to which human societies have been, as popularly believed, making steady progress in the quality of human life. Our look ahead attempts to use our understanding of sociocultural evolution over the past 10,000 years to project the human future over the next century or so. The chapter and the book conclude by briefly considering the importance of a general theory of world history as a reliable guide to thinking about the future.

## The Past 10,000 Years: Human Progress?

The most important evolutionary trends of the past 10,000 years in relation to the overall quality of human life concern the *standard of living*, the *quantity and quality of work*, *equality*, and *democracy and freedom*. To discuss these evolutionary trends in a meaningful way, an abstract concept known as the **average world person** is employed, and the implications of major evolutionary changes are judged from the perspective of this hypothetical individual. The average world person is the typical member of the typical type of human society prevailing in any given historical era. For example, 15,000 years ago, all humans lived in hunter-gatherer societies, and thus the average world person was a hunter or a gatherer. By contrast, some 3,000 years ago, the agrarian way of life had basically become the predominant form of social life on earth, and thus the average world person was a peasant farmer. Since most of the world's population currently lives in the underdeveloped nations, today's average world person is a Third World peasant or urban worker. It must be remembered that the employment of the concept of the average world person is a purely methodological device designed to simplify the discussion about the nature and meaning of broad evolutionary trends. To talk about an average world person is to talk about how evolutionary trends affect the majority of the world's population, if not all individuals, groups, and societies.

## The Standard of Living

Perhaps the best way of comparing different societies' standards of living is in terms of a universally desired good or state of affairs, something all humans need and desire and whose absence produces not only a subjective feeling of deprivation, but an actual objective condition of deprivation. The *quality of the diet* can be used as such a measure of the standard of living. Using this measure, we find an overall decline in the standard of living over the past 10,000 years, at least when judged from the perspective of our average world person. The most recent evidence suggests that ancient hunter-gatherers probably enjoyed diets that were abundant in calories, fully adequate in animal proteins, and highly nutritious. As argued in Chapter 3, hunter-gatherers probably constituted an "original affluent society"—a type of society in which people were able to satisfy their basic needs with a minimum of effort.

The decline in the standard of living began with the transition to the first agricultural (horticultural) communities. The real decline in the living standard, though, was brought about several thousand years later at about the time people were greatly intensifying their agricultural methods. By the time the average world person had become a peasant, the standard of living had dropped very sharply. The average peasant in the average agrarian society of the past had a diet markedly inferior to that of the average hunter-gatherer of earlier times. Peasant diets were notoriously deficient in calories, proteins, and nutrients, and they probably also had a stultifying monotony. As Lenski notes in regard to medieval England (1966:270–271), "The diet of the average peasant consisted of little more than the following: a hunk of bread and a mug of ale in the morning; a lump of cheese and bread with perhaps an onion or two to flavor it, and more ale at noon; a thick soup or pottage followed by bread and cheese at the main meal in the evening. Meat was rare, and the ale was usually thin." Things were just as bad or worse outside Europe (at least in the past few centuries). In China and Japan, little meat was eaten by the average peasant, and in India, virtually the entire population had been reduced to a state of obligatory vegetarianism. In China, even the rich mandarins ate little meat (Braudel, 1981).

Evolutionary trends in the standard of living can also be measured by *the level of health and the incidence of disease*. Here, a similar picture emerges. Hunter-gatherers were far healthier and freer from disease than commonly thought (M. Harris, 1977; Cohen and Armelagos, 1984; Cohen, 1989), and their life expectancies, although short, were comparable to those of horticulturalists and peasants. As Chapter 3 showed, paleopathological studies of ancient populations suggest that horticulturalists and peasants generally had poorer health than hunter-gatherers. Moreover, the great killer contagious diseases familiar to humankind were products of the high-density urban life of agrarian societies (McNeill, 1976).

There were two basic reasons for the overall decline in the standard of living as assessed in these ways. One was population growth. The increasing pressure of numbers compelled people to adopt more intensive methods of production. Yet, the adoption of such methods did not allow people to increase their living standard or even to maintain it, for the pressure of numbers drove the living standard ever downward. By intensifying their production methods, people were simply keeping their living standards from dropping to drastically low levels. The other basic cause of the decline in living standards was the rise of class stratification, itself due in part to the growth of population. As some individuals and groups gained control over productive resources, they were able to compel other individuals and groups to produce economic surpluses from which the members of dominant groups could live. In the preindustrial world, this process reached its peak in agrarian societies and contributed very heavily to the low living standard of the peasantry. In the modern world, exploitation remains severe in many Third World countries and is one of the most important causes of the low living standard of Third World peoples.

But what of the transition to modern industrial capitalist societies? People in these societies have experienced enormous improvements in the quality of the diet, and modern medicine has made great strides. Infant mortality rates have dropped dramatically and longevity has increased appreciably. Most of this improvement has occurred in the last century or so; the average life span in the United States in 1900, for example, was only 49 years. There have also been enormous advances in the standard of living as measured by the quality of housing (and all the conveniences that go with it, such as electric lighting, central heating, and flush toilets) and the possession of material goods, such as high-quality automobiles, elaborate labor-saving applicances, stereo systems, personal computers, and cell phones. With rapid technological advance, the quality of these products has continually improved, their prices have decreased, and they have become increasingly available to wider segments of the population. People seem to be very fond of these things and consume them eagerly when they have the means to do so. Even Marxist critics of capitalism consume these things and seem to enjoy them as much as the average person.

A very important question concerns whether or not people have some sort of innate desire for material possessions. In this book's predecessor, *Macrosociology: An Introduction to Human Societies* (4th ed. 1999a), the first author argued that they do not. But this argument was perhaps a bit hasty. Hunter-gatherers, horticulturalists, pastoralists, and agrarian peasants who know nothing of the existence of modern material possessions and conveniences do not necessarily feel deprived by not having them, but they usually accept them readily and enjoy them very much when given them. Humans desire things that allow them to reduce toil and to experience a wide range of comforts and pleasures. They do not *need* these things in any technical sense of that term, but they certainly seem to *want* them and feel that they improve the quality of life when they are available. So, the conclusion would seem to be that the standard of living, and the gratification it provides, has improved dramatically for the members of advanced industrial capitalist societies in recent centuries, especially the last century. This marks a reversal of the age-old trend of a declining standard of living.

## The Quantity and Quality of Work

There is little doubt that the quantity of work has increased and its quality has deteriorated over the past 10,000 years. Hunter-gatherers seem to work less and enjoy more leisure time than the members of all other types of societies. Evidence from contemporary hunter-gatherer societies indicates that they are resistant to advancing their subsistence technology when their standard of living is deemed adequate because they realize this will bring increases in their workload.

The members of horticultural societies do indeed appear to work somewhat harder and longer than people in hunting and gathering societies. But, as with the standard of living, the truly marked change seems to have occurred with the emergence of agrarian societies. The workload in agrarian societies was markedly greater than in all previous forms of preindustrial society. In the modern world, work levels are still very high in both the industrialized countries and the Third World nations (Minge-Klevana, 1980). The average member of an industrial society may spend on the order of 60 hours a week in subsistence activities, if we add to the 40 hours per week spent earning a living the time spent shopping for food and preparing it, as well as the time spent maintaining a household. This is about three to four times the average weekly workload of many hunter-gatherers. The average Third World worker probably spends considerably more time than this in all subsistence activities.

A basic assumption of the preceding discussion is that people seem to obey what has been called a *Law of Least Effort* (Zipf, 1965; Harris, 1979; Sanderson, 2001). This law holds that, other things being equal, people prefer to accomplish activities with a minimum amount of energy expenditure. This seems to be a basic feature of human nature. Thus, increasing their workload is something people normally wish to avoid. Under what conditions will people work harder and longer than would otherwise be the case? There are perhaps three basic reasons why people will increase their energy expenditure: political compulsion, economic necessity, and psychological conditioning. People will work harder and longer when other people gain power over them and force them to increase their workload. They will also increase their work activities if compelled by a declining standard of living to intensify their productive efforts. Finally, people can be conditioned to believe that hard work is a moral virtue, laziness a moral defect (this idea has been basic to the Protestant work ethic of Western civilization in recent centuries). The first two of these have been the leading causes of the intensification of the workload over the past several millennia.

What, then, of the quality of work? Marx argued that work is the primary means of human self-realization. Humans realize their humanity and achieve meaning in life when they manipulate the world according to their own purposes and designs. The primitive hunter and the agrarian craftsman were classic examples of self-fulfilled workers. To a large extent the same was true even of agrarian peasants. Despite their exploitation and low standard of living, they had considerable control over their work activities and worked in harmony with nature and the seasons. In precapitalist and preindustrial societies, then, work was not what Marx called *alienated labor*, or labor that lacked meaning, purpose, and satisfaction (Thomas, 1964). The real emergence of alienated labor began with the transition to modern industrial capitalism. Here, workers came to be reduced to instruments of production who performed routinized and fragmented tasks. They lost control over the means of production, had little control over their work activities, and had little sense of identification with the final product they produced. In the Third World, much work is also alienated labor, especially to the extent that capitalist methods of production and worker control have penetrated underdeveloped societies. Thus, the trend in the quality of human work—arguably one of the most basic of all human needs—has been negative.

The assertion that much work in modern industrial societies is alienated labor must be balanced by the recognition that changes in the occupational structure have also created extremely fulfilling forms of work for those talented enough and fortunate enough to obtain it. The work done by high-level business managers, computer technicians, scientists, and urban planners, for example, as well as by such learned professionals as physicians, lawyers, architects, and university professors is for the most part extremely rewarding in and of itself and has created a new kind of person—the "workaholic." Much manual work (especially its unskilled versions) and clerical work may be alienating and unpleasant, or at least not inherently rewarding, but these forms of work are not the only forms of work in modern capitalism. Marx hardly anticipated such things in his predictions about the future of capitalism.

## Equality

There is no mistaking the overall trend in social and economic equality. It has been decidedly in the direction of greater *inequalities*, particularly those based on access to economic resources. Most band and tribal societies are egalitarian societies in which the only real inequalities are those of status and influence. These inequalities are generally not socially inherited, and they are unrelated to control over economic resources or to political power. Influential and prestigious leaders in band and tribal societies have no greater wealth than others, nor do they have any capacity to compel the actions of others. In other words, in such societies class stratification does not exist.

Class stratification tends to emerge in more intensive horticultural societies, where population pressure has already reached significant levels. It is here that societies first come to be divided into groups possessing unequal levels of power and wealth, although the first forms of stratification usually do not impose severe economic penalties on the members of subordinate classes. But in high-density agrarian societies, class stratification becomes so extreme that the members of subordinate classes generally suffer from marked economic deprivations. It is in such societies that a great social and economic gap between rich and poor emerges.

Although contemporary industrial societies have reduced some of the extremes of stratification compared to agrarian societies of the past, the economic inequalities among nations within the world-capitalist economy are probably greater today than ever before. In the modern world, polarization in the world-economy has certainly been a prominent trend.

## Democracy and Freedom

Although there is a strong tendency in Western capitalist society to use the concepts of democracy and freedom more or less interchangeably, the terms, though related, should really carry different meanings. Pure democracy is a process of self-government, one whereby people decide their own affairs through open discussion and debate and in the absence of any individuals or groups who can command their actions.

Given this definition, human societies over the past ten millennia have moved more and more away from democracy. Many band and tribal societies are fundamentally democratic in that they lack elite groups capable of commanding the actions of others. Headmen and big men are leaders of some influence and respect, but they have no genuine power. People are under no obligation to obey their wishes, and such leaders have no possibility of imposing penalties on those who ignore their suggestions. Democracy is undermined at the same basic point in social evolution at which class stratification emerges. With the growth of large-scale agrarian societies and their elaborate stratification systems, democracy drops to a very low point. In such societies tiny elites rule the actions of others and have the capacity to impose severe penalties on them for disobedience.

In the modern world, a form of democracy, *parliamentary democracy*, has been created. Under this political arrangement, people gain a great deal of protection against the arbitrary exercise of power that is so common in agrarian societies. However, democracy conceived as the direct participation of the populace in the affairs of government is more an illusion than a reality. (In the totalitarian Communist states, of course, it was not even an illusion.) Modern Western parliamentary democracies are governed by elite groups whose actions are self-serving and to a very great extent beyond significant control by the masses.

But what of freedom? Assessing the evolutionary history of freedom depends crucially on what is meant by the concept, which has been subject to rather diverse definitions. In the Western tradition of thought, freedom has usually been conceptualized as **individual autonomy.** Freedom in this sense involves the absence of external constraints on individual thought and action. Autonomous individuals are those who follow their own courses of action relatively unimpeded by others.

Alexandra Maryanski and Jonathan Turner (1992) assert that there is a curvilinear relationship between individual autonomy and social evolution. Greatest autonomy occurs at the ends of the evolutionary spectrum—in hunter-gatherer and industrial societies—whereas people in horticultural and agrarian societies have the least autonomy. Maryanski and Turner claim that the main external constraint on individual autonomy in horticultural societies is the web of kinship, whereas in agrarian societies the leading constraint is that of power. They argue, in addition, that the constraints of kinship are more severe than those of power. We agree with

Maryanski and Turner's overall argument, but we would question their claim that it is in horticultural societies that individuals are subjected to the most severe constraints. We would nominate agrarian societies for that dubious honor. In these societies, people are subjected not only to the constraints of kinship ties and obligations but also to severe class domination and the overwhelming power of the state.

Another difficulty with Maryanski and Turner's argument is that they overlook the constraining influence of custom and tradition. Individuals in hunter-gatherer societies have a great deal of freedom from direct coercion by others, and individual autonomy is highly prized (Gardner, 1991), but they are hardly free to set their own normative standards of behavior. People are, in fact, highly coerced by what the French sociologist Emile Durkheim called the *collective conscience*—roughly, the will of the group. There is extremely strong group pressure to conform to the norms and values of the group, and the penalties for failure to conform are often severe, including either death or banishment from the group. What is true of hunter-gatherers is also true of people in horticultural and agrarian societies. In fact, concerning this dimension of freedom, what might be called **individualism,** it is clear that people in all forms of preindustrial societies are relatively unfree, and that it is modern capitalism and industrialism that have generated the highest levels of individualism. In modern industrial capitalist societies, there is government protection of individual rights and liberties and strong encouragement of individual self-expression. This individualistic conception of freedom pervades all of the basic social arrangements of modern Western capitalist societies (but not non-Western capitalist Japan).

There is yet a third form of freedom, one that might be called freedom as **human self-realization.** This conception of freedom is associated with the Marxian tradition of thought (cf. Elster, 1985). Freedom in this sense involves the equal opportunity of all individuals to realize their basic nature as members of the human species. For Marx, freedom existed when everyone had the full opportunity to achieve meaning and purpose in life, especially insofar as this could be achieved through work. Marx thought that freedom could be achieved only in a classless society with a very advanced level of technology—in the future socialist society. He believed that modern Western capitalist societies, even though they granted certain *political* freedoms to individuals, failed to achieve true *human* freedom because most of the population was exploited by the capitalist class and had no genuine opportunity for the realization of their human nature. If we follow this tradition of conceptualizing freedom, we can see that freedom has not been increasing in human history, and in a sense has been decreasing inasmuch as the members of precapitalist societies generally do have considerable opportunity to realize themselves through their labor. Even in modern industrial societies, most work provides little opportunity for individual self-fulfillment.

## The Concept of Progress Revisited

The preceding discussion suggests once again what was asserted early in the book: One must be extremely wary of using the concept of progress to characterize the major changes of the past 10,000 years. Indeed, it seems apparent that much of what has been happening over most of this period has actually been a form of cultural *regression*. How else is one to regard a general decline in the standard of living, an increase in the quantity of and a deterioration in the quality of work, the emergence of marked social and economic inequalities, and the undermining of democracy? Of course, as we have noted, not all of these changes apply to all persons, groups, or societies. For many individuals and groups, and for a number of societies, the standard of living has increased and work has become lighter, easier, and more gratifying. Many societies have achieved much greater equality and democracy than anything even remotely found in the agrarian past.

Moreover, improvements have been occurring in other areas as well. Humans have made enormous scientific, technological, intellectual, artistic, and literary achievements. Such achievements—those of Einstein, Darwin, Hawking, Rawls, Picasso, Mozart, Shakespeare, da Vinci, and others—cannot be swept aside as insignificant. It is possible to say, then, that humans have actually been making certain forms of progress over the past 10,000 years in spite of the very significant regressions that have been occurring.

## How to Judge a Society

This discussion gives rise to the basic question of whether or not we can truly judge societies, and, if so, how we can do it. If we can judge societies and rank them on a scale of moral worth and decency, what criteria shall we use?

Early in the twentieth century, anthropologists and sociologists developed a doctrine known as **cultural relativism.** It was developed to combat the problem of **ethnocentrism**—the common view that one's own culture is superior to all others and that other cultures can be judged only by reference to one's own. In its more extreme forms, ethnocentrism leads to intolerance, bigotry, and even hatred. Cultural relativism is the doctrine that no culture is inherently superior or inferior to others, but that, since every culture represents an adaptive solution to fundamental human problems, all cultures are "equally valid." Cultural relativists believe that there are no absolute or objective standards for judging cultures. Each culture can be evaluated only on its own terms—that is, by its own internal standards. If we were to apply this doctrine in judging the propriety of female infanticide (the selective killing of female infants) among the Yanomama, for example, all we could really say would be something like "Although it's wrong for us, it's right for them." And we would say this through recognition of the fact that infanticide "is right" for the Yanomama since it represents an adaptive solution to a problem of human living.

As a moral or ethical perspective, cultural relativism has been subjected to severe criticism, and it does not constitute a satisfactory system of ethics (Kohlberg, 1971; Patterson, 1977). The problems with it are fairly well known. For one thing, it can quickly collapse into "the disease of which it is the cure" (Kohlberg, 1971). That is, it easily leads to condoning or even approving practices that most people would consider inhumane and repellant (Hatch, 1983). For example, a strict cultural relativist perspective would have us endorse such practices as the Nazi effort to exterminate the Jews, Soviet forced labor camps, Roman slavery or black slavery in the New World, Yanomama gang rape of women, and countless other cultural phenomena that seem morally repellant by most reasonable standards—all in the name of tolerance toward other ways of life. In addition, cultural relativism seems to perpetuate a kind of "tyranny of custom" by leaving little or no room for the autonomy of the individual (Hatch, 1983).

In fact, the limitations of cultural relativism have appeared obvious even to many of the cultural relativists themselves, some of whom have actually violated their own principles in practice. For instance, Ruth Benedict, one of the major architects of cultural relativism, consistently undermined her own relativist stance when she discussed cultural differences (Hatch, 1983). In her well-known book, *Patterns of Culture* (1934), Benedict clearly showed a preference for certain cultural traits over others, displaying, for example, a particular dislike for cultures in which force played a major role.

Elvin Hatch (1983) suggests a way around cultural relativism that overcomes its basic deficiencies while at the same time retaining what seems to be of value in it: its general plea for tolerance. Hatch proposes what he calls a "humanistic principle" as a means of judging other cultures. This principle holds that cultures can be evaluated in terms of whether or not they harm persons by such means as torture, sacrifice, war, political repression, exploitation, and so on. It also judges them in terms of how well they provide for the material existence of their members—the extent to which people are free from poverty, malnutrition, disease, and the like.

Hatch makes some excellent points, but one can go further. One could add that cultures are good to the extent that they provide for self-realization. Cultures that allow their members opportunities to pursue intellectual life, science, music and the arts in general, and so on are preferable to cultures that do not allow for these things—either because they suppress them, or because they do not provide material opportunities for their attainment.

The most famous moral theorist of the second half of the twentieth century was the Harvard philosopher John Rawls. In his celebrated book, *A Theory of Justice* (1971), Rawls set forth two basic moral principles. The first principle states that *each person is to have an equal right to the most extensive basic liberty compatible with a similar liberty for others.* This idea is already familiar to Americans and the members of Western industrial societies generally, for it is enshrined in our political constitutions and our basic values. The second principle involves economic equality and states that *social and economic inequalities are to be arranged so that they are both (a) reasonably expected to be to everyone's advantage and (b) attached to positions and offices open to all.* Regarding this second principle, Rawls went on to say that inequalities are justified only to the extent that they improve the economic position of those persons at the bottom of the society.

Rawls's moral theory is not without flaws, but it is probably the best that has been developed in moral philosophy so far. What does his theory say about capitalist society? How does capitalist society measure up in light of this moral theory? Industrial capitalism measures up extremely well in terms of the first principle, since capitalism has, at least indirectly, promoted democracy in the form of liberties and rights. On this score, it is vastly superior to agrarian states and intensive horticultural chiefdoms, and certainly to the state socialist societies. It is also superior to hunter-gatherer and simple horticultural stateless societies because, although there is a great deal of individual autonomy in those societies, this is because of their very small scale—the inability of some to gain enough control to deprive others of autonomy—and, besides, such societies suffer from the constraints imposed by the web of kinship (Maryanski and Turner, 1992).

In terms of the second principle, industrial capitalist society also measures up quite well. Although it is true that industrial capitalist societies contain large inequalities of income and wealth, these are much smaller than in earlier agrarian societies and in contemporary less-industrialized Third World countries. Moreover, capitalism has led to a tremendous diffusion of income throughout the population and has improved the economic position of those at the bottom far beyond what it would otherwise be. The working class has lost all of its revolutionary potential in the United States, and nearly all of it in the other advanced capitalist societies, because workers have experienced a marked degree of *embourgeoisement* (to use that delightful French word)—they enjoy very high living standards and in many cases have adopted middle-class attitudes and lifestyles. Many social scientists would reply that income and wealth inequality have been increasing in recent years, at least in the United States. This is certainly true, but such increases in inequality have been associated with large increases in both income and wealth. In 1960, for example, total household assets in the United States amounted to approximately $8 trillion but had increased over sixfold, to $50 trillion, by 1999 (calculations are in constant 2000 dollars) (Keister, 2004).

But what of global capitalism? Peter Singer (2002) criticizes Rawls for focusing exclusively on nation-states, arguing that a just distribution of resources must be evaluated on a global level. Inequalities within capitalism are justified not simply if they elevate those at the bottom of any given nation-state, but only in terms of whether they elevate those at the bottom of the world capitalist system. How well has capitalism acquitted itself in this respect? As Chapters 9 and 10 were at pains to show, although the quality of life in the Third World continues to lag far behind its quality in the highly developed countries, major improvements were made in the twentieth century, and especially in the last three or four decades. Per capita GDP did increase dramatically, as did primary and secondary educational attainment, adult literacy, life expectancy, and access to consumer goods that reduced work and made life more pleasurable. By the same token, infant and child mortality fell dramatically, along with poverty, malnourishment, and starvation.

Truly democratic governments are much less common in the Third World than in the developed world, but they have become more numerous; real inroads against brutal dictatorships have been made in many less-developed countries. Moreover, less-developed societies that have chosen a socialist developmental path have fared far less well than those that have remained capitalist, and most who once chose socialism have abandoned it for capitalism. Despite many continuing problems, capitalism has acquitted itself in the Third World much better than was once thought.

Thus, industrial capitalism meets both of Rawls's principles fairly well, and even Third World capitalism meets his principles much better than agrarian societies of the past. Capitalism has elevated the level of the average member of most Third World societies, even if has yet to elevate the position of those at the absolute bottom. Despite the many critiques of it, capitalism has much to recommend it. Marxists and other radical critics of capitalism believe, however, that we can still do a lot better by developing a genuine socialist society—that socialism can create even more equality while maintaining the high standard of living capitalism has created. They have in mind not Marxian-inspired Communism Soviet-style, but socialist democracy. As we saw earlier, Boswell and Chase-Dunn (2000), for example, advocate the creation of a future society that will combine the strengths of both capitalist market principles and socialist command principles.

This is all very well and good in principle, but the actual record suggests that these critics may be unduly optimistic. As Peter Berger (1986) states, when judging capitalism in comparison with socialism we have to compare capitalism to the forms of socialism that have actually existed, not to some form of socialism that is purely imaginary and philosophical. We know that when the state takes total control of the means of production, the results are almost never good and usually a disaster, both politically and economically. Few would any longer advocate such a course of action. (Surprisingly, some still do, apparently oblivious to recent historical events!) But even the introduction of significant command principles into a market-based system may very well produce worse results, not better. It could move us back in the direction of the old state socialism, although, of course, stopping short of that. It might be best, then, to stick with capitalism. However, this should be "capitalism with a human face"—a form of capitalism that provides just enough state regulation of the economy to minimize poverty and to decommodify work (in Esping-Andersen's sense) as much as is feasible. To this point in history, this form of capitalism has been most fully achieved in northern Europe—in Sweden, Denmark, Norway, Finland, and the Netherlands.

As argued earlier, inequality per se is not always or necessarily bad. It is bad when it leads to a great deal of degradation and suffering, as in agrarian societies of the past, parts of the less-developed world of today, and industrial capitalist societies of the nineteenth and early twentieth centuries. Inequality can also be negative in that it can lead to much envy and political conflict. But there really is no reason to resent the rich and wealthy at the top if they create huge amounts of wealth whose fruits even those at the bottom can enjoy to some extent. You can be sure that the standard of living is exceptionally high when ordinary people will think little of paying $3 or more for a cup of coffee at Starbucks, or the same amount for an ice cream cone at Ben and Jerry's! Such a thing would have been unthinkable 50 years ago. This should demonstrate beyond any doubt how much the standard of living has increased just in recent decades.

Despite its deficiencies and drawbacks, capitalism is the best we have done so far in history in terms of the material quality of life and the possibilities for human self-realization. But we still must look at capitalism's future possibilities. As Marx pointed out, and as current Marxists never tire of reminding us, capitalism contains inherent *contradictions*—forces that continually inhibit its functioning and that may ultimately make it less workable or even destroy it. What might the future of world capitalist civilization bring?

## Future Trends: The Very Large Scale

Taking things on a very large scale, we predict the following major trends over the course of the next half-century to century.

**1.** *Technology will continue to advance, and to advance with increasing rapidity.* This prediction is a "no-brainer" if there ever was one, given the remarkable tendency of humans to engage in technological advance throughout social evolution and the enormous technological advances of the past century, and especially of recent decades. But what will the specific trends be?

The next major technological revolution will very likely occur at the molecular level, mostly in what is called *nanotechnology*. The prefix *nano* means one-billionth, and a *nanometer* is one-billionth of a meter in size, the size of the atom. Nanotechnology involves the manipulation of atoms one at a time in order to create a vast array of new, supersmall technological apparatuses. Its applications will be extraordinary. Douglas Mulhall (2002) summarizes the so-called nanotechnology revolution and speculates on the following developments sometime within the twenty-first century:

- The first nanocomputer will be built. It will weigh only a few ounces and can be carried in your hand or, more likely, worn on your body. Nanobased music players and other electronic devices will also become wearable.

*Nanotechnologists at work. The nanotechnological revolution now in its early stages is likely to produce extraordinary consequences for human social life.*

- Virtual reality will expand on a major scale. Virtual reality is based on the technology of holograms, which resemble photographs but with a dramatic difference. Photographs allow us to see only a flat image, but with a hologram we see in "3D." We are able to perceive depth and to see the "whole image." By wearing virtual reality helmets or suits, or by entering virtual reality rooms, people will have virtual offices that allow them to work from any location; will be able to attend virtual conferences and take virtual vacations; and will be able to experience virtual touch and extremely realistic virtual sex that will likely be more stimulating and pleasurable than regular sex. Some people— "virtual junkies"—will become addicted to virtual reality. This technology will revolutionize social relationships, and the difference between actual reality and virtual reality will eventually become blurred.
- Energy production and use will be radically transformed. Oil and gas will decline significantly as energy sources and will eventually disappear. Fuel cells using principles of photovoltaics will become widespread and will be used to heat and cool homes. Renewable energy sources will be easily renewed and will be extremely cheap.
- Nanocoatings and nanogears will eliminate the need for lubricants, and motors will shrink dramatically in size and become much more energy efficient. Nanocoatings will protect surfaces far better than ordinary paint, and their colors can be changed automatically as often as one desires. Nanosurfaces will be completely resistant to dirt, and so cleaning them will no longer be necessary.
- Dramatic changes in transportation will occur. Automobiles will be replaced by self-piloting flying cars that will maneuver through computerized air corridors. Worldwide supersonic tunnels will be built in which people can travel in pods at 2,500 miles per hour. Airplanes and airlines will become useless and disappear. It will be possible to travel from New York to London in 90 minutes, or from New York to Shanghai in five hours. People will simply give voice commands to their pods to tell them exactly where they want to go (city, hotel name, etc.). Self-replicating fractal robots will build these tunnels, and the capital cost will be only for software.
- The first molecular assembler or desktop fabricator will be built. This will allow most consumer goods to be made at home quickly, easily, and cheaply, and will spell the end of global manufacturing. Most things that are now consumer durables, such as washing machines or refrigerators, will become throwaway goods.
- Clothes will warm us up if we are too cold or cool us down if we are too hot. They will be able to change colors by voice command.
- Languages will become instantly translatable, thus eliminating language barriers. Every library in the world will become downloadable into a personal electronic book.
- Major developments in biotechnology will occur. These major advances in biotechnology, which are already beginning, are part of what has been called *biomedicalization* (Clarke et al., 2003). Biomedicalization involves not just in-

creasing control over conditions related to human health, but the actual transformation of the very bodies and lives of human beings in medical ways. Biomedicalization involves at its core such things as transplant medicine, DNA engineering, stem cell research, the mapping of the human genome, computer-based medical visualization technologies, and computer-assisted drug developments. Biomedicalization will soon allow heart disease and many cancers to be correctable before birth using gene therapy. We will eventually be able to grow our own organs from our own tissues to be used as replacement organs if and when we need them, and this will become outdated when artificial organs can be made. Nanobots will enter the body to clean arteries, make necessary repairs, and so on. And it is possible that we may soon be seeing life after complete heart failure, women giving birth many years after reaching menopause, walking without leg bones, the cloning of humans, and the capacity to genetically design life itself.

- Synthesized food will replace plant- and animal-based food, and the killing of animals for food, as well as for fashion, will end. Electronic paper that acts like a computer screen but looks like paper will be developed, thus helping to save our forests.

- Designer nanodrugs will be created that will be virtually undetectable and will be used extensively by both teenagers and adults. People may eventually spend much of their time taking nanodrugs and living in virtual reality.

- Instant communication with anyone at anytime and anywhere will become possible and will undoubtedly lead to major changes in social life. These technological advances will intensify globalization even more than it would have been intensified otherwise.

- Technology will be developed that can protect us against natural catastrophes, which may occur with greater frequency than we have thought. These include not only earthquakes but also asteroid collisions with the earth and tidal waves.

- Robots that can see, hear, feel, smell, and taste, as well as tell us about their experiences, will be created. These robots will be used for specialized purposes, such as household work, sex, or companionship. This will eventually lead to the development of a new species, *Robo sapiens*, that will be as intelligent as humans and highly autonomous. By using the same type of gene sequences that humans have, *Robo sapiens* will become self-replicating and eventually ask for rights.

- Advanced humans with genetically enhanced intelligence and bodies will become common. These humans, which Mulhall calls *Homo provectus*, will marry some *Robo sapiens*, and robot-human hybrids will emerge.

Although Mulhall says he is speculating rather than predicting, it seems clear that much of what he suggests will eventually happen, and probably sooner rather than later. Nanocomputing already exists. It made a dramatic advance in 2001 and now seems to be very close to the industrial production stage. In 2000, the United States government established the National Nanotechnology Initiative, and nanotechnology centers have been developed at a number of major U.S. universities. Europe and Japan are even slightly ahead of U.S. efforts. Venture capitalists are starting to enter the nanotechnology market, and the first nanoproducts are starting to become available. A nanotoothpaste, for example, has already been developed that contains enamel-like particles intended to fill nanocavities in teeth (Mulhall, 2002).

If even half of these technological possibilities become reality, social life may be transformed in extraordinary ways (Mulhall, 2002). Advances in biotechnology could make romantic and sexual relationships between 70-year-olds and 20-year-olds relatively common, because the 70-year-olds will have aged very slowly. Since women tend to seek men who have high status, intelligence, and wealth and other resources, young women may be highly attracted to biologically "young" older men who have had many decades to accumulate wisdom, status, and wealth. If people spend much of their time taking designer drugs and living in virtual reality, then social relationships could be radically altered, and largely in highly undesirable ways. This would undoubtedly increase the individualistic tendencies of modern societies, reducing social bonding even further than it has already been reduced. And what will happen to "real" relationships when they become increasingly virtual—that is, when people interact with each other mostly in virtual reality?

The end of global manufacturing through the widespread use of molecular assemblers will create massive unemployment on a scale heretofore unimaginable. What will people do? How will they spend their time (more designer drugs, more virtual sex)? How will capitalism be reorganized when few people do any work, when most resources are extremely cheap, and when people can produce almost every product that they need? And there will be enormous implications for government and for the military. As Mulhall notes (2002:248), "What are the military implications of having to fight individuals with the power of an army generated from a desktop factory, when biological weapons can be made and released at the flick of a switch"? And with people living much healthier lives for much longer, generational conflict will intensify as older people who have jobs fail to retire. Instant communication with anyone anywhere, combined with extremely rapid transportation all over the globe, have dramatic implications for social and cultural change. And the creation of intelligent and autonomous robots and "posthumans" will undoubtedly have enormous implications for the emergence of new forms of stratification. One could go on and on.

2. *Substantial democratization will occur throughout the semiperiphery and parts of the periphery.* Given the "new democratization" occurring throughout the Third World and the postsocialist societies in the 1980s and 1990s, and given the continued evolution of forces that are favorable for democratization—industrialization, mass education, and literacy—democratization will be a substantial evolutionary trend in many currently undemocratic or marginally democratic societies. However, this trend could be counterbalanced by what Robert Kaplan (2000) calls "the coming anarchy." Kaplan argues that, for a variety of reasons, we are beginning to witness increasing lawlessness, the erosion of nation-states and international borders, and increasing social disorder. Seeing contemporary sub-Saharan Africa as the leading

edge of these trends, he predicts they will intensify and spread more widely in the decades ahead. To the extent that Kaplan is right—and that is very much an open question—then on the heels of increasing democratization may arise a new authoritarianism designed to deal with rising and spreading disorder. Increasing democratization may be a short-lived process, or at least interrupted for a significant period of time.

**3.** *There will be increasing ethnic conflict on a global scale.* A major dimension of globalization has been a tremendous acceleration of international migration. There was a huge increase in immigration flows into the United States in the 1970s, 1980s, and 1990s, and annual immigration is now on the order of 4 to 5 million people. Most of the immigrants are coming from Latin America (mostly Mexico), the Caribbean, and Asia (Held, McGrew, Goldblatt, and Perraton, 1999). Many European countries, such as France, Germany, and Sweden, have also experienced considerable immigration in recent decades, as has Australia. In fact, as noted in the last chapter, there is now an enormous amount of immigration all over the world, mostly from less-developed to advanced industrial countries, and this is producing increasing ethnic heterogeneity. Tatu Vanhanen (1999) shows that the degree of ethnic heterogeneity in a society and its level of ethnic conflict are very closely related, and a high level of ethnic heterogeneity is far and away the major cause of ethnic conflict. Moreover, the greater the differences between ethnic groups (especially the extent to which the differences are physical as well as cultural), the greater the conflict. Given these facts, the increasing ethnic heterogeneity of societies is likely to cause an intensification of ethnic conflict in the future.

**4.** *Globalization will continue and will intensify to mind-numbing levels.* Although there is certainly nothing inevitable about continued globalization, as noted in the last chapter, it is very likely that globalization will continue on all levels: economic, political, and sociocultural. There will be increasing integration of world production and finance, increasing domination of the world-economy by a few gigantic corporations, an increasing number and importance of organizations devoted to international political regulation, and increasing destruction of local cultural traditions and the spread of a world culture. The world will increasingly become "one world," although of course there are limits to this as well. Anthony Giddens (2002) says that, because of globalization, we are already living in a "runaway world"; this world will continue to runaway faster and faster as time goes by.

In his book *The Condition of Postmodernity* (1989), David Harvey argues that increasing globalization has led to a continual shrinking of the psychological experience of time and space, a phenomenon he calls *time-space compression*. Harvey argues that in the history of capitalism there have been several surges of time-space compression. The latest episode began in the early 1970s, Harvey declares, and this episode, like the earlier ones, has psychologically disturbed and destabilized the individuals who have been experiencing it. The enormous acceleration in the global scale and pace of capitalist production in the past 30 years has led to a dramatic increase in the pace of social life more generally. This period of time-space

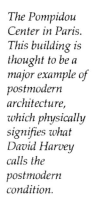

*The Pompidou Center in Paris. This building is thought to be a major example of postmodern architecture, which physically signifies what David Harvey calls the postmodern condition.*

compression has been accompanied by dramatic changes in personal life of a very disruptive nature. The continual acceleration of production has led to (Harvey, 1989:285–286)

> parallel accelerations in exchange and consumption. Improved systems of communication and information flow, coupled with rationalizations in techniques of distribution . . . , made it possible to circulate commodities through the market system with greater speed. . . .
>
> Of the many developments in the arena of consumption, two stand out as being of particular importance. The mobilization of fashion in mass (as opposed to elite) markets provided a means to accelerate the pace of consumption. . . . A second trend was a shift away from the consumption of goods and into the consumption of services—not only personal, business, educational, and health services, but also into entertainments, spectacles, happenings, and distractions. . . .
>
> Of the innumerable consequences that have flowed from this general speedup in the turnover times of capital [two stand out]. . . .
>
> The first major consequence has been to accentuate volatility and ephemerality of fashions, products, production techniques, labour processes, ideas and ideologies, values and established practices. The sense that "all that is solid melts into air" has rarely been more pervasive. . . .
>
> In the realm of commodity production, the primary effect has been to emphasize the values and virtues of instantaneity (instant and fast foods, meals, and other satisfactions) and of disposability (cups, plates, cutlery, packaging, napkins, clothing, etc.). . . . It meant more than just throwing away produced goods (creating a monumental waste-disposal problem), but also being able to throw away values, life-styles, stable relationships, and attachments to things, buildings, places, people, and received ways of doing and being. . . . Individuals were forced to cope with disposability, novelty, and the prospects for instant obsolescence. . . . And this im-

plies profound changes in human psychology. . . . The bombardment of stimuli, simply on the commodity front, creates problems of sensory overload.

Globalization has thus been having major psychological consequences. If Harvey's theory is correct, then the implications for the future are ominous. Time-space compression is built into the very logic of capitalist development, and the pace of production, consumption, and social life constantly increase. Future waves of time-space compression would be expected to be even more intense, and as such would likely produce even more severe forms of psychological destabilization. If this were to occur, then the time-space compression of the late twentieth and early twenty-first centuries may turn out in retrospect to seem relatively mild. As hardly needs to be said, that is not an enticing prospect.

5. *A world-annihilating war is a very real possibility.* Because of the extremely competitive interstate system that parallels the modern world-economy, and due to the presence of nuclear weapons of mass destruction, we could blow ourselves up. Many (e.g., Chase-Dunn, 1989b, 1990) think we will unless dramatic steps are taken immediately. If such a war were to occur, when might it happen?

Several scholars have been struck by the association between **Kondratieff waves,** or **K-waves,** in the history of capitalism and the incidence of war. In a major study of this problem, Joshua Goldstein (1988) shows that K-waves since 1495 have been remarkably correlated with the outbreak of major wars. Goldstein identifies 10 K-waves since 1495 and finds that a major war between powerful states has almost always occurred in the second half of the upturn phase of the cycle. The only exception to this striking regularity is World War II, which occurred at the beginning of an upturn. However, World War II may not be a genuine exception. Some social scientists regard World Wars I and II as really being two phases of one great war, not as two separate wars. If this is a valid interpretation, then the pattern identified by Goldstein is perfect. Although there are several possible ways of interpreting this empirical finding, Goldstein theorizes that powerful states fight truly major wars with one another only when they can bear the expense of doing so. Major wars occur near the end of an upswing, then, because it is only at that time that states are financially capable of undertaking such military efforts.

On the basis of his findings, Goldstein goes on to predict the timing of the next major war. The world-economy has been in a downturn phase since about 1970, and the next upturn should begin anytime. If it begins soon, this upturn will crest in approximately 2030, which would mean that the next major war can be expected to occur during the decade between 2020 and 2030. This prediction depends on the validity of the assumption that the basic features of the world political system will not change appreciably in the years ahead. Some world-system theorists, however, think that this assumption is not likely to hold (Wallerstein, 1982; Arrighi, 1982). They think that the presence of nuclear weapons changes everything. Since core states now have these weapons, war becomes unthinkable because it is recognized by all parties as unwinnable. But not all world-system theorists take such an optimistic position. Christopher Chase-Dunn and Kenneth O'Reilly (1989) examine a number of factors that they believe strongly bear on the likelihood of a major war in the near future, what they call a "core war." These factors include the K-wave, intensifying ecological problems, the declining position of the United States in the world-economy, efforts at nuclear disarmament, and the emergence of new international organizations designed to reduce the threat of war. They conclude that "developments that lower the probability of a core war are not great enough to offset those factors that will increase the chance of war in the coming decades. The probability of serious war among core states over the next four decades may be as much as fifty-fifty" (1989:61).

**6.** *Numerous efforts will be made to establish a world state.* If a major core war were to break out early in this century, it would not necessarily have to be a nuclear war, but in all probability nuclear weapons would be involved. What might be done to avert the unprecedented catastrophe that would result from such a war? Chase-Dunn (1989b, 1990, 2003) argues that the answer lies in the creation of a world state, or what he likes to call a "collectively rational democratic global commonwealth" (cf. Singer, 2002). This would be an overarching political system that would centralize political and economic decision making on a world scale. It would eliminate the system of competing and conflicting nation-states—the interstate system—that has characterized the capitalist world-economy for approximately 500 years. In Chase-Dunn's thinking, such a state would reduce if not eliminate the threat of world-destroying war; it could also be an extremely effective tool in eliminating gross inequalities in the worldwide distribution of economic resources, and thus could do much to promote economic development in the Third World.

Chase-Dunn suggests that a future world state should contain a centralized system of political and economic decision making, but at the same time be sufficiently decentralized to allow for local and national preferences and for important cultural differences. What Chase-Dunn really has in mind is a kind of federation that eliminates the worst and most dangerous forms of conflict between nation-states while simultaneously permitting them to retain a good deal of their identity. Thus, the world state is not a single political society, but an artificially imposed structure that oversees the political and economic functioning of various individual societies.

A number of scholars have predicted the eventual emergence of a world state, and there undoubtedly will be serious efforts made by various individuals and groups to create such a state. However, the creation of a world state seems highly unlikely. As Randall Collins notes, a world state is a contradiction in terms, since to some extent what we mean by a state is a political entity that engages in competition with other political entities. Moreover, humankind's obviously very strong nationalist tendencies, themselves rooted in powerful and often fierce ethnic attachments, mitigate against the formation of such a state. But even if, by chance, a world state were to emerge, it has clear potential for disaster. It would concentrate so much political and military power that it would be an extreme threat to human liberty. It could lead to the creation of a type of world empire similar to the classical empires of the past, and as such would greatly undermine the capitalist character of the modern world and lead to severe economic stagnation and a return to some of the economic characteristics of the classical empires (Snooks, 1997).

To his credit, Chase-Dunn recognizes that there are grave dangers inherent in the creation of a world state; he realizes that such a state could become a kind of Orwellian monster. He believes, nevertheless, that the risk is worth taking because the alternative risk—complete destruction of the human species—is just as great and so much more appalling. Moreover, if we know in advance the risks to freedom that a world state can pose, then we can take strong steps to try to avert this eventuality. Chase-Dunn's view, however, seems unduly optimistic. Nuclear weapons have existed for some 60 years, and the world has used them only once, and then on a small scale. (Two nuclear bombs were dropped on Japan by the United States in late 1945 as a means of ending World War II, killing 100,000 people and injuring many more.) It seems that we must know how to control them, or are afraid to use them because of their huge dangers. Therefore, the threat of nuclear war is probably not as great as Chase-Dunn believes. But the evidence is clear that when a state is able to concentrate enormous political and military power, it will not hesitate to do so. The negative consequences of a world state, then, seem to be more likely than what it is designed to prevent.

But even though a world state may not be created, it seems fairly clear that world-scale political organizations will play an increasing role in social life. Indeed, they already do and have for the past couple of decades. Alongside sovereign states, we have such IGOs and INGOs as the UN, the WTO, NATO, the EU, NAFTA, the G7 (seven advanced industrial countries: the United States, Canada, Germany, France, Italy, the United Kingdom, and Japan), APEC (Asia-Pacific Economic Cooperation), ACC (Arab Cooperation Council), and MERCOSUR (Southern Cone Common Market Organization). The growth in the importance of such groups was dramatic throughout the twentieth century. Early in that century there were 37 IGOs and 176 INGOs, but by 2000, the numbers had soared to 6,743 and 47,098, respec-

*A session of the United Nations General Assembly. The UN is the world political organization that most closely approximates a world state, but it lacks the "teeth" that a true world state would have. Some scholars doubt that a world state is either possible or desirable.*

tively (Held and McGrew, 2002). There is every reason to expect that such organizations will grow in both number and importance in the years ahead.

**7.** *An ecological and economic collapse does not appear likely; especially given technological advances, the environment seems sustainable throughout the twenty-first century.* Some years ago, the senior author predicted an ecological and economic collapse of world capitalist civilization (Sanderson, 1995). Few predictions work out very well, and this one now seems highly dubious. As we saw in Chapter 10, our environmental problems do not appear as ominous as many have thought. Population growth is declining significantly throughout the less-developed world, fossil fuels are still highly abundant, and pollution has been reduced in the industrialized world and is likely to be reduced in the less-developed world. The world appears sustainable for a very long time even without a great leap forward to a dramatically new technology. And, as discussed earlier in this chapter, that great leap forward may be only a few decades away. Even though we have enough fossil energy sources for some time to come, it is likely that these will play less and less a role in our energy use. The nanotechnology revolution to come will provide us with much cheaper sources of renewable energy. As the use of fossil fuels declines, global temperatures will rise only modestly and global warming will not become a serious problem.

## Future Trends: The Merely Large Scale

Now we turn to another set of predictions, but in this case on a somewhat smaller (although still very large) scale.

**1.** *There will be continuing economic development throughout the core, in much of the semiperiphery, and in parts of the periphery, but it will be very uneven.* Castells (1996) notes that the new global economy in which we now live is highly dynamic, strongly exclusionary, and very unstable in its boundaries. It is an exacting taskmaster that suffers no fools gladly. To succeed in this extremely competitive world, four basic traits are necessary: technological capacity; access to a large, well integrated, and affluent market (e.g., the European Union, the North American trade zone); a significant differential between cost of production at the production site and prices in the destination market; and the capacity of governments to steer the growth strategies of the economies that they regulate.

Societies that have these traits must use them to integrate themselves centrally into the global economy (or, as the case may be, to keep themselves centrally integrated). Those that can compete will do so, and those that cannot will be brutally excluded and marginalized. And to refuse to play the new global game is no option, for that will bring certain disaster. Many of the old patterns of domination and dependency will be perpetuated. The core will continue to thrive and to develop ever higher standards of living. Most of the semiperiphery, and parts of the periphery, will also develop economically. In the semiperiphery, much of South America, especially Brazil and Mexico, will improve, and substantial development will take place in southeast Asia, especially in Malaysia, Indonesia, and Thailand. Korea—a single Korea resulting from the reunification of the old North Korea and South Korea—will make its way into the core, as will a reunified China consisting of the old Mainland China, Taiwan, and Hong Kong. In the periphery, some of Central America might move into the semiperiphery. Most of Africa and parts of Latin America and Asia will continue to be marginalized, and their suffering may increase.

2. *Sub-Saharan Africa will continue to deteriorate and may eventually implode.* Despite continuing economic development throughout most of the world, some societies and regions within the world-economy will become completely marginalized, the most prominent of which will be sub-Saharan Africa (Castells, 1998). Not only will it become totally marginalized but it will likely implode. Sub-Saharan Africa no longer has anything to offer to the core and the richer semiperipheral countries. It is so poor that its level of demand is extremely low, and its extremely low literacy rates, predatory states, poor educational systems, extremely high levels of AIDS, and constant ethnic violence, make it an extremely poor choice for capitalist investment. Manuel Castells (1996:135–136) states,

> The systematic logic of the new global economy does not have much of a role for the majority of the African population in the new international division of labor. Most primary commodities are useless or low priced, markets are too narrow, investment too risky, labor not skilled enough, communication and telecommunication infrastructure clearly inadequate, politics too unpredictable, and government bureaucracies inefficiently corrupt. . . . Under the dominance of free market conditions, internationally and domestically, most of Africa ceased to exist as an economically viable entity in the informational/global economy.

As a result, Africa is largely being ignored and the situation can only get worse. Already virtually a basket case at the present time, it is difficult to imagine what the further deterioration of Africa will look like, but this deterioration will most surely continue. And none of this is even considering the continuing rapid spread of AIDS throughout the continent, the region that is by far the world leader in the incidence of this disease (it has an AIDS rate some 20 times higher than the rate of western Europe and North America and nearly 90 times higher than the rate of east Asia). This will only intensify what Manuel Castells calls "the human holocaust that threatens Africa."

3. *The economic decline of the United States will continue for decades to come.* As noted in Chapter 6, the United States lost its hegemonic position in the world-economy around 1970. It has remained the number-one economic and political power in the world, but it has not gone unchallenged. It helped to rebuild western Europe and Japan after World War II, but both became major economic competitors. It now faces the challenge of the European Union (see item number 4). The United States played a major role in facilitating the astonishing development of South Korea and Taiwan, and they too have become competitors. Russia and eastern Europe have reentered the sphere of market capitalism, and, although they cannot become strong competitors for some time, they will become competitors nonetheless. But the real

competitor will be China, which is already undergoing stunningly rapid capitalist development. In the decades to come it will become the chief economic antagonist of the United States.

As capitalist accumulation and commodification intensify to ever higher levels, the United States will continue to maintain a strong position, but will it stay where it is, decline even further, or rise again to a new hegemonic position? Wallerstein expects that it will continue to decline, although slowly. This is certainly a very real possibility. Chase-Dunn, Jorgenson, Reifer, Giem, Lio, and Rogers (2003), however, argue that it could experience a new hegemonic phase. They point out that the U.S. decline seemed to bottom out in the 1990s, and there are indications of a slight upturn. They also point to scholars (e.g., Rennstich, 2001) who think that the U.S. advantage in such leading economic sectors as information technology and biotechnology will likely lead to a "second American hegemony." On the other hand, Chase-Dunn and colleagues note that the United States continues to experience larger and larger trade deficits—it is buying more goods from abroad than it is selling—and that foreign investment in the U.S. economy is huge and continues to grow. This latter consideration suggests to us that a renewed U.S. hegemony is extremely unlikely, especially when we recognize that no hegemon has ever lost and then regained hegemonic status. The world-economy just does not seem to work this way.

4. *There will be growing conflict between the United States and the European Union as the latter struggles for economic dominance.* In 1993, the European Union (EU) was formally created, although its beginnings go all the way back to 1951 and there were several steps along the way (Snooks, 1997). The EU included 15 members for the decade beginning in 1993: Germany, France, Austria, Finland, Sweden, Belgium, Luxembourg, the Netherlands, the United Kingdom, Denmark, Italy, Spain, Portugal, Ireland, and Greece. On May 1, 2004, it added 10 more states from eastern and southern Europe: the Czech Republic, Estonia, Cyprus, Latvia, Lithuania, Hungary, Malta, Poland, Slovenia, and Slovakia. Eventually, Bulgaria, Romania, Turkey, and possibly even Russia will likely join. The EU has a parliament consisting of 626 members that the individual states elect every five years, a single European passport, a European flag and anthem, and a common economic policy that led to the adoption of a common currency, the Euro, in January of 2002 (Bradshaw and Wallace, 1996).

The real intent behind the creation of the EU is the establishment of a more powerful economic entity than each of the member countries themselves. The EU wants to compete more effectively with the United States and Japan and, possibly, to make a bid for hegemonic status in the world-economy. However, it is very doubtful that it can achieve this latter aim (Bradshaw and Wallace, 1996; Weede, 1999; Tausch, 2003). York Bradshaw and Michael Wallace (1996) identify three serious obstacles in the EU's path.

First, there are *economic obstacles.* There are major differences between the European economies, with some being very strong and others weak. Such differences make it very difficult if not impossible to create a unified policy that all the member states can agree on. Second, there are *language obstacles.* Some 20 different languages are spoken by the EU countries. Is there going to be an official language, and which one would it be? People have a natural preference for their own language, none more so than the French, who seem convinced that they have the greatest language of all time. Given the world dominance of English, and the historic antagonisms between the English and the French, one can see a significant conflict here. Finally, *national obstacles* loom large. These national differences between countries, along with ethnic differences and conflicts within the member states, create the most severe obstacle to unification. Recent survey research shows that less than 5 percent of respondents who were Europeans said that being European was their foremost identity, and 45 percent said they felt no European identity whatsoever. A full 88 percent claimed that their foremost identification was with their nation or a region within their nation (Reif, 1993; Held, McGrew, Goldblatt, and Perraton, 1999). On the basis of these considerations, it is extremely difficult to imagine that the EU could ever become a culturally or politically unified body even if it solved the first two problems.

As Manuel Castells (1998) points out, to achieve any degree of unity at all Europe must have a sense of common identity, but this will be very difficult to achieve. What would give Europeans a sense of common identity? It cannot be Christianity, as was the case in the Middle Ages, given the much more limited role of religion in general and the Church in particular in contemporary Europe. It cannot be a democratic mode of government or democratic ideals, since both of these extend far beyond Europe. It certainly cannot be ethnicity, as already noted. And, given the economic differences among European countries and the economic reality of continuing globalization, it cannot be economics. If Europe cannot achieve a sense of common identity, "and if identity remains exclusively national, regional or local, European integration may not last beyond the limits of a common market" (Castells, 1998:332–333). We suspect that this will more than likely be the outcome. As for the much more ambitious aim of achieving hegemony, that is far less likely; a hegemon requires a single state and a single, powerful military apparatus, and it is virtually impossible to imagine the EU ever developing these.

It is not even clear that EU membership is good for its individual members. Arno Tausch (2003) notes that belonging to the EU has many negative consequences for its member states. He presents statistical data to show that the longer a country has belonged to the EU, the higher its unemployment rate, the larger its prisoner population, the greater its consumption of alcohol, the lower its GNP growth rate, and the less its expenditure on health and education, among numerous other negative indicators.

Nevertheless, it is clear that most European countries think that EU membership is a positive thing, and the EU wants to achieve as much unity as possible and become as much of a competitor to the other leading core societies as it can. The first strong signs of a break between the United States and Europe came in 2003 in the debate over the intent of the United States to invade Iraq. The two most powerful members of the EU, Germany and France, strongly opposed this invasion, and this led to a substantial increase in U.S.-European tensions that may prove difficult to resolve. There are large cracks in the so-called Atlantic Alliance between the United States and Europe, and many observers expect these to grow in the years to come. The United States is clearly worried about the EU and the financial effect of its common currency and regards it as a serious economic competitor. However, the growing EU/US conflict could be substantially moderated by the rise of China (see item number 6). They could become significant allies again to counteract this trend.

**5.** *The remaining Leninist societies will collapse and the two Koreas will be reunified.* There are only five Leninist regimes left in the world (six if you count Ethiopia, which is officially a federal republic but still controlled by the Ethiopian People's Revolutionary Democratic Front). Given the collapse of Communism in eastern Europe in 1989 and the Soviet Union in 1991, these regimes have little future and will eventually give way to non-Leninist regimes leading essentially capitalist societies. Cuba, for example, will very likely abandon Leninism with the death of Fidel Castro, and the industrialization and rapid capitalist development occurring in China will eventually—within 20 years probably—undermine its Leninist regime. These developments will put an end once and for all to the state socialist experiment in its twentieth-century form.

Within the context of the collapse of the remaining Leninist societies, the two Koreas will sooner or later—probably sooner—reunify into a single Korea, as many Koreans fervently desire already. This will create a formidable state, because it will inherit the high level of economic development of South Korea and the tremendous military apparatus of North Korea. If this unified Korean state has nuclear weapons, China and Japan will be forced to respond accordingly, which may create a very dangerous world geopolitical situation.

**6.** *The center of the world-economy will shift from the United States and western Europe to East Asia, and a reunified China will emerge as the next great world power.* Andre Gunder Frank's (1998, 2003) prediction that the world-economy will shift back toward Asia in the twenty-first century will come true. Within the next 25 to 50 years, the dominant society in Asia—indeed, in the entire world—will be China. China has the world's largest population; with the exception of India, which is a close second, no other society comes even close to its huge size. With such a huge population, combined with the enormous economic strides China has made in recent years, it is poised to become the next great economic power. This will necessitate the throwing off of the current Leninist state that governs China, and that is likely within 20 years as China develops the internal conditions for democratization. Once China begins to democratize and to develop an increasing number of truly private enterprises, the antagonism toward it of Taiwan and Hong Kong will greatly diminish and the "three Chinas" will become a unified superstate. This superstate will probably become impossible to stop once it reaches a certain developmental threshold, and will become the next great hegemonic power.

## Conclusions: The Future from the Perspective of a General Theory of History

In a celebrated book, *The End of History and the Last Man* (1992), Francis Fukuyama offers a completely different scenario from any of those previously presented.

Fukuyama draws on Hegel's philosophy of history to argue that free-market capitalism and liberal democracy represent the final stage of human history, the grandest of all human achievements. Hegel argued that history was unfolding in a rational and progressive manner, and that ultimately a society would be achieved that was perfect, or at least as close to perfect as was possible. Fukuyama thinks we are there now, and thus that history has come fundamentally to an end. Any further changes will be mere fine-tuning of liberal capitalism.

Although Fukuyama is, politically speaking, a thinker of a completely different stripe than Marx and the Marxists, they all agree that history has an end. But, of course, this cannot be so. Liberal capitalism is simply what we have come to so far, and it has only been around for a century or two. It will undoubtedly be replaced by something else at some point, but no one knows, or can possibly know, what this might be. We cannot really know the future in any grand sense. But one thing is certain: If we do not have a good general theory of the past, then we have absolutely no hope of speculating intelligently about what is ahead.

This book has offered a materialist and evolutionary perspective in order to understand the past, and it may be suggested that such a perspective is our most reliable guide to the future. No one can know whether the predictions of Heilbroner, Goldstein, and Chase-Dunn, plus all the other ones we have made in this chapter, are good ones, but they do try to come to grips with the factors that are likely to be most centrally involved in shaping the future. Today, we live in a capitalist world-economy that has been expanding and evolving for half a millennium, and that is closely intertwined with an interstate system. Together, the two make up the modern world-system. It is the evolution of this world-system that is the principal driving force of the modern world, and, more than anything else, it is its dynamics that will determine what lies ahead.

There is an old Chinese saying: "May you live in interesting times." We do indeed live in extremely interesting times, since the world is changing in dramatic ways at an increasingly accelerating pace. Intelligent citizens have a special obligation to learn about the times in which we live, especially about the dangers and opportunities they present, in order to maximize the opportunities and minimize the dangers. We hope that this book has contributed in some way to this learning process.

## FOR FURTHER READING

Mark Cohen's *Health and the Rise of Civilization* (1989) provides an extremely detailed analysis of health, nutrition, and disease among many different types of societies. Cohen makes a persuasive case for the relatively good health and nutrition of ancient hunter-gatherer societies compared to the agricultural societies that evolved later. Minge-Klevana (1980) provides very useful data on workloads in various types of societies.

Galtung, Heiestad, and Rudeng (1980) compare the current state of the capitalist world-economy with that of the Roman Empire during the beginning of its decline. This is a provocative comparison, perhaps with considerable merit, but one that must be approached with caution. Stirring defenses of capitalism have been written by Berger (1986) and Seldon (1990). Fukuyama (1992) is another defense of capitalism, but in this case, with a provocative theoretical and historical backdrop and the argument that it is "the end of history." Maryanski and Turner (1992) argue for the superiority of industrial society as a form of social life based on the individualism it promotes, which they believe is consistent with human nature and human needs.

Elvin Hatch (1983) provides an excellent critique of the serious limitations of cultural relativism as a way of judging other cultures. John Rawls's *A Theory of Justice* (1971) is the best-known and probably the mostly widely accepted ethical theory of the last century. Rawls has recapitulated his argument in *Justice as Fairness: A Restatement* (2001a) and extended it in *The Law of Peoples* (2001b). Peter Singer's *One World: The Ethics of Globalization* (2002) accepts Rawls's basic principles but argues that Rawls has limited them unnecessarily by applying them to nation-states rather than to the world as a single moral community.

A stunning work on technological advance is Robert Mulhall's *Our Molecular Future* (2002). Mulhall focuses in particular on advances in nanotechnology and makes a number of extraordinary predictions for the next 50 to 100 years, some of which seem stranger than science fiction. See also Gross (1999). Christian (2004) makes bold predictions concerning the near, middle-range, long-range, and very long-range future.

Joshua Goldstein (1988) analyzes the relationship between economic cycles in the history of capitalism and major wars. This allows him to predict the timing of the next major war. Many have argued for the necessity of a world state to prevent nuclear annihilation and to create a more just world. See, in particular, Chase-Dunn (2003).

George Ayittey's *Africa in Chaos* (1998) is an excellent work on Africa's current problems and their likely causes. Ayittey, himself an African, is extremely critical of African state structures and puts most of the blame on them for Africa's failures. See also Castells (1998).

David Harvey (1989) has written an extremely influential book on the psychologically destabilizing consequences of globalization. Arrighi and Silver (1999) contains important essays on U.S. hegemonic decline. Castells (1998) looks at the European Union and its prospects, as do Bradshaw and Wallace (1996) and Tausch (2003). On the shift to Asia as the center of the world-economy, see Frank (2003). A popular work that makes very pessimistic predictions about the economic, ecological, and political future of the Third World is Robert Kaplan's *The Coming Anarchy* (2000). Kaplan foresees potential catastrophe in much of the Third World occurring in the near future.

Boswell and Chase-Dunn (2000) make about as good a case for socialism as can be made. Warren Wagar's *A Short History of the Future* (1999) uses world-system theory as the basis for an extraordinary work of fiction in which a historian from the twenty-third century narrates world history from the late twentieth century to his own time. By 2015, the world has fallen under the control of 12 megacorporations. Devastating nuclear war in 2044 leads to the creation of a socialist world commonwealth that regulates world affairs for the better part of a century, only to yield to the formation of thousands of tiny statelets and the reestablishment of some elements of capitalism.

# GLOSSARY

**absolutism**  See *absolutist monarchy*.

**absolutist monarchy**  A type of state found in late medieval and early modern Europe in which a centralized bureaucracy developed around the king. This bureaucratic centralization was associated with the general intensification of state power. Compare *national states*.

**adaptation**  The process whereby humans select social patterns because they are useful or effective in meeting their various needs and desires.

**adaptive**  See *adaptation*.

**agrarian society**  A society whose members make a living by using intensive and advanced agricultural methods, such as plows and animal energy for plowing.

**agriculture**  As distinguished from *horticulture*, a form of farming in which large plots of land (fields) are carefully prepared and then cultivated with the use of plows and traction animals.

**articulated economy**  One whose multiple economic sectors are highly interconnected so that changes in one sector contribute significantly to changes in other sectors. Such an economy has balance and diversification.

**authority**  The socially legitimated right to command the actions of others.

**average world person**  The typical member of the most common type of society predominant in the world in a given historical period.

**balanced reciprocity**  An obligation to repay others that is specific as to time and amount. See *reciprocity*.

**big men**  Men of considerable prestige and renown who perform important political and economic leadership roles in many horticultural societies, especially those of Melanesia.

**bourgeoisie**  In Marxian theory, the class owning capital.

**capitalism**  An economic system devoted to the production and sale of commodities on a market, with the objective of earning the maximum profit and accumulating profit over time.

**chiefdom**  A political system characterized by the integration of a number of villages into a larger whole that is administered by a class of ruling chiefs and their functionaries.

**civilization**  A complex and large-scale society characterized by such features as towns and cities, monumental architecture, craft specialization and occupational differentiation, writing and record keeping, and extreme social and economic inequalities. A civilization is usually politically ruled by a *state*.

**commodification**  The process whereby economic production is increasingly governed by considerations of profitability.

**commodified work**  Work that is organized in such a way that it contributes to the maximum profit and capital accumulation.

**contest-mobility educational system**  A type of educational system that does no formal channeling or tracking and that permits students to pursue as much education as their talents and inclinations allow.

**convergent evolution**  Changes in two or more originally dissimilar societies that make them increasingly alike.

**core**  Those societies within the capitalist world-economy that are the most technologically and economically advanced, that concentrate on the production of the most advanced commodities, and that usually contain the most powerful governments and military structures.

**corvée**  A system whereby the elite groups of highly stratified agrarian societies recruit large teams of laborers for special work projects.

**credential inflation**  A process whereby educational credentials (diplomas and degrees) decline in value over time because of an increase in the number of people who possess them.

**credentialism**  The process whereby an educational system comes to be oriented around the pursuit of education for its credential value rather than for its intrinsic merits. See also *credential inflation*.

**cultural relativism**  The doctrine developed by various anthropologists in the early twentieth century that there are no absolute or objective criteria for judging a society or culture; societies and cultures can be judged only by their own internal standards, and thus on their own terms all are "equally valid."

**deepening of capitalist development**  The process whereby capitalist relations and activities, especially commodification and proletarianization, become increasingly characteristic of an economy and society. See also *commodification* and *proletarianization*.

**demesne**  The "home farm" of the feudal manor, or the land held directly by the landlord and cultivated exclusively for his own use.

**democracy**  See *parliamentary democracy*.

**demographic transition**  A process associated with large-scale industrialization in which both death and birthrates drop sharply and family size declines markedly.

**dependency theory**  An approach to the problem of economic underdevelopment that holds that underdevelopment results from the economic dependency to which many nations have been historically subjected. See *economic dependency*.

**disarticulated economy**  One whose multiple sectors do not significantly interrelate such that growth in one sector contributes little or nothing to the growth of other sectors. Such an economy is characterized by a lack of diversification and by exaggerated specialization, typically of the raw-materials-production-for-export sector.

**divergent evolution**  Changes in two or more originally similar societies that make them increasingly different.

**economic dependency**  A process whereby one society's economy falls under the domination of a foreign society.

**economic globalization**  Increasing integration of the world-economy by means of greater international production, trade, finance, and migration. Compare *political* and *sociocultural globalization*.

**economic surplus**  A quantity of economic valuables above and beyond that necessary for the subsistence of the individuals who produce such valuables.

**economy**  The set of social relationships through which people organize the production, distribution, and exchange of valuables.

**egalitarian societies**  Societies that lack class divisions, or hereditary social groups possessing unequal amounts of power, privilege, and prestige.

**environmental depletion**  The exhaustion, or at least the substantial diminution, of environmen-

tal resources, either as the result of population pressure or the impact of technology on the environment.

**ethnocentrism**  The view, characteristic of most people in all societies, that one's own society or culture is the reference point for judging other ways of life and superior to all of those ways of life.

**evolution**  See *social evolution*.

**evolutionary materialism**  A general theoretical approach to the study of social evolution, which emphasizes that evolutionary changes occur primarily as the result of changing technological, economic, demographic, and ecological forces.

**evolutionary theory**  A theoretical strategy that attempts to describe and explain directional sequences of long-term social change. See also *evolutionary materialism*.

**expanding world commercialization**  Growth in the volume and density of world trade and commercial activity over the past 5,000 years.

**export-oriented industrialization**  A strategy of economic development or industrialization employed by less-developed countries involving producing goods to be sold in foreign markets. Compare *import-substitution industrialization*.

**feudalism**  An economic and political system found in some agrarian societies in which a private landlord class holds land in the form of fiefs. See also *fief*.

**fief**  A grant of land given by an overlord to a vassal (lesser lord) in return for the performance of such obligations as military service and personal protection.

**forced labor**  Any labor system in which workers are not free to negotiate the kind and amount of labor they will perform and their level of compensation.

**formal democracy**  A government that has established some of the recognized attributes of democracy but that fails to implement truly democratic practices. A formal democracy is thus a democracy in name only.

**generalized reciprocity**  An obligation to repay others that is vague and nonspecific as to the nature, time, and amount of repayment. See *reciprocity*.

**geopolitical**  See *geopolitics*.

**geopolitics**  The intersection of politics and geography. Geopolitical considerations are those that involve the territorial and diplomatic relations among states, either regionally or worldwide. See *interstate system.*

**globalization** The emergence of a worldwide interconnectedness among the economic, political, social, and cultural aspects of social life, accompanied by increased awareness among social actors on a worldwide scale. See *economic globalization, political globalization,* and *sociocultural globalization.*

**hegemon** See *hegemony.*

**hegemony** A situation in which a single capitalist state is dominant in the world-economy in regard to economic production, commerce, and finance. Such a state is known as a *hegemon.* A hegemon is so powerful economically that it can almost always impose its will on competing capitalist states.

**horticultural** See *horticulture.*

**horticulture** A simple form of agriculture in which small plots of land (gardens) are crudely prepared and cultivated through the use of hand tools. See *intensive horticultural society* and *simple horticultural society.*

**human self-realization** The equal opportunity of individuals to realize their basic nature as members of the human species and to gain meaning and fulfillment in life, especially through work.

**hunter-gatherer society** One whose members make a living exclusively or primarily through the hunting of wild animals and the collection of wild plants.

**idealism** In social science, the view that the human mind in the form of ideas governs social life and its evolution over time. Compare *materialism.*

**import-substitution industrialization** A strategy of economic development in which the aim is to produce goods to be sold in domestic markets by minimizing the importation of foreign goods.

**individual autonomy** The relative absence of constraints on individual thought and behavior, or the freedom of individuals to follow their own courses of action.

**individualism** The freedom of individuals to engage in personal self-expression, or the tolerance of a society for individual nonconformity.

**industrial capitalism** The form of economic activity that emerged in Europe with the Industrial Revolution and that today characterizes most of the societies of western Europe, North America,

Australia, and Japan. In Marx's formulation, it involves the making of profits through the exploitation of labor power in the very process of production itself.

**industrialization** The process by which a society comes to be characterized by an economic system and a mode of social life based around machinery and the factory system of manufacturing. See *mechanization.*

**industrial society** One having acquired a level of technology based on the use of machines to replace hand labor and the widespread use of these machines in the process of economic production.

**infrastructure** The raw materials and social forms used by the members of a society to meet their needs in regard to economic production and biological reproduction.

**intensification of agricultural production** An increase in energy expenditure with respect to agricultural practices. See *intensification of production.*

**intensification of production** An increase in the expenditure of energy involved in carrying out economic production. This may occur through greater work inputs, the use of more natural resources, an advancement in the level of technology, or any combination of these.

**intensive horticultural society** A horticultural society whose members have adopted more energy-intensive means of cultivation, such as shortening the fallow period of land or using more advanced tools and techniques of production.

**intergenerational mobility** The upward or downward movement of individuals within a stratification system relative to the class position of their parents.

**interstate system** The complex system of competing and conflicting nation-states that are closely intertwined with the capitalist world-economy.

**intragenerational mobility** The upward or downward movement of individuals within a stratification system with respect to the first job they hold.

**Kondratieff waves** Economic cycles of upturn and downturn that appear to be characteristic of the capitalist world-economy throughout its lifetime. Each upturn phase lasts about 20 to 30 years and is followed by a downturn phase of approximately the same length.

**K-waves**  See *Kondratieff waves.*

**labor-repressive agriculture**  An agricultural system in which peasants or serfs are compelled by landlords to provide certain labor services and to pay rent, taxation, and so on, for the right to use land controlled by those landlords.

**Law of Least Effort**  The principle that, other things being equal, people prefer to carry out activities with a minimum amount of energy expenditure.

**Leninist regime**  A form of government associated with state socialist societies in which the Communist party monopolizes power and represses the large mass of the population.

**Leninist societies**  See *Leninist regime.*

**lineage ownership**  Communal ownership of land by large-scale kinship groups.

**manor**  The lands and the labor force controlled by a feudal landlord.

**market**  An economic institution that involves the buying and selling of goods and services in a socially organized manner.

**market-dominated society**  A society having both markets and marketplaces and in which market principles govern economic activity.

**marketless society**  A society having neither markets nor marketplaces.

**marketplace**  A physical site where market activities occur.

**mass education**  An educational system that is devoted, at least at the primary level and usually at the secondary level, to educating virtually the entire population. Mass education is highly standardized and bureaucratized wherever it is found.

**materialism**  In social science, the viewpoint that the basic features of a society derive from the "material conditions of social life," such as the economy, the physical environment, and the level of technology. Compare *idealism.*

**materialist**  See *materialism.*

**mechanization**  The process whereby machinery and other advanced forms of technology are increasingly applied to economic production. See *industrialization.*

**mercantilism**  An economic practice in the seventeenth and early eighteenth centuries whereby governments granted monopolies to European trading companies so that they could make large profits from their trade with foreign colonies.

**merchant capitalism**  In Marx's formulation, an early form of capitalism, prevailing approximately in the years 1450–1750, in which trading companies made profits throughout the world by capitalizing on favorable terms of trade.

**mobility inflows**  The movement of individuals into social classes other than the class from which they originated.

**mobility outflows**  The movement of individuals out of the social class from which they originated.

**modernization theory**  An approach to the problem of economic underdevelopment that postulates that contemporary underdeveloped nations remain in a "traditional" state because they contain certain internal deficiences that constitute obstacles to development.

**monopoly capitalism**  That stage of capitalism, generally beginning in the last quarter of the nineteenth century, characterized by the rise of the giant corporation as the basic economic unit and the emergence of extensive foreign investment of core nations in the capitalist periphery.

**national states**  Those highly centralized, bureaucratically organized, and militarily powerful states that arose in Europe between the sixteenth and nineteenth centuries. Compare *absolutist monarchy.*

**Neolithic Revolution**  That major technological transformation, beginning about 10,000 years ago, most importantly associated with the beginnings of agriculture.

**parallel evolution**  Changes in two or more societies that are similar in form and in the rate of change.

**paramount ownership**  A form of property rights characterized by the (at least theoretical) ownership of land by a ruling chief and his royal family.

**parliamentary democracy**  A type of government resting on the existence of a parliamentary or congressional body to which other segments of government must be responsible; the regular, free, and fair election of government officials; and the granting of individual rights and freedoms to the mass of the population.

**partial redistribution**  A form of economic redistribution in which only some of what is received is returned to the original parties who provided it. See *redistribution*.

**pastoralism** A mode of subsistence in which people survive primarily through tending animal herds and living off their products. By necessity, pastoralists are nomadic rather than sedentary.

**patrimonial ownership** A form of seigneurial ownership in which land is privately owned by a landlord class and inherited in family lines. See *seigneurial ownership*.

**peasant** A farmer, ordinarily found in an agrarian or contemporary underdeveloped society, who typically exists in an economically and politically subordinate relationship to the principal owner or controller of the land from which he or she gains his or her subsistence.

**peripheral market society** A society having marketplaces, but in which market principles are not the primary organizers of economic life.

**periphery** The least economically developed part of the capitalist world-economy, extensively subjected to high levels of surplus expropriation by the core.

**political globalization** The increasing establishment of a "world polity" through growth in the number and importance of international agreements, accords, and alliances; political globalization also involves an increase in the number and importance of international nongovernmental organizations. Compare *economic globalization* and *sociocultural globalization*.

**political power** See *power*.

**population pressure** A level of population density that, for any given society at a given level of technology, produces a deterioration in the economic standard of living.

**postindustrial society** As conceived by certain social theorists, a type of society in which the economic system is primarily devoted to the production of services and in which a new class of highly educated professionals replaces capitalists as the dominant class.

**postsocialism** A term characterizing the economic and political situation of those Eastern European societies (including the former Soviet Union) that after 1989 experienced profound economic and political changes involving the delegitimation of the Communist party and the shift toward private ownership in the economy.

**postsocialist societies** See *postsocialism*.

**power** The capacity of one party to compel the actions of other parties even against their will.

**prebendal ownership** A form of seigneurial ownership in which land is owned by a powerful government that assigns officials to oversee its cultivation and make their living from it. See *seigneurial ownership*.

**precapitalist economy** See *precapitalist society*.

**precapitalist society** A type of society existing before the emergence of modern capitalism, or not yet significantly characterized by capitalist economic features.

**preindustrial society** One existing prior to the Industrial Revolution, or not yet having acquired an industrial level of technology.

**primitive communism** A form of economic ownership in which all individuals and groups have equal access to the resources of nature that sustain life.

**Principle of Infrastructural Determinism** The notion that the elements of the infrastructure have a logical priority in the creation of social life and a major influence on the nature of the structure and superstructure and the changes they undergo. Sanderson's version says that ecology and demography are the most important elements of the infrastructure in hunter-gatherer, horticultural, and pastoral societies; that these elements plus technology and economy are most important in agrarian societies; and that economy is the most important infrastructural element in modern capitalist societies and the capitalist world-system.

**progress** A betterment or improvement in social life and its various features.

**proletarianization** The process whereby the contractual form of labor known as wage labor increasingly becomes the dominant form of labor organization. See also *wage labor*.

**proletariat** In Marxian theory, the class that must sell its labor power to capitalists in order to earn a living.

**pure redistribution** A form of economic redistribution in which all that is funneled in one direction is refunneled in the other. See *redistribution*.

**qualificationism** See *credentialism*.

**rank society** An unstratified society in which there is a limited number of high-status social positions for which individuals vigorously compete.

**reciprocity** The obligation to repay others for what they have given to us, as well as the act of repayment itself. See also *balanced reciprocity* and *generalized reciprocity*.

**redistribution** A process of economic distribution in which goods are brought to a central source (person or group) and then returned in some manner to the points from which they originated. See also *partial redistribution* and *pure redistribution*.

**restricted democracy** A government that has democratic practices, including elections, but that restricts the right to vote to certain segments of the population, such as property owners, men, or members of certain racial groups.

**seigneurial ownership** Ownership of land by a class of landlords having the power to impose severe penalties on other persons for their use of the land.

**semiperiphery** That segment of the capitalist world-economy that is intermediate between the core and the periphery. This zone of the world-economy contains a mixture of core-like and periphery-like economic activities.

**serfdom** A form of forced labor in which peasants are tied to plots of land administered by landlords and compelled to provide rent, taxation, and labor services at the request of those landlords.

**simple horticultural society** One whose members earn a living through reliance upon the simplest agricultural techniques. Normally this involves long-fallow cultivation of small garden plots using hand tools.

**slash-and-burn cultivation** A form of cultivation in which forest land is cleared of vegetation and the vegetation is piled up, dried out, and burned. The remaining ashes are spread throughout the farming plot and serve as a fertilizer. Also known as *shifting cultivation*.

**slavery** A form of labor organization in which some persons are legally owned as a form of human property, are compelled to work by their owners, and are deprived of most or all political rights.

**social continuity** The preservation of the basic features of a society over time.

**social devolution** Social change resulting in the emergence of characteristics typical of an earlier stage of social evolution.

**social evolution** Qualitative structural transformations within a society (or one or more of its parts) that exhibit a directional pattern.

**social extinction** The elimination of a society, either through the death of its members or through its absorption into another society.

**social mobility** The upward or downward movement of individuals between positions in the class structure of a society.

**social stratification** The existence within a society (or world-system) of social groups that possess unequal levels of social power, privilege, and prestige.

**sociocultural globalization** Increased worldwide similarity in social institutions and cultural tastes, preferences, norms, values, and the objects and goals of cultural consumption. Compare *economic globalization* and *political globalization*.

**sponsored-mobility educational system** A type of educational system in which students are channeled into different educational tracks early in their careers based on their performance on standardized examinations.

**state** A political system claiming a monopoly over the use of the means of violence within a specified territory.

**state breakdown** A situation in which the capacity of a state to govern has been crippled or severely limited. State breakdowns sometimes lead to revolutions, or radical transformations of government and society.

**state socialism** A form of economy in which the government is the principal owner and manager of the means of production and production is carried out without a market mechanism.

**state socialist society** See *state socialism*.

**structure** The organized patterns of social behavior common to the members of a society.

**substantive democracy** A government that not only establishes the formal attributes of democracy but that also generally employs them in practice.

**superstructure** The organized set of beliefs, values, feelings, and symbols shared by the members of a society.

**surplus expropriation** The siphoning off of the economic surplus produced by one group into the hands of another group by means of one or another form of compulsion.

**systemic cycle of accumulation** A long economic cycle in which a capitalist hegemon shifts its investment away from production and commerce and more toward finance as the profitability of production and commerce decline.

**technology** The material means, which include tools, techniques, and knowledge, whereby humans meet their needs and desires.

**totalitarian dictatorship** A type of government, generally associated with modern state socialist societies, in which all power is concentrated in the hands of a governmental elite that rules the people without regard to any concept of popular sentiment or individual rights and liberties.

**transnational corporation** A company that has branches of production in several countries.

**tribe** A network of bands or villages sharing a common culture and speaking the same language. Also, a level of political evolution characterized by the absence of centralized authority and political leaders with the power to compel the actions of others.

**underdeveloped society** One of the least technologically and economically advanced societies within the capitalist world-economy; underdeveloped societies have low levels of economic development and a high percentage of the population working in agriculture.

**unrestricted democracy** A democratic government that permits the entire adult population to vote.

**wage labor** A labor relationship in which workers are legally free to bargain with employers for a specified rate of compensation for their work and the conditions under which they will perform that work.

**world-economy** A world-system lacking political centralization and that therefore contains within it a plurality of competing states. A world-economy is characterized by economic relations of production and exchange that serve to integrate it. See also *core, periphery,* and *semiperiphery.*

**world-empire** A world-system that is politically and militarily centralized or unified.

**world-system** Any relatively large social system having a high degree of autonomy, an extensive division of labor, and a plurality of societies and cultures.

**world-system theory** A theoretical approach designed to explain many features of the evolution of capitalism since the sixteenth century. It holds that capitalism has evolved as a hierarchical arrangement of exploiting and exploited nations, each of which can be properly understood only as part of the entire system.

# BIBLIOGRAPHY

Abonyi, Arpad. 1982. Eastern Europe's reintegration. In Christopher Chase-Dunn (ed.), *Socialist States in the World-System*. Beverly Hills, CA: Sage.

Abu-Lughod, Janet. 1988. The shape of the world system in the thirteenth century. *Studies in Comparative International Development* 22 (4):3–24.

_____. 1989. *Before European Hegemony: The World-System A.D. 1250–1350*. New York: Oxford University Press.

_____. 1991. *Can Japan become a hegemon? Revising (so soon?) the revisionist thesis*. Paper presented at the annual meetings of the American Sociological Association, Cincinnati.

Adams, Robert McC. 1966. *The Evolution of Urban Society*. Chicago: Aldine.

_____. 1972. Demography and the "Urban Revolution" in lowland Mesopotamia. In Brian Spooner (ed.), *Population Growth: Anthropological Implications*. Cambridge, MA: MIT Press.

Aganbegyan, Abel. 1988. New directions in Soviet economics. *New Left Review* 169:87–93.

_____. 1989. *Inside Perestroika: The Future of the Soviet Economy*. Trans. Helen Szamuely. New York: Harper & Row.

Altman, Dennis. 2001. *Global Sex*. Chicago: University of Chicago Press.

Amin, Samir. 1972. Underdevelopment and dependence in black Africa: Origins and contemporary forms. *Journal of Modern African Studies* 10:503–524.

_____. 1974. *Accumulation on a World Scale*. New York: Monthly Review Press.

_____. 1991. The ancient world-systems versus the modern capitalist world-system. *Review* 14:349–385.

_____. 1997. *Capitalism in the Age of Globalization*. London: Zed Books.

Anderson, Perry. 1974a. *Passages from Antiquity to Feudalism*. London: New Left Books.

_____. 1974b. *Lineages of the Absolutist State*. London: New Left Books.

Apter, David E. 1987. *Rethinking Development: Modernization, Dependency, and Post-Modern Politics*. Beverly Hills, CA: Sage.

Arriaga, P. 1985. Toward a critique of the information economy. *Media, Culture, and Society* 7:271–296.

Arrighi, Giovanni. 1982. A crisis of hegemony. In Samir Amin et al., *Dynamics of Global Crisis*. New York: Monthly Review Press.

_____. 1994. *The Long Twentieth Century*. New York: Verso.

Arrighi, Giovanni, Takeshi Hamashita, and Mark Selden (eds.). 2003. *The Resurgence of East Asia: 500, 150, and 50 Year Perspectives*. New York: Routledge.

Arrighi, Giovanni, and Beverly J. Silver. 1999. *Chaos and Governance in the Modern World System*. Minneapolis: University of Minnesota Press.

Aseniero, George. 1994. South Korean and Taiwanese development: The transnational context. *Review* 17:275–336.

_____. 1996. Asia in the world-system. In Sing Chew and Robert A. Denemark (eds.), *The Underdevelopment of Development: Essays in Honor of Andre Gunder Frank*. Thousand Oaks, CA: Sage.

Atkinson, A. B. 1983. *The Economics of Inequality* (2nd ed.). Oxford: Oxford University Press.

Ayittey, George B. N. 1998. *Africa in Chaos*. New York: St. Martin's Press.

Baran, Paul, and E. J. Hobsbawm. 1973. The stages of economic growth: A review. In Charles K. Wilber (ed.), *The Political Economy of Development and Underdevelopment*. New York: Random House.

Barfield, Thomas J. 1989. *The Perilous Frontier: Nomadic Empires and China*. Oxford, UK: Blackwell.

_____. 1993. *The Nomadic Alternative*. Upper Saddle River, NJ: Prentice-Hall.

Barnet, Richard J., and Ronald E. Müller. 1974. *Global Reach: The Power of the Multinational Corporations*. New York: Simon & Schuster (Touchstone).

Barrett, Richard E., and Martin King Whyte. 1982. Dependency theory and Taiwan: Analysis of a deviant case. *American Journal of Sociology* 87:1064–1089.

Barth, Fredrik. 1961. *Nomads of South Persia*. New York: Humanities Press.

Beals, Ralph L., and Harry Hoijer. 1971. *An Introduction to Anthropology* (4th ed.). New York: Macmillan.

Beauchamp, Edward R. (ed.). 1991. *Windows on Japanese Education*. Westport, CT: Greenwood Press.

Beaud, Michel. 1983. *A History of Capitalism, 1500–1980*. New York: Monthly Review Press.

Beckfield, Jason. 2003. Inequality in the world polity: The structure of international organization. *American Sociological Review* 68:401–424.

Bell, Daniel. 1973. *The Coming of Post-Industrial Society.* New York: Basic Books.

Benavot, Aaron, and Phyllis Riddle. 1988. The expansion of primary education, 1870–1940: Trends and issues. *Sociology of Education* 61:191–210.

Benedict, Ruth. 1934. *Patterns of Culture.* Boston: Houghton Mifflin.

Bennett, H. S. 1937. *Life on the English Manor: A Study of Peasant Conditions, 1150–1400.* Cambridge, UK: Cambridge University Press.

Berger, Peter L. 1986. *The Capitalist Revolution.* New York: Basic Books.

Berger, Stephen D. 1974. Review of Daniel Bell, the coming of post-industrial society. *Contemporary Sociology* 3:101–105.

Bergesen, Albert J., Roberto M. Fernandez, and Chintamani Sahoo. 1987. America and the changing structure of hegemonic production. In Terry Boswell and Albert Bergesen (eds.), *America's Changing Role in the World-System.* New York: Praeger.

Bergesen, Albert J., and John Sonnett. 2001. The global 500: Mapping the world economy at century's end. *American Behavioral Scientist* 44:1602–1615.

Bettinger, Robert L. 1991. *Hunter-Gatherers: Archaeological and Evolutionary Theory.* New York: Plenum.

Bienefeld, Manfred. 1981. Dependency and the newly industrialising countries (NICs): Towards a reappraisal. In Dudley Seers (ed.), *Dependency Theory: A Critical Assessment.* London: Frances Pinter.

Binford, Lewis R. 1968. Post-Pleistocene adaptations. In S. R. Binford and L. R. Binford (eds.), *New Perspectives in Archaeology.* Chicago: Aldine.

Blau, Peter, and Otis Dudley Duncan. 1967. *The American Occupational Structure.* New York: Free Press.

Blaut, J. M. 1993. *The Colonizer's Model of the World.* New York: Guilford Press.

Bloch, Marc. 1961. *Feudal Society.* Trans. L. A. Manyon. 2 volumes. Chicago: University of Chicago Press. (Originally published 1930.)

Blomstrom, Magnus, and Bjørn Hettne. 1984. *Development Theory in Transition.* London: Zed Books.

Bluestone, Barry, and Bennett Harrison. 1982. *The Deindustrialization of America.* New York: Basic Books.

Blumberg, Rae Lesser. 1978. *Stratification: Socioeconomic and Sexual Inequality.* Dubuque, IA: Wm. C. Brown.

Bogucki, Peter. 1999. *The Origins of Human Society.* Oxford: Blackwell.

Bohannan, Paul, and George Dalton (eds.). 1962. *Markets in Africa.* Evanston, IL: Northwestern University Press.

Boli, John, Francisco O. Ramirez, and John W. Meyer. 1985. Explaining the origins and expansion of mass education. *Comparative Education Review* 29:145–170.

Bornschier, Volker, and Christopher Chase-Dunn. 1985. *Transnational Corporations and Underdevelopment.* New York: Praeger.

Bornschier, Volker, Christopher Chase-Dunn, and Richard Rubinson. 1978. Cross-national evidence of the effects of foreign investment and aid on economic growth and inequality: A survey of findings and a reanalysis. *American Journal of Sociology* 84:651–683.

Boserup, Ester. 1965. *The Conditions of Agricultural Growth.* Chicago: Aldine.

_____. 1981. *Population and Technological Change.* Chicago: University of Chicago Press.

_____. 1986. Shifts in the determinants of fertility in the developing world: Environmental, technical, economic and cultural factors. In David Coleman and Roger Schofield (eds.), *The State of Population Theory: Forward from Malthus.* Oxford, UK: Blackwell.

Boswell, Terry, and Christopher Chase-Dunn. 2000. *The Spiral of Capitalism and Socialism.* Boulder, CO: Lynne Rienner.

Bourdieu, Pierre, and Jean-Claude Passeron. 1977. *Reproduction: In Education, Society and Culture.* Beverly Hills, CA: Sage.

Bowles, Samuel, and Herbert Gintis. 1976. *Schooling in Capitalist America.* New York: Basic Books.

Boyd, Robert, and Peter J. Richerson. 1985. *Culture and the Evolutionary Process.* Chicago: University of Chicago Press.

Bradshaw, York W., and Michael Wallace. 1996. *Global Inequalities.* Thousand Oaks, CA: Pine Forge Press.

Braudel, Fernand. 1981. *The Structures of Everyday Life.* (Volume 1 of *Civilization and Capitalism, 15th–18th Century.*) New York: Harper & Row.

_____. 1982. *The Wheels of Commerce.* (Volume 2 of *Civilization and Capitalism, 15th–18th Century.*) New York: Harper & Row.

_____. 1984. *The Perspective of the World.* (Volume 3 of *Civilization and Capitalism, 15th–18th Century.*) New York: Harper & Row.

Braverman, Harry. 1974. *Labor and Monopoly Capital: The Degradation of Work in the Twentieth Century.* New York: Monthly Review Press.

Brenner, Robert. 1977. The origins of capitalist development: A critique of neo-Smithian Marxism. *New Left Review* 104:25–92.

Brown, David K. 1995. *Degrees of Control: A Sociology*

*of Educational Expansion and Occupational Credentialism.* New York: Teachers College Press.

Burch, Ernest S., and Linda J. Ellanna (eds.). 1994. *Key Issues in Hunter-Gatherer Research.* Oxford, UK: Berg.

Burns, Edward McNall. 1973. *Western Civilizations* (Vol. 2, 8th ed.). New York: Norton.

Caldwell, John C. 1976. Toward a restatement of demographic transition theory. *Population and Development Review*: 2:321–366.

Cameron, Kenneth Neill. 1973. *Humanity and Society: A World History.* New York: Monthly Review Press.

Campbell, Donald T. 1965. Variation and selective retention in socio-cultural evolution. In Herbert R. Barringer, George I. Blanksten, and Raymond W. Mack (eds.), *Social Change in Developing Areas: A Reinterpretation of Evolutionary Theory.* Cambridge, MA: Schenkman.

Cardoso, Fernando Henrique. 1982. Dependency and development in Latin America. In Hamza Alavi and Teodor Shanin (eds.), *Introduction to the Sociology of "Developing Societies."* London: Macmillan.

———. 1986. Democracy in Latin America. *Politics and Society* 15:23–41.

———. 2001. *Charting a New Course: The Politics of Globalization and Social Transformation.* Lanham, MD: Rowman & Littlefield.

Cardoso, Fernando Henrique, and Enzo Faletto. 1979. *Dependency and Development in Latin America.* Berkeley: University of California Press.

Carneiro, Robert L. 1968. Slash-and-burn cultivation among the Kuikuru and its implications for cultural development in the Amazon Basin. In Yehudi A. Cohen (ed.), *Man in Adaptation: The Cultural Present.* Chicago: Aldine.

———. 1973. The four faces of evolution. In J. J. Honigmann (ed.), *Handbook of Social and Cultural Anthropology.* Chicago: Rand McNally.

———. 1981. The chiefdom: Precursor of the state. In Grant D. Jones and Robert R. Kautz (eds.), *The Transition to Statehood in the New World.* New York: Cambridge University Press.

———. 2003. *Evolutionism in Cultural Anthropology.* Boulder, CO: Westview Press.

Carnoy, Martin. 1984. *The State and Political Theory.* Princeton, NJ: Princeton University Press.

Cashdan, Elizabeth A. 1980. Egalitarianism among hunters and gatherers. *American Anthropologist* 82:116–120.

———. 1985. Coping with risk: Reciprocity among the Basarwa of northern Botswana. *Man* 20:454–474.

———. 1989. Hunters and gatherers: Economic behavior in bands. In Stuart Plattner (ed.), *Economic*

*Anthropology.* Stanford, CA: Stanford University Press.

Castells, Manuel. 1996. *The Information Age: Economy, Society, and Culture. Volume 1: The Rise of the Network Society.* Oxford, UK: Blackwell.

———. 1998. *The Information Age: Economy, Society, and Culture. Volume 3: End of Millennium.* Oxford, UK: Blackwell.

Cavalli-Sforza, L. L., and M. W. Feldman. 1981. *Cultural Transmission and Evolution.* Princeton, NJ: Princeton University Press.

Central Intelligence Agency. 1998. *World Factbook.* Washington, DC: CIA.

Chagnon, Napoleon A. 1983. *Yanomamö: The Fierce People* (3rd ed.). New York: Holt, Rinehart and Winston.

———. 1992. *Yanomamö: The Last Days of Eden.* San Diego: Harcourt Brace Jovanovich.

Champion, Timothy, Clive Gamble, Stephen Shennan, and Alasdair White. 1984. *Prehistoric Europe.* New York: Academic Press.

Chandler, Tertius. 1987. *Four Thousand Years of Urban Growth.* Lewiston, NY: St. David's University Press.

Chang, Kwang-chih. 1986. *The Archaeology of Ancient China* (4th ed.). New Haven, CT: Yale University Press.

Chase-Dunn, Christopher. 1975. The effects of international economic dependence on development and inequality: A cross-national study. *American Sociological Review* 40:720–738.

———. 1982. Socialist states in the capitalist world-economy. In Christopher Chase-Dunn (ed.), *Socialist States in the World-System.* Beverly Hills, CA: Sage.

——— (ed.). 1982. *Socialist States in the World-System.* Beverly Hills, CA: Sage.

———. 1989a. *Global Formation: Structures of the World-Economy.* Oxford, UK: Blackwell.

———. 1989b. *Is a world state necessary?* Paper presented at the joint meetings of the British and American International Studies Associations, London, March 24.

———. 1990. World-state formation: Historical processes and emergent necessity. *Political Geography Quarterly* 9:108–130.

———. 1998. *Global Formation: Structures of the World-Economy* (updated ed.). Lanham, MD: Rowman & Littlefield.

———. 2003. Globalization from below: Toward a collectively rational and democratic global commonwealth. In Gernot Köhler and Emilio José Chaves (eds.), *Globalization: Critical Perspectives.* New York: Nova Science.

Chase-Dunn, Christopher, and Thomas D. Hall. 1997.

*Rise and Demise: Comparing World-Systems*. Boulder, CO: Westview Press.

Chase-Dunn, Christopher, Andrew Jorgenson, Thomas Reifer, Rebecca Giem, Shoon Lio, and John Rogers. 2003. *The trajectory of the United States in the world-system: A quantitative reflection.* Paper presented at the annual meetings of the American Sociological Association, Atlanta.

Chase-Dunn, Christopher, Yukio Kawano, and Benjamin D. Brewer. 2000. Trade globalization since 1795: Waves of integration in the world-system. *American Sociological Review* 65:77–95.

Chase-Dunn, Christopher, and Kenneth O'Reilly. 1989. Core wars of the future. In Robert K. Schaeffer (ed.), *War in the World-System*. Westport, CT: Greenwood Press.

Chaudhuri, K. N. 1985. *Trade and Civilisation in the Indian Ocean*. Cambridge, UK: Cambridge University Press.

Chew, Sing C. 2001. *World Ecological Degradation: Accumulation, Urbanization, and Deforestation, 3000 B.C.–A.D. 2000*. Walnut Creek, CA: AltaMira Press.

Chew, Sing C., and Robert A. Denemark (eds.). 1996. *The Underdevelopment of Development: Essays in Honor of Andre Gunder Frank*. Thousand Oaks, CA: Sage.

Childe, V. Gordon. 1936. *Man Makes Himself*. London: Watts & Co.

_____. 1951. *Social Evolution*. London: Watts & Co.

_____. 1954. *What Happened in History*. Harmondsworth, UK: Penguin Books. (1st ed., 1942.)

Chirot, Daniel. 1977. *Social Change in the Twentieth Century*. New York: Harcourt Brace Jovanovich.

_____. 1985. The rise of the West. *American Sociological Review* 50:181–195.

_____. 1986. *Social Change in the Modern Era*. San Diego: Harcourt Brace Jovanovich.

_____ (ed.). 1989. *The Origins of Backwardness in Eastern Europe*. Berkeley: University of California Press.

_____. 1991. What happened in Eastern Europe in 1989? In Daniel Chirot (ed.), *The Crisis of Leninism and the Decline of the Left*. Seattle: University of Washington Press.

Chiswick, Barry R., and Timothy J. Hatton. 2003. International migration and the integration of labor markets. In Michael D. Bordo, Alan M. Taylor, and Jeffrey G. Williamson (eds.), *Globalization in Historical Perspective*. Chicago: University of Chicago Press.

Christian, David. 2004. *Maps of Time: An Introduction to Big History*. Berkeley: University of California Press.

Ciccantell, Paul S., and Stephen G. Bunker. 2003. *The economic ascent of China and the potential for restructuring the capitalist world-economy.* Paper presented at the annual meetings of the American Sociological Association, Atlanta.

Cipolla, Carlo M. 1993. *Before the Industrial Revolution: European Society and Economy, 1000–1700* (3rd ed.). New York: Norton.

Clark, Burton R. 1962. *Educating the Expert Society*. San Francisco: Chandler.

Clark, Robert P. 2000. *Global Life Systems: Population, Food, and Disease in the Process of Globalization*. Lanham, MD: Rowman & Littlefield.

Clarke, Adele E., Janet K. Shim, Laura Mamo, Jennifer Ruth Fosket, and Jennifer R. Fishman. 2003. Biomedicalization: Technoscientific transformations of health, illness, and U.S. biomedicine. *American Sociological Review* 68:161–194.

Clarke, William C. 1966. From extensive to intensive shifting cultivation: A succession from New Guinea. *Ethnology* 5:347–359.

Cohen, G. A. 1978. *Karl Marx's Theory of History: A Defence*. Princeton, NJ: Princeton University Press.

Cohen, Jere. 1980. Rational capitalism in Renaissance Italy. *American Journal of Sociology* 85:1340–1355.

Cohen, Mark N. 1977. *The Food Crisis in Prehistory*. New Haven, CT: Yale University Press.

_____. 1984. An introduction to the symposium. In Mark N. Cohen and George J. Armelagos (eds.), *Paleopathology at the Origins of Agriculture*. New York: Academic Press.

_____. 1985. Prehistoric hunter-gatherers: The meaning of social complexity. In T. Douglas Price and James A. Brown (eds.), *Prehistoric Hunter-Gatherers*. New York: Academic Press.

_____. 1989. *Health and the Rise of Civilization*. New Haven, CT: Yale University Press.

Cohen, Mark N., and George J. Armelagos. 1984. Paleopathology at the origins of agriculture: Editors' summation. In Mark N. Cohen and George J. Armelagos (eds.), *Paleopathology at the Origins of Agriculture*. New York: Academic Press.

Cohen, Ronald, and Elman R. Service (eds.). 1978. *Origins of the State*. Philadelphia: Institute for the Study of Human Issues.

Colchester, Marcus. 1984. Rethinking Stone Age economics: Some speculations concerning the pre-Columbian Yanoama economy. *Human Ecology* 12:291–314.

Collins, Randall. 1975. *Conflict Sociology: Toward an Explanatory Science*. New York: Academic Press.

_____. 1977. Some comparative principles of educational stratification. *Harvard Educational Review* 47:1–27.

_____. 1979. *The Credential Society: An Historical Sociology of Education and Stratification.* New York: Academic Press.

_____. 1980. Weber's last theory of capitalism: A systematization. *American Sociological Review* 45:925–942.

_____. 1986. *Weberian Sociological Theory.* New York: Cambridge University Press.

_____. 1988. *Theoretical Sociology.* San Diego: Harcourt Brace Jovanovich.

_____. 1994. *Four Sociological Traditions.* New York: Oxford University Press.

Collins, Randall, and David Waller. 1992. What theories predicted the state breakdowns and revolutions of the Soviet bloc? In Louis Kriesberg (ed.), *Research in Social Movements, Conflicts and Change* (Vol. 14). Greenwich, CT: JAI Press.

Collinwood, Dean W. (ed.) 2001. *Global Studies: Japan and the Pacific Rim* (6th ed.). Guilford, CT: McGraw-Hill/Dushkin.

Conelly, W. Thomas. 1992. Agricultural intensification in a Philippine frontier community: Impact on labor efficiency and farm diversity. *Human Ecology* 20:1–21.

Connah, Graham. 1987. *African Civilizations.* Cambridge, UK: Cambridge University Press.

Courtois, Stéphane, Nicolas Werth, Jean-Louis Panné, Andrzej Paczkowski, Karel Bartosek, and Jean Louis Margolin. 1999. *The Black Book of Communism.* Trans. Jonathan Murphy and Mark Kramer. Cambridge, MA: Harvard University Press.

Cowgill, George L. 1975. On causes and consequences of ancient and modern population changes. *American Anthropologist* 77:505–525.

Crane, George T. 1982. The Taiwanese ascent: System, state, and movement in the world-economy. In Edward Friedman (ed.), *Ascent and Decline in the World-System.* Beverly Hills, CA: Sage.

Cribb, Roger. 1991. *Nomads in Archaeology.* Cambridge, UK: Cambridge University Press.

Critchley, John. 1978. *Feudalism.* London: Allen & Unwin.

Crone, Patricia. 1989. *Pre-Industrial Societies.* Oxford, UK: Blackwell.

Cumings, Bruce, 1984. The origins and development of the northeast Asian political economy: Industrial sectors, production cycles, and political consequences. *International Organization* 38:1–40.

Curtin, Philip D. 1984. *Cross-Cultural Trade in World History.* New York: Cambridge University Press.

Dallin, Alexander, and Gail W. Lapidus (eds.). 1995.

*The Soviet System: From Crisis to Collapse* (2nd ed.). Boulder, CO: Westview Press.

Davis, Howard, and Richard Scase. 1985. *Western Capitalism and State Socialism: An Introduction.* Oxford, UK: Blackwell.

de Vries, Jan, and Ad van der Woude. 1997. *The First Modern Economy: Success, Failure, and Perseverence of the Dutch Economy, 1500–1815.* Cambridge, UK: Cambridge University Press.

Deininger, Klaus, and Lyn Squire. 1996. A new data set measuring income inequality. *World Bank Economic Review* 10:565–591.

Delacroix, Jacques, and Charles C. Ragin. 1981. Structural blockage: A cross-national study of economic dependency, state efficacy, and underdevelopment. *American Journal of Sociology* 86:1311–1347.

Diamond, Jared. 1997. *Guns, Germs, and Steel: The Fates of Human Societies.* New York: Norton.

Dixon, William J., and Terry Boswell. 1996a. Dependency, disarticulation, and denominator effects: Another look at foreign capital penetration. *American Journal of Sociology* 102:543–562.

_____. 1996b. Differential productivity, negative externalities, and foreign capital: Reply to Firebaugh. *American Journal of Sociology* 102:576–584.

Djilas, Milovan. 1957. *The New Class.* New York: Praeger.

Dobb, Maurice. 1963. *Studies in the Development of Capitalism* (rev. ed.). New York: International Publishers.

Domhoff, G. William. 1970. *The Higher Circles.* New York: Random House.

_____. 1978. *The Powers That Be: Processes of Ruling Class Domination.* New York: Random House (Vintage Books).

_____. 1983. *Who Rules America Now?* New York: Simon & Schuster (Touchstone).

_____. 1990. *The Power Elite and the State: How Policy is Made in America.* Hawthorne, NY: Aldine.

Doorenspleet, Renske. 2000. Reassessing the three waves of democratization. *World Politics* 52:384–406.

Dore, Ronald. 1976. *The Diploma Disease: Education, Qualification, and Development.* Berkeley: University of California Press.

Dos Santos, Theotonio. 1970. The structure of dependence. *American Economic Review* 60:231–236.

Duby, Georges. 1968. *Rural Economy and Country Life in the Medieval West.* Trans. Cynthia Postan. Columbia: University of South Carolina Press.

Durham, William H. 1991. *Coevolution: Genes, Culture,*

*and Human Diversity*. Stanford, CA: Stanford University Press.

Earle, Timothy. 1997. *How Chiefs Come to Power: The Political Economy in Prehistory*. Stanford, CA: Stanford University Press.

_____. (ed.). 1991. *Chiefdoms: Power, Economy, and Ideology*. New York: Cambridge University Press.

Eckstein, Susan. 1986. The impact of the Cuban revolution: A comparative perspective. *Comparative Studies in Society and History* 28:502–534.

*Economist, The*. 2000. 355(8165), April 8.

Ekholm, Kajsa, and Jonathan Friedman. 1982. "Capital" imperialism and exploitation in ancient world-systems. *Review* 4:87–109.

Elster, Jon. 1985. *Making Sense of Marx*. Cambridge, UK: Cambridge University Press.

Elvin, Mark. 1973. *The Pattern of the Chinese Past*. Stanford, CA: Stanford University Press.

Ember, Carol. 1978. Myths about hunter-gatherers. *Ethnology* 17:439–448.

Engels, Friedrich. 1963. Speech at the graveside of Karl Marx. In Howard Selsam and Harry Martel (eds.), *Reader in Marxist Philosophy*. New York: International Publishers. (Originally given 1883.)

_____. 1973. *The Condition of the Working Class in England*. Moscow: Progress Publishers. (Originally published 1845.)

Ericson, Richard E. 1995. The Russian economy since independence. In Gail W. Lapidus (ed.), *The New Russia: Troubled Transformation*. Boulder, CO: Westview Press.

Erikson, Robert, and John H. Goldthorpe. 1993. *The Constant Flux: A Study of Class Mobility in Industrial Societies*. Oxford, UK: Oxford University Press (Clarendon Press).

Esping-Andersen, Gøsta. 1990. *The Three Worlds of Welfare Capitalism*. Princeton, NJ: Princeton University Press.

Evans, Peter B. 1979. *Dependent Development: The Alliance of Multinational, State, and Local Capital in Brazil*. Princeton, NJ: Princeton University Press.

_____. 1987. Class, state, and dependence in east Asia: Lessons for Latin Americanists. In Frederic C. Deyo (ed.), *The Political Economy of the New Asian Industrialism*. Ithaca, NY: Cornell University Press.

Evans, Peter B., Dietrich Rueschemeyer, and Theda Skocpol (eds.). 1985. *Bringing the State Back In*. New York: Cambridge University Press.

Evans-Pritchard, E. E. 1940. *The Nuer*. Oxford, UK: Oxford University Press (Clarendon Press).

Eyal, Gil. 2003. *The Origins of Postcommunist Elites: From Prague Spring to the Breakup of Czechoslovakia*. Minneapolis: University of Minnesota Press.

Fagan, Brian M. 1989. *People of the Earth: An Introduction to World Prehistory* (6th ed.). Glenview, IL: Scott, Foresman.

Featherman, David L., and Robert M. Hauser. 1978. *Opportunity and Change*. New York: Academic Press.

Fiedel, Stuart J. 1987. *Prehistory of the Americas*. New York: Cambridge University Press.

Firebaugh, Glenn. 1992. Growth effects of foreign and domestic investment. *American Journal of Sociology* 98:105–130.

_____. 1996. Does foreign capital harm poor nations? New estimates based on Dixon and Boswell's measures of capital penetration. *American Journal of Sociology* 102:563–575.

_____. 1999. Empirics of world income inequality. *American Journal of Sociology* 104:1597–1630.

_____. 2000. The trend in between-nation income inequality. *Annual Review of Sociology* 26:323–339.

_____. 2003. *The New Geography of Global Income Inequality*. Cambridge, MA: Harvard University Press.

Flannery, Kent V. 1973. The origins of agriculture. *Annual Review of Anthropology* 2:271–310.

Flora, Peter. 1983. *State, Economy, and Society in Western Europe, 1815–1975* (Vol. 1). Frankfurt: Campus Verlag.

Folger, J. K., and C. B. Nam. 1964. Trends in education in relation to the occupational structure. *Sociology of Education* 38:19–33.

*Fortune Magazine*. 1998. Fortune's Global 500: The world's largest corporations. *Fortune* 138(5).

Fossier, Robert. 1988. *Peasant Life in the Medieval West*. Trans. Juliet Vale. Oxford, UK: Blackwell.

Frank, Andre Gunder. 1966. The development of underdevelopment. *Monthly Review* 18(4):17–31.

_____. 1967. Sociology of development and underdevelopment of sociology. *Catalyst* 3:20–73.

_____. 1969. *Capitalism and Underdevelopment in Latin America*. New York: Monthly Review Press.

_____. 1978. *World Accumulation, 1492–1789*. New York: Monthly Review Press.

_____. 1979. *Dependent Accumulation and Underdevelopment*. New York: Monthly Review Press.

_____. 1980. *Crisis: in the World Economy*. New York: Holmes & Meier.

_____. 1981. *Crisis: in the Third World*. New York: Holmes & Meier.

_____. 1990. A theoretical introduction to 5,000 years of world system history. *Review* 13:155–248.

_____. 1991. A plea for world system history. *Journal of World History* 2:1–28.

_____. 1998. *ReOrient: Global Economy in the Asian Age*. Berkeley: University of California Press.

_____. 2003. Asian meltdown or startup? In Gernot

Köhler and Emilio José Chaves (eds.), *Globalization: Critical Perspectives*. New York: Nova Science.

Frank, Andre Gunder, and Barry K. Gills (eds.). 1993. *The World System: Five Hundred Years or Five Thousand?* London: Routledge.

Freedom House Survey Team. 2003. *Freedom in the World: The Annual Review of Political Rights and Civil Liberties, 2003*. New York: Freedom House.

Freeman, Richard B. 1976. *The Overeducated American*. New York: Academic Press.

Fried, Morton H. 1967. *The Evolution of Political Society*. New York: Random House.

Fröbel, Folker, Jürgen Heinrichs, and Otto Kreye. 1980. *The New International Division of Labour*. Cambridge: Cambridge University Press.

Fukuyama, Francis. 1992. *The End of History and the Last Man*. New York: Free Press.

Galtung, Johan, Tore Heiestad, and Erik Rudeng. 1980. On the decline and fall of empires: The Roman Empire and Western imperialism compared. *Review* 4:91–153.

Gardner, Peter. 1991. Foragers' pursuit of individual autonomy. *Current Anthropology* 32:543–572.

Gastil, Raymond D. 1978. *Freedom in the World*. Boston: G. K. Hall.

_____. 1989. *Freedom in the World: Political Rights and Civil Liberties, 1988–89*. New York: Freedom House.

Geertz, Clifford. 1963. *Agricultural Involution: The Processes of Ecological Change in Indonesia*. Berkeley: University of California Press.

Gereffi, Gary, and Donald L. Wyman (eds.). 1990. *Manufacturing Miracles: Paths of Industrialization in Latin America and East Asia*. Princeton, NJ: Princeton University Press.

Gershenkron, Alexander. 1962. *Economic Backwardness in Historical Perspective*. Cambridge, MA: Harvard University Press.

Gibbs, James L., Jr. 1965. The Kpelle of Liberia. In James L. Gibbs, Jr. (ed.), *Peoples of Africa*. New York: Holt, Rinehart and Winston.

Gibson, Campbell J., and Emily Lennon. 1999. Historical census statistics on the foreign-born population of the United States: 1850–1990. U.S. Census Bureau, Population Division, Working Paper No. 29. Washington, DC: U.S. Census Bureau.

Giddens, Anthony. 1973. *The Class Structure of the Advanced Societies*. New York: Harper & Row.

_____. 1980. *The Class Structure of the Advanced Societies* (2nd ed.). London: Hutchinson.

_____. 1990. *The Consequences of Modernity*. Stanford, CA: Stanford University Press.

_____. 2002. *Runaway World: How Globalization Is Reshaping Our Lives* (rev. ed.). London: Routledge.

Giddens, Anthony, and David Held (eds.). 1982. *Classes, Power, and Conflict: Classical and Contemporary Debates*. Berkeley: University of California Press.

Gilbert, D., and J. Kahl. 1993. *The American Class Structure* (4th ed.). Belmont, CA: Wadsworth.

Gills, Barry K., and Andre Gunder Frank. 1991. 5000 years of world system history: The cumulation of accumulation. In Christopher Chase-Dunn and Thomas D. Hall (eds.), *Core/Periphery Relations in Precapitalist Worlds*. Boulder, CO: Westview Press.

_____. 1992. World system cycles, crises, and hegemonial shifts, 1700 B.C. to 1700 A.D. *Review* 15:621–687.

Goesling, Brian. 2001. Changing income inequalities within and between nations: New evidence. *American Sociological Review* 66:745–761.

Goldfrank, Walter L. 1983. The limits of analogy: Hegemonic decline in Great Britain and the United States. In Albert Bergesen (ed.), *Crises in the World-System*. Beverly Hills, CA: Sage.

Goldman, Minton F. (ed.). 2001. *Global Studies: Russia, the Eurasian Republics, and Central/Eastern Europe* (8th ed.). Guilford, CT: McGraw-Hill/Dushkin.

Goldschmidt, Walter. 1959. *Man's Way: A Preface to the Understanding of Human Society*. New York: Holt.

Goldstein, Joshua S. 1988. *Long Cycles: Prosperity and War in the Modern Age*. New Haven. CT: Yale University Press.

Goldstein, Melvyn, and Cynthia Beall. 1989. *Nomads of Western Tibet*. Berkeley: University of California Press.

Goldstone, Jack. 1991. *Revolution and Rebellion in the Early Modern World*. Berkeley: University of California Press.

Goldthorpe, John H. 1980. *Social Mobility and Class Structure in Modern Britain*. Oxford: Oxford University Press (Clarendon Press).

Good, Kenneth. 1993. *Foraging and farming among the Yanomami: Can you have one without the other?* Paper presented at the 7th International Conference on Hunting and Gathering Societies, Moscow.

Goodwin, Paul B. (ed.). 2000. *Global Studies: Latin America* (9th ed.). Guilford, CT: McGraw-Hill/Dushkin.

Goody, Jack. 1996. *The East in the West*. Cambridge, UK: Cambridge University Press.

Gorin, Zeev. 1985. Socialist societies and world system theory: A critical survey. *Science and Society* 49:332–366.

Granovetter, Mark. 1979. The idea of "advancement" in theories of social evolution and development. *American Journal of Sociology* 85:489–515.

Green, Daniel M. 1999. Liberal moments and democracy's durability: Comparing global outbreaks of democracy—1918, 1945, 1989. *Studies in Comparative International Development* 34:83–120.

Gross, Michael. 1999. *Travels to the Nanoworld*. New York: Plenum.

Haas, Jonathan. 1982. *The Evolution of the Prehistoric State*. New York: Columbia University Press.

Haggard, Stephan. 1990. *Pathways from the Periphery: The Politics of Growth in the Newly Industrializing Countries*. Ithaca, NY: Cornell University Press.

Hahn, Gordon M. 2002. *Russia's Revolution from Above*. New Brunswick, NJ: Transaction Publishers.

Hall, John A. 1985. *Powers and Liberties: The Causes and Consequences of the Rise of the West*. Berkeley: University of California Press.

Hall, John Whitney. 1970. *Japan: From Prehistory to Modern Times*. New York: Delacorte Press.

Halliday, Jon. 1975. *A Political History of Japanese Capitalism*. New York: Monthly Review Press.

Hallpike, C. R. 1986. *The Principles of Social Evolution*. Oxford, UK: Clarendon Press.

Handwerker, W. Penn. 1986. The modern demographic transition: An analysis of subsistence choices and reproductive consequences. *American Anthropologist* 88:400–417.

Hane, Mikiso. 1992. *Modern Japan: A Historical Survey* (2nd ed.). Boulder, CO: Westview Press.

Hanley, Susan B., and Kozo Yamamura. 1972. Population trends and economic growth in pre-industrial Japan. In D.V. Glass and Roger Revelle (eds.), *Population and Social Change*. London: Edward Arnold.

Harner, Michael J. 1970. Population pressure and the social evolution of agriculturalists. *Southwestern Journal of Anthropology* 26:67–86.

_____. 1975. Scarcity, the factors of production, and social evolution. In Steven Polgar (ed.), *Population, Ecology, and Social Evolution*. The Hague: Mouton.

Harris, David R. 1977. Alternative pathways toward agriculture. In Charles A. Reed (ed.), *Origins of Agriculture*. The Hague: Mouton.

Harris, Marvin. 1964. *Patterns of Race in the Americas*. New York: Norton.

_____. 1968. *The Rise of Anthropological Theory*. New York: Crowell.

_____. 1971. *Culture, Man, and Nature: An Introduction to General Anthropology*. New York: Crowell.

_____. 1974. *Cows, Pigs, Wars, and Witches: The Riddles of Culture*. New York: Random House.

_____. 1975. *Culture, People, Nature: An Introduction to General Anthropology* (2nd ed.). New York: Crowell.

_____. 1977. *Cannibals and Kings: The Origins of Cultures*. New York: Random House.

_____. 1979. *Cultural Materialism: The Struggle for a Science of Culture*. New York: Random House.

_____. 1980. *Culture, People, Nature: An Introduction to General Anthropology* (3rd ed.). New York: Harper & Row.

_____. 1981. *America Now: The Anthropology of a Changing Culture*. New York: Simon & Schuster.

_____. 1985a. *Good to Eat: Riddles of Food and Culture*. New York: Simon & Schuster.

_____. 1985b. *Culture, People, Nature: An Introduction to General Anthropology* (4th ed.). New York: Harper & Row.

_____. 1989. *Our Kind*. New York: Harper & Row.

Harris, Marvin, and Eric B. Ross. 1987. *Death, Sex and Fertility: Population Regulation in Preindustrial and Developing Societies*. New York: Columbia University Press.

Harvey, David. 1989. *The Condition of Postmodernity*. Oxford, UK: Blackwell.

Hassig, Ross. 1985. *Trade, Tribute, and Transportation: The Sixteenth-Century Political Economy of the Valley of Mexico*. Norman: University of Oklahoma Press.

Hatch, Elvin. 1983. *Culture and Morality: The Relativity of Values in Anthropology*. New York: Columbia University Press.

Hatton, Timothy J., and Jeffrey G. Williamson. 1998. *The Age of Mass Migration: Causes and Economic Impact*. New York: Oxford University Press.

Hawkes, Kristen, and James F. O'Connell. 1985. Optimal foraging models and the case of the !Kung. *American Anthropologist* 87:401–405.

Hayden, Brian. 1981. Research and development in the Stone Age: Technological transitions among hunter-gatherers. *Current Anthropology* 22:519–548.

_____. 1992. Models of domestication. In Anne B. Gebauer and T. Douglas Price (eds.), *Transitions to Agriculture in Prehistory*. Madison, WI: Prehistory Press.

Hegel, Georg Wilhelm Friedrich. 1953. *Reason in History*. Trans. Robert S. Hartman. New York: Liberal Arts Press. (Originally published 1837.)

_____. 1956. *The Philosophy of History*. Trans. J. Sibree. New York: Dover. (Originally published 1830–31.)

Heilbroner, Robert. 1972. *The Making of Economic Society* (4th ed.). Englewood Cliffs, NJ: Prentice-Hall.

_____. 1980. *An Inquiry into the Human Prospect*. New York: Norton.

_____. 1985. *The Making of Economic Society* (7th ed.). Englewood Cliffs, NJ: Prentice-Hall.

Held, David, and Anthony McGrew. 2002. *Globalization/Anti-Globalization*. Cambridge, UK: Polity Press.

Held, David, Anthony McGrew, David Goldblatt, and Jonathan Perraton. 1999. *Global Transformations: Politics, Economics, and Culture*. Stanford, CA: Stanford University Press.

Henry, Donald O. 1989. *From Foraging to Agriculture: The Levant at the End of the Ice Age*. Philadelphia: University of Pennsylvania Press.

Hill, Kim, Hillard Kaplan, Kristen Hawkes, and Ana Magdelena Hurtado. 1985. Men's time allocation to subsistence work among the Aché of eastern Paraguay. *Human Ecology* 13:29–47.

Hilton, Rodney (ed.). 1976. *The Transition from Feudalism to Capitalism*. London: New Left Books.

Hobsbawm, Eric J. 1968. *Industry and Empire*. New York: Pantheon.

_____. 1991. Goodbye to all that. In Robin Blackburn (ed.), *After the Fall: The Failure of Communism and the Future of Socialism*. London: Verso.

Hodges, Richard. 1988. *Primitive and Peasant Markets*. Oxford, UK: Blackwell.

Hogbin, H. Ian. 1964. *A Guadalcanal Society: The Kaoka Speakers*. New York: Holt, Rinehart and Winston.

Hole, Frank. 1977. *Studies in the Archaeological History of the Deh Luran Plain*. Ann Arbor: University of Michigan Museum of Anthropology, Memoir No. 9.

Holton, Robert J. 1985. *The Transition from Feudalism to Capitalism*. New York: St. Martin's Press.

Hoogvelt, Ankie M. M. 1982. *The Third World in Global Development*. London: Macmillan.

_____. 1997. *Globalization and the Postcolonial World*. Baltimore, MD: Johns Hopkins University Press.

Hopkins, Terence K., Immanuel Wallerstein, and associates. 1982. Patterns of development of the modern world-system. In Terence K. Hopkins, Immanuel Wallerstein, and associates (eds.), *World-Systems Analysis: Theory and Methodology*. Beverly Hills, CA: Sage.

Hornik, Richard. 1994. Bursting China's bubble. *Foreign Affairs* 73(3):28–42.

Hrdy, Sarah Blaffer. 1999. *Mother Nature: A History of Mothers, Infants, and Natural Selection*. New York: Pantheon.

Huber, Evelyne, and John D. Stephens. 2001. *Development and Crisis of the Welfare State: Parties and Politics in Global Markets*. Chicago: University of Chicago Press.

International Organization for Migration. 2003. *World Migration Report 2003*. Geneva: International Organization for Migration.

International Telecommunications Union. 2002. *Yearbook of Statistics: Chronological Time Series 1992–2001*. Geneva: International Telecommunications Union.

Israel, Jonathan I. 1989. *Dutch Primacy in World Trade, 1585–1740*. Oxford, UK: Oxford University Press (Clarendon Press).

James, Harold. 2001. *The End of Globalization: Lessons from the Great Depression*. Cambridge, MA: Harvard University Press.

Jannetta, Ann Bowman. 1987. *Epidemics and Mortality in Early Modern Japan*. Princeton, NJ: Princeton University Press.

Johansen, J. H., H. W. Collins, and J. A. Johnson. 1986. *American Education* (5th ed.). Dubuque, IA: Wm. C. Brown.

Johnson, Allen W., and Timothy Earle. 1987. *The Evolution of Human Societies: From Foraging Group to Agrarian State*. Stanford, CA: Stanford University Press.

Jones, E. L. 1987. *The European Miracle* (2nd ed.). Cambridge, UK: Oxford University Press (Clarendon Press).

_____. 1988. *Growth Recurring: Economic Change in World History*. Oxford, UK: Clarendon Press.

_____. 2000. *The Evolution of Human Societies: From Foraging Group to Agrarian State* (2nd ed.). Stanford, CA: Stanford University Press.

Jowitt, Kenneth. 1978. *The Leninist Response to National Dependency*. Berkeley: Institute of International Studies.

_____. 1992. *New World Disorder: The Leninist Extinction*. Berkeley: University of California Press.

Kaneda, Tatsuo. 1988. Gorbachev's economic reforms. In P. Juviler and H. Kimura (eds.), *Gorbachev's Reforms*. New York: Aldine.

Kaplan, Hilliard S. 1994. Evolutionary and wealth-flows theories of fertility: Empirical tests and new models. *Population and Development Review* 20:753–791.

_____. 1996. A theory of fertility and parental investment in traditional and modern human societies. *Yearbook of Physical Anthropology* 39:91-135.

Kaplan, Hilliard S., and Kim Hill. 1992. The evolutionary ecology of food acquisition. In Eric Alden Smith and Bruce Winterhalder (eds.), *Evolutionary Ecology and Human Behavior*. New York: Aldine.

Kaplan, Robert D. 2000. *The Coming Anarchy: Shattering the Dreams of the Post Cold War.* New York: Random House (Vintage).

Kargarlitsky, Boris. 2002. *Russia Under Yeltsin and Putin.* London: Pluto Press.

Kautsky, John H. 2002. *Social Democracy and the Aristocracy.* New Brunswick, NJ: Transaction Publishers.

Keister, Lisa. 2000a. *Wealth in America: Trends in Wealth Inequality.* New York: Cambridge University Press.

_____. 2000b. *Chinese Business Groups.* New York: Oxford University Press.

_____. 2004. Wealth inequality. In James Ciment (ed.), *Social Issues: An Encyclopedia of Controversy, History, and Debates.* Armonk, NY: M. E. Sharpe.

Keister, Lisa, and Stephanie Moller. 2000. Wealth inequality in the United States. *Annual Review of Sociology* 26:63–81.

Kelly, Robert L. 1995. *The Foraging Spectrum: Diversity in Hunter-Gatherer Lifeways.* Washington, DC: Smithsonian Institution Press.

Kennedy, Paul. 1993. *Preparing for the Twenty-first Century.* New York: Random House.

Keynes, John Maynard. 1920. *The Economic Consequences of the Peace.* New York: Harcourt, Brace and Howe.

Kiljunen, Kimmo. 2003. Global governance. In Gernot Köhler and Emilio José Chaves (eds.), *Globalization: Critical Perspectives.* New York: Nova Science.

Kingston, Paul W. 2000. *The Classless Society.* Stanford, CA: Stanford University Press.

Kirch, Patrick Vinton. 1984. *The Evolution of the Polynesian Chiefdoms.* New York: Cambridge University Press.

Kitamura, Kazuyuki. 1991. The future of Japanese higher education. In Edward R. Beauchamp (ed.), *Windows on Japanese Education.* Westport, CT: Greenwood Press.

Klein, Richard G. 1999. *The Human Career: Human Biological and Cultural Origins* (2nd ed.). Chicago: University of Chicago Press.

Kohl, Philip L. 1978. The balance of trade in southwestern Asia in the mid-third millennium. *Current Anthropology* 19:463–492.

_____. 1989. The use and abuse of world-systems theory: The case of the "pristine" west Asian state. In C. C. Lamberg-Karlovsky (ed.), *Archaeological Thought in America.* Cambridge, UK: Cambridge University Press.

Kohlberg, Lawrence. 1971. From is to ought: How to commit the naturalistic fallacy and get away with it in the study of moral development. In

Theodore Mischel (ed.), *Cognitive Development and Epistemology.* New York: Academic Press.

Köhler, Gernot, and Emilio José Chaves (eds.). 2003. *Globalization: Critical Perspectives.* New York: Nova Science.

Kolko, Gabriel. 1962. *Wealth and Power in America.* New York: Praeger.

Kondratieff, Nikolai. 1984. *The Long Wave Cycle.* New York: Richardson and Snyder. (Originally published 1928.)

Koo, Hagen. 1987. The interplay of state, social class, and world system in east Asian development: The cases of South Korea and Taiwan. In Frederic C. Deyo (ed.), *The Political Economy of the New Asian Industrialism.* Ithaca, NY: Cornell University Press.

Kornai, János. 1992. *The Socialist System: The Political Economy of Communism.* Princeton, NJ: Princeton University Press.

Korzeniewicz, Roberto P., and Timothy P. Moran. 1997. World-economic trends in the distribution of income, 1965–1992. *American Journal of Sociology* 102:1000–1039.

Krader, Lawrence. 1963. *Social Organization of the Mongol-Turkic Pastoral Nomads.* The Hague: Mouton.

Kriedte, Peter. 1983. *Peasants, Landlords and Merchant Capitalists: Europe and the World Economy, 1500–1800.* Cambridge, UK: Cambridge University Press.

Kumar, Krishan. 1988. *The Rise of Modern Society: Aspects of the Social and Political Development of the West.* Oxford, UK: Blackwell.

_____. 1992. The revolutions of 1989: Socialism, capitalism, and democracy. *Theory and Society* 21:309–356.

_____. 1995. *From Post-Industrial to Post-Modern Society: New Theories of the Contemporary World.* Oxford, UK: Blackwell.

_____. 2001. *1989: Revolutionary Ideas and Ideals.* Minneapolis: University of Minnesota Press.

Kurzman, Charles. 1998. Waves of democratization. *Studies in Comparative International Development* 33:42–64.

Kushnirsky, F. I. 1988. Soviet economic reform: An analysis and a model. In S. Linz and W. Moskoff (eds.), *Reorganization and Reform in the Soviet Economy.* Armonk, NY: M. E. Sharpe.

Lancaster, William. 1981. *The Rwala Bedouin Today.* Cambridge, UK: Cambridge University Press.

Landes, David S. 1969. *The Unbound Prometheus: Technological Change and Industrial Development in Western Europe from 1750 to the Present.* New York: Cambridge University Press.

_____. 1998. *The Wealth and Poverty of Nations*. New York: Norton.

Lane, David. 1985. *Soviet Economy and Society*. Oxford, UK: Blackwell.

Langton, John. 1979. Darwinism and the behavioral theory of sociocultural evolution: An analysis. *American Journal of Sociology* 85:288–309.

Lapidus, Gail W. 1988. Gorbachev's agenda: Domestic reforms and foreign policy reassessments. In P. Juviler and H. Kimura (eds.), *Gorbachev's Reforms*. Hawthorne, NY: Aldine.

_____ (ed.). 1995. *The New Russia: Troubled Transformation*. Boulder, CO: Westview Press.

Larrain, Jorge. 1989. *Theories of Development*. Cambridge, UK: Polity Press.

Le Goff, Jacques. 1988. *Medieval Civilization, 400–1500*. Trans. Julia Barrow. Oxford, UK: Blackwell.

Lee, Richard B. 1968. What hunters do for a living, or, how to make out on scarce resources. In Richard B. Lee and Irven DeVore (eds.), *Man the Hunter*. Chicago: Aldine.

_____. 1972. The !Kung bushmen of Botswana. In M. G. Bicchieri (ed.), *Hunters and Gatherers Today*. New York: Holt, Rinehart and Winston.

_____. 1978. Politics, sexual and nonsexual, in an egalitarian society. *Social Science Information* 17:871–895.

_____. 1979. *The !Kung San: Men, Women, and Work in a Foraging Society*. New York: Cambridge University Press.

_____. 1984. *The Dobe !Kung*. New York: Holt, Rinehart and Winston.

Leggett, Robert E. 1988. Gorbachev's reform program: "Radical" or more of the same? In S. Linz and W. Moskoff (eds.), *Reorganization and Reform in the Soviet Economy*. Armonk, NY: M. E. Sharpe.

Lenski, Gerhard E. 1966. *Power and Privilege: A Theory of Social Stratification*. New York: McGraw-Hill.

_____. 1970. *Human Societies: A Macro-level Introduction to Sociology*. New York: McGraw-Hill.

Lenski, Gerhard, and Patrick Nolan. 1984. Trajectories of development: A test of ecological-evolutionary theory. *Social Forces* 63:1–23.

Leupp, Gary P. 1992. *Servants, Shophands, and Laborers in the Cities of Tokugawa Japan*. Princeton, NJ: Princeton University Press.

Leys, Colin. 1982. African economic development in theory and practice. *Daedalus* 111(2):99–124.

Livi-Bacci, Massimo. 1992. *A Concise History of World Population*. Trans. Carl Ipsen. Oxford: Blackwell.

Lollock, Lisa. 2001. *The Foreign Born Population of the United States: March 2000. Current Population Reports, P20-535*. Washington, DC: U.S. Census Bureau.

Lomborg, Bjørn. 2001. *The Skeptical Environmentalist: Measuring the Real State of the World*. Cambridge, UK: Cambridge University Press.

Lopez, Robert S. 1971. *The Commercial Revolution of the Middle Ages, 950–1350*. Englewood Cliffs, NJ: Prentice-Hall.

Low, Bobbi S. 1991. Reproductive life in nineteenth century Sweden: An evolutionary perspective on demographic phenomena. *Ethology and Sociobiology* 12:411–448.

_____. 1993. Ecological demography: A synthetic focus in evolutionary anthropology. *Evolutionary Anthropology* 1:177–187.

Lumsden, Charles J., and Edward O. Wilson. 1981. *Genes, Mind, and Culture: The Coevolutionary Process*. Cambridge, MA: Harvard University Press.

Lyotard, Jean-Francois. 1985. *The Postmodern Condition*. Minneapolis: University of Minnesota Press.

McCorriston, Joy, and Frank Hole. 1991. The ecology of seasonal stress and the origins of agriculture in the Near East. *American Anthropologist* 93:46–69.

McMichael, Philip. 2004. *Development and Social Change: A Global Perspective* (3rd ed.). Thousand Oaks, CA: Pine Forge Press.

McNeill, William H. 1976. *Plagues and Peoples*. Garden City, NY: Doubleday (Anchor Books).

_____. 1982. *The Pursuit of Power: Technology, Armed Force, and Society Since A.D. 1000*. Chicago: University of Chicago Press.

MacNeish, Richard. 1978. *The Science of Archaeology*. North Scituate, MA: Duxbury Press.

Mahoney, James. 2003. Long-run development and the legacy of colonialism in Spanish America. *American Journal of Sociology* 109:50–106.

Mair, Lucy. 1964. *Primitive Government*. Baltimore: Penguin Books.

_____. 1974. *African Societies*. Cambridge, UK: Cambridge University Press.

Mandel, Ernest. 1989. *Beyond Perestroika: The Future of Gorbachev's USSR*. Trans. Gus Fagan. London: Verso.

Mann, Michael. 1986. *The Sources of Social Power. Volume 1: A History of Power from the Beginning to A.D. 1760*. Cambridge, UK: Cambridge University Press.

_____. 1988. *States, War and Capitalism*. Oxford, UK: Blackwell.

Markoff, John. 1996. *Waves of Democracy*. Thousand Oaks, CA: Pine Forge Press.

Marx, Karl. 1963. *Karl Marx: Early Writings*. Tom Bottomore (ed.). New York: McGraw-Hill. (Originally written 1843–1844.)

_____. 1967. *Capital* (Vol. 1). New York: International Publishers. (Originally published 1867.)

_____. 1978. The eighteenth brumaire of Louis Bonaparte. In Robert C. Tucker (ed.), *The Marx-Engels Reader* (2nd ed.). New York: Norton. (Originally published 1852.)

_____. 1979. Letter to Engels. In Saul K. Padover (ed.), *The Letters of Karl Marx*. Englewood Cliffs, NJ: Prentice-Hall. (Originally written June 18, 1862.)

Marx, Karl, and Friedrich Engels. 1978. Manifesto of the Communist party. In Robert C. Tucker (ed.), *The Marx-Engels Reader* (2nd ed.). New York: Norton. (Originally published 1848.)

_____. 1970. *The German Ideology*. C. J. Arthur (ed.). New York: International Publishers. (Originally written 1846.)

Maryanski, Alexandra, and Jonathan H. Turner. 1992. *The Social Cage: Human Nature and the Evolution of Society*. Stanford, CA: Stanford University Press.

Meadows, Donella H., Dennis L. Meadows, and Jørgen Randers. 1992. *Beyond the Limits*. Post Mills, VT: Chelsea Green.

Meadows, Donella H., Dennis L. Meadows, Jørgen Randers, and William W. Behrens III. 1972. *The Limits to Growth*. New York: Universe Books.

Mellars, Paul A. 1985. The ecological basis of social complexity in the Upper Paleolithic of southwestern France. In T. Douglas Price and James A. Brown (eds.), *Prehistoric Hunter-Gatherers*. New York: Academic Press.

Meyer, John W., John Boli, George M. Thomas, and Francisco O. Ramirez. 1997. World society and the nation-state. *American Journal of Sociology* 103:144–181.

Meyer, John W., Francisco O. Ramirez, Richard Rubinson, and John Boli-Bennett. 1977. The world educational revolution, 1950–1970. *Sociology of Education* 50:242–258.

Meyer, John W., David Tyack, Joane Nagel, and Audri Gordon. 1979. Public education as nation-building in America: Enrollments and bureaucratization in the American states, 1870–1930. *American Journal of Sociology* 85:591–613.

Milisauskas, Sarunas. 1978. *European Prehistory*. New York: Academic Press.

Minge-Klevana, Wanda. 1980. Does labor time decrease with industrialization? A survey of time-allocation studies. *Current Anthropology* 21:279–298.

Modelski, George, and William R. Thompson. 1996. *Leading Sectors and World Powers*. Columbia: University of South Carolina Press.

Moller, Stephanie, David Bradley, Evelyne Huber, François Nielsen, and John D. Stephens. 2003. Determinants of relative poverty in advanced capitalist democracies. *American Sociological Review* 68:22–51.

Moore, Barrington, Jr. 1966. *Social Origins of Dictatorship and Democracy*. Boston: Beacon Press.

Morgan, David. 1987. *The Mongols*. Oxford, UK: Blackwell.

Morgan, Lewis Henry. 1974. *Ancient Society, or Researches in the Lines of Human Progress from Savagery through Barbarism to Civilization*. Gloucester, MA: Peter Smith. (Originally published 1877.)

Moseley, K. P., and Immanuel Wallerstein. 1978. Precapitalist social structures. *Annual Review of Sociology* 4:259–290.

Moulder, Frances V. 1977. *Japan, China and the Modern World Economy*. New York: Cambridge University Press.

Mulhall, Douglas. 2002. *Our Molecular Future: How Nanotechnology, Robotics, Genetics, and Artificial Intelligence Will Transform Our World*. Amherst, NY: Prometheus Books.

Murdock, George Peter. 1967. *Ethnographic Atlas*. Pittsburgh: University of Pittsburgh Press.

Murphy, Raymond. 1988. *Social Closure: The Theory of Monopolization and Exclusion*. Oxford, UK: Clarendon Press.

Murthi, Mamta, Anne-Catherine Guio, and Jean Dreze. 1995. Mortality, fertility, and gender bias in India: A district-level analysis. *Population and Development Review* 21:745–782.

Nag, Moni, Benjamin N. F. White, and R. Creighton Peet. 1978. An anthropological approach to the study of the economic value of children in Java and Nepal. *Current Anthropology* 19:293–306.

National Center for Education Statistics. 2001. *Digest of Educational Statistics 2000*. Washington, DC: U.S. Department of Education.

National Research Council. 2000. *Beyond Six Billion: Forecasting the World's Population*. Washington, DC: National Academy Press.

Nef, John U. 1964. *The Conquest of the Material World*. Chicago: University of Chicago Press.

North, Douglass C., and Robert Paul Thomas. 1973. *The Rise of the Western World: A New Economic History*. New York: Cambridge University Press.

Norton, James H. K. (ed.). 2001. *Global Studies: India and South Asia* (5th ed.). Guilford, CT: McGraw-Hill/Dushkin.

Nove, Alec. 1989. *Glasnost in Action: Cultural Renaissance in Russia*. London: Unwin Hyman.

Oates, Joan. 1978. Comment on "The balance of trade in southwestern Asia in the mid-third millennium." *Current Anthropology* 19:480–481.

Obstfeld, Maurice, and Alan M. Taylor. 2003. Globalization and capital markets. In Michael D. Bordo, Alan M. Taylor, and Jeffrey G. Williamson (eds.) *Globalization in Historical Perspective.* Chicago: University of Chicago Press.

O'Donnell, Guillermo. 1973. *Modernization and Bureaucratic Authoritarianism.* Berkeley: University of California Institute of International Studies.

Office of Management and the Budget. 1973. *Social Indicators 1973.* Washington, DC: U.S. Government Printing Office.

Oliver, Douglas. 1955. *A Solomon Island Society: Kinship and Leadership among the Siuai of Bougainville.* Cambridge, MA: Harvard University Press.

O'Rourke, Kevin H., and Jeffrey G. Williamson. 1999. *Globalization and History: The Evolution of a Nineteenth-Century Atlantic Economy.* Cambridge, MA: MIT Press.

Parkin, Frank. 1971. *Class Inequality and Political Order: Social Stratification in Capitalist and Communist Societies.* New York: Holt, Rinehart and Winston.

_____. 1979. *Marxism and Class Theory: A Bourgeois Critique.* New York: Columbia University Press.

Parsons, Talcott. 1966. *Societies: Evolutionary and Comparative Perspectives.* Englewood Cliffs, NJ: Prentice-Hall.

_____. 1971. *The System of Modern Societies.* Englewood Cliffs, NJ: Prentice-Hall.

Patterson, Orlando. 1977. *Ethnic Chauvinism: The Reactionary Impulse.* New York: Stein and Day.

Pearson, M. N. 1991. Merchants and states. In James D. Tracy (ed.), *The Political Economy of Merchant Empires.* New York: Cambridge University Press.

Penn, Dustin. 1999. *Why do empowered women have fewer offspring?* Paper presented at the annual meetings of the Human Behavior and Evolution Society, University of Utah, Salt Lake City.

Petras, James. 1987. The anatomy of state terror: Chile, El Salvador and Brazil. *Science and Society* 51:314–338.

Phillipson, David W. 1985. *African Archaeology.* Cambridge, UK: Cambridge University Press.

Plattner, Stuart (ed.). 1989. *Economic Anthropology.* Stanford, CA: Stanford University Press.

Pomeranz, Kenneth. 2000. *The Great Divergence: China, Europe, and the Making of the Modern World Economy.* Princeton, NJ: Princeton University Press.

Popkin, Samuel L. 1979. *The Rational Peasant.* Berkeley: University of California Press.

Possehl, Gregory L. 1990. Revolution in the Urban Revolution: The emergence of Indus urbanization. *Annual Review of Anthropology* 19:261–282.

Price, T. Douglas, and James A. Brown (eds.). 1985. *Prehistoric Hunter-Gatherers.* San Diego: Academic Press.

Ramsay, E. Jeffress (ed.). 2001. *Global Studies: Africa* (9th ed.). Guilford, CT: McGraw-Hill/Dushkin.

Rasler, Karen A., and William R. Thompson. 1994. *The Great Powers and Global Struggle, 1490–1990.* Lexington: University Press of Kentucky.

Rawls, John. 1971. *A Theory of Justice.* Cambridge, MA: Harvard University Press.

_____. 2001a. *Justice as Fairness: A Restatement.* Cambridge, MA: Harvard University Press (Belknap Press).

_____. 2001b. *The Law of Peoples.* Cambridge, MA: Harvard University Press.

Reif, K. 1993. Cultural convergence and cultural diversity as factors in European identity. In S. Garcia (ed.), *European Identity and the Search for Legitimacy.* London: Pinter.

Reischauer, Edwin O. 1956. Japanese feudalism. In Rushton Coulborn (ed.), *Feudalism in History.* Princeton, NJ: Princeton University Press.

Remnick, David. 1997. *Resurrection: The Struggle for a New Russia.* New York: Random House.

Rennstich, Joachim K. 2001. The future of great power rivalries. In Wilma Dunaway (ed.), *New Theoretical Directions for the 21st Century World-System.* New York: Greenwood Press.

Robertson, Roland. 1992. *Globalization: Social Theory and Global Culture.* London: Sage.

Robinson, William I. 1996. *Promoting Polyarchy: Globalization, U.S. Intervention, and Hegemony.* New York: Cambridge University Press.

Roemer, John E. 1994. A future for socialism. *Politics and Society* 22:451–478.

Ross, Robert J. S., and Kent C. Trachte. 1990. *Global Capitalism: The New Leviathan.* Albany: State University of New York Press.

Rossides, Daniel. 1976. *The American Class System: An Introduction to Social Stratification.* Boston: Houghton Mifflin.

_____. 1990. *Social Stratification: The American Class System in Comparative Perspective.* Englewood Cliffs, NJ: Prentice-Hall.

Rostow, W. W. 1960. *The Stages of Economic Growth: A Non-Communist Manifesto.* New York: Cambridge University Press.

Roxborough, Ian. 1979. *Theories of Underdevelopment.* London: Macmillan.

Rubinson, Richard, and Deborah Holtzman. 1981. Comparative dependence and economic development. *International Journal of Comparative Sociology* 22:86–101.

Rueschemeyer, Dietrich, Evelyne Huber Stephens, and John D. Stephens. 1992. *Capitalist Develop-*

*ment and Democracy*. Chicago: University of Chicago Press.

Runciman, W. G. 1989. *A Treatise on Social Theory. Volume II: Substantive Social Theory*. Cambridge, UK: Cambridge University Press.

Ruyle, Eugene E. 1973. Slavery, surplus, and stratification on the Northwest Coast: The ethnoenergetics of an incipient stratification system. *Current Anthropology* 14:603–631.

Sahlins, Marshall. 1958. *Social Stratification in Polynesia*. Seattle: University of Washington Press.

_____. 1960. Evolution: Specific and general. In Marshall Sahlins and Elman R. Service (eds.), *Evolution and Culture*. Ann Arbor: University of Michigan Press.

_____. 1963. Poor man, rich man, big man, chief: Political types in Melanesia and Polynesia. *Comparative Studies in Society and History* 5:285–303.

_____. 1968. *Tribesmen*. Englewood Cliffs, NJ: Prentice-Hall.

_____. 1972. *Stone Age Economics*. Chicago: Aldine.

Sanders, William T. 1972. Population, agricultural history, and societal evolution in Mesoamerica. In Brian Spooner (ed.), *Population Growth: Anthropological Implications*. Cambridge, MA: MIT Press.

Sanderson, Stephen K. 1985. The provincialism of introductory sociology. *Teaching Sociology* 12:397–410.

_____. 1990. *Social Evolutionism: A Critical History*. Oxford, UK: Blackwell.

_____. 1994a. The transition from feudalism to capitalism: The theoretical significance of the Japanese case. *Review* 17:15–55.

_____. 1994b. Expanding world commercialization: The link between world-systems and civilizations. *Comparative Civilizations Review* 30:91–103.

_____. 1994c. Evolutionary materialism: A theoretical strategy for the study of social evolution. *Sociological Perspectives* 37:47–73.

_____. 1995. *Social Transformations: A General Theory of Historical Development*. Oxford, UK: Blackwell.

_____. 1997. Evolutionism and its critics. *Journal of World-Systems Research* 3:94–114.

_____. 1999a. *Macrosociology: An Introduction to Human Societies* (4th ed.). New York: Addison Wesley Longman.

_____. 1999b. *Social Transformations: A General Theory of Historical Development* (expnd. ed.). Lanham, MD: Rowman & Littlefield.

_____. 2001. *The Evolution of Human Sociality: A Darwinian Conflict Perspective*. Lanham, MD: Rowman & Littlefield.

_____. 2004. *World democratization, 1850–2000: A cross-national test of modernization and power resource theories*. Paper presented at the annual meetings of the American Sociological Association, San Francisco.

Sanderson, Stephen K., and Joshua Dubrow. 2000. Fertility decline in the modern world and in the original demographic transition: Testing three theories with cross-national data. *Population and Environment* 21:511–537.

Sansom, George. 1961. *A History of Japan, 1334–1615*. Stanford, CA: Stanford University Press.

Schaeffer, Robert K. 1997. *Power to the People: Democratization Around the World*. Boulder, CO: Westview Press.

Schama, Simon. 1997. *The Embarrassment of Riches: An Interpretation of Dutch Culture in the Golden Age*. New York: Random House (Vintage).

Schultz, T. Paul. 1998. Inequality in the distribution of personal income in the world: How it is changing and why. *Journal of Population Economics* 11:307–344.

Schumpeter, Joseph A. 1947. *Capitalism, Socialism, and Democracy* (2nd ed.). New York: Harper & Row.

Scott, James C. 1976. *The Moral Economy of the Peasant*. New Haven, CT: Yale University Press.

_____. 1990. *Domination and the Arts of Resistance*. New Haven, CT: Yale University Press.

Seldon, Arthur. 1990. *Capitalism*. Oxford, UK: Blackwell.

Service, Elman R. 1963. *Profiles in Ethnology*. New York: Harper & Row.

_____. 1966. *The Hunters*. Englewood Cliffs, NJ: Prentice-Hall.

_____. 1971. *Primitive Social Organization: An Evolutionary Perspective* (2nd ed.). New York: Random House.

Shannon, Thomas Richard. 1996. *An Introduction to the World-System Perspective* (2nd ed.). Boulder, CO: Westview Press.

Sheldon, Charles David. 1958. *The Rise of the Merchant Class in Tokugawa Japan, 1600–1868*. (Monographs of the Association for Asian Studies, V.) Locust Valley, NY: J. J. Augustin.

Shreeve, James. 1995. *The Neandertal Enigma: Solving the Mystery of Modern Human Origins*. New York: William Morrow.

Silver, Morris. 1985. *Economic Structures of the Ancient Near East*. London: Croom Helm.

Simon, Julian. 1981. *The Ultimate Resource*. Princeton, NJ: Princeton University Press.

Singer, Peter. 2002. *One World: The Ethics of Globalization*. New Haven, CT: Yale University Press.

Sjoberg, Gideon. 1960. *The Preindustrial City*. New York: Free Press.

Skidmore, Thomas E., and Peter H. Smith. 2001. *Mod-*

ern *Latin America* (5th ed.). New York: Oxford University Press.

Skocpol, Theda. 1977. Wallerstein's world capitalist system: A theoretical and historical critique. *American Journal of Sociology* 82:1075–1090.

Smith, Alan K. 1991. *Creating a World Economy: Merchant Capital, Colonialism, and World Trade, 1400–1825.* Boulder, CO: Westview Press.

Smith, Thomas C. 1959. *The Agrarian Origins of Modern Japan.* Stanford, CA: Stanford University Press.

Snooks, Graeme Donald. 1996. *The Dynamic Society: Exploring the Sources of Global Change.* London: Routledge.

_____. 1997. *The Ephemeral Civilization: Exploding the Myth of Social Evolution.* London: Routledge.

_____. 1998. *The Laws of History.* London: Routledge.

So, Alvin Y. 1990. *Social Change and Development: Modernization, Dependency, and World-System Theories.* Newbury Park, CA: Sage.

So, Alvin Y., and Stephen W. K. Chiu. 1995. *East Asia and the World Economy.* Thousand Oaks, CA: Sage.

Somit, Albert, and Steven A. Peterson. 1997. *Darwinism, Dominance, and Democracy.* Westport, CT: Praeger.

Spencer, Daniel Lloyd. 1958. Japan's pre-Perry preparation for economic growth. *American Journal of Economics and Sociology* 17:195–216.

Spencer, Herbert. 1972. *Herbert Spencer on Social Evolution.* J. D. Y. Peel (ed.). Chicago: University of Chicago Press.

Spencer, William (ed.). 2001. *Global Studies: The Middle East.* Guilford, CT: McGraw-Hill/Dushkin.

Stearns, Peter N. 1993. *The Industrial Revolution in World History.* Boulder, CO: Westview Press.

Steel, Ronald. 1992. Europe after the superpowers. In Charles W. Kegley, Jr., and Eugene R. Wittkopf (eds.), *The Future of American Foreign Policy.* New York: St. Martin's Press.

Stephens, Evelyne Huber. 1989. Capitalist development and democracy in South America. *Politics and Society* 17:281–352.

Stevenson, Paul. 1974. Monopoly capital and inequalities in Swedish society. *Insurgent Sociologist* 5(1):41–58.

_____. 1982. Capitalism and inequality: The negative consequences for humanity. *Contemporary Crises* 6:333–372.

Steward, Julian H. 1949. Cultural causality and law: A trial formulation of the development of early civilizations. *American Anthropologist* 51:1–27.

_____. 1955. *Theory of Culture Change: The Methodology of Multilinear Evolution.* Urbana: University of Illinois Press.

_____. 1977. Cultural evolution. In Julian H. Steward, *Evolution and Ecology: Essays on Social Transformation.* Jane C. Steward and Robert F. Murphy (eds.). Urbana: University of Illinois Press. (Originally published 1956.)

Stiglitz, Joseph E. 2003. *Globalization and its Discontents* (rev. ed.). New York: Norton.

Stringer, Christopher, and Clive Gamble. 1993. *In Search of the Neanderthals.* London: Thames & Hudson.

Sutton, Mark Q., and E. N. Anderson. 2004. *Introduction to Cultural Ecology.* Walnut Creek, CA: AltaMira Press.

Sweezy, Paul. 1976. A critique. In Rodney Hilton (ed.), *The Transition from Feudalism to Capitalism.* London: New Left Books. (Originally published 1950.)

_____. 1980. *Post-Revolutionary Society.* New York: Monthly Review Press.

Szelenyi, Ivan. 1992. Social and political landscape, Central Europe, fall 1990. In Ivo Banac (ed.), *Eastern Europe in Revolution.* Ithaca, NY: Cornell University Press.

Szelenyi, Ivan, and Balazs Szelenyi. 1992. *Why socialism failed: Causes of the disintegration of East European state socialism.* Paper presented at the annual meetings of the American Sociological Association, Pittsburgh.

Szymanski, Albert. 1978. *The Capitalist State and the Politics of Class.* Cambridge, MA: Winthrop.

_____. 1981. *The Logic of Imperialism.* New York: Praeger.

_____. 1982. The socialist world-system. In Christopher K. Chase-Dunn (ed.), *Socialist States in the World-System.* Beverly Hills, CA: Sage.

_____. 1983. *Class Structure: A Critical Perspective.* New York: Praeger.

Taeuber, Irene B. 1958. *The Population of Japan.* Princeton, NJ: Princeton University Press.

Tainter, Joseph A. 1988. *The Collapse of Complex Societies.* New York: Cambridge University Press.

Tausch, Arno. 2003. The European Union: Global challenge or global governance? 14 world system hypotheses and two scenarios on the future of the Union. In Gernot Köhler and Emilio José Chaves (eds.), *Globalization: Critical Perspectives.* New York: Nova Science.

Testart, Alain. 1982. The significance of food storage among hunter-gatherers: Residence patterns, population densities, and social inequalities. *Current Anthropology* 23:523–537.

_____. 1988. Some major problems in the social anthropology of hunter-gatherers. *Current Anthropology* 29:1–32.

Therborn, Göran. 2000a. Introduction: From the

universal to the global. *International Sociology* 15:149–150.

\_\_\_\_. 2000b. Globalizations: Dimensions, historical waves, regional effects, normative governance. *International Sociology* 15:151–179.

Thomas, Keith. 1964. Work and leisure in pre-industrial society. *Past and Present* 29:50–66.

Tilly, Charles. (ed.). 1975. *The Formation of National States in Western Europe*. Princeton, NJ: Princeton University Press.

\_\_\_\_. 1983. Flows of capital and forms of industry in Europe, 1500–1900. *Theory and Society* 12:123–142.

\_\_\_\_. 1984. The old new social history and the new old social history. *Review* 7:363–406.

\_\_\_\_. 1990. *Coercion, Capital, and European States, A.D. 990–1990*. Oxford, UK: Basil Blackwell.

\_\_\_\_. 1998. *Durable Inequality*. Berkeley: University of California Press.

Tilly, Charles, and Wim P. Blockmans (eds.). 1994. *Cities and the Rise of States in Europe, A.D. 1000 to 1800*. Boulder, CO: Westview Press.

Trigger, Bruce G. 1998. *Sociocultural Evolution*. Oxford, UK: Blackwell.

Trow, Martin. 1966. The second transformation of American secondary education. In Reinhard Bendix and Seymour Martin Lipset (eds.), *Class, Status, and Power* (2nd ed.). New York: Free Press.

Tucker, Robert C. (ed.). 1978. *The Marx-Engels Reader* (2nd ed.). New York: Norton.

Turke, Paul W. 1989. Evolution and the demand for children. *Population and Development Review* 15:61–90.

Turnbull, Colin. 1972. *The Mountain People*. New York: Simon & Schuster (Touchstone).

Turner, Ralph H. 1960. Modes of social ascent through education: Sponsored and contest mobility. *American Sociological Review* 25:121–139.

Tylor, Edward Burnett. 1871. *Primitive Culture: Researches into the Development of Mythology, Philosophy, Religion, Language, Art, and Custom* (2 vols.). London: John Murray.

\_\_\_\_. 1878. *Researches into the Early History of Mankind*. New York: Holt.

\_\_\_\_. 1924. *Primitive Culture: Researches into the Development of Mythology, Philosophy, Religion, Language, Art, and Custom* (7th ed.). New York: Brentano's.

UNESCO. 1996. *Statistical Yearbook*. Paris: UNESCO.

\_\_\_\_. 1998. *Statistical Yearbook*. Paris: UNESCO.

United Nations. 1992. *Human Development Report*. New York: Oxford University Press.

\_\_\_\_. 2001. *Human Development Report*. New York: Oxford University Press.

\_\_\_\_. 2002. *Human Development Report*. New York: Oxford University Press.

Upham, Steadman (ed.). 1990. *The Evolution of Political Systems: Sociopolitics in Small-Scale Sedentary Societies*. New York: Cambridge University Press.

U.S. Bureau of the Census. 1982. *Statistical Abstract of the United States*. Washington, DC: U.S. Government Printing Office.

\_\_\_\_. 1984. *Current Population Reports, Series P-60, No. 142. Money Income of Households, Families and Persons in the United States: 1982*. Washington DC: U.S. Government Printing Office.

van den Berghe, Pierre L. 1978. *Man in Society: A Biosocial View* (2nd ed.). New York: Elsevier.

van den Berghe, Pierre L., and Joseph Whitmeyer. 1990. Social class and reproductive success. *International Journal of Contemporary Sociology* 27:29–48.

Vanhanen, Tatu. 1997. *Prospects of Democracy: A Study of 172 Countries*. London: Routledge.

\_\_\_\_. 1999. *Ethnic Conflicts Explained by Ethnic Nepotism*. Stamford, CT: JAI Press.

\_\_\_\_. 2003. *Democratization: A Comparative Analysis of 170 Countries*. London: Routledge.

Wagar, W. Warren. 1999. *A Short History of the Future* (3rd ed.). Chicago: University of Chicago Press.

Walker, R.A. 1985. Is there a service economy? The changing capitalist division of labor. *Science and Society* 49:42–83.

Wallerstein, Immanuel. 1974a. The rise and future demise of the world capitalist system: Concepts for comparative analysis. *Comparative Studies in Society and History* 16:387–415.

\_\_\_\_. 1974b. *The Modern World-System: Capitalist Agriculture and the Origins of the European World-Economy in the Sixteenth Century*. New York: Academic Press.

\_\_\_\_. 1979. *The Capitalist World-Economy*. New York: Cambridge University Press.

\_\_\_\_. 1980. *The Modern World-System II: Mercantilism and the Consolidation of the European World-Economy, 1600–1750*. New York: Academic Press.

\_\_\_\_. 1982. Crisis as transition. In Samir Amin et al., *Dynamics of Global Crisis*. New York: Monthly Review Press.

\_\_\_\_. 1983. *Historical Capitalism*. London: Verso.

\_\_\_\_. 1984. *The Politics of the World-Economy*. New York: Cambridge University Press.

\_\_\_\_. 1989. *The Modern World-System III: The Second Era of Great Expansion of the Capitalist World-Economy, 1730–1840s*. San Diego: Academic Press.

\_\_\_\_. 1998. *Utopistics: Or Historical Changes of the Twenty-First Century*. New York: New Press.

Warren, Bill. 1980. *Imperialism: Pioneer of Capitalism.* London: Verso.

Weber, Max. 1958. *The Protestant Ethic and the Spirit of Capitalism.* New York: Charles Scribner's Sons. (Originally published 1905.)

———. 1978. *Economy and Society* (2 vols.). Guenther Roth and Claus Wittich (eds.). Berkeley: University of California Press. (Originally published 1923.)

Weede, Erich. 1999. Future hegemonic rivalry between China and the West? In Volker Bornschier and Christopher Chase-Dunn (eds.), *The Future of Global Conflict.* London: Sage.

Weil, Robert. 1996. *Red Cat, White Cat: China and the Contradictions of "Market Socialism."* New York: Monthly Review Press.

Weissner, Polly. 1982. Risk, reciprocity, and social influence on !Kung San economies. In Eleanor Leacock and Richard B. Lee (eds.), *Politics and History in Band Societies.* Cambridge, UK: Cambridge University Press.

Wenke, Robert J. 1990. *Patterns in Prehistory: Mankind's First Three Million Years* (3rd ed.). New York: Oxford University Press.

———. 1996. *Patterns in Prehistory: Mankind's First Three Million Years* (4th ed.). New York: Oxford University Press.

Westergaard, John, and Henrietta Resler. 1975. *Class in a Capitalist Society: A Study of Contemporary Britain.* New York: Basic Books.

White, Benjamin. 1973. Demand for labor and population growth in colonial Java. *Human Ecology* 2:217–236.

———. 1976. Population, involution and employment in rural Java. *Development and Change* 7:267–290.

———. 1982. Child labor and population growth in rural Asia. *Development and Change* 13:587–610.

White, Leslie A. 1943. Energy and the evolution of culture. *American Anthropologist* 45:335–356.

———. 1945. History, evolutionism, and functionalism. *Southwestern Journal of Anthropology* 1:221–248.

———. 1949. *The Science of Culture.* New York: Grove Press.

———. 1959. *The Evolution of Culture.* New York: McGraw-Hill.

White, Lynn, Jr. 1962. *Medieval Technology and Social Change.* New York: Oxford University Press.

Wilber, Charles K. (ed.) 1973. *The Political Economy of Development and Underdevelopment.* New York: Random House.

Wilensky, Harold L. 2002. *Rich Democracies: Political Economy, Public Policy, and Performance.* Berkeley: University of California Press.

Wiley, Andrea S., and Leslie C. Carlin. 1999. Demographic contexts and the adaptive role of mother-infant attachment. *Human Nature* 10:135–161.

Wilk, Richard R. 1996. *Economies and Cultures: Foundations of Economic Anthropology.* Boulder, CO: Westview Press.

Wilkinson, David. 1992. Cities, civilizations, and oikumenes: I. *Comparative Civilizations Review* 27:51–87.

———. 1993. Cities, civilizations, and oikumenes: II. *Comparative Civilizations Review* 28:41–72.

Wilkinson, Richard G. 1973. *Poverty and Progress: An Ecological Perspective on Economic Development.* New York: Praeger.

Winterhalder, Bruce. 1986a. Diet choice, risk, and food sharing in a stochastic environment. *Journal of Anthropological Archaeology* 5:369–392.

———. 1986b. Optimal foraging: Simulation studies of diet choice in a stochastic environment. *Journal of Ethnobiology* 6:205–223.

———. 1987. The analysis of hunter-gatherer diets: Stalking an optimal foraging model. In Marvin Harris and Eric B. Ross (eds.), *Food and Evolution: Toward a Theory of Human Food Habits.* Philadelphia: Temple University Press.

———. 1993. Work, resources, and population in foraging societies. *Man* 28:321–340.

Winterhalder, Bruce, and Eric Alden Smith (eds.). 1981. *Hunter-Gatherer Foraging Strategies: Ethnographic and Archaeological Analyses.* Chicago: University of Chicago Press.

Wittfogel, Karl. 1957. *Oriental Despotism.* New Haven, CT: Yale University Press.

Wolf, Eric. 1966. *Peasants.* Englewood Cliffs, NJ: Prentice-Hall.

———. 1982. *Europe and the People Without History.* Berkeley: University of California Press.

Wolff, Edward N. 1995. How the pie is sliced: America's growing concentration of wealth. *American Prospect* 22:58–64.

Woodburn, James. 1968. An introduction to Hadza ecology. In Richard B. Lee and Irven DeVore (eds.), *Man the Hunter.* Chicago: Aldine.

———. 1982. Egalitarian societies. *Man* 27:431–451.

World Bank. 1984. *World Development Report.* New York: Oxford University Press.

———. 1997. *World Development Report.* New York: Oxford University Press.

———. 2001. *World Development Report.* New York: Oxford University Press.

———. 2002. *World Development Indicators.* Washington, DC: World Bank.

———. 2003. *World Development Report.* New York: Oxford University Press.

World Trade Organization. 2001. *International Trade*

*Statistics 2001*. Geneva: World Trade Organization.

Worldwatch Institute. 2003. *State of the World 2003*. New York: Norton.

Wright, Erik Olin. 1983. Giddens's critique of Marxism. *New Left Review* 138:11–35.

———. 1985. *Classes*. London: Verso.

Yamamura, Kozo. 1980. The agricultural and commercial revolution in Japan, 1550–1650. In Paul Uselding (ed.), *Research in Economic History* (Vol. 5). Greenwich, CT: JAI Press.

Yellen, J. E. 1977. *Archaeological Approaches to the Present: Models for Reconstructing the Past*. New York: Academic Press.

Yesner, David R. 1994. Seasonality and resource "stress" among hunter-gatherers: Archaeological signatures. In Ernest S. Burch, Jr., and Linda J. Ellanna (eds.), *Key Issues in Hunter-Gatherer Research*. Oxford, UK: Berg.

Yoshihara, Kunio. 1986. *Japanese Economic Development* (2nd ed.). Tokyo: Oxford University Press.

Zaslavsky, Victor. 1995. From redistribution to marketization: Social and attitudal change in post-Soviet Russia. In Gail W. Lapidus (ed.), *The New Russia: Troubled Transformation*. Boulder, CO: Westview.

Zeitlin, Irving. 1973. *Rethinking Sociology: A Critique of Contemporary Theory*. Englewood Cliffs, NJ: Prentice-Hall.

———. 1984. *The Social Condition of Humanity* (2nd ed.). New York: Oxford University Press.

Zemtsov, Ilya, and John Farrar. 1989. *Gorbachev: The Man and the System*. New Brunswick, NJ: Transaction Books.

Zipf, George Kingsley. 1965. *Human Behavior and the Principle of Least Effort*. New York: Hafner. (Originally published 1949.)

Zolberg, Aristide R. 1981. Origins of the modern world system: A missing link. *World Politics* 33:253–281.

# INDEX

Mechanization of production, 105

Medieval Europe:
emergence of modern capitalism in, 98–100
and peripheral markets, 83–84

Mercantilism, 91–93, 100

Merchant capitalism, 89–90

Merchant class of agrarian societies, 63

Mesopotamian civilization, 4

Militant societies, definition of (Spencer), 9–10

Mobility inflows and outflows, definitions of, 133

Modern capitalism, origins of, 87–100
capitalist world-economy, 95–97
commercial expansion, 88–89
European feudalism, 87–88
feudalism to capitalism transition, 98–100
in Japan, 97–98
mercantilism, 91–93
nature of, 89–90
rise of, 5–7
seventeenth century, 91–93
thirteenth to sixteenth centuries, 90–91
as world-system, 93–95

Modern Communist state, 166–171

Modernity (Parsons), 19

Modernization theory, 191–194

Monopoly capitalism, definition of, 111

Moore, B., 136

Morgan, L. H., 10

Moulder, F., 114

Mulhall, D., 255–258

Multilinear evolutionism, definition of, 16

Mundurucu of South America, 16–17

Nanotechnology, 255–258

National states, formation of, 101–103

Nation-building theory and mass education, 144

Natural resources, depleting, 233–235

Neolithic Revolution (Childe), 2–3, 14–15

New World-African slave trade, 211

*Nomenklatura* class in state socialism, 165

Nonegalitarian classlessness and state socialism, 164

Nonowning classes in U.S. society, 131

Nonrationality of precapitalist markets, 85

North, D., 87–88

Northwest Coast hunter-gatherer societies, 42

Nuclear weapons in future, 261–262

Nuer, 69–70, 71–72

Occupation as determinant of class position, 131

Oil and gas reserve, 235

Old World civilizations vs. Mesoamerica, 2–5

Oliver, D., 48–49

Olmec civilization, 4

Outdated business techniques and practices in underdeveloped societies, 191–192

Owning classes in U.S. society, 131

Parallel evolution, definition of, 27

Paramount ownership, definition of, 51

Parkin, F., 164, 165

Parliamentary democracy, 134–139, 249

Parsons, T., 17–20

Partial redistribution:
economies, 46
vs. expropriation, 60–61

Pastoral societies, 67–73
categories of, 68–69

political economy, 71–73
subsistence technology, 67–70

Patrimonial ownership, definition of, 60

Peasant class of agrarian societies, 58–61, 64–65

*Perestroika*, 161, 163, 164, 171, 172

Peripheral market societies, 82–84

Peripheral segment of world-economy, 94

Peripheralization of Africa, 212

Perraton, J., 219

Political changes in Soviet Union, 171–173

Political globalization, 222–223

Politics:
agrarian society, 66–67
evolution of, 79–81
hunter-gatherers, 42–43
intensive horticulturalists, 54–55
pastoralists, 71–73
postsocialist countries, 178–180
simple horticulturalists, 48–49

Polynesian intensive horticulturalists, 50

Pompidou Center in Paris, 260

Population growth, 24
in underdeveloped countries, 232–233

Population living in poverty, 187, 189

Population pressure, definition of, 73

Postindependence in Latin America, 208

Postindustrial society, rise of, 151–153

Postrevolutionary Communist party, 166–171

Postsocialism, 175–180
economy, 175–177
politics, 178–180
stratification, 177–178

Poverty:
in Africa, 212
in underdeveloped countries, 189, 199

Lenski, 21
Sanderson, 26–27
Sociocultural globalization, 223–225
South Korea and economic development, 203–204
Southern Bantu, 53
Soviet Union (*see* State socialism, rise and demise)
Specialization of labor, 6
Spencer, H., 9–10
Sponsored-mobility educational systems, 145–146
Stalin, J., 164
Stalinist terrorism, 169–170
Standard of living:
    evolutionary trends, 245–246
    and population growth, 246
    in underdeveloped societies, 187
State breakdown, definition of, 173
State socialism, rise and demise, 155–182
    and capitalist world-economy, 158–160
    collapse of Communism, 171–175
    current status, 156
    future of socialism, 181–182
    Leninist regimes, 166–171
    modern Communist state, 166–171
    origin and nature of, 155–158
    postsocialism, 175–180
    reform and transition to postsocialism, 160–163
    stratification, 163–166
States, definition of, 4
Stearns, P., 105–106, 108
Steel, R., 178–179
Stephens, E. H., 134–135, 137–138
Stephens, J. D., 134–135, 137–138
Steward, J., 16–17
Stiglitz, J., 177, 226, 230, 231
Stratification in industrial capitalist societies, 125–134
    class structure, 130–132
    income inequalities, 125–128

social mobility, 132–134
    wealth inequalities, 128–130
Stratification in postsocialist countries, 177–178
Stratification and standard of living, 246
Stratification within state socialism, 163–166
Structural distortion, 197
Structure of society:
    Harris, 23
    Sanderson, 26
Sub-Saharan Africa:
    failure of economic development, 211–213
    future of, 265
    intensive horticultural societies, 52–53
Subsistence technology:
    agrarian society, 57–60
    evolution of, 73–78
    hunter-gatherers, 32–36
    intensive horticulturalists, 49–51
    pastoralists, 67–70
    simple horticulturalists, 43–45
Substantive democracy, definition of, 135
Superstructure of society:
    Harris, 23
    Marx and Engels, 11–12
    Sanderson, 26
Surplus expropriation, definition of, 60–61
Systemic cycle of accumulation (SCA), 122
Szymanski, A., 136–137, 158–160

Tahitian intensive horticulturalists, 50–51
Taiwan and economic development, 203–204
Takeoff of underdeveloped countries, 192
Taxation:
    in industrial capitalist societies, 127
    of peasants of agrarian societies, 64–65
Technological advancement

measured by use of electricity, 186
Technological development, levels of (Morgan), 10
Technological evolutionism (Lenski), 20–22
Technology:
    definition of, 15, 332
    growth in future, 255–258
Testart, A., 41–42
Therborn, G., 219
Third World societies, 183–184
    (*see also* Underdeveloped societies)
Thomas, R., 87–88
Tilly, C., 101
Tokugawa period, 97–98
Totalitarian dictatorships, 170
Trade networks, 86–87
Trade-to-output ratio, 220–221, 239
Trading companies, 91–92
Transnational corporations, 112–113
Transportation in future, 256
Trebly compound societies, definition of, 9
Tribe, definition of, 33
Tsembaga Maring of New Guinea, 44
Turner, J., 249–250
Tylor, E. B., 10

Underdeveloped societies, 183–184
    internal deficiencies of, 191
    lack of consciousness or mentality that promotes development, 192
Unilinear evolutionism, definition of, 16
United Nations General Assembly, 263
United States:
    economic decline of, 265–266
    and European Union, conflict in future, 266–268
    hegemony, 117–119
    investment in peripheral capitalist countries, 158